P9-DXT-666

The
Reflective Woman

Seventh Edition

COLLEGE *of* ST. CATHERINE

Development of The Reflective Woman *was supported in part by grants from the National Endowment for the Humanities and the Bush Foundation.*

Copley Custom Textbooks

An imprint of XanEdu Custom Publishing

Copyright © 2008 by the College of St. Catherine.
All rights reserved
Printed in the United States of America

ISBN 13: 978-1-58152-582-3
ISBN 10: 1-58152-582-6

No part of this book may be reproduced in any manner without permission in writing from the publisher.

College of St. Catherine Web site: www.stkate.edu

Printed on recycled paper with soy ink.

Copley Custom Textbooks
An imprint of XanEdu Custom Publishing
138 Great Road
Acton, MA 01720
800-562-2147

Editors

Martha M. Phillips
Professor, Biology

Russell B. Connors Jr.
Professor, Theology

Marla Martin Hanley
Associate Dean for Integrated Learning

Michael J. Baynes
Associate Director of Student Life

Nancy A. Heitzeg
Associate Professor, Sociology

Lise R. Roy
Associate Professor, French

William Andrew Myers
Professor, Philosophy

Contents

Unit 3—Working toward Community and Justice 259

Resources 383

Acknowledgements

The Reflective Woman course, the Core Curriculum as a whole, and this seventh edition of the reader in particular, have all developed through the collaboration of many people over at least seventeen years, and we are grateful for their many insights and contributions. We recognize our deep indebtedness to the work of previous Core Committees and Core Directors: Brian Fogarty, Cecilia Konchar Farr, and Suzanne Hendricks. Thank you, also, to the students, teaching assistants, staff, and faculty who have participated over the last two years in focus groups and conversations about course and reader revisions. Using their feedback, we have attempted to clarify how each reading contributes to course objectives, and to align those goals with the College's Liberal Arts Goals. Based on the suggestions of many teachers and learners, this edition reduces the units to three, integrating readings on art throughout as students explore the role of art in self-expression, understanding truths, and in community identity and change. Because of the input of so many, however, this reader will still seem quite familiar, building on the wisdom and successes of the previous editions.

Materials in the Resources section: the writing and researching guides, the College Mission, Leadership, and Roman Catholic Identity Statements, the Liberal Arts Learning Goals, and the Catherine Connection, all originated in initiatives and projects outside the Core Curriculum. For these contributions, we extend a heart-felt thanks to all our colleagues in both Academic and Student Affairs, whose service to the college in a spirit of mutual respect makes such creative work together possible.

Thank you, also, to our college authors for their contributions and revisions to articles in this edition, and to our cover artist, Juliana Nagan, whose entry was selected from submissions from Professor Patricia Olson's Fall 2007 Publication and Computer Design class. Our particularly deep gratitude goes to the Core Administrative Assistant, Jacquelyn Schroeder, for the patience and skill she brings to her work.

Members of The Reflective Woman Reader Revision Subcommittee:

Russ Connors and Martha Phillips, Co-Chairs
Michael Baynes, Marla Hanley, Nancy Heitzeg,
Lise Hoy, and William Myers

Introduction

Moving to music not yet written . . .

Welcome to the College of St. Catherine and the unique liberal arts education it offers you. We believe real education begins, as Adrienne Rich describes, by "refusing to let others do your thinking, talking, and naming for you; it means learning to respect and use your own brains and instinct." This is the work of a lifetime. You began this learning before you came to college, of course, and none of us can know where it will ultimately take you. At St. Kate's, both in and out of the classroom, you will have opportunities to affirm what you know, to test it, to deepen it, to revise it. Through courses, campus organizations and activities, groups of friends and teams of co-workers, internships or activism in the wider community, a St. Catherine education supports you and challenges you to move beyond what is known and familiar. You are invited to explore further a vast universe of knowledge, values, and skills: where they come from, how well they work, how to create them, how they fit together, and how to use them.

Our vision for a St. Catherine education has been developing, since the Sisters of St. Joseph of Carondelet founded the college in 1905, through braiding together three interlocking threads: Catholic, liberal arts, and women. Just as the Sisters in France taught lace making to help women support themselves, St. Kate's helps you weave an education by drawing together Catholic intellectual traditions and social teachings with the liberating disciplines of the arts and sciences in a learning environment uniquely suited to women. To prepare women to lead and influence, we have developed a set of Liberal Arts Goals to guide both curriculum (courses) and co-curriculum (programs available outside the classroom). These Liberal Arts Goals and the college Mission, Leadership, and Roman Catholic Identity Statements are in the Resources section of this text.

Many students enter college with the main goal of completing a major, and studying deeply in one field is certainly important. However, a liberal arts education prepares you for much more than a job. It prepares you to navigate a complex and constantly changing world, to understand issues no one is yet discussing, to make decisions none of us can predict, to take on work that has not even been invented, and to enrich your life with meaning, purpose, and satisfaction. To learn to "move to music not yet written" requires rigorous study in a variety of subjects, taking risks to try new and challenging experiences, and a commitment to excellence—expecting the very best of yourself. In this kind of education, you invest your time and energy in learning that will be valuable no matter what life brings you. The goals of a College of St. Catherine's liberal arts education are to learn how to collaborate with others; how to act ethically; how to understand and honor diversity; how to gather, analyze, and use information to support your positions and decisions; how to communicate your ideas; and how to continue growing intellectually throughout your life.

This course, The Reflective Woman, introduces you to liberal arts learning at St. Kate's. We require it because the College believes that a common experience helps to build a community and to accomplish our unique mission. As the first step in our "core curriculum," The Reflective Woman is designed for these specific liberal arts goals:

1. Critical and creative inquiry

    - to understand and use different kinds of information
    - to reflect on the meaning of your experiences, observations, passions, and imagination
    - to begin to analyze complex issues and arguments
    - to explore how different disciplines approach learning

2. Effective communication

    - to improve your reading, listening, and discussion skills
    - to better organize and present your ideas in writing
    - to explore expression through the arts

3. Understanding diversity

    - to understand the experiences of women
    - to understand how race/ethnicity, gender, social class, and other differences affect identity and contribute to systems of power and privilege

Certainly, other goals are also addressed in this course; we believe it can affect your self-concept, enhance your ability to work in groups, and appreciate different ways of learning. It introduces ideas about justice and ways of working to improve our communities. Like any course, however, meeting the goals of The Reflective Woman relies largely on students taking responsibility for their own learning. There is no expert lecturing while you sit passively writing down the "right" answers for a test. Rather, as a discussion-based course taught by instructors from all over the college, it depends on each class member reading carefully, discussing actively, and contributing to everyone's learning. *The Reflective Woman* reader has been designed to assist you in preparing for class. Each unit begins with an introduction explaining the focus of that section, and each reading starts with information about the writer and some questions to ponder as you read the selection.

This approach to learning will continue throughout the courses you take at St. Kate's to complete a baccalaureate degree. The baccalaureate includes study of a variety of liberal arts subjects, which we call the "liberal arts distribution requirements." One strategy to completing these requirements is a Core Minor, which links several courses together with a common theme. While not required, core minors are designed to help students make clearer connections between subjects and learn to approach complex issues from multiple perspectives. If you major or minor in a liberal arts discipline, you will explore the liberal arts in a deeper and more disciplined way than the core curriculum offers. However, all majors here build on a liberal arts foundation, and our programs in professional and health fields are richer because of the strength of our liberal arts requirements. In addition, the College of St. Catherine offers a rich variety of opportunities outside the classroom to develop your interests and skills, which we encourage you to explore with your advisor throughout your years here. Finally, regardless of your major, in your final core course, The Global Search for Justice, you will be able to analyze a justice issue in depth, such as environmental concerns, racism, or health disparities, and explore the responsibility of global citizens to work for change.

Education at St. Kate's may seem similar in many ways to what is offered at other colleges and universities, but much you will find here, beginning with The Reflective Woman, is unique. We believe this difference is essential in an education that prepares women to lead and influence. To meet this mission, we design our liberal arts education with *you* at its heart, respecting your own uniqueness, appreciating the perspectives you bring, and trusting in your capacity to claim this education for your own.

Marla Martin Hanley

Associate Dean for Integrated Learning

June 2008

UNIT I

Composing a Life

listen
somebody need a map
to understand you

Lucille Clifton

Introduction to Composing a Life

This first unit explores identity—what are the choices we make in order to compose a life that expresses who we really are?—and it explores, also, the challenges and supports we encounter around us in that process of becoming ourselves.

The College of St. Catherine itself has an identity, composed around its mission and the mission of the Sisters of Carondelet who founded it. The first two readings in this unit introduce you to St. Kate's, and by describing the work of the Sisters of St. Joseph and the early days of the College, reveal how history has shaped us and how stories continue to have a powerful influence on who we think we are.

The main goals of this unit are to provide a variety of such stories about identity so that you have the opportunity to reflect further on your own authentic self and the many creative processes—including our educations—that combine throughout a lifetime to form us. These personal narratives introduce us to many diverse voices, as authors describe who they are and what forces have contributed to and hindered their developing, understanding, and expressing who they are. Gender, class, race/ethnicity, sexual orientation, and language are just some of the differences these writers explore.

The processes of composing a life and expressing who we are transpire both within us as individuals and within our social contexts. The interplay of the individual and her social and physical environment is a central theme throughout literature and the arts, and a key question that theories in science and the social sciences explore as well. In these stories about identity, you will have the opportunity to consider many perspectives through reading a variety of literary styles. In journals and classroom discussions, you and others may decide to explore your own unique experiences of being invisible, empowered, oppressed, privileged. How do we discover our authentic selves? In what ways do you express your uniqueness as an individual? How do we safeguard others' rights to discover and express themselves authentically? What importance does knowing oneself have for claiming an education?

Joan Mitchell, CSJ (b. 1940), is a CSC alumna. The following text served as a presentation she delivered at the College of St. Catherine Faculty/Staff Workshop in 1994. In it she addresses both her own identity as one of the Sisters of St. Joseph as well as the identity of the college as an institution of higher learning unique in its dedication to Catholic ideas of social justice and to the education and empowerment of women. As you read, consider the ways in which Mitchell emphasizes both the individual and community. What values, perspectives, and choices (individual or otherwise) have contributed to the making of the CSC community?

All Women Can Be: The Spirit of the Sisters of St. Joseph

Joan Mitchell, CSJ

I feel a personal passion for St. Catherine's because I found my life here in my undergraduate years 1958–1962. My four years were a journey of empowerment. I came undereducated and afraid; I left able to write, think, and perform. I also found a community of women, the Sisters of St. Joseph of Carondelet, with whom to invest my life in service.

Empowering is what Sisters of St. Joseph have been about from their beginning in 1650. Pre-revolutionary France had terrible social and economic inequalities. With wealth concentrated in the church and nobility the country suffered much the same chronic problems as Third World countries today. The desperate needs of the people at the bottom gave birth to *apostolic* orders, whose cloisters became the streets, whose prayer became the works of mercy.

Among their ministries the first sisters helped young women forced to support themselves through prostitution to learn lacemaking and become self-supporting. Many marriageable young men had gone to the New World, leaving many young women without the possibility of marriage. The sisters gave these women at the bottom of society a stepping stone to their own place in its economic life beyond the social norm of their day.

The College of St. Catherine has educated and empowered most of the present members of the Sisters of St. Joseph of the St. Paul Province. Most sisters attended St. Catherine as beleaguered teachers coming on Saturday mornings or during the hot days of summer sessions, to finish degrees on the twenty-year plan. Many attended in the days before the Second Vatican Council, when we were forbidden to talk to the other students and cut off from the community life of the college. Many sisters have returned to St. Catherine's to do graduate work, for example, in the Master of Arts in Organizational Leadership, theology, and spirituality, and their work has nurtured the community.

However, norms for women also affected us. Our community educated many women to the doctoral level but never in medicine, nor did we train our own women in advanced theology degrees until after Vatican II. Sister Rosalie Ryan led that small revolution toward the college theology department of today. In her research and writing she is one of the pioneering women bible scholars who have recovered the importance of women among Jesus's disciples, those women who follow and serve him and are with him from the beginning in Galilee but whose presence was lost to us in the scant two and three verses the gospel gives to their presence.

The Sisters of St. Joseph College Consortium, which has twelve member colleges, funded a study of their mission and image, surveying 480 people, twenty-five on this campus, four of them sisters. Sister Karen Kennelly, formerly academic dean on the St. Paul Campus and now president of Mount St. Mary's in Los Angeles, chairs this consortium. Their study reports five distinctive characteristics of these colleges, which include St. Catherine:

1) Hospitality and caring community
2) Concern for all without distinction
3) Addressing the needs of the time
4) Striving for excellence in all endeavors
5) Making a difference in local and world community

These same characteristics reach back to our beginnings as a community. Our houses were to be hubs of hospitality, caring, and outreach to our neighbors. The first foundation of the Sisters of St. Joseph was a secret society. It lasted only two years. This was a small group of pious women who wanted to help others. The Jesuit Father Medaille, who articulated the spirituality of these women, describes the community as a "little design," called by the name of St. Joseph, a model of hidden service, like the self-emptying humility of Jesus hidden in the tabernacle among the people. What lasted of this first foundation is its identity with Joseph, of whom little is known but his care for Mary and Jesus. From this name we take an ethic of *charity to the dear neighbor without distinction*.

To address the needs of the time was why the community of St. Joseph began anew in 1650 in LePuy, France, with the support of Bishop de Maupas, in a hospital. The first sisters formed a hub from which the spokes of the wheel of ministry went out. Our first constitutions directed the sisters to "divide the city into various sections, and either by visiting the sick personally or through the lay associates of the congregation . . . make every effort to learn what disorders prevail in each quarter so that they may remedy them either by their own efforts or by the intermediary of those who have some power over the person engaged in these disorders."

Striving for excellence is an ethic at the heart of St. Catherine. Seventeenth-century piety used the word *zeal* and the concept of *the more* to express this value that we know so well from the history of the St. Paul campus where Mother Antonia sent six young sisters to study in European universities. They became the living endowment of the college's early years. We know this quality well, too, from the history of the Minneapolis campus where the faculty practically had to teach in the stairwells as second and third year nursing students contended for space with the first class of the junior college Sister Ann Joachim founded.

The *more* is an ethic of liberation that envisioned the sisters being all women could be and envisioned people at the bottom of society empowered to be all they could be. At our general chapter as a congregation in 1993 we asked ourselves again, "What more is being asked of us now in our commitment to justice?" You see the clear common roots of the two campuses in these characteristics:

- Hospitality and caring
- Concern for the dear neighbor without distinction
- Addressing the needs of the time
- Striving for excellence

They add up to making a difference.

Sometimes when I hear people talk about *the sisters*, I sense they are not talking about me or sisters today but about women farther back, perhaps those who founded St. Catherine's or those who formed the academic community in the past. I share reverence for these sisters, but I suspect they seem wise and foresighted rather than dangerous and single-minded because they are safely dead. We laud Mother Antonia today but would we have sided with her when she put up Mendel Hall to stop Prior from going through the St. Paul Campus? Where beyond the status quo would her passion for excellence and education for women lead her today? Perhaps where it has led our 1989 general chapter, which declared, "We support the exercise of the gifts of all the baptized for ministry." And what more? Conflict, conversation, argument—these are creative processes.

George Arbunckle, a cultural anthropologist, Marist priest, and New Zealander, says the Catholic Church missed the modern era. At the Council of Trent, which met twenty-five times between 1546 and 1563, the Church responded to the Protestant Reformation by effectively freezing itself in a medieval time warp that lasted until the Second Vatican Council 402 years later.

In the Church's fixed self-understanding prior to Vatican II, sisters' permanent vowed commitment gave them a special, privileged place in the structure of the Church, lower than the clergy but higher than the faithful laity. The Second Vatican Council radically flattened these hierarchical gradations by stressing the common call to holiness all Christians share, none more than others, by reason of the baptism.

Thirty years ago we sisters lived our higher spiritual vocation by being set apart from lay people. Today we are part of the ordinary life of the human community rather than apart from it. We understand ourselves not only as a community of vowed members but a vast inclusive network of relationships with colleagues in ministry, former members, families, and friends. We share life, prayer, ministry, and companionship with consociates who link themselves with us through interest and shared charism rather than vows.

There are positives in missing the modern era. Catholic consciousness remains very shaped by the communal experience that antedates the Enlightenment focus on individual subjectivity. Books such as *Habits of the Heart* call for churches to become the glue of fragmented postmodern society. Catholic tradition and sisters' experience in creating community together have something to offer the civic community toward this need, not in going backward to a community that buries the individual but forward to communities of mutuality and interdependence. In fact, in Latin America a base-community movement has arisen reinventing Christian community at the grassroots level. This movement is spreading here in the U.S., too.

The Second Vatican Council called Christians to serve the poor and make a difference in this world. "The joys and the hopes, the griefs and the anxieties of the people of this age, especially those who are poor or are in any way afflicted, those too are the joys and hopes, the griefs and anxieties of the followers of Christ," it said (*Pastoral Constitution on the Church in the Modern World, #1*). Our ministries as a community have radically broadened in response to this call. Our history in this century had been one of participating in the building of the Catholic school system in this country and the Catholic health care system. Things were gained in this national endeavor—immigrant Catholics were educated and assimilated into the American culture. This era also made us semi-cloistered in our convents and limited to staffing schools and hospitals. Since Vatican II we have rediscovered we are an order founded to serve on the streets and form partnerships with lay people. We were founded to "divide the city in various sections."

At first, this emphasis strained relations between people who moved out of their classroom to give direct service to the poor and those who stayed in institutions such as the college. Now, thirty years later, we see very clearly the importance of higher education in people's journey out of poverty, welfare, and hunger. I'll bet anyone who heard the student from the Minneapolis campus with the six children and the disabled husband who spoke one year at our Student/Board of Trustees Dialog still remembers her and the difference her education was making for all of them. I remember Anita Pampusch remarking at the tenth anniversary of Weekend College that those who established educational policies in large corporations probably did not have in mind educating the numbers of women in secretarial work who took advantage of these programs to earn bachelors' degrees.

The Sisters of St. Joseph have profoundly changed in the last thirty years and we want you to know who we are today. We continue to have sisters on the college faculty and staff, but fewer than in the past. In the past thirty years sisters have developed new ministries that offer sites for volunteer work, internships, and mentoring programs. Sisters are actively involved with Peace House, where Rose Tillemans welcomes and shares lunch and prayer with street people in a community of respect right next to the Dairy Queen near Franklin and Portland. Down Portland is St. Joseph House, which Char Madigan helped start and so many keep going as a place that welcomes battered women and nurtures clients as staff members. HOPE, Homes on Portland Enterprises, has refurbished former crack houses on the same block. At Incarnation House sisters helped found and staff this place for women with young children; at Ascension Place, women are struggling out of addictions. Sisters are teaching in literacy programs in the Frogtown area and at the Administration Center and Carondelet Center next door. In these new ministries as in our earliest ministries we partner with lay people.

Few people in the Church have changed more than sisters as a group. We were readied to respond to the needs of the time by good educations. We have roared through modern consciousness into the postmodern. Today we pursue our own talents and gifts in ministry rather than getting educated to fill a waiting position. Today we are working out new forms of governance that build vision from the bottom up by hearing into words all our voices.

The Second Vatican Council was part of the social change and challenge of the 1960's that also revived the women's movement. This movement began in the last century among Quaker and Unitarian women who joined the cause for abolition and moved on to women's suffrage. In the

last twenty years Catholic women have taken their place in the movement, especially in the theological fields.

Elisabeth Schussler Fiorenza has put feminist methodologies to work
retrieving the importance of women in the bible, theorizing that the first
Christian communities formed a discipleship of equals and aiming to
make the scriptures no longer tablets of stone but bread to nourish
women and men today.

Rosemary Radford Ruether, pioneer Catholic woman historian, god-
mothers younger feminists. She insists women rape victims in her classes
can relate to Jesus because of his experience of violence. He is Christ and
Christa. Mary Daly's prodigious research chronicles violence to women
in many cultures and creates new language for women's experience. Elizabeth Johnson is a Sister of St. Joseph of Brentwood and professor at
Fordham who suggests, in her book *She Who Is* that we no longer neglect
the feminine imagery of God as Spirit and recognize the imminent presence of God as Spirit cogiven with all life. Hispanic sisters have formed
Las Hermanas to further the struggle for liberation among Hispanic
women. The Black Sisters Conference has contributed its own voices—
Toinette Eugene, Jamie Phelps, Thea Bowman.

Catholic women and men stand at a threshold today. People ask sisters,
"How can you stay in the Catholic Church? It's so patriarchal. How can
you let the pope tell you what to do?" How can one care about educating
men and women for interdependency and community and stay in the
church? I should point out that these are not only women's questions. St.
Catherine honored Bishop Raymond Lucker for his support of women
during the debates about the women's pastoral.

At the last board retreat I attended we had to draw an image of St.
Catherine. I found myself drawing the stacks of books in the library and
beside them the big doors of the chapel. I drew the shelves open but put
a lock on the chapel. How does a Catholic college educate women to be
all they can be when the church does not welcome their gifts for ministry?

Withdrawing from the church is the easiest answer. It's the answer of
preference among Catholics in their twenties. It's not mine. It's not a lot
of people's. As a Sister of St. Joseph I am a publicly committed woman of
the church. I say, "We are the Church. This is our home. We won't be put
out." More than that, women have always belonged here. Scripture gives
us evidence of women disciples, apostles, deacons, prophets. Church history tells us Hilda of Whitby and Brigid of Ireland were abbesses of double monasteries of men and women. Shawn Madigan's research identifies
women mystics in every age.

What do the Sisters of St. Joseph ask and offer this college toward the future? We are here today asking for dialog. We have to offer our struggle to change since Vatican II and a long history as an alternative Christian community within the Church. Feminist and other liberation theologies locate authority in the voices of the oppressed struggling for justice. These liberation theologies call us to speak the truth of our experience and to make room for others through listening them into speech.

A cultural anthropologist looks at the current movement to restore the pre-Vatican II Catholic Church and says that it's surprising the backlash isn't worse because the social upheaval and chaos have been so profound. This is the restoration church. On the other side, another kind of church is taking form in small Christian communities of lay men and women who break open the word together, do justice together, seek equality together. This is the emergent church.

The restoration church says the conversation is over. The emergent church says we must begin a conversation that includes everyone and invites all to speak for themselves as their most fundamental act of being human. We are asking for dialog and engagement in improvising a useful future.

Pope John Paul II's statement on Catholic education, *Ex Corde Ecclesiae*, has renewed conversation about what Catholic means in the missions of institutions of higher learning. In *America*, for May 28, 1994, Father Joseph Feeney of St. Joseph University in Philadelphia asks familiar questions: "While Jesuit colleges do and should welcome students of all faiths and no faith, has a diverse student body clouded institutional vision? How is Jesuit education defined? As liberal-arts based? Humanistic? Christian humanistic? Faith and justice based? How to link campus ministry and classroom? How to cherish diversity and build community?"

The Sisters of St. Joseph who came to the United States in 1836 from France to New Orleans, up the Mississippi to St. Louis, to the town of Carondelet just south of St. Louis, came to do what had to be done in the New World. In 1851 sisters came upstream to St. Paul to teach Indians, but they wound up founding the first hospital in the state, St. Joseph's, because a cholera epidemic demanded their school become a hospital. They improvised a useful future.

Sister Rita Steinhagen is a legend among the sisters for all she has initiated as a result of Father Harry Bury taking her to the streets of Cedar Riverside, where she began hearing people's needs and started a Free Store, the West Bank Clinic, the Bridge for runaway kids, and with Char Madigan St. Joseph House for Battered Women. Rita and Char taught us to listen to the needs of the dear neighbor without distinction as the con-fraternities of mercy had done in France in the beginning.

At our last all-community gathering Sister Marian Louwaige brought to the eucharistic table a piece of Belgian lace. She saw in its airy pattern a symbol of room for all in the design of the community and its future. Sister Sharon Howell brought to the altar a piece of kinte cloth, a tightly woven African cloth. She saw in the weave a symbol of the solidarity in which we must stand together. What we really ask of you is to continue the lacemaking with us, to weave a future that continues to reintegrate those who have least with those who have most, that makes of the threads of our lives a pattern of grace that is both open to all and tight enough not to come undone, or fray, but last as an intricacy where sisters cared and joined hands with lasting friends in entwining circles of learning and care, love and service.

A 1936 graduate of CSC, Rosalie Ryan, CSJ, began her tenure at the College in 1948 as professor of English. She later served as admissions director and academic dean and retired in 1985 from the theology department. John Christine Wolkerstorfer, CSJ, is also a CSC graduate. She was professor of American history at CSC, with special interests in oral history and in the U.S. Civil War. She retired in 1997. The following excerpt is taken from their work, More than a Dream: Eighty-five Years at the College of St. Catherine, *published in 1992. They present a detailed history of the College calling attention to a number of key figures who played essential roles in making the college what it is today. What do you find noteworthy in this history? How does this history affect your thinking about your education here?*

from More than a Dream
Eighty-five Years at the College of St. Catherine

Rosalie Ryan, CSJ, and John Christine Wolkerstorfer, CSJ

Chapter One: A Vision of Excellence

Early in 1905, a bulletin announced that a new Catholic college for women would introduce "the third epoch in the development of the educational work of the Sisters of St. Joseph in the Northwest. In 1851 they opened the first Catholic elementary school . . . some years later they built St. Joseph's Academy, the first preparatory school; and finally they founded St. Catherine's . . . the purpose of those in charge is to make this college the best and highest school of its kind in the Northwest." Twenty-seven sisters had already begun to fulfill this vision in a single building on isolated farmland west of St. Paul.

The College of St. Catherine opened to students in January 1905, but the project had been long in the making. Archbishop John Ireland had begun to plan for the college in the early 1890s, helping his sister Ellen—Mother Seraphine Ireland—acquire 110 acres of land at the corner of Randolph and Cleveland avenues. A financial panic in 1893 postponed the project, and ten years passed before the work continued. Not everyone greeted plans for the new college with enthusiasm. Institutions for the higher education of women had not found favor in the United States in the late 1800s. Women's education was carried on chiefly by "female seminaries," which gave courses in "domestic training": needlework, manners, and a host of other topics intended to prepare a woman for her place in the home. Toward the end of the century, individual women began asking for more, and the heads of some colleges moved towards providing education in literature and the sciences to prepare women for teaching and other professions. George Schmidt wrote of what this entailed in *The Liberal Arts College: A Chapter in American Cultural History*: "To reach the college level . . . it would be necessary to slough off the many fashionable and vocational scraps of knowledge and concentrate on the solid subjects which sharpened the understanding and disciplined the mind. This meant the higher reaches of Latin, Greek, mathematics, mental and moral philosophy." Efforts to create greater intellectual challenge for women often met with shock, alarm, or derision. "Such an experience," said one critic, "can only be hardening and deforming." Another said, "This borders on the vulgar."

Historian Thomas Woody wrote that the Reverend John Todd, a Protestant minister, absolutely denounced the idea: "As for training young ladies through a long intellectual course, as we do young men, it can never be done. They will die in the process . . . The poor thing has her brain crowded with history, grammar, arithmetic, geography, natural history, chemistry . . . metaphysics, French, often German, Latin, perhaps Greek. . . . She must be on the strain all the school hours, study in the evening till her eyes ache, her brain whirls, her spine yields and gives way, and she comes through the process of education enervated, feeble, without courage or vigor, elasticity or strength."

The naysayers deterred neither the sisters nor Archbishop Ireland, who had already given material as well as moral support. In 1900 he had signed over to the sisters the rights to his book, *The Church and Modern Society*, which they peddled from door to door, selling 20,000 copies and raising $60,000 for the college building fund. In 1902, Hugh Derham, a wealthy farmer from Rosemount, asked the archbishop to name a special charity. Ireland suggested he support the effort toward a new Catholic liberal arts college for women. Derham donated $20,000 toward the erection of the first building and $5,000 for a scholarship. Later, Mother Seraphine said of the gift: "It may not seem very large . . . but it gave us courage to go on. He well deserved to have Derham Hall named for him."

Because of problems with construction, the school, scheduled to open in September 1904, was not ready for occupancy until the end of that year. On December 26, 1904, twenty-seven sisters walked a mile in a snowstorm from St. Joseph's Academy in downtown St. Paul to board the Grand Avenue streetcar at Seven Corners. They got off the bus at Cleveland Avenue, then walked another mile south to Randolph Avenue. The elements did not discourage their excitement over the new building. Sister Bridget Bohan later reminisced that on December 27 Archbishop Ireland came out with a team of horses. With him were Mother Seraphine and Sister Celestine Howard. Promptly at 7:00 A.M., the archbishop offered the first Mass. Then he blessed the rooms of Derham. Hall: "They had lanterns to light their way around the house . . . a cat followed . . . Sister Jarlath [Noonan] said that Sister Eulalia [Dress] brought the cat from the academy in a bag . . . The cat went into all the rooms as they were being blessed. Whenever the archbishop shook the holy water, the cat went up to receive . . . Finally he said, 'What's that doing here?'" Because of the continuing snow, the three guests left after breakfast. A few days later the boarding students from St. Joseph's Academy arrived to become students of Derham Hall.

The sisters had started from scratch in furnishing the new school, and they sometimes came up short. According to Sister Bridget: "We had about ninety boarders, and when their trunks came out with everything, we had sheets enough for about forty-eight or fifty beds . . . And this was the Christmas holidays. Sister Hyacinth [Werden] said, 'I don't know what to do.' 'Well,' I said, 'give us some money, and we'll do the buying.' Sister Edith [Hogan] and I went over to Minneapolis, and you couldn't get sheets ready-made. You had to buy the bolt of unbleached muslin . . . We rented [sewing] machines and Sister Antonia [McHugh] and I sat at those machines from dawn to dark, and Sister Monica [Berghs] made up the sheets. And the boarders took them without being laundered. They made nothing of it . . . Unbleached, oh, it was unspeakable!" Nevertheless, the school shortly offered an "academic" (college preparatory) course, music, art, and domestic arts. In September 1905, college courses formally began, with seven students registered as freshmen.

The challenge of building enrollment engaged the sisters from the start. Brochures extolled the beauty of the campus, and, later, paid advertisements in the *Catholic Bulletin* lured prospective students. The first printed materials read: "On this spot Nature has poured her beauty with a prodigal hand. To the west of the college is the Mississippi, just recovering from its dash over the Falls [of St. Anthony]; further still to the west, the laughing waters of Minnehaha make constant melody, and on all sides alternating stretches of unkempt forest and billowy greensward complete the beauty of the scene."

Later notices stressed the healthfulness of the site. In 1906: "No school in the United States for the education of young ladies is more favorably situated . . . in regard to the healthfulness and sanitation . . . The drainage and plumbing are as nearly perfect as can be found anywhere." Another ad read: "In the construction of the college building the comfort and safety of its inmates were taken into consideration . . . The wide corridors which extend through the whole length of the building afford space for recreation and exercise in inclement weather." And in 1907, signed by Charles Meade, physician for the college: "The site is exceptionally healthful, and the extensive grounds afford ample opportunity for free outdoor life and exercise in the bracing Minnesota air." Would such claims refute accusations of the likes of the Reverend Todd?

The earliest catalog stated plainly the college's objectives:

- to give the students a liberal education to train and develop all their powers simultaneously
- to train Catholic "girls" to be solidly virtuous and religious—to teach all, irrespective of their denominational differences, to respect, appreciate, and encourage religion and Christian morality.

Despite the publicity, enrollment grew slowly, and for the first six years the College of St. Catherine was really a small high school with just a handful of "specials" doing postsecondary work. Most students wishing to continue beyond the sophomore year transferred to the University of Minnesota. Finally in 1911, two students who had completed the sophomore year, Gertrude Malloy and Marguerite McCusker (Testor), returned as juniors. They remained to graduate in 1913. . . . That year Sisters Frances Clare Bardon, Margaret Kerby, and Antonia McHugh filed a certificate of incorporation for the College of St. Catherine to promote letters, sciences, and the arts through the care, protection, housing, and instruction of students in subjects including the practice of religion.

The next year, at the insistence of Archbishop Ireland, Sister Antonia McHugh was appointed the first dean (chief administrative officer). Building a great college for women was the object of her unceasing labor for the next twenty-four years.

Fit for Pioneer Work

Sister Antonia's background fitted her for pioneering work. She was born Anna McHugh in Omaha in 1873 of an itinerant frontier family. Her father, Patrick McHugh, after several moves in the Dakotas, settled in Langdon, North Dakota, to serve as mayor, postmaster, and bank director. He was elected a commissioner of Cavalier County, then to the territorial legislature for three terms and to the North Dakota legislature for four. Patrick McHugh often took young Anna with him on his business and political travels in the territory.

When she was twelve years old, Anna's father took her to St. Joseph's Academy in St. Paul to study and prepare for her first Holy Communion. During the next three years, she attended St. Mary's Academy in Winnipeg, which was closer to home. Sister Mary Joseph Calasenz, SNJM, remembered Anna McHugh from her days in high school: "She was remarkable in her practical piety, application to study, and generosity. Her outspokenness was proverbial among her companions; her frankness was of a nature to abash those who were not lovers of the truth." Said Sister Teresa Toomey: "During the whole of her life as an educator, Sister Antonia showed herself to be a true daughter of pioneers, alert, eager, undaunted by difficulties, and bold in her dreams of what Catholic schools in the Northwest could mean for both the Church and the nation she loved."

In 1890 Anna entered the novitiate of the Sisters of St. Joseph in St. Paul, then began teaching third and fourth grades at St. Joseph's Academy. She was among the first group of sisters at the new college. There she threw herself into a routine of cleaning and housekeeping, teaching, supervising resident students, and attending daily prayers. She continued her education with classes at the University of Chicago in summer and correspondence courses during the school year. . . Sister Antonia attended four successive seminars beginning in 1905, with a full year of study arranged for 1908. By December of that year, she had a bachelor's degree in philosophy and education. In 1909 she received a master's degree in history. . . .

Sister Antonia had returned from studies in Chicago to teach at the College of St. Catherine with characteristic enthusiasm. Her classes in history were filled with love of the classical age of Greece and Rome. For study of the Middle Ages she had collected hundreds of pictures of cathedrals and castles. She had spent much time in the study of geology and geography, so the map of Europe became familiar to her students. Her knowledge of music and art was extensive.

Sister Antonia sprinkled her teaching with dozens of maxims and phrases. When she said, "energize yourself," the student moved. She considered some responses "clear as mud" or "windy." Outside of class she might comment that "things for sale are in windows" or "only horses hang their heads" or "she who would be a woman must avoid mediocrity." From Room 12, she impartially handed out apples and advice. Her classroom was a place where young women found out what was the matter with them even when they didn't want to know. But there was also talk about books and stars and music and pictures. The seriousness of a particular conference with a student could be gauged by whether the door to Room 12 was open or closed.

In these ways Sister Antonia impressed students deeply: "I certainly knew, from the minute I set my foot here, that she was the most important one on the campus. She was the one I loved most, respected most, feared most, and she certainly was running things," said Sister Marie Philip Haley '21.

Spreading the News

When Sister Antonia became dean in 1914, eighteen students were enrolled in the college, but the sisters were determined to attract more. News items, articles, and full-page advertisements in the *Catholic Bulletin* helped make the public aware of the college's facilities: "Come to the College of St. Catherine. Don't put it off. Decide now. If you need financial help, write to us. We will do all we can. Many students earn their way through college. A college education is worth a big sacrifice. Come." On June 3, 1916, pictures first graced an ad. Around the same time, the college began placing ads in the St. Paul *Pioneer Press* and St. Paul *Dispatch* and publishing more and better brochures. The start of a regular run of the no-fare "dinky" from Snelling to Cleveland on Randolph in 1916 supported recruitment for day students, too. Earlier, the nearest streetcar lines were a mile east and north, on Snelling and Grand Avenues. . . .

Students in area elementary and secondary schools were advised by their teachers of opportunities at the college. Family members, friends, and acquaintances of students spoke highly of it. Sometimes a parish priest recommended a student, and alumnae visitors also spread the news. In response to laws passed in Minnesota and North Dakota requiring all teachers in elementary and high schools to meet requirements for state certification, Sister Antonia assisted the sisters in her congregation as well as those of others. She received letters from sisters in all parts of the country, asking for help in evaluating credits and meeting the new requirements, usually including a bachelor's degree. She gave advice and education, tuition-free at the college, in the hope that the recipients would send future students to their alma mater. In 1921–22, for example, five Sisters of the Holy Names from Vancouver, two Missionary Sisters of the Most Holy Trinity from Alabama, and two Sisters of St. Joseph from Crookston, Minnesota, registered at the college.

These strategies all helped toward increasing enrollment from 30 students in 1914 to 218 in 1920. But the most direct recruiting method—the personal visit—met with the most success. Genevieve Lamb (Oberly) recalled that every year the sisters stayed at her grandmother's home while visiting her hometown of Michigan, North Dakota. A teenager of fourteen or fifteen, she was called upon to drive a surrey carrying the sisters and their lunches to neighboring towns such as Crary. Obtaining the names of Catholic girls from the parish priest, the sisters then visited them in their homes. With no Catholic college in the state, North Dakota was a rich field for recruitment, and enrollment from the area increased from one in 1911 to thirty-one in 1919.

The sisters traveled to Minnesota towns, branching out to Wisconsin and Montana. They went to and from the coast on the Northern Pacific and

Great Northern railways on passes granted by the railroads on the assumption that students would come back as paying fares. Each pair of sisters carried fifty dollars in cash to cover six weeks' travel expenses. They stopped in every fair-sized town along the way, staying without cost in convents or hospitals and in the homes of students or alumnae. They visited the homes of those who had inquired about the college or who were known as prospective recruits by students or alumnae from the town. Difficulties were compensated for by their success at bringing in registrants and the chance to see the West—including Yellowstone and Glacier parks, as arranged by alumnae or parents of students.

The college took a step forward in recruiting techniques in 1924–25 with the production of a movie on campus life called *A Day at St. Catherine's*. Its plot centered on the adventures of a new student. Athletic events (including a field day and a tennis tournament), music classes, the dedication of the chapel, and a commencement procession were shown. Two years later, the college announced the availability of honor tuition scholarships in Catholic high schools throughout Minnesota and surrounding states. This strategy, coupled with a student service program initiated in 1922, helped to increase enrollment even during the economic depression of the 1930s.

Sister Antonia clearly was not interested in enrollment for enrollment's sake, however, and she carefully planned for every facet of college development. Sister Teresa remembered that she labored, usually in several areas at once, to carry through this fourfold program:

1. to obtain national and international recognition for the scholastic work
2. to offer to the sisters of the college the opportunity for a wide cultural background and for professional education at outstanding American and European centers of learning
3. to work out a schedule of study and activity ensuring education at once religious, humanistic, and professional
4. to secure funding for the erection of new buildings, the maintenance of an adequate library, and the establishment of an endowment fund.

Official Recognition

Between 1916 and 1920, the college was accredited by the North Central Association of Colleges, the National Educational Association, the National Catholic Educational Association, and the Association of American Colleges. . . . Accreditation by the North Central Association of Colleges had been particularly complicated, since the financial organization of public universities and colleges differed from that of private colleges, especially Catholic ones. During the winter of 1915–16, the college prepared a self-study and was visited by an accrediting team from the association. The sticking point was the matter of endowment. The college had very little, most of its resources being invested in buildings and faculty development. Sister Antonia worked to convince team members that the contributed services of the sisters constituted a considerable endowment. Team member Charles Judd, a friend from the University of Chicago, seemed to understand the concept, for he wrote in his North Central report: "These teachers do not receive any pay and have no private contracts with the institution but are under the general control of the orders to which they belong. Many of the institutions undoubtedly receive in this way services that represent a large endowment."

But the larger commission did not at first accept the concept. Judd wrote to Sister Antonia: "The committee . . . is not including the name of your institution on the tentative list . . . on the grounds set forth in this report." She replied immediately, on March 18, 1916: "I note with complete satisfaction your just appreciation of the endowment question for Catholic schools. . . . With this matter settled in our favor, I am at a loss to know why our name is not included on your approved list, as I know we more than meet every other standard recommended by the Association."

The committee evidently reversed itself; the Spring 1916 *Ariston* crowed: "On Saturday, March 25, the announcement was made to us that our college had been placed upon its list of schools accredited by the North Central Association of Colleges." That year college recruitment ads replaced the line "accredited by the Minnesota State Board of Public Instruction and by several prominent universities" with "the only college for women in the Northwest belonging to the North Central Association, which places it educationally on a par with Vassar, Wellesley, and Smith."

Professional Educators

Indeed, the teaching services of the sisters constituted an extraordinary endowment. Sister Antonia had given high priority to the professional and cultural education of the faculty. The teaching sisters were to be as well educated as their equals at other colleges and universities. To Sister Antonia, that meant attending and receiving degrees at great universities in the United States as well as travel and study abroad, and the process had begun before the college opened. Sisters Hyacinth, who taught German, and Bridget, who taught music, had studied in France and Germany in 1903. Sister Antonia had begun her correspondence course at the University of Chicago, unheard of for Catholic sisters at the time. But with the cooperation of the superiors of the Sisters of St. Joseph, Sister Antonia sent many young sisters for further study as soon as they left the novitiate, conveniently constructed just east of the college in 1912. As they finished their graduate work, these sisters became the core of the St. Catherine faculty. Sometimes they started teaching before finishing their studies, working on dissertations in their free hours or while sitting up to check in residents returning from concerts and other events.

Sister Agnes Rita Lingl reflected: "To the horror of some people, sometimes bishops, Sister Antonia sent the sisters out to many non-Catholic or rather secular universities. . . . We studied at the University of Chicago, and [when the university] wanted to start a three-year master's program, they picked out a number of colleges—I think only thirty-seven across the country—St. Catherine's was the Catholic representative . . . the sisters from other communities were all being sent to the Catholic University or to Notre Dame."

•   •   •

With the well-educated sisters donating their teaching services, the college had little need for full-time lay teachers. The earliest years saw a succession of part-time teachers for subjects such as piano and violin, voice and elocution. Sister Antonia brought in competent part-time instructors from the University of Minnesota, St. Thomas and the St. Paul Seminary for areas in which the sisters were not yet prepared to teach. . . . George Klasse from the Minneapolis Symphony Orchestra also taught part-time. . . .

Among the most loved teachers from the University of Minnesota was author and scholar Mary Ellen Chase. She taught English at the college for three school years beginning in 1929 and for three additional summers. She devoted a chapter in her book *A Goodly Fellowship* to the college and the friends she made there, saying: "I have never seen happier people, or funnier for that matter, than the nuns at St. Catherine's. Many of them were Irish by inheritance, some by birth, and their sense of humor was inimitable. I have never known so much laughter elsewhere or such good, rich cause for it. I like the thought, which I learned first at St. Catherine's, that those virtues resulting in sainthood are, first of all, simplicity and joy in the Lord rather than meekness, humility, patience, and other less attractive forms of holiness. Knowledge of the saints was not encouraged in my Maine upbringing; but in the years since then I have had a great good time in reading of some of them, and they have added immeasurably to my enjoyment of life.

"St. Catherine's, so far as I know, never looked upon me as either a heretic or a heathen. I shared, in so far as my 'heresy' allowed me, in its life, from which I gained blessings immeasurable. I liked the peace of its chapel, the quiet of its garden, the friendliness and fun of its nuns, the good manners of its students. I liked the shuffling off of a hundred trivialities, the release of which seemed not only possible but inevitable within its gates . . . I liked the single-mindedness . . . the sense that religion was not something to be seized upon in uneasy moments, but natural, like one's hands and feet, and waiting only to be discovered.". . .

Religious, Humanistic, and Professional

. . . Sociology and social work curricula . . . developed remarkably in the 1920s and 1930s. The College Bulletin announced: "The new part that women must take in solving social problems makes it imperative that the department of social and political science furnish a standard of judgment, and include courses like 'Racial Backgrounds and Americanization'." To help meet the need for specially trained workers in the field of social service and to encourage students to become interested in social work, the department listed four senior courses in applied sociology, later called "social case work." The dean's report for June 1932 announced the addition of an organized course in social service work, leading to a social service major. The course consisted of one quarter of social psychology, one of social psychiatry, and one of supervised field work.

Interest in the social sciences on campus reflected the growing involvement of women in fields of social service in the United States. . . . Sister Marie Philip, later reflecting on social work experiences of students in the 1920s, said that a social worker named Ruby Boughman was teaching at the college during that period. She took students to visit a street along the Mississippi River called "The Levee": "There was something like a frame schoolhouse—just one room, as I can remember. And you would go in there and there would be . . . just the nicest Italian chefs and bakers—all men. The women didn't go out at night. . . . We were trying to teach them. Of course, we knew nothing about teaching English to foreigners— absolutely nothing. . . . But I remember those nights, the warmth of them and the gratitude of those men. . . . We kind of prepared them for Americanization. For citizenship papers you need to know a little civics. And we felt perfectly safe. Nobody worried about us walking from Seventh Street to the Levee and back."

New emphasis was also placed on educating teachers for preschool children. Particularly gifted in teaching young children, Sister Ann Harvey, who had earned a master's degree in childhood education at Columbia in 1930, took over the nursery school opened by Ruby Blackhurst in 1929, continuing until her retirement in 1974. Over the years she taught several thousand children, some of whom became prominent St. Paul professionals.

•　•　•

Of Buildings, Bucks, and Books

Increased enrollment and expanding programs necessitated buildings in addition to Derham Hall, and Sister Antonia had embarked on a large-scale construction program. With friends from the University of Chicago and elsewhere, Sister Antonia set out for New York more than once to submit proposals for new buildings to various funding institutions.

When Sister Antonia was appointed dean in 1914, work on a second major building for the college had already begun. With the Derham Hall dormitories filled to overflowing, some provision had to be made for housing. The November 12, 1912, *Catholic Bulletin* commented: "The excavation of the new building to be added to St. Catherine's College is about completed and work on the basement walls has begun. It will have a frontage of 198 feet on Randolph Street, near Prior, and will have a depth of 173 feet. It will be a brick building of reenforced concrete, and will have four stories and a basement." In the fall of 1914, College Hall (at first called simply "the other building"), for housing college students and college facilities, was opened. The central section of the first story was designated Music Hall, East Hall housed the art department, the west wing—Science Hall—housed home economics and science. The residence corridors could accommodate 250 students. Jeanne d'Arc Auditorium, an extension, soon welcomed students, teachers, and speakers, as well as music department concerts and dramatic productions.

Ecstatic about its lovely new building, members of the St. Catherine community watched the beginnings of war on the other side of the world. Sentiment was strong against U.S. involvement both across the country and on campus until, after some provocation, Congress voted to help France fight Germany, on April 2, 1917. Then, much of the discussion on campus turned towards how best to serve. The Summer 1917 *Ariston* included an editorial called "College Women and War" as well as poems such as "War Hymn to Mary" and "Flag of Peace." A later editorial countered a suggestion that the college close so students could work for the war effort. After all, well-trained minds would be needed to put the world back together: To continue school, pray for peace, and join the Red Cross effort seemed the better course.

The college stayed open. Sister Eleanore Michel worked to retain the teaching of German and build the department despite the growing regulation of German texts by the Minnesota Commission of Public Safety. Students variously put on war benefits or continued antiwar efforts, expressing their positions in poems and editorials. And though not all students and faculty members agreed on American involvement in the war, almost everyone on campus became involved in knitting or making dressings for the St. Paul Red Cross, setting up the Derham Hall dining room every Friday afternoon for the purpose. All were happy to hear "The Great War is Over" ringing through the hall at midday on Friday, November 8, 1918. A bit prematurely, Sister Antonia gave the rest of the day off, but on the following Monday, the armistice was signed.

Despite suggestions that college students go to work, the war had in fact brought enrollment up. On December 14, 1918, the *Catholic Bulletin* noted that "twenty music rooms have been converted into dormitories and thirty single rooms have been transformed into double rooms. The intention of young women to prepare themselves to fill positions of men who have gone to the front is thought to be one of the reasons for breaking all records." Sister Antonia was ready. To make her vision concrete, she had drawn up a complete building and landscape plan. The next step would be a building for the music department, to be named for the patron of music, St. Cecilia. She set out on one of several visits to George Vincent at the Rockefeller Foundation, returning from New York with the promise of financial help and advice to establish a board of trustees.

On January 27, 1919, the Board of Trustees of the College of St. Catherine met for the first time, in the "Alumnae Parlour" of College Hall. . . . The twelve-member board was to hold and invest endowment funds and to approve mortgages, indebtedness, purchase and sale of property, and the erection of buildings. . . . They appointed a committee to plan an endowment campaign to raise $200,000 as a match for a $100,000 grant from the Rockefeller Foundation and planned to entertain Wallace Buttrick, president of the foundation's General Education Board. At the next two meetings, they agreed with Buttrick on the terms of the grant, including that it not be used for theological instruction, and approved plans for the new music hall. . . . In the fall of 1921, Caecilian Hall opened with studios for the faculty, practice rooms for students, and a recital hall for performances.

The first college homecoming, sponsored by the St. Catherine Alumna Association in June 1923, marked the twentieth anniversary of the laying of the college cornerstone. . . . Also in 1923, the entire campus was enclosed by a wrought-iron fence with elaborate gates, and planning was initiated for a separate chapel. It would be large, Romanesque, and beautiful—from the high bell tower to the tiled roof and tile facing on interior walls and pillars. H. A. Sullwold was chosen as architect and Paul Steenberg as contractor. Sullwold was sent to Europe to visit Spanish and French medieval cathedrals so he would understand what the chapel should look like. He visited the Church of St. Trophime at Arles, France, which Sister Antonia had admired in 1922. She told him that with a few adaptations, the chapel at the college must follow suit.

Work on the chapel progressed rapidly, with many conferences among Sister Antonia, the architect, and the contractor. When the workers laying concrete for the floor were unable to finish before Thanksgiving of 1923, Sister Antonia promised to provide Thanksgiving dinner if they would work through the holiday to finish. And so they did. On another occasion, when the tile company did not want to work on Saturday, contractor Paul Steenberg persuaded the carpentry foreman and bricklayer foremen to lay tiles themselves. Sister Antonia was so pleased she gave each of them a box of cigars. Years later, Steenberg wrote: "I was much pleased with doing this chapel for many reasons. First, it was a place to worship God. It was a beautiful chapel, and I believe I had satisfied Sister Antonia's wish, which I was told could not be done. [She] was a woman who knew what she wanted and was pleased when she got a real job."

On October 7, 1924, the chapel was complete, and it was dedicated on the feast of Our Lady of Victory, for whom it was named. Three days earlier, the *Catholic Bulletin* had given fourteen pages almost exclusively to the college and its new chapel. Archbishop Dowling reportedly said: "Sister Antonia asked to build a chapel, but she built a cathedral." Sister Lioba, an enthusiastic observer, wrote to Sister Ste. Helene at Oxford University in England: "That great day dawned . . . summer sun, summer warmth, summer green on all sides—and through this loveliness of combined beauty there passed from College Hall to the Chapel of Our Lady of Victory, the procession of dedication—the Archbishop in Cappa Magna, monsignori in such a blaze of glory that it communicated itself to the entire line, priests to the number of at least seventy, the college student body, and people world without end . . . Father [Francis] Missia and the seminarians sang the litany all the way down the aisle, and the reverence of students and congregation can never be forgotten.

"Father [Aloysius] Ziskowsky presided in the sanctuary and his prowess in the church service kept things moving with both grace and precision, but with no sign of obtrusiveness . . . Some of the college girls were ushers in the true sense of the word, for they seated a throng which must have numbered 1,000. All the pews were full with six in a pew besides hundreds of chairs. Mr. [Leopold] Bruenner's Mass was divine—parts of it like the Agnus Dei really inspired—and never did Anna [Goulet] play nor the sisters sing as on last Tuesday. The seminarians sang the gradual and the proper of the Mass in Gregorian chant and the change from their voices to the choir was most affecting . . . there is no telling when [Anna] will again come down to foot locomotion." Sister Anna had first use of what the *Catholic Bulletin* described as: "a fine, three-manual organ . . . That this organ might thoroughly harmonize with the beautiful new building, the Reuter Organ Company sent their experts to St. Paul to go over the plans and details of the building with the architects . . . It . . . has character, one that is admirably well fitted for concert purposes as well as for chapel services."

With the dedication complete, faculty and staff helped move the library from Derham Hall to the ground floor of the new chapel. A new closed stack system meant that student assistants in large numbers paged books to waiting patrons. The library science department, at first called the "School of Library Science," moved there, too. Beginning in 1918 with a nine-credit course in school librarianship, the program had quickly grown. . . . In 1926 a principal sequence, distributed over the junior and senior years and leading to a bachelor's degree in library science, was offered.

• • •

In the meantime, Sister Antonia had attended to the construction of a new building for the sciences. A second grant of $100,000 from the Rockefeller Foundation in 1926 made possible the erection of Mendel Hall, named for the great Austrian biologist and discoverer of the laws of heredity. The *Catholic Bulletin* noted upon its opening in September 1927: "Mendel Hall is to be used exclusively by the science departments. It is a five-story building of variegated red and terra cotta brick . . . The building is divided by a tower, the center of which is ninety-four feet from the east end . . . The new hall was designed to hold approximately fifteen laboratories, as well as lecture rooms, study hall, and faculty office." But Mendel Hall soon accommodated the art department, the education department, and a Montessori child care facility as well. . . .

In 1929, the Rockefeller Foundation granted $300,000 to help develop the health program at the college. The new building, at first known as the Health Center and later as Fontbonne Hall, particularly was to provide space for training in basic sciences for nurses and in physical education for teachers. Sister Antonia, in the president's report for 1931–32, stated that the new Health Center, open that year, "embodies the complete realization . . . of the health unit in our expansion program." The burgeoning library school also moved to the Health Center. The new office for the department chair, a laboratory room for technical processes, and a large classroom there meant more room for the crowded library beneath the chapel.

Praise with Pots and Pans . . .

The care and maintenance of six buildings and the hundreds of students filling them demanded much of the nonteaching staff of the college. Among those working behind the scenes was Sister Georgia Morrisson, beloved friend and counselor of students living in Whitby Hall. She had greeted the first students arriving from St. Joseph's Academy in 1905. Among other responsibilities, she had charge of the laundry, which at that time meant washing all the students' clothes. Sister Georgia assigned each sister, including faculty members, a part of the laundry work according to her own estimate of the other's intelligence. When a task was not well done, she might say: "And you with your Ph.D.!"

•　•　•

Well known among students, too, were several Sisters of St. Joseph who had come to America from Ireland as lay missionaries. (The United States was considered mission territory until 1921.) The Irish sisters—Odelia Murphy, Jarlath Noonan, Candida Gallahue, Elerius Hennessy, and others—provided a warm, loving atmosphere, consoling many a homesick freshman with an extra cookie or piece of cake. Magdalen (later Sister Marie David) Schimanski, a student in the late 1930s, remembered: "Sister Odelia . . . used to provide our work-a-day spreads on a summer evening because we always stayed during summers and vacations . . . the painters, the electricians would have to work in the buildings, so we would move every month to a different building . . . I was very fond of all those kitchen sisters from Ireland: Sister Candida, Elerius, Jarlath. I remember them standing in the chapel—it would be the grand entrance to the chapel overlooking the Dew Drop. They'd be looking at the sunset there. I could almost draw them from memory—those silhouettes of those great big women. There was something beautiful about their peacefulness and their joy and the way they were friendly to us students."

Another admirer, Mary Ellen Chase, wrote in *A Goodly Fellowship*: "They praised the Lord with pots and pans as cymbals and harps and with good food. I used to go into their huge kitchen below the chapel cloister and talk with them as they beat, stirred, and kneaded. The four of them were ample women of great good humor. They wore large gray aprons over their black habits and usually had a touch of flour somewhere on their black veils. As they bustled about in their convent garb intent upon the means of existence, they somehow connected the religious life with the ageless, and surely religious, necessity of daily bread."

•　•　•

And Beyond

Sister Antonia oversaw the construction of five college buildings from 1914 to 1932, but her vision for the students reached beyond buildings, beyond campus, beyond city and nation. To her mind, one could not be fully educated without travel in Europe. She emphasized that basic to preparation for travel was intensive study of the appropriate language: "I am quite sure of this, that encouragement should be given to our young people in schools to acquire a language sense. They should be encouraged to learn at least one or two modern languages which they could use with facility—other than our mother tongue.

Many times I have had parents ask me, 'What is the good of learning French or German? Our daughter will not speak these languages here in America.' True, there is rare occasion for their use, but let us hope that most of our boys and girls will have a chance to visit the countries where these languages are spoken. Certainly it makes for cultural background in every way."

If students could not get to other countries, she found a way to bring other countries to them. One way to accomplish that was to offer scholarships to international students. Several students from Canada and one from Mexico had attended the college earlier, but the first European students were Lucienne and Angele Petit, at the college from 1918 to 1920. Emerging from the postwar devastation of France, they had had little preparation for the United States. Sister Mona Riley recalled: "I can remember them sitting with babushkas over their heads, not knowing any English, but they turned out beautifully. Lucienne finished at one of the universities—I think it was Columbia—and then she taught at Adelphi College on Long Island."

After these first two students from France, a steady stream of students— from Puerto Rico, Panama, Peru, and Brazil, from Germany, Hungary, Italy, Spain, Greece, the Philippines, Iraq, Israel, and Japan—registered at the college. In the 1970s and 1980s many students came from Africa— Kenya, Tanzania, Nigeria—and from the Orient—Japan, China, Malaysia, and Pakistan. . . . Sister Antonia also encouraged international-mindedness by inviting teachers from other countries as native speakers to help students improve their language skills.

•　　•　　•

Students unable to travel abroad learned much from international students and teachers on campus, as well as from other visitors and events of the day. In the vanguard of American women preparing for new participation in the world, they were independent in spirit and sometimes broke college rules designed to limit "radical behavior." Lucy Sanschagrin '25 (later Sister Marie Ursule), for instance, was almost expelled for bobbing her hair, and Mary O'Brien '27 (Sister Antonine's sister) was accused of "suffragetteism" for carrying a swagger stick. There seems to have been little activity related to women's suffrage (most students were not old enough to vote), but after women's right to vote was ratified in 1919, mock presidential elections were held. The first, apparently in response to the election of Calvin Coolidge, was described in the 1924 student yearbook: "Not to be outstripped by any other independent women in America, we of the College of St. Catherine decided to use our privilege of franchise and held our own election. It was with much agitation and anxiety that the girls gathered at eleven o'clock on a certain Wednesday morning in the auditorium. After several days electioneering the students met ready to assert their opinions and support their candidates. In fact, the meeting resembled a Republican caucus."

Then interest in social and political events grew, and with faculty members returning from study in other lands, the discussion of world issues flourished. . . . A *Wheel* editorial on April 12, 1935, discussed a speaker at the Woman's Club of Minneapolis: "Dame Rachel Crowdy, head of the humanitarian committee of the League of Nations, was scheduled to speak on 'Women in International Affairs.' She was astonished when told of her topic and said, 'I could not speak for five minutes on *women* in international affairs. There are none.' We, who are vitally interested in international peace, will some day answer Dame Crowdy's challenge and give her ample opportunity."

Some students combined artistic, entertainment and economic activities to good effect. Proceeds from a grassroots attempt to produce plays on campus were donated to a fund for a new elevator in Derham Hall in the early 1920s, for example. . . . Among the more formal musical and dramatic productions was *The Messiah*, presented by the Choral Club and assisted by the men of the St. Paul Municipal Chorus. On March 2, 1926, the *Lantern* (a weekly published by the sophomores for one year only) mentioned Austrian composer and pianist Percy Grainger's visit and the two programs he gave in Jeanne d'Arc Auditorium. Inspired by Edvard Grieg, he had collected English and Irish folksongs and arranged them for concert use. Sister Antonia's voice rang forth: "This event is one of the greatest privileges which are given to the students, probably a privilege which to some may not again be granted . . . It is your duty, girls, to let the public know of his coming and invite them."

•   •   •

Despite her many responsibilities, Sister Antonia kept in touch with the students, making sure the world of each was expanded through cultural activities outside the classroom. Sister Ann Harvey recalled: "Someone sent Mother Antonia four tickets to the symphony, and the seats were very good. She asked me if I wanted one and I said 'Yes,' because I was a poor little girl and did not have any money . . . a telephone call came from Mother Antonia about twenty minutes after she gave me the ticket, to please come to her office because she wanted to tell me what to wear, and how to look. She told me to wear a hat and bring my purse and wear gloves . . . In true Sister-Antonia-fashion, she waited up for us after the symphony and got our enthusiastic ideas on the music. It was my first symphony, and I thought I was in heaven."

According to Sister Antonia, the accumulation of knowledge was not the sole purpose of a college education. Character training or "the building of a life" was most often the subject of her assembly talks. Sister Marie Philip noted: "Wednesday after Wednesday she lashed us into a fairly homogeneous student group. She drove at practice, at homely virtues— honesty, cleanliness, industry, dependableness, a nice consideration for others. Who could ever forget her urging us to chisel our characters, to accomplish hard things, to be women of good sense? She taught us that the ideal of sound and strong Catholic womanhood is big, simple, noble, and practicable."

Mary Ellen Chase wrote in *A Goodly Fellowship:* " Sister Antonia went at the realization of St. Catherine's College with everything she had in her . . . *Laborare est orare* was sound doctrine to her . . . She saw architects and remade their plans; she sat on stone heaps and inspired workmen. She laid out grounds and planted trees . . . She had read widely and seemingly she had forgotten nothing that she had ever read. She was the best of teachers . . . Her feverish activity made her not only apparently omnipresent, but completely master of every scene and situation as well . . . In the chapel she could be intent upon her own devotions and aware of any lack of devotion in her girls . . . She was a handsome woman with an alert, eager face and a fine carriage. When she swept down the corridors of her college in her black habit on her way to the chapel, or the garden or the kitchen or the powerhouse, everyone upon her swift approach straightened head and shoulders."

In 1936, Sister Antonia became ill, suffering several strokes. In 1937 she resigned because of increasing disability, to live quietly in Whitby 106. Friends and alumnae still visited, and the honors poured in as before: President Herbert Hoover invited her to the White House Conference on Child Health and Protection. Pope Pius XI awarded her the *Pro Ecclesia et Pontifice* medal. She was elected president of the Association of Minnesota Colleges and awarded an honorary degree of Doctor of Laws by the University of Minnesota.

Sister Antonia McHugh died quietly on October 11, 1944. The Spring 1927 *Ariston* had written of her: "Sister Antonia succeeded in building up not only the physical plant but the curriculum and the faculty as well . . . Our development in every line is due to her farsightedness, her zeal in furthering the course of Catholic education in America. Under her wise guidance, courses of study have been organized and the college standardized until it is now recognized by the highest authorities. All the best in American universities, all the advantages, all the benefits of foreign travel, have been utilized . . . in the preparation of superior teachers."

Five years after her death, *Ariston* was still paying her tribute: "Always to her St. Catherine's has been a great college. Even when it was only a dream. Never just a building on a hill, it was a growing family of build-ings: Caecilian, Mendel, the Health Center, the Chapel. All these she planned, built, and peopled in her mind long before the architects were ever summoned. The pews of Our Lady of Victory Chapel were filled with girls in cap and gown when the old chapel on fourth Derham was still adequate to the college needs. It is that vision for the future, that aspi-ration for excellence, and the creative power to convert vision into reality that has distinguished Mother Antonia's work." That vision of excellence was her legacy.

Adrienne Rich (b. 1929) is an American poet, essayist, feminist activist, and speaker. The following passage comes from On Lies, Secrets and Silence: Selected Prose 1966–1978 (1979). *Here Rich addresses a group of students gathered for a convocation at an all women's college. What key words does she define in this essay on the responsibility of women to be actively engaged in shaping their own education? For example, what is the difference between "claiming" and "receiving" here? What does "responsibility" mean in this particular context? What does this notion of "claiming an education" mean to you as a student at an all women's college?*

Claiming an Education

Adrienne Rich

For this convocation, I planned to separate my remarks into two parts: some thoughts about you, the women students here, and some thoughts about us who teach in a women's college. But ultimately, those two parts are indivisible. If university education means anything beyond the processing of human beings into expected roles, through credit hours, tests, and grades (and I believe that in a women's college especially it *might* mean much more), it implies an ethical and intellectual contract between teacher and student. This contract must remain intuitive, dynamic, unwritten, but we must turn to it again and again if learning is to be reclaimed from the depersonalizing and cheapening pressures of the present day academic scene.

The first thing I want to say to you who are students, is that you cannot afford to think of being here to *receive* an education; you will do much better to think of yourselves as being here to *claim* one. One of the dictionary definitions of the verb "to claim" is: *to take as the rightful owner; to assert in the face of possible contradiction.* "To receive" is *to come into possession of; to act as receptacle or container for; to accept as authoritative or true.* The difference is that between acting and being acted-upon, and for women it can literally mean the difference between life and death.

One of the devastating weaknesses of university learning, of the store of knowledge and opinion that has been handed down through academic training, has been its almost total erasure of women's experience and thought from the curriculum, and its exclusion of women as members of the academic community. Today, with increasing numbers of women students in nearly every branch of higher learning, we still see very few women in the upper levels of faculty and administration in most institutions. Douglass College itself is a women's college in a university administered overwhelmingly by men, who in turn are answerable to the state

legislature, again composed predominantly of men. But the most significant fact for you is that what you learn here, the very texts you read, the
lectures you hear, the way your studies are divided into categories and
fragmented one from the other—all this reflects to a very large degree,
neither objective reality, nor an accurate picture of the past, nor a group
of rigorously tested observations about human behavior. What you can
learn here (and I mean not only at Douglass but any college in any university) is how *men* have perceived and organized their experience, their
history, their ideas of social relationships, good and evil, sickness and
health, etc. When you read or hear about "great issues," "major texts,"
"the mainstream of Western thought," you are hearing about what men,
above all white men, in their male subjectivity have decided is important.

Black and other minority peoples have for some time recognized that
their racial and ethnic experience was not accounted for in the studies
broadly labeled human; and that even the sciences can be racist. For
many reasons, it has been more difficult for women to comprehend our
exclusion, and to realize that even the sciences can be sexist. For one
thing, it is only within the last hundred years that higher education has
grudgingly been opened up to women at all, even to white, middle-class
women. And many of us have found ourselves poring eagerly over books
with titles like: *The Descent of Man; Man and His Symbols; Irrational Man;
The Phenomenon of Man; The Future of Man; Man and the Machine; From Man
to Man; May Man Prevail?; Man, Science and Society;* or *One-Dimensional
Man*—books pretending to describe a "human" reality that does not
include over one-half the human species.

Less than a decade ago, with the rebirth of a feminist movement in this
country, women students and teachers in a number of universities began
to demand and set up women's studies courses—to *claim* a woman-
directed education. And, despite the inevitable accusations of "unschol-
arly," "group therapy," "faddism," etc., despite backlash and budget cuts,
women's studies are still growing, offering to more and more women a
new intellectual grasp on their lives, new understanding of our history, a
fresh vision of the human experience, and also a critical basis for evaluating what they hear and read in other courses, and in the society at large.

But my talk is not really about women's studies, much as I believe in their
scholarly, scientific, and human necessity. While I think that any Douglass
student has everything to gain by investigating and enrolling in women's
studies courses, I want to suggest that there is a more essential experience
that you owe yourselves, one which courses in women's studies can
greatly enrich, but which finally depends on you, in all your interactions
with yourself and your world. This is the experience of *taking responsibility toward yourselves.* Our upbringing as women has so often told us that
this should come second to our relationships and responsibilities to other

people. We have been offered ethical models of the self-denying wife and
mother; intellectual models of the brilliant but slapdash dilettante who
never commits herself to anything the whole way, or the intelligent
woman who denies her intelligence in order to seem more "feminine," or
who sits in passive silence even when she disagrees inwardly with everything that is being said around her.

Responsibility to yourself means refusing to let others do your thinking,
talking, and naming for you; it means learning to respect and use your own
brains and instincts; hence, grappling with hard work. It means that you do
not treat your body as a commodity with which to purchase superficial
intimacy or economic security; for our bodies and minds are inseparable in
this life, and when we allow our bodies to be treated as objects, our minds
are in mortal danger. It means insisting that those to whom you give your
friendship and love are able to respect your mind. It means being able to
say, with Charlotte Bronte's *Jane Eyre*: "I have an inward treasure born with
me, which can keep me alive if all the extraneous delights should be with-
held or offered only at a price I cannot afford to give."

Responsibility to yourself means that you don't fall for shallow and easy
solutions—predigested books and ideas, weekend encounters guaranteed
to change your life, taking "gut" courses instead of ones you know will
challenge you, bluffing at school and life instead of doing solid work, marrying early as an escape from real decisions, getting pregnant as an evasion
of already existing problems. It means that you refuse to sell your talents
and aspirations short, simply to avoid conflict and confrontation. And this,
in turn, means resisting the forces in society which say that women should
be nice, play safe, have low professional expectations, drown in love and
forget about work, live through others, and stay in the places assigned to
us. It means that we insist on a life of meaningful work, insist that work be
as meaningful as love and friendship in our lives. It means, therefore, the
courage to be "different"; not to be continuously available to others when
we need time for ourselves and our work; to be able to demand of others—
parents, friends, roommates, teachers, lovers, husbands, children—that
they respect our sense of purpose and our integrity as persons. Women
everywhere are finding the courage to do this, more and more, and we are
finding that courage both in our study of women in the past who possessed
it, and in each other as we look to other women for comradeship, community, and challenge. The difference between a life lived actively, and a life
of passive drifting and dispersal of energies, is an immense difference.
Once we begin to feel committed to our lives, responsible to ourselves, we
can never again be satisfied with the old, passive way.

Now comes the second part of the contract. I believe that in a women's college you have the right to expect your faculty to take you seriously. The
education of women has been a matter of debate for centuries, and old,

negative attitudes about women's role, women's ability to think and take leadership, are still rife both in and outside the university. Many male professors (and I don't mean only at Douglass) still feel that teaching in a women's college is a second-rate career. Many tend to eroticize their women students—to treat them as sexual objects—instead of demanding the best of their minds. (At Yale a legal suit [*Alexander v. Yale*] has been brought against the university by a group of women students demanding a stated policy against sexual advances toward female students by male professors.) Many teachers, both men and women, trained in the male-centered tradition, are still handing the ideas and texts of that tradition on to students without teaching them to criticize its anti-woman attitudes, its omission of women as part of the species. Too often, all of us fail to teach the most important thing, which is that clear thinking, active discussion, and excellent writing are all necessary for intellectual freedom, and that these require *hard work*. Sometimes, perhaps in discouragement with a culture which is both anti-intellectual and anti-woman, we may resign ourselves to low expectations for our students before we have given them half a chance to become more thoughtful, expressive human beings. We need to take to heart the words of Elizabeth Barrett Browning, a poet, a thinking woman, and a feminist, who wrote in 1845 of her impatience with studies which cultivate a "passive recipiency" in the mind, and asserted that "women want to be made to *think actively*: their apprehension is quicker than that of men, but their defect lies for the most part in the logical faculty and in the higher mental activities." Note that she implies a defect which can be remedied by intellectual training; *not* an inborn lack of ability.

I have said that the contract on the student's part involves that you demand to be taken seriously so that you can also go on taking yourself seriously. This means seeking out criticism, recognizing that the most affirming thing anyone can do for you is demand that you push yourself further, show you the range of what you can do. It means rejecting attitudes of "take-it-easy," "why-be-so-serious," "why-worry-you'll-probably-get-married-anyway." It means assuming your share of responsibility for what happens in the classroom, because that affects the quality of your daily life here. It means that the student sees herself engaged *with* her teachers in an active, ongoing struggle for a real education. But for her to do this, her teachers must be committed to the belief that women's minds and experience are intrinsically valuable and indispensable to any civilization worthy of the name; that there is no more exhilarating and intellectually fertile place in the academic world today than a women's college—*if* both students and teachers in large enough numbers are trying to fulfill this contract. The contract is really a pledge of mutual seriousness about women, about language, ideas, methods, and values. It is our shared commitment toward a world in which the inborn potentialities of so many women's minds will no longer be wasted, raveled-away, paralyzed, or denied.

Parker J. Palmer (b. 1939) is a Quaker writer, teacher, and activist for education, spirituality, and social change. What follows is excerpted from his Let Your Life Speak: Listening for the Voice of Vocation *(2000). He discusses the complicated and often elusive relationship between selfhood and identity. What does Palmer mean by "authenticity" and "vocation"? Like Mitchell, he insists on both the individual and the community. How? Consider the exploration of the self that Palmer encourages in this essay. How might it relate to Rich's call for women to "claim an education"?*

Now I Become Myself

Parker J. Palmer

A Vision of Vocation

With twenty-one words, carefully chosen and artfully woven, May Sarton evokes the quest for vocation—at least, my quest for vocation—with candor and precision:

> Now I become myself.
>
> It's taken time, many years and places.
>
> I have been dissolved and shaken,
>
> Worn other people's faces. . . .[1]

What a long time it can take to become the person one has always been! How often in the process we mask ourselves in faces that are not our own. How much dissolving and shaking of ego we must endure before we discover our deep identity—the true self within every human being that is the seed of authentic vocation.

I first learned about vocation growing up in the church. I value much about the religious tradition in which I was raised: its humility about its own convictions, its respect for the world's diversity, its concern for justice. But the idea of "vocation" I picked up in those circles created distortion until I grew strong enough to discard it. I mean the idea that vocation, or calling, comes from a voice external to ourselves, a voice of moral demand that asks us to become someone we are not yet—someone different, someone better, someone just beyond our reach.

That concept of vocation is rooted in a deep distrust of selfhood, in the belief that the sinful self will always be "selfish" unless corrected by external forces of virtue. It is a notion that made me feel inadequate to the task of living my own life, creating guilt about the distance between who

34

I was and who I was supposed to be, leaving me exhausted as I labored to close the gap.

Today I understand vocation quite differently—not as a goal to be achieved but as a gift to be received. Discovering vocation does not mean scrambling toward some prize just beyond my reach but accepting the treasure of true self I already possess. Vocation does not come from a voice "out there" calling me to become something I am not. It comes from a voice "in here" calling me to be the person I was born to be, to fulfill the original selfhood given me at birth by God.

It is a strange gift, this birthright gift of self. Accepting it turns out to be even more demanding than attempting to become someone else! I have sometimes responded to that demand by ignoring the gift, or hiding it, or fleeing from it, or squandering it—and I think I am not alone. There is a Hasidic tale that reveals, with amazing brevity, both the universal tendency to want to be someone else and the ultimate importance of becoming one's self: Rabbi Zusya, when he was an old man, said, "In the coming world, they will not ask me: 'Why were you not Moses?' They will ask me: 'Why were you not Zusya?'"[2]

If you doubt that we all arrive in this world with gifts and as a gift, pay attention to an infant or a very young child. A few years ago, my daughter and her newborn baby came to live with me for a while. Watching my granddaughter from her earliest days on earth, I was able, in my early fifties, to see something that had eluded me as a twenty-something parent: my granddaughter arrived in the world as *this* kind of person rather than *that*, or *that*, or *that*.

She did not show up as raw material to be shaped into whatever image the world might want her to take. She arrived with her own gifted form, with the shape of her own sacred soul. Biblical faith calls it the image of God in which we are all created. Thomas Merton calls it true self. Quakers call it the inner light, or "that of God" in every person. The humanist tradition calls it identity and integrity. No matter what you call it, it is a pearl of great price.

In those early days of my granddaughter's life, I began observing the inclinations and proclivities that were planted in her at birth. I noticed, and I still notice, what she likes and dislikes, what she is drawn toward and repelled by, how she moves, what she does, what she says.

I am gathering my observations in a letter. When my granddaughter reaches her late teens or early twenties, I will make sure that my letter finds its way to her, with a preface something like this: "Here is a sketch of who you were from your earliest days in this world. It is not a definitive picture—only you can draw that. But it was sketched by a person who loves you very much. Perhaps these notes will help you do sooner something your grandfather did only later: remember who you were when you first arrived and reclaim the gift of true self."

We arrive in this world with birthright gifts—then we spend the first half of our lives abandoning them or letting others disabuse us of them. As young people, we are surrounded by expectations that may have little to do with who we really are, expectations held by people who are not trying to discern our selfhood but to fit us into slots. In families, schools, work-places, and religious communities, we are trained away from true self toward images of acceptability; under social pressures like racism and sex-ism our original shape is deformed beyond recognition; and we ourselves, driven by fear, too often betray true self to gain the approval of others.

We are disabused of original giftedness in the first half of our lives. Then—if we are awake, aware, and able to admit our loss—we spend the second half trying to recover and reclaim the gift we once possessed.

When we lose track of true self, how can we pick up the trail? One way is to seek clues in stories from our younger years, years when we lived closer to our birthright gifts. A few years ago, I found some clues to myself in a time machine of sorts. A friend sent me a tattered copy of my high school newspaper from May 1957 in which I had been interviewed about what I intended to do with my life. With the certainty to be expected of a high school senior, I told the interviewer that I would become a naval aviator and then take up a career in advertising.

I was indeed "wearing other people's faces," and I can tell you exactly whose they were. My father worked with a man who had once been a navy pilot. He was Irish, charismatic, romantic, full of the wild blue yon-der and a fair share of the blarney, and I wanted to be like him. The father of one of my boyhood friends was in advertising, and though I did not yearn to take on his persona, which was too buttoned-down for my taste, I did yearn for the fast car and other large toys that seemed to be the accessories of his selfhood!

These self-prophecies, now over forty years old, seem wildly misguided for a person who eventually became a Quaker, a would-be pacifist, a writer, and an activist. Taken literally, they illustrate how early in life we can lose track of who we are. But inspected through the lens of paradox, my desire to become an aviator and an advertiser contain clues to the core of true self that would take many years to emerge: clues, by definition, are coded and must be deciphered.

Hidden in my desire to become an "ad man" was a lifelong fascination with language and its power to persuade, the same fascination that has kept me writing incessantly for decades. Hidden in my desire to become a naval aviator was something more complex: a personal engagement with the problem of violence that expressed itself at first in military fantasies and then, over a period of many years, resolved itself in the pacifism I aspire to today. When I flip the coin of identity I held to so tightly in high school, I find the paradoxical "opposite" that emerged as the years went by.

If I go farther back, to an earlier stage of my life, the clues need less deciphering to yield insight into my birthright gifts and callings. In grade school, I became fascinated with the mysteries of flight. As many boys did in those days, I spent endless hours, after school and on weekends, designing, crafting, flying, and (usually) crashing model airplanes made of fragile balsa wood.

Unlike most boys, however, I also spent long hours creating eight- and twelve-page books about aviation. I would turn a sheet of paper sideways; draw a vertical line down the middle; make diagrams of, say, the cross-section of a wing; roll the sheet into a typewriter; and peck out a caption explaining how air moving across an airfoil creates a vacuum that lifts the plane. Then I would fold that sheet in half along with several others I had made, staple the collection together down the spine, and painstakingly illustrate the cover.

I had always thought that the meaning of this paperwork was obvious: fascinated with flight, I wanted to be a pilot, or at least an aeronautical engineer. But recently, when I found a couple of these literary artifacts in an old cardboard box, I suddenly saw the truth, and it was more obvious than I had imagined. I didn't want to be a pilot or an aeronautical engineer or anything else related to aviation. I wanted to be an author, to make books—a task I have been attempting from the third grade to this very moment!

From the beginning, our lives lay down clues to selfhood and vocation, though the clues may be hard to decode. But trying to interpret them is profoundly worthwhile—especially when we are in our twenties or thirties or forties, feeling profoundly lost, having wandered, or been dragged, far away from our birthright gifts.

Those clues are helpful in counteracting the conventional concept of vocation, which insists that our lives must be driven by "oughts." As noble as that may sound, we do not find our callings by conforming ourselves to some abstract moral code. We find our callings by claiming authentic selfhood, by being who we are, by dwelling in the world as Zusya rather than straining to be Moses. The deepest vocational question is not "What ought I to do with my life?" It is the more elemental and demanding "Who am I? What is my nature?"

Everything in the universe has a nature, which means limits as well as potentials, a truth well known by people who work daily with the things of the world. Making pottery, for example, involves more than telling the clay what to become. The clay presses back on the potter's hands, telling her what it can and cannot do —and if she fails to listen, the outcome will be both frail and ungainly. Engineering involves more than telling materials what they must do. If the engineer does not honor the nature of the steel or the wood or the stone, his failure will go well beyond aesthetics: the bridge or the building will collapse and put human life in peril.

The human self also has a nature, limits as well as potentials. If you seek vocation without understanding the material you are working with, what you build with your life will be ungainly and may well put lives in peril, your own and some of those around you. "Faking it" in the service of high values is no virtue and has nothing to do with vocation. It is an ignorant, sometimes arrogant, attempt to override one's nature, and it will always fail.

Our deepest calling is to grow into our own authentic selfhood, whether or not it conforms to some image of who we *ought* to be. As we do so, we will not only find the joy that every human being seeks—we will also find our path of authentic service in the world. True vocation joins self and service, as Frederick Buechner asserts when he defines vocation as "the place where your deep gladness meets the world's deep need."[3]

Buechner's definition starts with the self and moves toward the needs of the world: it begins, wisely, where vocation begins—not in what the world needs (which is everything), but in the nature of the human self, in what brings the self joy, the deep joy of now knowing that at we are here on earth to be the gifts that God created.

Contrary to the conventions of our thinly moralistic culture, this emphasis on gladness and selfhood is not selfish. The Quaker teacher Douglas Steere was fond of saying that the ancient human question "Who am I?" leads inevitably to the equally important question "Whose am I?"—for there is no selfhood outside of relationship. We must ask the question of selfhood and answer it as honestly as we can, no matter where it takes us. Only as we do so can we discover the community of our lives.

As I learn more about the seed of true self that was planted when I was born, I also learn more about the ecosystem in which I was planted—the network of communal relations in which I am called to live responsively, accountably, and joyfully with beings of every sort. Only when I know both seed and system, self and community, can I embody the great commandment to love both my neighbor and myself.

•   •   •

Selfhood, Society, and Service

By surviving passages of doubt and depression on the vocational journey, I have become clear about at least one thing: self-care is never a selfish act—it is simply good stewardship of the only gift I have, the gift I was put on earth to offer to others. Anytime we can listen to true self and give it the care it requires, we do so not only for ourselves but for the many others whose lives we touch.

There are at least two ways to understand the link between selfhood and service. One is offered by the poet Rumi in his piercing observation: "If you are here unfaithfully with us, you're causing terrible damage."[7] If we are unfaithful to true self, we will extract a price from others. We will make promises we cannot keep, build houses from flimsy stuff, conjure dreams that devolve into nightmares, and other people will suffer—if we are unfaithful to true self.

I will examine that sort of unfaithfulness, and its consequences, later in this book. But a more inspiring way of understanding the link between selfhood and service is to study the lives of people who have been here *faithfully* with us. Look, for example, at the great liberation movements that have served humanity so well—in eastern Europe, Latin America, and South Africa, among women, African Americans, and our gay and lesbian brothers and sisters. What we see is simple but often ignored: the movements that transform us, our relations, and our world emerge from the lives of people who decide to care for their authentic selfhood.

The social systems in which these people must survive often try to force them to live in a way untrue to who they are. If you are poor, you are supposed to accept, with gratitude, half a loaf or less; if you are black, you are supposed to suffer racism without protest; if you are gay, you are supposed to pretend that you are not. You and I may not know, but we can at least imagine, how tempting it would be to mask one's truth in situations of this sort—because the system threatens punishment if one does not.

But in spite of that threat, or because of it, the people who plant the seeds of movements make a critical decision: they decide to live "divided no more." *They decide no longer to act on the outside in a way that contradicts some truth about themselves that they hold deeply on the inside.* They decide to claim authentic selfhood and act it out—and their decisions ripple out to transform the society in which they live, serving the selfhood of millions of others.

I call this the "Rosa Parks decision" because that remarkable woman is so emblematic of what the undivided life can mean. Most of us know her story, the story of an African American woman who, at the time she made her decision, was a seamstress in her early forties. On December 1, 1955,

in Montgomery, Alabama, Rosa Parks did something she was not supposed to do: she sat down at the front of a bus in one of the seats reserved
for whites—a dangerous, daring, and provocative act in a racist society.

Legend has it that years later a graduate student came to Rosa Parks and
asked, "Why did you sit down at the front of the bus that day?" Rosa
Parks did not say that she sat down to launch a movement, because her
motives were more elemental than that. She said, "I sat down because I
was tired." But she did not mean that her feet were tired. She meant that
her soul was tired, her heart was tired, her whole being was tired of playing by racist rules, of denying her soul's claim to selfhood.[8]

Of course, there were many forces aiding and abetting Rosa Parks's decision to live divided no more. She had studied the theory and tactics of
nonviolence at the Highlander Folk School, where Martin Luther King Jr.
was also a student. She was secretary of the Montgomery chapter of the
National Association for the Advancement of Colored People, whose
members had been discussing civil disobedience.

But in the moment she sat down at the front of the bus on that December
day, she had no guarantee that the theory of nonviolence would work or
that her community would back her up. It was a moment of existential
truth, of claiming authentic selfhood, of reclaiming birthright giftedness—and in that moment she set in motion a process that changed both
the lay and the law of the land.

Rosa Parks sat down because she had reached a point where it was essential to embrace her true vocation—not as someone who would reshape
our society but as someone who would live out her full self in the world.
She decided, "I will no longer act on the outside in a way that contradicts
the truth that I hold deeply on the inside. I will no longer act as if I were
less than the whole person I know myself inwardly to be."

Where does one get the courage to "sit down at the front of the bus" in a
society that punishes anyone who decides to live divided no more? After
all, conventional wisdom recommends the divided life as the safe and
sane way to go: "Don't wear your heart on your sleeve." "Don't make a
federal case out of it." "Don't show them the whites of your eyes." These
are all the clichéd ways we tell each other to keep personal truth apart
from public life, lest we make ourselves vulnerable in that rough-and-
tumble realm.

Where do people find the courage to live divided no more when they
know they will be punished for it? The answer I have seen in the lives of
people like Rosa Parks is simple: these people have transformed the
notion of punishment itself. They have come to understand that *no punishment anyone might inflict on them could possibly be worse than the punishment they inflict on themselves by conspiring in their own diminishment.*

In the Rosa Parks story, that insight emerges in a wonderful way. After she had sat at the front of the bus for a while, the police came aboard and said, "You know, if you continue to sit there, we're going to have to throw you in jail."

Rosa Parks replied, "You may do that...," which is a very polite way of saying, "What could your jail of stone and steel possibly mean to me, compared to the self-imposed imprisonment I've suffered for forty years—the prison I've just walked out of by refusing to conspire any longer with this racist system?"

The punishment imposed on us for claiming true self can never be worse than the punishment we impose on ourselves by failing to make that claim. And the converse is true as well: no reward anyone might give us could possibly be greater than the reward that comes from living by our own best lights.

You and I may not have Rosa Parks's particular battle to fight, the battle with institutional racism. The universal element in her story is not the substance of her fight but the selfhood in which she stood while she fought it—for each of us holds the challenge and the promise of naming and claiming true self.

But if the Rosa Parks story is to help us discern our own vocations, we must see her as the ordinary person she is. That will be difficult to do because we have made her into superwoman—and we have done it to protect ourselves. If we can keep Rosa Parks in a museum as an untouchable icon of truth, we will remain untouchable as well: we can put her up on a pedestal and praise her, world without end, never finding ourselves challenged by her life.

Since my own life runs no risk of being displayed in a museum case, I want to return briefly to the story I know best—my own. Unlike Rosa Parks, I never took a singular, dramatic action that might create the energy of transformation around the institutions I care about. Instead, I tried to abandon those institutions through an evasive, crablike movement that I did not want to acknowledge, even to myself.

But a funny thing happened on the way to my vocation. Today, twenty-five years after I left education in anger and fear, my work is deeply related to the renewal of educational institutions. I believe that this is possible only because my true self dragged me, kicking and screaming, toward honoring its nature and needs, forcing me to find my rightful place in the ecosystem of life, to find a right relation to institutions with which I have a lifelong lover's quarrel. Had I denied my true self, remaining "at my post" simply because I was paralyzed with fear, I would almost certainly be lost in bitterness today instead of serving a cause I care about.

Rosa Parks took her stand with clarity and courage. I took mine by diversion and default. Some journeys are direct, and some are circuitous; some are heroic, and some are fearful and muddled. But every journey, honestly undertaken, stands a chance of taking us toward the place where our deep gladness meets the world's deep need.

As May Sarton reminds us, the pilgrimage toward true self will take "time, many years and places." The world needs people with the patience and the passion to make that pilgrimage not only for their own sake but also as a social and political act. The world still waits for the truth that will set us free—my truth, your truth, our truth—the truth that was seeded in the earth when each of us arrived here formed in the image of God. Cultivating that truth, I believe, is the authentic vocation of every human being.

Notes

[1] May Sarton, "Now I Become Myself," in *Collected Poems, 1930–1973* (New York: Norton, 1974), 156.

[2] Martin Buber, *Tales of the Hasidim: The Early Masters* (New York: Schocken Books, 1975), 251.

[3] Frederick Buechner, *Wishful Thinking: A Seeker's ABC* (San Francisco: Harper San Francisco, 1993), 119.

[4] Phil Cosineau, *The Art of Pilgrimage* (Berkeley: Conari Press 1998), xxiii.

[5] Parker J. Palmer, *The Company of Strangers: Christians and the Renewal of America's Public Life* (New York: Crossroads, 1981).

[6] See Howard H. Brinton, *The Pendle Hill Idea: A Quaker Experiment in Work, Worship, Study* (Wallingford, PA: Pendle Hill, 1950), and Eleanor Price Mather, *Pendle Hill: A Quaker Experiment in Education and Community* (Wallingford, PA: Pendle Hill, 1980).

[7] Rumi, "Forget Your Life," in *The Enlightened Heart*, ed. Stephen Mitchell (New York: HarperCollins, 1989), 56.

[8] Rosa Parks, *Rosa Parks: My Story* (New York: Dial Books, 1992), 116.

Maya Lin (b. 1959) is best known as the artist whose winning design for the Vietnam Veterans Memorial in Washington, DC, was submitted when she was a college senior at Yale University. She combines her heritage as a Chinese-American with culturally diverse sources such as works by American earthworks artists of the 1960s and 1970s and Japanese gardens to create her sculptures and other architectural projects. "On Making" comes from Lin's book, Boundaries *(2000). In this text, Lin describes her creative process, one in which she purposefully attempts to achieve a balance between the analytical and the intuitive. Lin's narrative about her own artistic process serves as an example of how we might reflect on ourselves, our values, perspectives, and choices. Indeed, it offers a model as to how we might develop the articulation of our own self-knowledge. What essential components contribute to Lin's process as described here? What metaphors describe this process? What role does writing play for Lin?*

On Making

Maya Lin

I begin by imagining an artwork verbally. I try to describe in writing what the project is, what it is trying to do. I need to understand the artwork without giving it a specific materiality or solid form.

I try not to find the form too soon. Instead, I try to think about it as an idea without a shape.

Most of my art and architectural works are commissioned for a specific site by a specific individual or group. And with these commissioned works I have often started with a written description of what I think the work is about or what its purpose should be. When making these works, I spend much time researching the site—not just the physical aspects of the site but the cultural context of it as well: who will use the site, the history of the place, the nature of the people who live there. I spend the first few months researching a multitude of facts, history, and materials, not knowing if anything I am studying will be of use to me in the artwork.

Sometimes, as with the memorials, I see a very specific and clearly defined purpose to the project. With the *Vietnam Veterans Memorial*, I needed to ask myself the question "What is the purpose of a war memorial at the close of the twentieth century?" My question led me to a study of war memorials, from the earliest funereal stelae to the monuments of the great world wars. I felt that the design should focus on the individuals who died and not on the politics surrounding that war. I sought a design that would bring the viewer to an honest acceptance of the deaths of those individuals.

For the *Civil Rights Memorial*, the sponsor, the Southern Poverty Law Center, felt the need for such a memorial but left it to me to define what such a memorial would specifically entail. I had to ask myself what its purpose should be. As I began to learn more about the civil rights movement, I was surprised at how little I knew about the history surrounding the struggle for racial equality. I decided early on that a memorial to civil rights had to evoke the history of that period. Just listing the names of those killed in the movement would not give a visitor a true idea of what that struggle for equality had been about. I felt the goal of the memorial would be to present a brief idea of what that time period had been about (as a teaching tool), so that the struggles and sacrifices would not be forgotten.

For both these memorials, my research and study led me in the general direction I wanted to take before I had visited the sites, and when I did visit the sites, the idea that I brought with me helped me to imagine almost instantly the form each memorial would take. In both instances, I waited until I knew my direction partly because I was afraid that if I saw the site too soon, I might react to it in a more formal way and imagine a design onto which I would then have to force a function.

At other times, as with most of my outdoor artworks, the project takes its purpose or shape from a combination of my research of the site and my aesthetic interests. The *Wave Field*, which is sited at an aerospace engineering building at the University of Michigan, is based on an image I found while researching the mechanics of flight, whereas in *Reading a Garden*, a sculpture for the Cleveland Public Library, I had been waiting for a library as a site so that I could collaborate with a writer to create a garden of words.

For most of the works, I make an initial visit to a site, put it somewhere in the back of my mind, then return to my studio and start researching the project. I never know what I am looking for at this point and I never try to focus too directly or self-consciously on the search for an idea for the artwork. The research, in fact, is more about my curiosity about a new subject, such as flight dynamics or computer technology. Perhaps this is because of my academic background, or perhaps I just miss school. In any case, each project allows me to learn about a new subject.

But I rarely arrive at an idea by consciously sitting down at a desk and trying to figure out what I want to do. Once I start thinking about a project, though, it doesn't really leave my focus until I have come up with an idea.

I cannot force a design; I do not see this process as being under my conscious control. It is a process of percolation, with the form eventually finding its way to the surface.

Sometimes the idea takes initial shape as an essay. *10 Degrees North* began as an essay on balancing and mobiles. *Reading a Garden* began as a collaborative essay between a poet and a sculptor. Or it can start as a sketch with text, as in the very first sketches for the *Women's Table*. But most of the time my artworks begin as models.

I will make a model of a work without trying to draw it or plan how to make the model; they are made instantaneously. Sometimes I just wake up and without really thinking make a model—as with the *Women's Table* or *Eclipsed Time*, this "automatic act" takes place after many months of letting the project sit in my head.

I think with my hands.

These models, which I also refer to as sketches, have a clue or thread that will give me an understanding of what I am trying to do. Yet to most who are used to looking at models as finished miniature representations of actual work, they are sometimes indecipherable. But I am blind without these models.

I never fully realized how atypical this reliance on three-dimensional modeling was to my training as an architect until quite recently—most architects are trained to design in drawings. Yet I have always relied on the making of models to see and create my work; drawings for anything other than plans are harder for me to see or, more importantly, to feel what a space or place is.

I was never drawn to two-dimensional processes but always to three-dimensional arts: sculpture, metalsmithing, anything I could physically work with my hands. Growing up near Ohio University, where my father was a ceramicist and the dean of fine arts, I was able to experiment with most arts and crafts mediums before I left high school.

Watching my father pull a pot from a mound of clay, seeing the immediacy of making a form—without plans, drawings, blueprints—has had a profound impact on my creative process.

I do not think that we can fully understand how one makes a specific mark upon a page—at some point one has to trust one's eye, one's intuition. I do not think that that implies a lack of rational thought. I just think that one cannot understand why one makes a specific move, that the creative act is a combination of conscious and subconscious thoughts that cannot or should not be deciphered.

My creative process balances analytic study, based very much on research, with, in the end, a purely intuited gesture. It is almost as if after months of thinking I shut that part of my brain down and allow the nonverbal side to react. It is this balance between the analytical and the intuitive, or between the left side and the right side of the brain, that is so much a part of these works.

The phrase that some people have used to describe my process is that I lay an "egg." It is a rather strange metaphor, but an accurate one. My idea appears very quickly and is fully formed when it arrives. I do not work and rework the idea. And in looking at the final work, I think it is most successful when it captures the spirit of those first sketches or models.

But no matter how often I have gone through this process, I am never sure when I am going to find the form. Or, more accurately, when the form is going to find me.

The fact that these works are almost always commissioned, rather than made in the studio, requires that I present the design to others at an early stage. In order to get them built, I must go through a fairly public process. I have always relied on writing a description of the artwork or architectural work because I feel writing is the best way to convey what the project will be. It allows me to describe not just the physicality of the works but how one will experience the works. These essays become an integral part of each piece, helping to define for me what each work is. I consider them verbal sketches—like the models or drawings—and they are invaluable to me. I do not see the artwork as something that can be described in image alone, just as I feel the finished work cannot be understood from a single picture. Instead the experience of the work is critical to its understanding, and writing is the clearest form in which to capture what the work is about. I use the essays to clarify and distill the intentions of the work.

The essays for the Rockefeller Foundation's *10 Degrees North* and for *Sounding Stones* are not finished texts but sketches that give me a sense of what I am searching for. Defining the work in words sets the concept that I will follow throughout the development of the idea—the words are my guide.

The development of the design and its realization is a long, drawn-out process. Depending upon the complexity of the work, and how integrated the project is with existing architecture, this process can take years. The difficulty in translating idea into reality varies considerably from artwork to artwork. There are always technical problems to be worked out—getting the water in the *Civil Rights Memorial* to flow upside down or designing the clock mechanism for *Eclipsed Time*—but these problems did not pose a real difficulty for me (though my technical consultants might disagree). The challenge, for me, is not technical but emotional: the attempt to capture the essence of the idea that is so much a part of the original model. The *Wave Field* existed first as a photograph and then as a small model. I tried to stay close to the power of the original photos and models, but as the scale of the models increased, they began to lose the fluidity and poetry of those first images. I found it was impossible to predict or model or visualize its final shape until we actually built it; the piece literally changed, becoming too stiff with every increase in scale. I finally realized that I would not understand it or be able to predict if the form would work until I built it at its actual scale. After months of analyzing the form of a water wave—how it begins and ends—I just had to go out into the field and shape it.

Creating these works is never simply a process of replication. If the end result looks identical to the smaller-scale versions, then something has failed in the development. Architecture that looks like a blown-up version of its scale model has lost something in its translation. Obviously, the process of building architecture does not allow for as much spontaneity in the actual construction—nor would I want it to—but in those works as well, the early conceptual models have a presence that I try not to lose as the design develops.

No matter how many iterations—research, sketches, models—precede it, I am trying to capture that instantaneous act of making in the final piece, much the same way those first models or sketches convey a certain character or feeling. Perhaps it marks the presence of the human hand or the free-form creative act—something we are familiar with in smaller works, such as paintings or small-scaled sculptures, but is difficult to capture in the larger scale—when the method to construct these larger works involves teams of people, blueprints, engineered documents . . .

The last thing that I make about each work is its name. I don't feel the piece is complete until I have named it, yet I cannot even begin to think about its name until I have seen it finished.

There are always clues in the writings I have already made and in the drawings about the works. I need to return to the original text descriptions to find the clues. Each work always gives a descriptive clue to what it is.

Sometimes, as in *Sounding Stones*, the working title becomes the name, but only at the last minute. The piece changed, transformed into a fountain, and I saw it as something else. But then when I experienced the piece, its earlier name fit it; as I heard the echoes of the city noises and the water traveling through the drilled holes, I returned to its earlier name.

Other names . . . *Water Tables, 10 Degrees North, A Shift in the Stream, Phases of the Moon, The Earth is (not) Flat; Longitude, Equator, Latitude, Stones, Avalanche, Craters*. Whether large scale or small, these artworks and their names all speak of place, geography, naturally occurring phenomena, the environment.

I see the name as its final shape. And once it has its name, it's on its own. I have moved on both mentally and emotionally from it.

Linda (Olenik) Pastan (b. 1932) is a writer, teacher, and poet. She was poet laureate of Maryland from 1991–1995. Her poetry relies on imagery and metaphor to portray the complexity of domestic life and the tension inherent in the rites and roles of motherhood and housekeeping. "Marks," written in 1977, appears in Pastan's Carnival Evening: New and Selected Poems 1968–1998 *(1999). How does Pastan use specific vocabulary to make her point in this poem? What is her point? In what ways does this poem seem to articulate a certain knowledge of self? How does it suggest certain "systemic" challenges to the poet's notion of self?*

Marks

Linda Pastan

My husband gives me an A
for last night's supper,
an incomplete for my ironing,
a B plus in bed.
My son says I am average
an average mother, but if
I put my mind to it
I could improve.
My daughter believes
in Pass/Fail and tells me
I pass. Wait 'til they learn
I'm dropping out.

1977

Lucille Clifton (b. 1936) is a widely published African-American poet. Her poems generally focus on racial issues or on the strength that women draw upon during adversity. Her work also includes several children's books. The following two poems are included in her collection, Good Woman: Poems and a Memoir 1969–1980 *(1987), which was nominated for a Pulitzer Prize. Clifton uses images of the body to structure her two poems. What other images and metaphors appear in the poems? How does the form of the poems seem to reflect their meaning? In what ways are these poems an (artistic) expression of self?*

homage to my hips

Lucille Clifton

these hips are big hips.
they need space to
move around in.
they don't fit into little
petty places. these hips
are free hips.
they don't like to be held back.
these hips have never been enslaved,
they go where they want to go
they do what they want to do.
these hips are mighty hips.
these hips are magic hips.
i have known them
to put a spell on a man and
spin him like a top!

what the mirror said

Lucille Clifton

listen,
you a wonder.
you a city
of a woman.
you got a geography
of your own.
listen,
somebody need a map
to understand you.
somebody need directions
to move around you.
listen,
woman,
you not a noplace
anonymous
girl;
mister with his hands on you
he got his hands on
some
damn
body!

Kristina Anderson (b. 1978) graduated from the College of St. Catherine in 2000 with a B.A. in English and philosophy. She wrote the following personal narrative for the 2002 edition of the TRW reader. Her postscript was added to the current edition. With honesty and sensitivity, Anderson describes her experience as a lesbian on the CSC campus including both the pain and joy involved in coming out during her years here. Consider the ways in which Anderson expresses her authentic selfhood here. What can we learn about ways to speak our own truths, whatever they may be, in examining her story? What does Anderson teach us about GLBT issues both on campus and off?

Where I Belong

Kristina Anderson

I didn't even know what a lesbian was until I was twelve or thirteen. As I began to connect the word and its meaning with what I was feeling as a young adolescent, my world collapsed around me. Like many people in junior high and high school, the only references I heard to homosexuality were negative. "Dyke," "fag," "homo," and "fairy" were just a few of the hurtful words hurled at anyone a little different. I hid quietly, trying to blend into the crowd of ordinariness, hoping that no one could tell I might be a lesbian. I grasped early on that my confused sexual feelings must never be revealed, for I knew that homosexuality was not acceptable. In desperation and fear, I made an ultimatum with myself: if I discovered I truly was a lesbian, I would end my life. It sounded simple enough, and in many senses it comforted me to know that I could escape from what I perceived to be an unforgivable evil. I was certain that no one could live happily or productively as a lesbian, and if that turned out to be who I was, I had no choice but to die.

With time and the positive influence of others I reluctantly began to observe and even speak about my sexual orientation. I was still very much confused and filled with guilt and shame. Nonetheless, the more I dared to speak the more I came to understand that what I was feeling was not evil. The ultimatum I had made began to fade in my mind as I gained more confidence in myself. As high school came to an end, I knew I needed to find a college where I could openly discover myself in an environment that was both supportive and challenging.

I thought that by attending a women's college I would find the freedom to be myself, to be open about my sexual orientation. The College of St. Catherine was an immediate first choice because of its urban location, beautiful campus, and women-centered educational philosophy. I imagined St.

51

Kate's to be a place where women, regardless of sexual orientation, were encouraged in their goals and dreams. The first day I arrived on campus St. Kate's seemed to be all I had imagined. As my family and I pulled into the parking lot of the dorm I was to live in, two women stood on the side-walk holding hands. They appeared relaxed in their affection for one another, laughing and smiling. I stared at them from the window of the car, trying not to visibly display my excitement. "This is it!" I thought. These two women are being open about who they are, right in front of the first year dorm on moving in day. I felt a small sense of hope and excite-ment as I moved into the dorm, knowing I was not alone.

Within a few days I began to wonder if the lesbians I had seen on the side-walk were not lesbians at all, or rather the only two such women who existed at St. Kate's. The first year dorm in which I resided was a stifling atmosphere of heterosexuality. I was inundated by glossy pictures of scantily clad male figures each time I entered the bathroom. It wasn't that I cared that many of the other residents enjoyed having male company while brushing their teeth, but rather that many women never considered the possibility that some of us were not attracted to men. Talk in the hall-ways and dorm rooms was not much better. Many of the women had boyfriends back home or were pursuing males they had met at parties. I began to feel resentful at the very sight of a woman and her boyfriend being able to express their affection for one another in the halls and lounges of the dorm.

One day after becoming exasperated by the hetero-ness on my floor, I decided to try a little experiment. If the bathroom had been claimed as heterosexual territory, then I was going to claim the walls of the elevator as a more woman friendly environment. I carefully searched through magazines that did not promote sexualized waifs and found pictures of strong, intelligent, beautiful women. There was nothing about these women that made them look dyke-ish; they were just women, sexual ori-entation undefined. I made several trips to the elevator throughout the day to check on the condition of the pictures taped to the walls. No more than four or five hours had passed before I found them torn from the walls, violently I imagined, and discarded in a crumpled heap on the floor. I did try again, cutting out more pictures and taping them up, just as determined as before. I was rewarded with the same results. I had expected this reaction from the beginning, but even so there still existed within me the tiniest bit of hope that no one would care. If we had to look at handsome men all the while brushing our teeth, could we not look at beautiful women while riding the elevator? You certainly do not have to be a lesbian to think women are beautiful. But somebody did not under-stand this. Someone was offended, perhaps disgusted, or maybe even frightened by their own reaction to the pictures.

The silence among my classmates was unnerving, as if I were walking around with some hideous malfunction that everyone pretended did not exist out of politeness. Some of the people around me were aware of my sexual orientation because I had found the courage to tell them, yet for whatever reason the subject was taboo. People rarely spoke about it directly to me, but rumors circulated freely. It was a strange feeling that people who knew nothing about me knew I was a lesbian. It didn't make much of a difference to them that I was active in campus groups striving for social justice, involved in campus ministry, that I loved outdoor activities, enjoyed writing poetry, or that my favorite thing to do on the weekends was watch movies. For some, none of these commonly shared activities made any difference because my sexual orientation was all they knew of me, perhaps all they allowed themselves to know. There was a certain group of students on campus, I discovered, who were deeply opposed to homosexuality. Someone within this group told me in confidence that I had been identified as a lesbian among these students; they had been informed not to have any contact with me. I was deeply hurt by this, and in many ways still am, because I have always been overly sensitive to the opinions of others. I try very hard to be liked by everyone. I am especially bothered when people do not like me before they truly know me. I felt ashamed any time I encountered these people around campus because I could only imagine what they were thinking of me (what I imagined them to be thinking were the same horrible things I had thought of my own self for so long). I am certain they held within their minds a negative notion of lesbianism and applied this to me. I wanted desperately to speak with them and let them know that lesbianism is only one part of my identity. And yet, I never really did. I stayed in my comfortable corner, as did they. This benefited neither of us. I was too frightened and intimidated to share other parts of myself with them, as were they to receive from me. I do not think it is my duty to prove to others that there is nothing wrong with homosexuality, but if no one takes the initiative to educate others about our common differences, divisions will remain. If I had been more comfortable with my own sexual orientation, perhaps I could have attempted to dispel the fears and myths this group had.

Even among some of my friends, people I should have felt comfortable and safe with, lesbianism was a topic rarely discussed. I *wanted* to talk about it. I wanted to know what people felt and thought. I wanted to tell people how excited and scared and confused and thrilled I was at the process of accepting a part of myself I had detested for so long. I wanted to share with my friends the amazing music, literature, poetry, films, and art that the LGBT (lesbian, gay, bisexual, transgender) community produced. Yet as long as my friends appeared accepting of my sexual orientation, few of them felt it necessary to ever discuss the matter or become involved in active support. I recall an incident in which I was telling one of my friends about an Indigo Girls concert that attracted protesters because of the musicians' sexual orientation. I was angry and discouraged by yet another attack on homosexuality. I went to my friend looking for some encouragement. Instead, she curtly replied, "Is that all you ever talk about?!?" It took all my energy not to scream at her and say, "I listen to you talk about your guy problems every night! Why is it that any time I mention anything having to do with lesbianism, which is not often, I am suddenly talking about it all the time?" She never questioned talking about guys and everything heterosexual because this was a privilege she took for granted. If I was a lesbian that was fine with her, as long as I did not talk about it.

One of my greatest struggles in dealing with my sexual orientation was how to do so in the academic arena. While there are many important aspects of college life, academics was always my top priority. I worked hard to receive good grades. I yearned for a student/professor relationship in which I could drop in during office hours and chat in depth about class discussions and related issues. Yet, I was fearful my emerging sexual orientation might jeopardize my grade or a relationship with a professor. I was a chameleon of sorts, changing attitudes and interests with each professor I met. It may seem trivial that professors ignore or refuse to acknowledge the possibility that some of their students may not be heterosexual, but it never felt trivial to me. If you have ever been the minority in a room of people praised and given attention to because of the color of their skin, religious beliefs, political affiliations, race, educational background, ability level, socioeconomic status, gender, age, or sexual orientation, you are familiar with the feeling of invisibleness. I felt invisible to a professor when she excluded me from class examples by using heterosexist language, knowing full well I was not heterosexual. I was not asking her, or anyone else, to accept my sexual orientation, simply to acknowledge it. I wanted to be seen and spoken to as a whole person. I did not want parts of my identity to be ignored. There is nothing more painful or life threatening than being invisible because of your mere creation.

It came as a great relief, a secret celebration, each time I found supportive students and professors in my classes. I always looked for professors' doors that were decorated with a sign or symbol indicating they were an ally of the LGBT community. Those signs were a friendly sight when walking down a hallway of dismally blank doors that showed no indication my whole self was welcome. Certainly many professors who do not display LGBT support are themselves supportive, but it is often difficult to discern this. I listened for subtle clues in class lectures that signaled to me a professor was okay with homosexuality. I remember the first time I was sitting in a class and the professor used the word "significant other" in place of boyfriend. My heart burst out of my chest upon hearing these two simple words. Finally, at last, my entire being had been acknowledged. My invisibility was beginning to melt away and the silence had been broken.

As I had yet to feel accepted in the residence halls, I reached outside of the dorm life and my straight friends to find what I thought I was looking for. I suppose it is like anyone who does not feel welcome in a community and turns elsewhere to find what it is they need. I met other lesbians on campus and tried to bring myself to be like them. Many of the women were what I considered to be very "out," both in appearance and attitude. Some were the stereotypical dyke in appearance with hair cut short and masculine attire. Some had freedom rings in their ears or eyebrows and others wore jewelry emblazoned with the black triangle, all symbols of pride in their sexual orientation. Some talked freely about their girlfriends, others questioned their like for women and even the necessity for labeling sexual orientation. They all appeared to have a confidence in themselves that allowed them to talk about their sexual orientation and say such words as "dyke" and "lesbian" in a positive, almost righteous way. I seemed to come in on the middle of this ongoing conversation because I could not yet utter such words, nor did I feel comfortable in the presence of those who could. I wanted to be "out," but I also wanted to be me. I felt as if these two identities were in conflict, especially since I was still figuring out who I was.

I knew I was a white girl who grew up in a middle class Christian family of rather conservative values. I knew the things I was hearing among the lesbians I met, and even the things I was feeling, were not in line with what I had been taught to believe. But somehow I wanted to embrace these things. I cut my hair short in the middle of the winter and began wearing a black triangle in my ear. I tried to be more assertive in counteracting the heterosexist language in classes, among my friends, and in the dorms. I thought that if I forced this upon myself it would eventually feel natural. There were times, however, when I didn't have the energy to notice the heterosexism, when I took my earring out around certain people, or when I didn't even correct people if they asked if I had a boyfriend. I was finding that I didn't feel like I belonged among the lesbians on our campus either. I questioned where I belonged.

It never occurred to me during my first years at St. Kate's that I did not have to give up my values, hobbies, taste in music, spiritual and religious beliefs, etc., to be a lesbian. I was so concerned with being a "real" lesbian that everything I valued and held to be true slipped away. I thought you had to look a certain way, act a certain way, dress a certain way, be a certain way to be a lesbian. As I tried to do all these things, I began to realize what little investment I had in *myself*. I simply wanted to fit in with a certain crowd, and if that meant being dishonest with myself, then I was willing to do this. However, I became increasingly unhappy as everything familiar and comforting was discarded for new ways of doing things. It wasn't that the new way was wrong or bad, it was simply different, and it wasn't always me. I do not know exactly what it was, perhaps the enormous amount of energy it took to be someone I was not, that made me realize I did not have to be a certain way to be a lesbian. I can be a lesbian who likes classical music, goes to church, reads literature, and goes fishing. As I again embraced those things that were important to me, while integrating some of my new interests, I became more confident among my lesbian and straight peers alike. First and foremost I discovered I am who I am, my sexual orientation is simply another element of my identity.

As time progressed, I began to create a place for myself at St. Kate's. I experimented with who I was and how I was going to portray myself to the world. I failed many times at this, made many mistakes, but always I found the courage and support to try again. I discovered I did not have to be like any other lesbian at St. Kate's, or any other lesbian in the world, to be a lesbian. I could be a self-described lesbian. I realized I could be a successful student, as well as an "out" lesbian. While this has never been easy, it has come to be less painful then pretending to be someone I am not. St. Kate's became what I made it: an environment in which to grow, discover, change, and voice opinions. This certainly did not come without great struggle and effort, but what St. Kate's offers, if you dare to find it, is a place to form definitions of who you are and find meaning in yourself, others, and the world.

2008 Postscript: Lesbian in Latin America

On September 1, 2001, almost a year after graduating from college, I boarded a plane headed for Guatemala to fulfill my childhood dream of working in missions and fighting for social justice for the poor and marginalized. I had been to Guatemala before as a student in a Global Search for Justice course and I had fallen in love with the Mayan people: their generosity and hospitality, their humility and simplicity, and their smiles, often toothless, radiating from dark faces even in times of hardship and suffering. I was going back to Guatemala for a three-year stint as a volunteer missionary with the dream of living and working among the poor. I was full of optimism and idealism as the plane bounced through the dark night sky, millions of blinking lights coming into view as we approached Guatemala City. I slipped a wisp of hair behind my ear, chewing a piece of tasteless gum with exaggerated force, and tried to ignore the anxiousness that was settling in the pit of my stomach. I was leaving behind everything and everyone I knew. No one I had previously made contact with in Guatemala knew anything about my sexual orientation, nor the years of struggle I had gone through to come to terms with myself. I was going to be working in a Catholic charitable hospital in a highly macho and conservative culture. It wasn't that I hadn't thought about this before; obviously I was hesitant and frightened about leaving behind the freedom I had found in finally accepting my sexual orientation and sharing it with others. Nevertheless, I had decided that if I had to choose between fulfilling my dream of working in missions or being an "out" lesbian, I would choose missions and go back into the closet. I didn't realize at that moment, as the plane came to a jolting stop on the runway, that my life was going to be jolted too, and that I was about to re-enter one of the darkest and loneliest closets of my life.

The first few months flew by in a sort of dreamlike reality. I was consumed with improving my Spanish in language school, learning the cultural customs of the Guatemalan people, and just trying to adjust to all the newness that surrounded me. Within the first few days of being in Guatemala I slipped back into my old role of pretending to be someone I was not. It became clear to me early on through conversations with Guatemalans that homosexuality was something not discussed, nor accepted, in fact, divulging one's sexual orientation could be dangerous within certain circles. I tried not to let this bother me. I was so focused on beginning my mission assignment that I let a lot of things go. I grimaced, yet remained quiet when Guatemalan men made sexist remarks towards women, or more specifically towards me—catcalling and whistling in the streets. I tried to disappear when sexually explicit language and jokes were told among my coworkers at the charitable hospital. Derogatory gay jokes or the use of the local vernacular for fag, *hueco* (coincidently the word *hueco* means hole in Spanish, like a hole in the ground, but it has become slang for a gay male in Guatemala) or *maricon*, peppered every conversation, especially when groups of men were together and a woman might be listening nearby. The jokes, the whistles and the comments were painful, but I found myself responding appropriately with a smile or smirk, never actually commenting or adding to a conversation, yet never speaking up either. I was a silent bystander with a fake smile pasted on my face and my silence was suffocating me. I didn't want to be noticed and I didn't want to be more different than I already was in this new country. I surprised even myself with my passivity. I thought I had traded it for assertiveness during my years at St. Kate's. I was ashamed by my cowardliness. The self-hatred I had worked so hard to kill was coming out of its hibernation and now it was hungry.

My work became my refuge and my salvation. I spent long hours in the operating room working as a translator for medical mission teams that came from North America, assisting them when they needed to communicate with the Guatemalan operating room staff. I also found a place for myself at the bedside of patients waiting for surgery. The majority of patients had come from small villages where no medical care was available to receive life-changing surgery at the hospital. Many of the patients were campesinos or indigenous that had never left their fields or remote villages, so the shock of being in a hospital was overwhelming. They were old men, brown and wrinkled like raisins waiting to have hernias the size of footballs removed from their bellies, fifty year-old women with deeply creased and cracked faces looking forward to the day they could walk without a prolapsed uterus hanging between their knees, and babies with dark eyes full of hope and love, their mouths grotesquely deformed by cleft lips waiting for a new smile: these were the people I spent my days with. Their graciousness and gratitude nourished me. In addition, I often visited the residential patients of the hospital, all of whom had some type of severe physical or mental disability. Many of them were tied into wheelchairs, adults and children alike, and spent the day in front of the droning television or sitting in a hallway. They lacked stimulation and would sometimes scream out or cry if they could not speak, hoping for some attention. I fell in love with the residential patients of the hospital. They desired nothing more than a hug, a listening ear, someone to hold their hand when they were in pain. I became that person for them, and in turn they did the same for me.

Most days my sexual orientation didn't even come to mind because my work was so consuming. After awhile it became a non-issue for me as it didn't even seem to be relevant when all around me people were struggling just to survive. I thought I could just let it go and be happy. Yet the constant denial of myself, making up excuses for why I didn't have a boyfriend, inventing boyfriends from the past to be part of a conversation, pretending I liked being gawked at and propositioned, it brought me down and began tearing me apart little pieces at a time. The joy and fulfillment I found in my work wasn't enough. While my sexual orientation is certainly not my defining feature as a person, it remains part of me, and denying that one part of my identity created chaos within me as a person. The closet I had chosen to re-enter was killing me. The darkness began to consume me and I couldn't see to get out. I didn't realize it until a few years later, but denying and lying about my sexual orientation actually caused me to fall into a profound depression.

There are many more stories about my time in Guatemala, both happy and sad, but what I came away learning from the whole experience is that truth is the greatest freedom, being honest about who you are and embracing and accepting that person is the first step on the path to happiness. I thought I had learned this while at St. Kate's, but my world changed so dramatically when I went to Guatemala that I threw away all I had learned. I was afraid; I was so fearful that I preferred crawling back into the darkness rather than risk rejection. I don't know what would have happened to me if I had been honest about my sexual orientation. A Guatemalan friend of mine, a woman in her early thirties, went through the coming out process while I was in Guatemala. Her family literally kicked her out of the house and disowned her when she told them she was a lesbian. They threatened her to the point that she sought and was granted asylum in the United States. After this experience I realized how fortunate and truly blessed I am to be from a more tolerant country and have the loving support of my family.

After a year and half reprieve and recovery in the United States, I am currently living in Colombia, where I teach English at a Catholic girls' school. I live in Bogota, the capital city, and have found that it is more open and tolerant of sexual orientation. I am able to have discussions about sexual orientation with my high school classes and I secretly cheer in my head when I hear my students talk about their gay friends. Nonetheless, I have to pick and choose with whom I share my life and I don't ever foresee being completely "out" while in this country. Some people might say I am a "sell-out," that I am embarrassed or ashamed of being a lesbian. I wonder and worry about this too, but I am proud to say the closet door is open. I am no longer trapped in the darkness and I think the experiences I have had are teaching me the importance of owning self-identity. I am a lesbian. I do not deny it, and in fact, I am learning to rejoice in who God has made me. It has not been an easy road, and I know it will never be, but it is a road I am choosing to take because it is the only road that will lead me to truth, freedom, and perhaps even a bit of happiness.

Alia Ganaposki's interests include the development of projects that incorporate storytelling with social justice and peace issues. Her personal narrative about being poor in college appeared in the journal About Campus *in 2001. In it she expresses the pain and difficulties she experienced as a low-income student at a private college. She offers up her story as a means of challenging the assumptions prevalent on many college campuses about the relationship between poverty and race in particular. How does this autobiographical text relate to the theme of the composition of one's life? How does it compare to some of the other personal stories included in this unit?*

Being Poor
A Look Inside This Secret Society

Alia Ganaposki

The good thing about being poor in college is you can hide it; you can pass as middle class as long as you hang out with people who think thrift store chic is a lifestyle choice and not a lifestyle necessity. Poverty is a secret club. In our rich, by-the-bootstraps society, being poor is a mortal sin and a blight on you and your family. So if you can pass, you do. Because of this secrecy and shame I don't think those who live in a land of plenty understand the real levels of poverty that exist on college campuses.

It wasn't until my final year of high school that I outed myself as poor. I had sat silently through a Friday afternoon economics class in my rural town, where my peers denounced welfare and kept talking about the inner-city-black-single-mother-welfare-cheat problem. By the end, tears were running down my face. In polite words edged with aggrieved righteousness and patronizing philanthropy, my classmates were attacking both my mother and my right to exist.

The next Monday, I walked into class, gripping a speech I had spent all weekend polishing. In the speech, I pointed out that poverty was not an urban, racial, or faraway problem. It was about not having money, about needing money in order to buy groceries, Christmas trees, and everything they took for granted. When they attacked welfare mothers, they were attacking my mother. I went on for several angry pages, and when I was done, there was silence. After class, many people came up to me, shocked that I wasn't like them and embarrassed that they had been called out on politically incorrect assumptions voiced in front of the "minority" they were attacking. Tentatively, they assured me that they didn't mean me, but some of them apologized and even seemed to alter their worldview a fraction.

During my senior year of high school I stopped feeling the need to protect myself by pretending I fit in economically with my peer group. By the time I got to college, I wasn't ashamed and felt I could take advantage of a new, student-formed Low Income Student Alliance (LISA). I was so excited to meet other people who might understand what it was like to send my mother an allowance from my wages rather than the other way around, who would laugh knowingly when I told the story about her response to the pamphlet I received during orientation on the expensive college medical plan: "Well, honey, don't get sick."

We shared stories—about roommates who didn't understand that we couldn't take our dirty laundry home to Mom during holidays, because she didn't have a washer and dryer—and frustrations—like how our small liberal arts college had canceled need-blind admissions during my freshman year and what further damage that would do to the already skewed representation of economic class on campus.

It was wrong and it made us angry—but between our part-time jobs and academic schedules, we didn't have time or energy to pursue it. In fact, LISA eventually ceased to exist because we weren't able to fit it into our lives. But there were people who understood and tried to help. One person I am particularly grateful to was a resident of the African Heritage House, who mentioned a grant for needy students who had to spend the winter term at school. There were posters up all over her house but none anywhere else on campus. My high school experience rushed back to me. The white liberal establishment wanted to help, but they had already decided who needed their help and in what manner. Needy person equals black person. She knew that poverty is color-blind. I did get the grant, though the department secretary informed me, when I asked about the allowance, that it was "for people who really needed it." But if I hadn't received the grant, I would not have been able to fulfill my winter term requirement on campus. I couldn't afford to do it anywhere else, and so I would have failed to meet the college's requirements and been kicked out.

In my final two years at college, I became a residential coordinator, responsible for the care and nurture of a floor of students in a dorm. I made it loudly clear from the beginning that I was poor, so that later, quietly, people who needed to could come to me and ask for help of the kind that LISA had given me. One of my residents in particular came to me often. I pointed her to all the sympathetic people in high places I knew, but in the end it wasn't enough. She had to leave college when the money she expected didn't come through, and the college couldn't bend anymore. I grieved for my personal loss, as she had been one of my charges and I felt that I had failed her—but I grieved more for this college that traded on its historically liberal reputation and yet couldn't understand that, yes, some people really were that poor. The college had become truly need-blind—it couldn't see need at all.

When the establishment finally did recognize me as being poor—in my fourth and final year—it was in the form of a mysterious invitation to go to the student support center. I had been getting excellent grades while holding down two part-time jobs, teaching classes on storytelling, and being a member of a busy campuswide committee. Why would I need support? I arrived and was greeted by a slightly patronizing woman who told me she was there for me because my file indicated my family was poor. And that was all. Despite all my achievements both academic and personal, I had a scarlet letter—a green dollar sign, even—hanging around my neck. The powers that be had suddenly decided I needed special help. Granted, perhaps some students did, and I shouldn't bash this attempt at recognizing low-income needs. But we didn't need counseling or coaching or support. What we needed was money. That didn't make us stupid; it didn't even make us less academically prepared. By my fourth year, it was a damn sight late for that kind of support, anyway. I politely declined her offer and rushed to my next class. Despite experiences like these, I loved my alma mater and got a lot out of my college years, and I know it could have been far worse elsewhere.

For example, when I was choosing a college, at that time when first impressions are crucial, one big-name college dropped off my top five list immediately after I received its standard financial aid form. One of the first blank spaces was for the needy student to list all the cars (plural!) her family owned and what model and make they were. The question led me to believe that the base level of poverty that this university anticipated in its applicants was so far above mine that it would be impossible for me to fit in. Forget diversity, inclusion, support. If this school assumed students needed financial aid if their family could afford only two cars, I couldn't see how I—with my family's single automobile—could navigate its hallowed halls.

On the other hand, we low-income students had a different view of those same halls, which allowed us to escape the stereotypical ivory tower trip. Although some students never left campus during their four years unless they needed a pack of cigarettes, I and the low-income students I knew tried much harder to interact with the town because we had more in common with that world than the world of our more privileged classmates.

Some volunteered in the schools; some worked at the stores. As part of my student aid package, I worked at a local museum and met wonderful old women and bustling old men, struggling but cheerful moms, and school trips by the busload. My college experience was much richer and more real because my friendships were not limited to people aged eighteen to twenty-one. Some of my most cherished, vivid memories of that time— and greatest learning experiences—happened far away from those hallowed halls of learning. My low-income friends were proof that students' political passion had not died out. We just took it out of the classroom and integrated it into our lives.

People are fond of saying, "Give a man a fish and feed him for a day. Teach him how to fish and feed him for a lifetime." This looks very good on a poster. But when the man is too hungry to concentrate on what his well-fed teacher thinks he should know, it just sounds gross.

There are many reasons people are poor, and when all the sources of poverty are understood and eradicated, it will be a great day for humanity. Until then, ask your low-income students what they need, and believe them when they tell you. Ask them what they know and what they want to learn. Maybe they will show you a new way to fish and change your worldview a fraction.

Kari Smalkoski (b. 1972) currently teaches at the University of Minnesota. She wrote "Notes on Hunger" when she was a senior in college. Though it is a fictionalized account of one woman's experiences as an adopted Korean, Smalkoski based it both on her own experiences and observations as an adopted Korean raised in Minnesota. It is an epistolary tale, fiction written in the form of letters. A double narrative voice thus structures the text. There are two I's here as well as two you's. Indeed, it is a written dialogue between two characters of Asian descent, Mia and E. Consider the ways in which the complexity of these two characters' ethnic identity is expressed through their first- and second-person dialogue. What role do both ethnicity and gender play in their conception of themselves as well as of each other?

Notes on Hunger

Kari Smalkoski

A given place becomes our temporary home, and yet we preserve a sufficient distance to feel its strangeness, not perceived by those who live there permanently.

—Czeslaw Milosz

Dear E.,

I've felt severed my entire life, literally, as if a part of me was cut off or more appropriately, taken away. I'm missing this entire part of myself that is Korean. People ask when it was I realized I was adopted and I tell them I always knew.

A friend of mine, also an adopted Korean, is learning Korean so she can meet other Koreans in an attempt to reclaim what it is she's lost. I've known other Korean adoptees who have tried this but it's been more than frustrating for them. Most Korean nationals they've encountered don't accept them and neither do many Korean Americans. They look down on us and consider us charity cases. Perhaps my resentment for you all those times we argue about Asian American identity issues is not because I disagree with you (I disagree with you on many points, but that's another letter), but because I am envious that you have in your family, in your life, something I will never possess or know, no matter how hard I try, no matter what it is I do, in my own. I often feel you take this for granted because you can.

There was a time, not so long ago, that I didn't know any Asians and I went out of my way not to be associated with them. Now, I know many Asians, particularly Asian Americans, a few who have become friends, like you. Even so, I can't help but feel I'm living a huge lie when I'm with them because they see me as them and I am not and can never be. I don't know if it's more an issue of not feeling accepted by Asians or still thinking of myself as so different from them. I don't look in the mirror anymore and see my mother and sister with their Eastern European features staring back at me. However, it does still get confusing when Asians assume I am just like them and whites shy away from me—act awkward in my presence because they think of me as completely different from them.

Have I ever mentioned anything to you about my first year of college? I was seventeen years old, idealistic and, most importantly, still thought I was a white girl. There was a woman who worked behind the cafeteria counter at the dorms who asked for our student IDs before every meal so she could check our name off a list. I took an instant liking to her because it was my first time away from home and she reminded me of a mother and I missed my own mother terribly. Over a month later, I noticed she wasn't asking for anybody's ID besides mine and one day she said quite innocently to me, "I still have to see *your* ID because your name just doesn't match your face." I recall walking very matter of factly to my dorm room, locking the door behind me and crying the rest of the day. I'll never forget how it felt to hear that—to realize that it was true.—Mia.

Dear M.—

I have more than one confession to make to you. Do you recall when it was I first saw you? You were sitting in that cafe, way back in November. I spent most of the evening trying to decide if I was interested in you because you were the only other Asian in the place and if I would have still been interested if I would have seen you at a predominately Asian place, like a Chinese restaurant. When I saw you sitting in Dr. Harrison's class, I felt an immediate paradox. I remembered you instantly, only I was quite aware that you and I stood out somehow. I've always fit in, or at least, I've always thought I have. It was the first time I felt like I didn't.

Most of my life I have believed that any Asian woman would be glad to date a guy like me. I apologize for sounding arrogant, which you accuse me of being all the time anyway, but, it's true. My mother believes this about me as well. She always identified much more with being an "American" than my father who still identifies strongly with being Chinese, even though he is third generation. When I learned you were an adopted Korean, you intrigued me even more. In my mind, I transformed you into a sort of oddity: not white but not Asian. I'm not saying I saw you as Amerasian or anything like that. Perhaps I saw you as a white woman in disguise. A friend of mine in college once commented that adopted Korean women were the ideal because they were actually white women who looked Asian. Perfect to bring home to an Asian mother and father!

I've never sensed you wished you had been born a white woman, although I've never sensed you're thrilled being who you are. Perhaps, like me, you believe that if you had been born white, your life somehow would have been less complicated. You wouldn't have to think so much all the time about every goddamn thing that's happening to you. You wouldn't always have to read into everything and everyone all the time. Being adopted Korean is complicated. If a white guy or any other guy of another race (besides Asian) is attracted to you, you have to second guess his intentions. You have to figure out if he has an Asian woman thing because maybe *he* doesn't even realize he does. If he's white, it becomes more confusing to you because you still see yourself as a white person, in a lot of ways. If you are attracted to some white guy and he isn't attracted to you, you have to figure out if your race has something to do with it. In my high school, Asian American women were either completely rejected by guys, particularly white guys, because they *were* Asian, or, completely obsessed over because they were.

Now, if an Asian guy is attracted to you, you have to get over the idea of it feeling inter-racial somehow, realizing that he sees you as an Asian woman and that he sees you as he sees himself. Still, he knows he can't just bring you home to meet his mom and pop, particularly if he's Korean. We both know what the "real" Koreans think about adopted Koreans. It isn't pretty.

You say I grew up believing I was really a white person, that I am in complete denial about who I am and where I come from. I disagree with you. It is true, I haven't given these issues much thought until we met, but with me it has been an entirely different experience. My family is Chinese American. I grew up with the culture, the language, the food—and unlike you, it matched my face. You once said I am the only person you know who likes eating the kind of Chinese food that *Chinese* really eat, not that white people eat. I'd never thought about it like that before. Eating things that you can't even stand to look at always seemed normal to me like turkey and stuffing were to you at Christmas.

Perhaps my Dear M., you think of me as a mild version of one of those born again Asian Americans that the politically conscious Asian Americans keep discussing. What does it mean to be a politically conscious Asian American? I find the criteria preposterous. When I was growing up, we were the only Asian American family in our neighborhood in Connecticut. My father was colleagues with many of the men on our block and so we never had any trouble, that is, nobody said anything to us or seemed to have a problem with us being there. I went to predominately white schools with kids who came from old money, real blue blood families, WASP types and I seemed to fit in fine. Although, I never had any serious relationships in high school and looking back on it now, I suppose I could say it was because I was Asian, or more specifically, not WASP, but I was never ostracized, at least I don't think I was.

Early in our friendship you accused my race as being 'invisible' to people and quite honestly, I did not know what you were implying. I decided I'd finally met my match, that there was someone else walking around the world taking themselves much too seriously and thinking about things too much. I suppose, like anyone, I wished to fit in and I did. I never had trouble fitting in. I wasn't teased like you, wasn't called *chink* and *gook* and *jap* every day. I don't think people understand the severity of what that can do to a kid who eventually turns into an adult. People don't realize how it gets internalized, how it's carried around inside of you, eating away at you your entire life.

Look, perhaps what this all boils down to is that I put unfair expectations on you because you are Asian. But then maybe, ideally, it has nothing to do with us being Asian at all, maybe it just has to do with us. But can it ever have to do with us, without us acknowledging our race? Can we ever just have the luxury of simply being Mia and Elliot? You know, that girl from Minneapolis and that guy from Connecticut? *Not* the adopted Korean woman or the Chinese American guy? It's funny, I thought I knew everything about this Asian American thing before I met you.—E.

Dear E.—

I ran into an old friend, Charles, the other day. We decided to have coffee and after sitting across from him for a few minutes, it became apparent to me that we had nothing to say to one another. There was a time when we were extremely close friends, the best of friends. There never seemed enough time for us to say everything we wanted. We met five years ago as sophomores in college. He was my father's wet dream, my mother's idea of marrying well, my grandmother's idea of good sperm for offspring and a product of East Coast society and the good ol' boys network. *Good stock* as my father calls Charles, spent his developing years at the fine boarding school called *Andover*, moved to Minnesota when his father, also a CEO and coincidentally a member of the same country club as my father, was permanently relocated, had been the president of his fraternity in college and is presently in his first year in medical school— not because he worked hard or is even smart for that matter, but because his father is friends with the Vice Chancellor.

"You know what a man really wants in a woman when you ask him to describe his favorite car, just like you know what a woman wants in a man when you ask her to describe her ideal house," was what Charles said to me over coffee, breaking a ten minute bantering called *small talk*. I changed the subject quickly, although I could tell he wanted to put his theory to test. I told him I thought I'd seen him walking down the street the other day. "Could have been. I'm white, male and in my twenties, it happens all the time," he said defensively.

I said to him, "the same could be said for me, you know, Asian American, female in her twenties." I watched his face go noticeably blank. It was the first time he'd ever heard me refer to myself as Asian American and the closest we'd ever come to discussing the fine subject of race, particularly mine. "I've had my fair share of people who come up to me and start talking really slow, like they know I can't speak English—the whole time they think I'm someone else. It's *so* bizarre," I said.

Charles appeared baffled. He crossed his arms and said, "I take it for granted, not having to worry about people making assumptions like that." Only, he hadn't said it as if a light bulb had come on in his head, rather, his tone was full of arrogance and sarcasm. There was a tone in his voice that said, *I'm really sick of all this multicultural, diversity shit, so could you just shut up please?* "Maybe I actually learned something in those waste of my time diversity seminars they forced us to go to in college," he laughed to himself and then said, "nah, I didn't."

A navy blue Land Rover is Charles' ideal car and in twenty minutes I found myself describing his ideal woman. Afterwards, I described my ideal house at which he took the liberty of describing my ideal man. What struck me about his preposterous theory was that when describing his ideal woman, I described myself with the physical attributes of women who look very much like my mother and sister and most of my friends. When describing my ideal man, he described himself, my father, brother and every man who would never consider me at all (including Asian men who claim they do not find Asian women attractive) and who would never describe me as their ideal. This was only a week ago. This scares the shit out of me.

I guess I've always known why Charles and I never had anything more than friendship, why it was he kept such a calculated distance and why, sadly, I entertained thoughts of him being what I wished to include in my long term plans; sadly, realizing as girls do, that they cannot marry their fathers; sadly, realizing I still wanted to end up with mine, as much as I hate and resent and love him as eldest daughters often do. I am, as far as I know, the only person of Asian descent my father has ever known. I am the only person of Asian descent anyone in my family or their friends, have ever personally known. I, the Korean adoptee, have insight that many Asians do not, which is truly no blessing or curse. It's simply the way it is.—M.

Dear E.

Vladimir's good friend, Yurri, from his hometown in Russia, is staying with Vladimir for a week. Ever since he got off the plane, Vladimir has been speaking Russian non-stop. I can't tell you what it's been like since it's the first time I've ever heard Vladimir speak Russian. It is also the first time I've understood the intimate connection Vladimir and I have shared from the beginning. I've always known he's experienced an immeasurable loss, similar to mine and I can't explain it the way I want to, not even in words—particularly not in words.

When Vladimir speaks Russian there's this almost secretive tone in his voice, this fluidness in language, an expressiveness I've never heard before. It has nothing to do with language, rather, it's a confidence and comfort I've never witnessed in him before. There are times when we are trying to communicate and we get stuck. He cannot say what he wants to and cannot understand what I'm trying to convey on a deeper level. But I've always trusted that he understands somehow, because he has this depth to him that has nothing to do with what he says.

There's a new aura about him since Yurri arrived. It is a similar feeling that adopted adults experience when they find their birth parents and meet them for the first time: the missing link has finally been found. Last week they went to a baseball game and asked me to come along. I didn't go because they were going with a group of Russian guys and their Russian girlfriends and I felt Vladimir needed time alone with them. Vladimir needs to spend time with his Russian friends without me. And yet, there's this part of me that feels deeply left out, more so than say, my sister Maddy would ever feel. I know this is due to my hunger for a culture that is everything I've never had or known.—Mia.

My dear Mia,

You are angry with me for the assumptions I made about Vladimir over the phone last week and I know I deserve your silence. However, this letter is not a feeble attempt to ask for your forgiveness. In all truth, I have many more confessions to make, things I've wanted to confess for some time.

Before moving to Minnesota, a Korean American colleague of mine at Yale had informed me that all Asians in Minnesota were Hmong and Vietnamese refugees and boat people who were uneducated, on welfare and spoke no English. It didn't hit me until after settling here, that he had actually been warning me that I may be mistaken for one of them. And of course, it really hit me while standing across from you in Dr. Harrison's office, that early on I had made similar presumptions about you that a naive white person or a naive Asian American, might make.

I realize now this and other events led to my unusual harshness with you in regards to your relationship with Vladimir. I have been much harder on you than I would be with a white woman—even a white woman who is dating an Asian guy. All those same expectations Asians have of you for "looking" the part, I've subconsciously had of you all along. I used to want to say, particularly when I first was getting to know you, "stop thinking like a white woman!" I am glad I never did, but I doubt it would have been half as bad as some of the judgments I've since made about you and about your and Vladimir's relationship. Even when something appears to be cut and dry, it never can be, can it?

I could not understand the camaraderie you shared with Vladimir from the beginning, because he's Russian Jewish born and bred and because his family's immigration to this country was one of exile; how it is you and he share an immeasurable loss in language and culture, amongst other things. I couldn't understand it because I didn't want to. I didn't want to accept the notion that someone with an Asian face like yours could grow up identifying much more with being Polish, even *if* your father was a Polish immigrant and you grew up immersed in the culture. I couldn't accept how it was for many years, you identified more with the writing of someone such as Czeslaw Milosz rather than Maxine Hong Kingston.

I spent the night at Kelly's and at three in the morning woke because I'd just come up with this brilliant line for a poem I'm working on. I tried to wake her so I could share the line before I forgot it but she just mumbled something incomprehensible and turned over. I shook her again and she looked at the clock and said, "Elliot, it's three in the morning, I have to be at work at seven-thirty, can't this wait?! I mean really, it's just a stupid poem!" By then, I'd already forgotten the line and I'm uncertain now what bothers me most, that I forgot it or that I couldn't share it with my girlfriend or even more significantly that she couldn't see the value in why I had woke her. It's not that I expected her to understand the line or even like it. What I wanted her to understand was why it was important to me and I guess I wanted *that* to be important to her.

How I miss you, Mia. Please come back.—E.

Amy Tan (b. 1952) is the author of many works for children and adults, includ-
ing the award-winning novels The Joy Luck Club *(1989) and* The Bonesetter's
Daughter *(2001). Tan's parents emigrated to the U.S. from China in the late*
1940s. Her personal experience as a first-generation Chinese-American informs
the following text, which first appeared in The Three-penny Review *(1990). In*
"Mother Tongue" Tan explores the complex and reciprocal relationship between
language, culture, family, and identity through a personal narrative about her
experience with what she calls several "different Englishes." How has Tan's expe-
rience with English affected her conception of self as well as her assessment of her
own work as a fiction writer in English? How would you describe the relationship
you perceive between the language(s) you use, the culture(s) and family(ies) you
come from, and your identity?

Mother Tongue

Amy Tan

I am not a scholar of English or literature. I cannot give you much more than personal opinions on the English language and its variations in this country or others.

I am a writer. And by that definition, I am someone who has always loved language. I am fascinated by language in daily life. I spend a great deal of my time thinking about the power of language—the way it can evoke an emotion, a visual image, a complex idea, or a simple truth. Language is the tool of my trade. And I use them all—all the Englishes I grew up with.

Recently, I was made keenly aware of the different Englishes I do use. I was giving a talk to a large group of people, the same talk I had already given to half a dozen other groups. The nature of the talk was about my writing, my life, and my book, *The Joy Luck Club*. The talk was going along well enough, until I remembered one major difference that made the whole talk sound wrong. My mother was in the room. And it was per-haps the first time she had heard me give a lengthy speech, using the kind of English I have never used with her. I was saying things like, "The intersection of memory upon imagination" and "There is an aspect of my fiction that relates to thus-and-thus"—a speech filled with carefully wrought grammatical phrases, burdened, it suddenly seemed to me, with nominalized forms, past perfect tenses, conditional phrases, all the forms of standard English that I had learned in school and through books, the forms of English I did not use at home with my mother.

Just last week, I was walking down the street with my mother, and I again found myself conscious of the English I was using, and the English I do use with her. We were talking about the price of new and used furniture and I heard myself saying this: "Not waste money that way." My husband was with us as well, and he didn't notice any switch in my English. And then I realized why. It's because over the twenty years we've been together I've often used that same kind of English with him, and sometimes he even uses it with me. It has become our language of intimacy, a different sort of English that relates to family talk, the language I grew up with.

So you'll have some idea of what this family talk I heard sounds like, I'll quote what my mother said during a recent conversation which I video-taped and then transcribed. During this conversation, my mother was talking about a political gangster in Shanghai who had the same last name as her family's, Du, and how the gangster in his early years wanted to be adopted by her family, which was rich by comparison. Later, the gangster became more powerful, far richer than my mother's family, and one day showed up at my mother's wedding to pay his respects. Here's what she said in part:

"Du Yusong having business like fruit stand. Like off the street kind. He is Du like Du Zong—but not Tsung-ming Island people. The local people call putong, the river east side, he belong to that side local people. That man want to ask Du Zong father take him in like become own family. Du Zong father wasn't look down on him, but didn't take seriously, until that man big like become a mafia. Now important person, very hard to inviting him. Chinese way, came only to show respect, don't stay for dinner. Respect for making big celebration, he shows up. Mean gives lots of respect. Chinese custom. Chinese social life that way. If too important won't have to stay too long. He come to my wedding. I didn't see, I heard it. I gone to boy's side, they have YMCA dinner. Chinese age I was nineteen."

You should know that my mother's expressive command of English belies how much she actually understands. She reads the *Forbes* report, listens to *Wall Street Week*, converses daily with her stockbroker, reads all of Shirley MacLaine's books with ease—all kinds of things I can't begin to understand. Yet some of my friends tell me they understand 50 percent of what my mother says. Some say they understand 80 to 90 percent. Some say they understand none of it, as if she were speaking pure Chinese. But to me, my mother's English is perfectly clear, perfectly natural. It's my mother tongue. Her language, as I hear it, is vivid, direct, full of observation and imagery. That was the language that helped shape the way I saw things, expressed things, made sense of the world.

Lately, I've been giving more thought to the kind of English my mother speaks. Like others, I have described it to people as "broken" or "fractured"

English. But I wince when I say that. It has always bothered me that I can think of no way to describe it other than "broken," as if it were damaged and needed to be fixed, as if it lacked a certain wholeness and soundness. I've heard other terms used, "limited English," for example. But they seem just as bad, as if everything is limited, including people's perceptions of the limited English speaker.

I know this for a fact, because when I was growing up, my mother's "limited" English limited *my* perception of her. I was ashamed of her English. I believed that her English reflected the quality of what she had to say. That is, because she expressed them imperfectly her thoughts were imperfect. And I had plenty of empirical evidence to support me: the fact that people in department stores, at banks, and at restaurants did not take her seriously, did not give her good service, pretended not to understand her, or even acted as if they did not hear her.

My mother has long realized the limitations of her English as well. When I was fifteen, she used to have me call people on the phone to pretend I was she. In this guise, I was forced to ask for information or even to complain and yell at people who had been rude to her. One time it was a call to her stockbroker in New York. She had cashed out her small portfolio and it just so happened we were going to go to New York the next week, our very first trip outside California. I had to get on the phone and say in an adolescent voice that was not very convincing, "This is Mrs. Tan."

And my mother was standing in the back whispering loudly, "Why he don't send me check, already two weeks late. So mad he lie to me, losing me money."

And then I said in perfect English, "Yes, I'm getting rather concerned. You had agreed to send the check two weeks ago, but it hasn't arrived."

Then she began to talk more loudly. "What he want, I come to New York tell him front of his boss, you cheating me?" And I was trying to calm her down, make her be quiet, while telling the stockbroker, "I can't tolerate any more excuses. If I don't receive the check immediately, I am going to have to speak to your manager when I'm in New York next week." And sure enough, the following week there we were in front of this astonished stockbroker, and I was sitting there red-faced and quiet, and my mother, the real Mrs. Tan, was shouting at his boss in her impeccable broken English.

We used a similar routine just five days ago, for a situation that was far less humorous. My mother had gone to the hospital for an appointment, to find out about a benign brain tumor a CAT scan had revealed a month ago. She said she had spoken very good English, her best English, no mistakes. Still, she said, the hospital did not apologize when they said they had lost the CAT scan and she had come for nothing. She said they did not seem to have any sympathy when she told them she was anxious to know the exact diagnosis, since her husband and son had both died of brain tumors. She said they would not give her any more information until the next time and she would have to make another appointment for that. So she said she would not leave until the doctor called her daughter. She wouldn't budge. And when the doctor finally called her daughter, me, who spoke in perfect English—lo and behold—we had assurances the CAT scan would be found, promises that a conference call on Monday would be held, and apologies for any suffering my mother had gone through for a most regrettable mistake.

I think my mother's English almost had an effect on limiting my possibilities in life as well. Sociologists and linguists probably will tell you that a person's developing language skills are more influenced by peers. But I do think that the language spoken in the family, especially in immigrant families which are more insular, plays a large role in shaping the language of the child. And I believe that it affected my results on achievement tests, IQ tests, and the SAT. While my English skills were never judged as poor, compared to math, English could not be considered my strong suit. In grade school I did moderately well, getting perhaps B's, sometimes B-pluses, in English and scoring perhaps in the sixtieth or seventieth percentile on achievement tests. But those scores were not good enough to override the opinion that my true abilities lay in math and science, because in those areas I achieved A's and scored in the ninetieth percentile or higher.

This was understandable. Math is precise; there is only one correct answer. Whereas, for me at least, the answers on English tests were always a judgment call, a matter of opinion and personal experience. Those tests were constructed around items like fill-in-the-blank sentence completion, such as, "Even though Tom was ____, Mary thought he was ____." And the correct answer always seemed to be the most bland combinations of thoughts, for example, "Even though Tom was shy, Mary thought he was charming," with the grammatical structure "even though" limiting the correct answer to some sort of semantic opposites, so you wouldn't get answers like, "Even though Tom was foolish, Mary thought he was ridiculous." Well, according to my mother, there were very few limitations as to what Tom could have been and what Mary might have thought of him. So I never did well on tests like that.

The same was true with word analogies, pairs of words in which you were supposed to find some sort of logical, semantic relationship—for example, "*Sunset* is to *nightfall* as ____ is to ____." And here you would be presented with a list of four possible pairs, one of which showed the same kind of relationship: *red* is to *stoplight*, *bus* is to *arrival*, *chills* is to *fever*, *yawn* is to *boring*. Well, I could never think that way. I knew what the tests were asking, but I could not block out of my mind the images already created by the first pair, "*sunset* is to *nightfall*"—and I would see a burst of colors against a darkening sky, the moon rising, the lowering of a curtain of stars. And all the other pairs of words—red, bus, stoplight, boring—just threw up a mass of confusing images, making it impossible for me to sort out something as logical as saying: "A sunset precedes nightfall" is the same as "a chill precedes a fever." The only way I would have gotten that answer right would have been to imagine an associative situation, for example, my being disobedient and staying out past sunset, catching a chill at night, which turns into feverish pneumonia as punishment, which indeed did happen to me.

I have been thinking about all this lately, about my mother's English, about achievement tests. Because lately I've been asked, as a writer, why there are not more Asian Americans represented in American literature. Why are there few Asian Americans enrolled in creative writing programs? Why do so many Chinese students go into engineering? Well, these are broad sociological questions I can't begin to answer. But I have noticed in surveys—in fact, just last week—that Asian students, as a whole, always do significantly better on math achievement tests than in English. And this makes me think that there are other Asian-American students whose English spoken in the home might also be described as "broken" or "limited." And perhaps they also have teachers who are steering them away from writing and into math and science, which is what happened to me.

Fortunately, I happen to be rebellious in nature and enjoy the challenge of disproving assumptions made about me. I became an English major my first year in college, after being enrolled as pre-med. I started writing nonfiction as a freelancer the week after I was told by my former boss that writing was my worst skill and I should hone my talents toward account management.

But it wasn't until 1985 that I finally began to write fiction. And at first I wrote using what I thought to be wittily crafted sentences, sentences that would finally prove I had mastery over the English language. Here's an example from the first draft of a story that later made its way into *The Joy Luck Club*, but without this line: "That was my mental quandary in its nascent state." A terrible line, which I can barely pronounce.

Fortunately, for reasons I won't get into today, I later decided I should envision a reader for the stories I would write. And the reader I decided upon was my mother, because these were stories about mothers. So with this reader in mind—and in fact she did read my early drafts—I began to write stories using all the Englishes I grew up with: the English I spoke to my mother, which for lack of a better term might be described as "simple"; the English she used with me, which for lack of a better term might be described as "broken"; my translation of her Chinese, which could certainly be described as "watered down"; and what I imagined to be her translation of her Chinese if she could speak in perfect English, her internal language, and for that I sought to preserve the essence, but neither an English nor a Chinese structure. I wanted to capture what language ability tests can never reveal: her intent, her passion, her imagery, the rhythms of her speech and the nature of her thoughts.

Apart from what any critic had to say about my writing, I knew I had succeeded where it counted when my mother finished reading my book and gave me her verdict: "So easy to read."

Raymond Carver (1938–1988) is credited as being one of a handful of contemporary writers who revived the dying short story genre. In addition to short stories, he authored several novels, poems, and essays. His short story, "Cathedral" (1983), received a Pulitzer Prize nomination in 1984. This first-person narrative evolves through a number of metaphors about seeing involving the narrator, a sighted person, and another character, a blind man. What does this story tell us about the differences in the experiences of an able-bodied person and one with a disability? How do the acts of looking, seeing, and watching compare to those of listening and feeling here? What value seems to be assigned to these different ways of engaging with the world around us?

Cathedral

Raymond Carver

This blind man, an old friend of my wife's, he was on his way to spend the night. His wife had died. So he was visiting the dead wife's relatives in Connecticut. He called my wife from his in-laws'. Arrangements were made. He would come by train, a five-hour trip, and my wife would meet him at the station. She hadn't seen him since she worked for him one summer in Seattle ten years ago. But she and the blind man had kept in touch. They made tapes and mailed them back and forth. I wasn't enthusiastic about his visit. He was no one I knew. And his being blind bothered me. My idea of blindness came from the movies. In movies, the blind moved slowly and never laughed. Sometimes they were led by seeing-eye dogs. A blind man in my house was not something I looked forward to.

That summer in Seattle she had needed a job. She didn't have any money. The man she was going to marry at the end of the summer was in officer's training school. He didn't have any money, either. But she was in love with the guy, and he was in love with her, etc. She'd seen something in the paper: Help Wanted—Reading for Blind Man, and a telephone number. She phoned and went over, was hired on the spot. She'd worked with this blind man all summer. She read stuff to him, case studies, reports, that sort of thing. She helped him organize his little office in the county social service department. They'd become good friends, my wife and the blind man. How do I know these things? She told me. And she told me something else. On her last day in the office, the blind man asked if he could touch her face. She agreed to this. She told me he ran his fingers over every part of her face, her nose—even her neck! She never forgot it. She even tried to write a poem about it. She was always writing a poem. She wrote a poem or two every year, usually after something really important had happened to her.

When we first started going out together, she showed me the poem. In the poem she recalled his fingers and the way they had moved around over her face. In the poem she talked about what she had felt at the time, about what went through her mind as he touched her nose and lips. I can recall I didn't think much of the poem. Of course I didn't tell her that. Maybe I just don't understand poetry. I admit it's not the first thing I reach for when I pick up something to read.

Anyway, this man who'd first enjoyed her favors, the officer-to-be, he'd been her childhood sweetheart. So okay. I'm saying that at the end of the summer she let the blind man run his hands over her face, said good-bye to him, married her childhood etc., who was now a commissioned officer, and she moved away from Seattle. But they'd kept in touch, she and the blind man. She made the first contact after a year or so. She called him up one night from an Air Force base in Alabama. She wanted to talk. They talked. He asked her to send him a tape and tell him about her life. She did this. She sent the tape. On the tape she told the blind man about her husband and about their life together in the military. She told the blind man she loved her husband but she didn't like it where they lived and she didn't like it that he was a part of the military-industrial complex. She told the blind man she'd written a poem and he was in it. She told him that she was writing a poem about what it was like to be an Air Force officer's wife in the Deep South. The poem wasn't finished yet. She was still writing it. The blind man made a tape. He sent her the tape. She made a tape. This went on for years. My wife's officer was posted to one base and then another. She sent tapes from Moody AFB, McGuire, McConnell, and finally Travis, near Sacramento, where one night she got to feeling lonely and cut off from people she kept losing in that moving-around life. She balked, couldn't go it another step. She went in and swallowed all the pills and capsules in the medicine cabinet and washed them down with a bottle of gin. Then she got into a hot bath and passed out.

But instead of dying she got sick. She threw up. Her officer—Why should he have a name? He was the childhood sweetheart, and what more does he want?—came home from a training mission, found her, and called the ambulance. In time, she put it on the tape and sent the tape to the blind man. Over the years she put all kinds of stuff on tapes and sent the tapes off lickety-split. Next to writing a poem every year, I think it was her chief means of recreation. On one tape she told the blind man she'd decided to live away from her officer for a time. On another tape she told him about her divorce. She and I began going out, and of course she told her blind man about this. She told him everything, so it seemed to me. Once she asked me if I'd like to hear the latest tape from the blind man. This was a year ago. I was on the tape, she said. So I said okay, I'd listen to it. I got us drinks and we settled down in the living room. We made ready to listen. First she inserted the tape into the player and adjusted a couple of dials. Then she pushed a lever. The tape squeaked and someone began to talk in this loud voice. She lowered the volume. After a few minutes of harmless chitchat, I heard my own name rasped out by this stranger, this man I didn't even know! And then this: "From all you've said about him, I can only conclude—" But we were interrupted, a knock at the door, something, and we didn't get back to the tape. Maybe it was just as well. I'd heard enough, anyway.

Now this same blind stranger was coming to sleep in my house.

"Maybe I could take him bowling," I said to my wife. She was at the draining board doing scalloped potatoes. She put down the knife she was using on the onion and turned around.

"If you love me," she said, "you can do this for me. If you don't love me, okay. But if you had a friend, any friend, and the friend came to visit, I'd make him feel comfortable." She wiped her hands with the dish towel.

"I don't have any blind friends," I said.

"You don't have *any* friends," she said. "Period. Besides," she said, "god-damnit, his wife's just died! Don't you understand that? The man's lost his wife!"

I didn't answer. She'd told me a little about the blind man's wife. The wife's name was Beulah. Beulah! That's a name for a colored woman.

"Was his wife a Negro?" I asked.

"Are you crazy?" my wife said. "Have you just flipped or something?" She picked up the onion. I saw it hit the floor, then roll under the stove. "What's wrong with you?" she said. "Are you drunk?"

"I'm just asking," I said.

Right then my wife filled me in with more detail than I cared to know. I made a drink and sat at the kitchen table to listen. Pieces of the story began to fall into place.

Beulah had gone to work for the blind man the summer after my wife had stopped working for him. Pretty soon Beulah and the blind man had themselves a church wedding. It was a little wedding—who'd be anxious to attend such a wedding in the first place?—just the two of them, and the minister and the minister's wife. But it was a church wedding just the same. What Beulah had wanted, he'd said. But even then Beulah must have been carrying cancer in her lymph glands. After they had been inseparable for eight years—my wife's word, *inseparable*—Beulah's health went into a rapid decline. She died in a Seattle hospital room, the blind man sitting beside the bed and holding on to her hand. They'd married, lived and worked together, slept together—had sex, sure—and then the blind man buried her. All this without his having ever seen what the goddamned woman looked like. It was beyond my understanding. Hearing this, I felt sorry for the blind man for a minute. And then I found myself thinking what a pitiful life this woman must have led. Imagine a woman who could never see herself reflected in the eyes of her loved one. A woman who could go on day after day and never receive the smallest compliment from her beloved. A woman whose husband would never read the expression on her face, be it misery or something better. Someone who could wear make-up or not—what difference to him? She could, if she wanted, wear green eye shadow around one eye, a straight pin in her nostril, yellow slacks and burgundy pumps, no matter. And then to slip off into death, the blind man's hand on her hand, his blind eyes streaming tears—I'm imagining now—her last thought maybe this: that her beloved never knew what she looked like, and she on an express to the grave. Robert was left with a small insurance policy and half of a twenty-peso Mexican coin. The other half of the coin went into the box with her. Pathetic.

So when the time rolled around, my wife went to the rail station. With nothing to do but wait—and sure, I blamed him for that—I was having a drink and watching TV when I heard the car pull into the drive. I got up from the sofa with my drink and went to the window to have a look.

I saw my wife laughing as she parked the car. I saw her get out of the car and shut the door. She was still wearing a smile. Just amazing. She went around to the other side of the car to where the blind man was already starting to get out. This blind man, feature this, he was wearing a full beard! A beard on a blind man! Too much, I say. The blind man reached into the back seat and dragged out a suitcase. My wife took his arm, shut the car door, and, talking all the way, moved him down the drive and then up the steps to the front porch. I turned off the TV. I finished my drink, rinsed the glass, dried my hands. Then I went to the door.

My wife said, "I want you to meet Robert. Robert, this is my husband. I've told you all about him." She closed the porch screen. She was beaming. She had this blind man by his coat sleeve.

The blind man let go of his suitcase and up came his hand.

I took it. He squeezed hard, held my hand, and then he let it go.

"I feel like we've already met," he boomed.

"Likewise," I said. I didn't know what else to say. Then I said, "Welcome. I've heard a lot about you." We began to move then, a little group, from the porch into the living room, my wife guiding him by the arm. He carried his suitcase in his other hand. My wife said things like, "To your left here, Robert. That's right. Now watch it, there's a chair. That's it. Sit down right here. This is the sofa. We just bought this sofa two weeks ago."

I started to say something about the old sofa. I'd liked that old sofa. But I didn't say anything. Then I wanted to say something else, small talk, about the scenic Hudson River. How going *to* New York, sit on the right-hand side of the train, and coming *from* New York, the left-hand side.

"Did you have a good train ride?" I said. "Which side of the train did you sit on, by the way?"

"What a question, which side!" my wife said. "What's it matter which side?" she said.

"I just asked," I said.

"Right side," the blind man said. "For the sun. Until this morning," the blind man said, "I hadn't been on a train in nearly forty years. Not since I was a kid. With my folks. That's been a long time. I'd nearly forgotten that sensation. I have winter in my beard now," he said. "So I've been told, anyway. Do I look distinguished, my dear?" he said to my wife.

"You look distinguished, Robert," she said. "Robert," she said.

"Robert, it's just so good to see you." My wife finally took her eyes off the blind man and looked at me.

I had the distinct feeling she didn't like what she saw. I shrugged.

I've never met or personally known anyone who was blind. This blind man was late forties, a heavyset, balding man with stooped shoulders, as if he carried a great weight there. He wore brown slacks, brown cordovan shoes, a light brown shirt, a tie, a sports coat. Spiffy. He also had this full beard. But he didn't carry a cane and he didn't wear dark glasses. I'd always thought dark glasses were a must for the blind. Fact was, I wished he had a pair. At first glance, his eyes looked like anyone else's eyes. But if you looked close there was something different about them. Too much white in the iris, for one thing, and the pupils seemed to move around in the sockets without his knowing it or being able to control it. Creepy. As I stared at his face, I saw the left pupil turn in toward his nose, while the other made a futile effort to keep in one place. But it was only an effort, for that eye was on the roam without his knowing it or wanting it to be.

I said, "Let me get you a drink. What's your pleasure? We have a little of everything. It's one of our pastimes."

"Bub, I'm a Scotch man myself," he said fast enough, in this big voice.

"Right," I said. Bub! "Sure you are. I knew it."

He let his fingers touch his suitcase, which was sitting alongside the sofa. He was taking his bearings. I didn't blame him for that.

"I'll move that up to your room," my wife said.

"No, that's fine," he said loudly. "It can go up when I go up."

"A little water with the Scotch?" I said.

"Very little," he said.

"I knew it," I said.

He said, "Just a tad. The Irish actor, Barry Fitzgerald? I'm like that fellow. When I drink water, Fitzgerald said, I drink water. When I drink whiskey, I drink whiskey." My wife laughed. The blind man brought his hand up under his beard. He lifted his beard slowly and let it drop.

I did the drinks, three big glasses of Scotch with a splash of water in each. Then we made ourselves comfortable and talked about Robert's travels. First the long flight from the West Coast to Connecticut, we covered that. Then from Connecticut up here by train. We had another drink concerning that leg of the trip.

I remembered having read somewhere that the blind didn't smoke because, speculation had it, they couldn't see the smoke they exhaled. I thought I knew that much and that much only about blind people. But this blind man smoked his cigarette down to the nubbin and then lit another one. This blind man filled his ashtray and my wife emptied it.

When we sat down to the table for dinner we had another drink. My wife heaped Robert's plate with cube steak, scalloped potatoes, green beans. I buttered him up two slices of bread. I said, "Here's bread and butter for you." I swallowed some of my drink. "Now let us pray," I said, and the blind man lowered his head. My wife looked at me, her mouth agape. "Pray the phone won't ring and the food doesn't get cold," I said.

We dug in. We ate everything there was to eat on the table. We ate like there was no tomorrow. We didn't talk. We ate. We scarfed. We grazed that table. We were into serious eating. The blind man had right away located his foods, he knew just where everything was on his plate. I watched with admiration as he used his knife and fork on the meat. He'd cut two pieces of meat, fork the meat into his mouth, and then go all out for the scalloped potatoes, the beans next, and then he'd tear off a hunk of buttered bread and eat that. He'd follow this up with a big drink of milk. It didn't seem to bother him to use his fingers once in a while, either. He used his bread to scoop beans.

We finished everything, including half of a strawberry pie. For a few moments we sat as if stunned. Sweat beaded on our faces. Finally, we got up from the table and left the dirty plates. We didn't look back. We took ourselves into the living room and sank into our places again. Robert and my wife sat on the sofa. I took the big chair. We had us two or three more drinks while they talked about the major things that had transpired for them in the past ten years. For the most part, I just listened. Now and then I joined in. I didn't want him to think I'd left the room, and I didn't want her to think I was feeling left out. They talked of things that had happened to them—to them!—these past ten years. I waited in vain to hear my name on my wife's sweet lips: "And then my dear husband came into my life"—something like that. But I heard nothing of the sort. More talk of Robert. Robert had done a little of everything, it seemed, a regular blind jack-of-all-trades. But most recently he and his wife had had an Amway distributorship, from which, I gathered, they'd earned their living, such as it was. The blind man was also a ham radio operator. He talked in his loud voice about conversations he'd had with fellow opera-tors in Guam, the Philippines, Alaska, even Tahiti. He said he'd have a lot of friends there if he ever wanted to go visit those places. From time to time he'd turn his blind face toward me, put his hand under his beard, ask me something. How long had I been at my present position? (Three years.) Did I like my work? (I didn't.) Was I going to stay with it? (What were the options?)

Finally, when I thought he was beginning to run down, I got up and turned on the TV.

My wife looked at me with irritation. She was heading toward a boil. Then she looked at the blind man and said, "Robert, do you have a TV?"

The blind man said, "My dear, I have two TVs. I have a color set and a black-and-white thing, an old relic. It's funny, but if I turn the TV on, and I'm always turning it on, I turn the color set on. Always. It's funny."

I didn't know what to say to that. I had absolutely nothing to say about that. No opinion. So I watched the news program and tried to listen to what the announcer was saying.

"This is a color TV," the blind man said. "Don't ask me how, but I can tell."

"We traded up a while ago," I said.

The blind man had another taste of his drink. He lifted his beard, sniffed it, and let it fall. He leaned forward on the sofa. He positioned his ashtray on the coffee table, then put the lighter to his cigarette. He leaned back on the sofa and crossed his legs at the ankles.

My wife covered her mouth, and then she yawned. She stretched. She said, "I think I'll go upstairs and put on my robe. I think I'll change into something else. Robert, you make yourself comfortable," she said.

"I'm comfortable," the blind man said.

"I want you to feel comfortable in this house," she said.

"I am comfortable," the blind man said.

After she'd left the room, he and I listened to the weather report and then to the sports roundup. My wife had been gone so long I didn't know if she was going to come back. I thought she might have gone to bed. I wished she'd come back downstairs. I didn't want to be left alone with a blind man. I asked him if he wanted another drink, and he said sure. Then I asked if he wanted to smoke dope with me. I said I'd just rolled a number. I hadn't, but I planned to do so in about two shakes.

"I'll try some with you," he said.

"Damn right," I said. "That's the stuff."

I got our drinks and sat down on the sofa with him. Then I rolled us two fat numbers. I lit one and passed it. I brought it to his fingers. He took it and inhaled.

"Hold it as long as you can," I said. I could tell he didn't know the first thing.

My wife came back downstairs wearing her robe and pink slippers. "What do I smell?" she said.

"We thought we'd have us some cannabis," I said.

My wife gave me a purely savage look. Then she looked at him and said, "Robert, I didn't know you smoked."

He said, "I do now, my dear. First time for everything," he said. "But I don't feel anything yet."

"This stuff is pretty mellow," I said. "This stuff is mild. It's dope you can reason with. It doesn't mess you up."

"Not much it doesn't, bub," he said, and laughed.

My wife sat on the sofa between the blind man and me. I passed her the number. She took it and inhaled and then passed it back to me. "Which way is this going?" she said. Then she said, "I shouldn't be smoking this. I can hardly keep my eyes open as it is. That dinner did me in. I shouldn't have eaten so much."

"It was the strawberry pie," the blind man said. "That's what did it," he said, and he laughed his big laugh. Then he shook his head.

"There's more strawberry pie," I said.

"Do you want some more, Robert?" my wife asked.

"Maybe in a little while," he said.

We gave our attention to the TV. My wife yawned again. She said, "Your bed is made up when you feel like going to bed, Robert. I know you must have had a long day. When you're ready to go to bed, say so." She pulled his arm. "Robert?"

He came to and said, "I've had a real nice time. This beats tapes, doesn't it?"

I said, "Coming at you," and I put the number between his fingers. He inhaled, held the smoke, and then let it go. It was like he'd been doing it since he was nine years old.

"Thanks, bub," he said. "But I think this is all for me. I think I'm beginning to feel it," he said. He held the burning roach out for my wife.

"Same here," she said. "Ditto. Me too." She took the roach and passed it to me. "I may just sit here for a while between you two guys with my eyes closed. But don't let me bother you, okay? Either one of you. If it bothers you, say so. Otherwise, I may just sit here with my eyes closed until you're ready to go to bed," she said. "Your bed's made up, Robert, when you're ready. It's right next to our room at the top of the stairs. We'll show you up when you're ready. You wake me up now, you guys, if I fall asleep." She said that and then she closed her eyes and went to sleep.

The news program ended. I got up and turned the channel. I sat back down on the sofa. I wished my wife hadn't pooped out. Her head lay across the back of the sofa, her mouth open. She'd turned so that her robe had slipped away from her legs, exposing a juicy thigh. I reached to draw her robe over the thigh, and it was then I glanced at the blind man. What the hell! I flipped the robe open again.

"You say when you want some strawberry pie," I said.

"I will," he said.

I said, "Are you tired? Do you want me to take you up to your bed? Are you ready to hit the hay?"

"Not yet," he said. "No, I'll stay up with you, bub. If that's all right. I'll stay up until you're ready to turn in. We haven't had a chance to talk. Know what I mean? I feel like me and her monopolized the evening." He lifted his beard and he let it fall. He picked up his cigarettes and his lighter.

"That's all right," I said. Then I said, "I'm glad for the company." And I guess I was. Every night I smoked dope and stayed up as long as I could before I fell asleep. My wife and I hardly ever went to bed at the same time. When I did go to sleep, I had these dreams. Sometimes I'd wake up from one of them, the heart going crazy.

Something about the Church and the Middle Ages, narrated by an Englishman, was on the TV. Not your run-of-the-mill TV fare. I wanted to watch something else. I turned to the other channels.

But there was nothing on them, either. So I turned back to the first channel and apologized.

"Bub, it's all right," he said. "It's fine with me. Whatever you want to watch is okay. I'm always learning something. Learning never ends. It won't hurt me to learn something tonight. I got ears," he said.

We didn't say anything for a time. He was leaning forward with his head turned at me, while his right ear was aimed in the direction of the set. Very disconcerting. Now and then his eyelids drooped and then they snapped open again. Now and then he put his fingers into his beard and tugged, as if thinking about something he was hearing on the television.

On the screen a group of men wearing cowls was being set upon and tormented by men dressed in skeleton costumes and men dressed as devils. The men dressed as devils wore devil masks, horns, and long tails. This pageant was part of a procession. The Englishman said it all took place in Málaga Spain, once a year. I tried to explain to the blind man what was happening.

"Skeletons," he said. "I know about skeletons," he said, and he nodded.

The TV showed Chartres Cathedral. Then there was a long slow look at Sainte-Chapelle. Finally the picture switched to Notre-Dame, with its flying buttresses, its spires reaching toward clouds. The camera pulled away to show the whole of the cathedral rising above the skyline.

There were times when the Englishman who was telling the thing would shut up, would simply let the camera move around over the cathedrals. Or else the camera would tour the countryside, men in fields walking behind oxen. I waited as long as I could. Then I felt I had to say something. I said, "They're showing the outside of this cathedral now. Gargoyles. Little statues carved to look like monsters. Now I guess they're in Italy. Yeah, they're in Italy. There's fresco paintings on the walls of this one church."

"What's fresco painting, bub?" he asked, and he sipped from his drink.

I reached for my glass. But it was empty. I tried to remember what I could remember about frescoes. "You're asking me what are frescoes?" I said. "That's a good question. I don't know."

The camera moved to a cathedral outside Lisbon, Portugal. The differences in the Portuguese cathedral compared with the French and Italian were not that great. But they were there. Mostly the interior stuff. Then something occurred to me and I said, "Something has occurred to me. Do you have an idea what a cathedral is? What they look like, that is? Do you follow me? If somebody says *cathedral* to you, do you have any notion what they're talking about? Do you know the difference between that and a Baptist church, say? Or that and a mosque, or synagogue?"

He let the smoke issue from his mouth. "I know they took hundreds of workers fifty or a hundred years to build," he said. "I just heard the man say that, of course. I know generations of the same families worked on a cathedral. I heard him say that, too. The men who began their life's work on them, they never lived to see the completion of their work. In that wise, bub, they're no different from the rest of us, right?" He laughed. Then his eyelids drooped again. His head nodded. He seemed to be snoozing. Maybe he was imagining himself in Portugal. The TV was showing another cathedral now. This one was in Germany. The Englishman's voice droned on. "Cathedrals," the blind man said. He sat up and rolled his head back and forth. "If you want the truth, bub, that's about all I know. What I just said. What I heard him say. But maybe you could describe one to me? I wish you'd do it. I'd like that. If you want to know, I really don't have a good idea."

I stared hard at the shot of the cathedral on the TV. It held a minute. Then it was gone, and the view was of the inside with rows of benches and high windows. How could I even begin to describe it? But say my life depended on it. Say my life was being threatened by an insane Turkish bey.

They took the camera outside again. I stared some more at the cathedral before the picture flipped off into the countryside. There was no use. I turned to the blind man and said, "To begin with, they're very tall. Very, very tall." I was looking around the room for clues. I tried again. "They reach way up. Up and up. Toward the sky. They soar. They're like poetry, that's what they're like. They're so big, some of them, they have to have these supports. To help hold them up, so to speak. These supports are called buttresses. They remind me of viaducts for some reason. But maybe you don't know viaducts, either? Sometimes the cathedrals have devils and such carved into the front. Sometimes great lords and ladies. Don't ask me why this is," I said. He was nodding. The whole upper part of his body seemed to be moving back and forth. "I'm not doing so good, am I?" I said.

He stopped nodding and leaned forward on the edge of the sofa. As he listened to me, he was running his fingers through his beard. I wasn't getting through to him though, I could see that. But he waited for me to go on just the same. He nodded, as if trying to encourage me. I tried to think what else I could say. "They're really big. They're massive. They're built of stone. Marble, too, sometimes. In those old days, when they built cathedrals, men aspired to be close to God. In those days God was an important part of everyone's life. This was reflected in their cathedral building. I'm sorry," I said, "but it looks like that's the best I can do for you. I'm just no good at it."

"That's all right, bub," he said. "Hey, listen. I hope you don't mind my asking you. Can I ask you something? Let me ask you a simple question, yes or no. I'm just curious and there's no offense. You're my host. But let me ask if you are in any way religious? You don't mind my asking?"

I shook my head. He couldn't see that, though. A wink is the same as a nod to a blind man. "I guess I'm agnostic or something. No, the fact is, I don't believe in it. Anything. Sometimes it's hard. You know what I'm saying?"

"Sure, I do," he said.

"Right," I said.

The Englishman was still holding forth. My wife sighed in her sleep. She drew a long breath and continued with her sleep.

"You'll have to forgive me," I said. "But I can't tell you what a cathedral looks like. It just isn't in me to do it. I can't do any more than I've done." The blind man sat very still, his head down, as he listened to me. "The truth is, cathedrals don't mean anything special to me. Nothing. Cathedrals. They're something to look at on late-night TV. That's all they are."

It was then he cleared his throat, He brought something up. He took a handkerchief from his back pocket. In a minute he said, "I get it, bub. It's okay. It happens. Don't worry about it," he said. "Hey, listen to me. Will you do me a favor? I got an idea. Why don't you find us some heavy paper? And a pen. We'll do something. An experiment. Sure, you can do it. You can. We'll draw one together. Get us a pen and some heavy paper. Go on, bub, get the stuff," he said.

So I went upstairs. My legs felt like they didn't have any strength in them. They felt like they did sometimes after I'd run a couple miles. In my wife's room I looked around. I found some ballpoints in a little basket on her table. And then I tried to think where to look for the kind of paper he was talking about.

Downstairs, in the kitchen, I found a shopping bag with onion skins in the bottom of the bag. I emptied the bag and shook it. I brought it into the living room and sat down with it near his legs. I moved some things, smoothed the wrinkles from the bag, spread it out on the coffee table. The blind man got down from the sofa and sat next to me on the carpet.

He ran his fingers over the paper. He went up and down the sides of the paper and the edges, top and bottom. He fingered the corners. "All right," he said. "All right. Let's do her."

He found my hand, the hand with the pen. He closed his hand over my hand. "Go ahead, bub, draw," he said. "Draw. You'll see. I'll follow along with you. It'll be all right. Just begin now, like I'm telling you. You'll see. Draw," he said.

So I began. First I drew a box that resembled a house. It could have been the house I lived in. Then I put a roof on the house. At either end of the roof I drew spires. Crazy.

"Swell," he said. "Terrific. You're doing fine," he said. "Never thought anything like this could happen in your lifetime, did you? Well, it's a strange life, bub, we all know that. Go on now. Keep it up."

I put in windows with arches. I drew flying buttresses. I hung great doors. I couldn't stop. The TV station went off the air. I put down the pen and closed and opened my fingers. The blind man felt around over the paper. He moved the tips of his fingers slowly over the paper, over what I'd drawn, and he nodded. "Doing fine," he said.

I took up the pen, and he found my hand once more. I kept at it. I'm no artist. But I kept drawing just the same.

My wife opened her eyes and gazed at us. She sat up on the sofa, her robe hanging open. She said, "What are you doing? What in the world are you doing?"

I didn't answer her. The blind man said, "We're drawing a cathedral, dear. Me and him are working on something important. Press hard now," he said to me. "That's right. That's good," he said. "Sure. You got it, bub. I can tell. You didn't think you could. But you can, can't you? You're cooking with Crisco now. You'll see. Know what I'm saying? We're going to have us something here in a minute. How's the old arm?" he said. "Put some people in there now. What's a church without people, bub?"

"What's going on?" my wife said. "Robert, what are you doing? What's going on?"

"It's all right," he said to her. "Close your eyes now, bub," he said.

I did that. I closed them just like he said.

"Are they closed?" he said, "Don't fudge."

"They're closed," I said.

"Keep them that way," he said. He said, "Don't stop now." So we kept on with it. His fingers rode my fingers as my hand went over the rough paper. It was like nothing else in my life up to now.

In a minute he said, "I think that's enough. I think you got the idea," he said. "Take a look. What do you think?"

But I had my eyes closed. I thought I'd keep them closed a little longer. I thought it was something I ought not to forget.

"Well?" he said. "Are you looking?"

My eyes were still closed. I was in my house and I knew that. But I didn't feel inside anything.

"It's really something," I said.

Peggy McIntosh is a professor and the associate director of the Wellesley College Center for Research on Women, and is founder and co-director of the national S.E.E.D. (Seeking Educational Equity and Diversity) Project on Inclusive Curriculum. Her many articles have examined different aspects of race and the integration of feminist theories into traditional curricula. In the following essay (1988) McIntosh is careful to say that this text is more of a personal record of her observations than a scholarly analysis. She uses the metaphor of an "invisible weightless knapsack" to specify the nature of white privilege. Can you explain how this metaphor works? How does she relate white privilege to male privilege? Why does she do this? What does she mean by hegemony? Systemic racism? Meritocracy? Taboos? How do McIntosh's ideas correspond to other texts in this unit, in particular to Rich's "Claiming an Education"?

White Privilege and Male Privilege
A Personal Account of Coming to See Correspondences through Work in Women's Studies

Peggy McIntosh

Through work to bring materials and perspectives from Women's Studies into the rest of the curriculum, I have often noticed men's unwillingness to grant that they are overprivileged in the curriculum, even though they may grant that women are disadvantaged. Denials that amount to taboos surround the subject of advantages that men gain from women's disadvantages. These denials protect male privilege from being fully recognized, acknowledged, lessened, or ended.

Thinking through unacknowledged male privilege as a phenomenon with a life of its own, I realized that since hierarchies in our society are interlocking, there was most likely a phenomenon of white privilege that was similarly denied and protected, but alive and real in its effects. As a white person, I realized I had been taught about racism as something that puts others at a disadvantage, but had been taught not to see one of its corollary aspects, white privilege, which puts me at an advantage.

I think whites are carefully taught not to recognize white privilege, as males are taught not to recognize male privilege. So I have begun in an untutored way to ask what it is like to have white privilege. This paper is a partial record of my personal observations and not a scholarly analysis. It is based on my daily experiences within my particular circumstances.

I have come to see white privilege as an invisible package of unearned assets that I can count on cashing in each day, but about which I was "meant" to remain oblivious. White privilege is like an invisible weightless knapsack of special provisions, assurances, tools, maps, guides, code-books, passports, visas, clothes, compass, emergency gear, and blank checks.

Since I have had trouble facing white privilege, and describing its results in my life, I saw parallels here with men's reluctance to acknowledge male privilege. Only rarely will a man go beyond acknowledging that women are disadvantaged to acknowledging that men have unearned advantage, or that unearned privilege has not been good for men's development as human beings, or for society's development, or that privilege systems might ever be challenged and *changed*.

I will review here several types or layers of denial that I see at work protecting, and preventing awareness about, entrenched male privilege. Then I will draw parallels, from my own experience, with the denials that veil the facts of white privilege. Finally, I will list forty-six ordinary and daily ways in which I experience having white privilege, by contrast with my African American colleagues in the same building. This list is not intended to be generalizable. Others can make their own lists from within their own life circumstances.

Writing this paper has been difficult, despite warm receptions for the talks on which it is based.[1] For describing white privilege makes one newly accountable. As we in Women's Studies work reveal male privilege and ask men to give up some of their power, so one who writes about having white privilege must ask, "Having described it, what will I do to lessen or end it?"

The denial of men's overprivileged state takes many forms in discussions of curriculum change work. Some claim that men must be central in the curriculum because they have done most of what is important or distinctive in life or in civilization. Some recognize sexism in the curriculum but deny that it makes male students seem unduly important in life. Others agree that certain *individual* thinkers are male oriented but deny that there is any *systemic* tendency in disciplinary frameworks or epistemology to overempower men as a group. Those men who do grant that male privilege takes institutionalized and embedded forms are still likely to deny that male hegemony has opened doors for them personally. Virtually all men deny that male overreward alone can explain men's centrality in all the inner sanctums of our most powerful institutions. Moreover, those few who will acknowledge that male privilege systems have overempowered them usually end up doubting that we could dismantle these privilege systems. They may say they will work to improve women's status, in the society or in the university, but they can't or won't support the idea of lessening men's. In curricular terms, this is the point at which they say that they regret they cannot use any of the interesting new scholarship on women because the syllabus is full. When the talk turns to giving men less cultural room, even the most thoughtful and fair-minded of the men I know will tend to reflect, or fall back on, conservative assumptions about the inevitability of present gender relations and distributions of power, calling on precedent or sociobiology and psychobiology to demonstrate that male domination is natural and follows inevitably from evolutionary pressures. Others resort to arguments from "experience" or religion or social responsibility or wishing and dreaming.

After I realized, through faculty development work in Women's Studies, the extent to which men work from a base of unacknowledged privilege, I understood that much of their oppressiveness was unconscious. Then I remembered the frequent charges from women of color that white women whom they encounter are oppressive. I began to understand why we are justly seen as oppressive, even when we don't see ourselves that way. At the very least, obliviousness of one's privileged state can make a person or group irritating to be with. I began to count the ways in which I enjoy unearned skin privilege and have been conditioned into oblivion about its existence, unable to see that it put me "ahead" in any way, or put my people ahead, overrewarding us and yet also paradoxically damaging us, or that it could or should be changed.

My schooling gave me no training in seeing myself as an oppressor, as an unfairly advantaged person, or as a participant in a damaged culture. I was taught to see myself as an individual whose moral state depended on her individual moral will. At school, we were not taught about slavery in any depth; we were not taught to see slaveholders as damaged people. Slaves were seen as the only group at risk of being dehumanized. My schooling followed the pattern which Elizabeth Minnich has pointed out: whites are taught to think of their lives as morally neutral, normative, and average, and also ideal, so that when we work to benefit others, this is seen as work that will allow "them" to be more like "us." I think many of us know how obnoxious this attitude can be in men.

After frustration with men who would not recognize male privilege, I decided to try to work on myself at least by identifying some of the daily effects of white privilege in my life. It is crude work, at this stage, but I will give here a list of special circumstances and conditions I experience that I did not earn but that I have been made to feel are mine by birth, by citizenship, and by virtue of being a conscientious law-abiding "normal" person of goodwill. I have chosen those conditions that I think in my case *attach somewhat more to skin-color privilege* than to class, religion, ethnic status, or geographical location, though these other privileging factors are intricately intertwined. As far as I can see, my Afro-American co-workers, friends, and acquaintances with whom I come into daily or frequent contact in this particular time, place, and line of work cannot count on most of these conditions.

1. I can, if I wish, arrange to be in the company of people of my race most of the time.

2. I can avoid spending time with people whom I was trained to mistrust and who have learned to mistrust my kind or me.

3. If I should need to move, I can be pretty sure of renting or purchasing housing in an area which I can afford and in which I would want to live.

4. I can be reasonably sure that my neighbors in such a location will be neutral or pleasant to me.

5. I can go shopping alone most of the time, fairly well assured that I will not be followed or harassed by store detectives.

6. I can turn on the television or open to the front page of the paper and see people of my race widely and positively represented.

7. When I am told about our national heritage or about "civilization," I am shown that people of my color made it what it is.

8. I can be sure that my children will be given curricular materials that testify to the existence of their race.

9. If I want to, I can be pretty sure of finding a publisher for this piece on white privilege.

10. I can be fairly sure of having my voice heard in a group in which I am the only member of my race.

11. I can be casual about whether or not to listen to another woman's voice in a group in which she is the only member of her race.

12. I can go into a book shop and count on finding the writing of my race represented, into a supermarket and find the staple foods that fit with my cultural traditions, into a hairdresser's shop and find someone who can deal with my hair.

13. Whether I use checks, credit cards, or cash, I can count on my skin color not to work against the appearance that I am financially reliable.

14. I could arrange to protect our young children most of the time from people who might not like them.

15. I did not have to educate our children to be aware of systemic racism for their own daily physical protection.

16. I can be pretty sure that my children's teachers and employers will tolerate them if they fit school and workplace norms; my chief worries about them do not concern others' attitudes toward their race.

17. I can talk with my mouth full and not have people put this down to my color.

18. I can swear, or dress in secondhand clothes, or not answer letters, without having people attribute these choices to the bad morals, the poverty, or the illiteracy of my race.

19. I can speak in public to a powerful male group without putting my race on trial.

20. I can do well in a challenging situation without being called a credit to my race.

21. I am never asked to speak for all the people of my racial group.

22. I can remain oblivious to the language and customs of persons of color who constitute the world's majority without feeling in my culture any penalty for such oblivion.

23. I can criticize our government and talk about how much I fear its policies and behavior without being seen as a cultural outsider.

24. I can be reasonably sure that if I ask to talk to "the person in charge," I will be facing a person of my race.

25. If a traffic cop pulls me over or if the IRS audits my tax return, I can be sure I haven't been singled out because of my race.

26. I can easily buy posters, postcards, picture books, greeting cards, dolls, toys, and children's magazines featuring people of my race.

27. I can go home from most meetings of organizations I belong to feeling somewhat tied in, rather than isolated, out of place, out-numbered, unheard, held at a distance, or feared.

28. I can be pretty sure that an argument with a colleague of another race is more likely to jeopardize her chances for advancement than to jeopardize mine.

29. I can be fairly sure that if I argue for the promotion of a person of another race, or a program centering on race, this is not likely to cost me heavily within my present setting, even if my colleagues disagree with me.

30. If I declare there is a racial issue at hand, or there isn't a racial issue at hand, my race will lend me more credibility for either position than a person of color will have.

31. I can choose to ignore developments in minority writing and minority activist programs, or disparage them, or learn from them, but in any case, I can find ways to be more or less protected from negative consequences of any of these choices.

32. My culture gives me little fear about ignoring the perspectives and powers of people of other races.

33. I am not made acutely aware that my shape, bearing, or body odor will be taken as a reflection on my race.

34. I can worry about racism without being seen as self-interested or self-seeking.

35. I can take a job with an affirmative action employer without having my co-workers on the job suspect that I got it because of my race.

36. If my day, week, or year is going badly, I need not ask of each negative episode or situation whether it has racial overtones.

37. I can be pretty sure of finding people who would be willing to talk with me and advise me about my next steps, professionally.

38. I can think over many options, social, political, imaginative, or professional, without asking whether a person of my race would be accepted or allowed to do what I want to do.

39. I can be late to a meeting without having the lateness reflect on my race.

40. I can choose public accommodation without fearing that people of my race cannot get in or will be mistreated in the places I have chosen.

41. I can be sure that if I need legal or medical help, my race will not work against me.

42. I can arrange my activities so that I will never have to experience feelings of rejection owing to my race.

43. If I have low credibility as a leader, I can be sure that my race is not the problem.

44. I can easily find academic courses and institutions that give attention only to people of my race.

45. I can expect figurative language and imagery in all of the arts to testify to experiences of my race.

46. I can choose blemish cover or bandages in "flesh" color and have them more or less match my skin.

I repeatedly forgot each of the realizations on this list until I wrote it down. For me, white privilege has turned out to be an elusive and fugitive subject. The pressure to avoid it is great, for in facing it I must give up the myth of meritocracy. If these things are true, this is not such a free country; one's life is not what one makes it; many doors open for certain people through no virtues of their own. These perceptions mean also that my moral condition is not what I had been led to believe. The appearance of being a good citizen rather than a troublemaker comes in large part from having all sorts of doors open automatically because of my color.

A further paralysis of nerve comes from literary silence protecting privilege. My clearest memories of finding such analysis are in Lillian Smith's unparalleled *Killers of the Dream* and Margaret Andersen's review of Karen and Mamie Fields' *Lemon Swamp*. Smith, for example, wrote about walking toward black children on the street and knowing they would step into the gutter; Andersen contrasted the pleasure that she, as a white child, took on summer driving trips to the south with Karen Fields' memories of driving in a closed car stocked with all necessities lest, in stopping, her black family should suffer "insult, or worse." Adrienne Rich also recognizes and writes about daily experiences of privilege, but in my observation, white women's writing in this area is far more often on systemic racism than on our daily lives as light-skinned women.[2]

In unpacking this invisible knapsack of white privilege, I have listed conditions of daily experience that I once took for granted, as neutral, normal, and universally available to everybody, just as I once thought of a male-focused curriculum as the neutral or accurate account that can speak for all. Nor did I think of any of these perquisites as bad for the holder. I now think that we need a more finely differentiated taxonomy of privilege, for some of these varieties are only what one would want for everyone in a just society, and others give license to be ignorant, oblivious, arrogant, and destructive. Before proposing some more finely tuned categorization, I will make some observations about the general effects of these conditions on my life and expectations.

In this potpourri of examples, some privileges make me feel at home in the world. Others allow me to escape penalties or dangers that others suffer. Through some, I escape fear, anxiety, insult, injury, or a sense of not being welcome, not being real. Some keep me from having to hide, to be in disguise, to feel sick or crazy, to negotiate each transaction from the position of being an outsider or, within my group, a person who is suspected of having too close links with a dominant culture. Most keep me from having to be angry.

I see a pattern running through the matrix of white privilege, a pattern of assumptions that were passed on to me as a white person. There was one main piece of cultural turf; it was my own turf, and I was among those who could control the turf. I could measure up to the cultural standards and take advantage of the many options I saw around me to make what the culture would call a success of my life. *My skin color was an asset for any move I was educated to want to make.* I could think of myself as "belonging" in major ways and of making social systems work for me. I could freely disparage, fear, neglect, or be oblivious to anything outside of the dominant cultural forms. Being of the main culture, I could also criticize it fairly freely. My life was reflected back to me frequently enough so that I felt, with regard to my race, if not to my sex, like one of the real people.

 Whether through the curriculum or in the newspaper, the television, the economic system, or the general look of people in the streets, I received daily signals and indications that my people counted and that others *either didn't exist or must be trying, not very successfully, to be like people of my race.* I was given cultural permission not to hear voices of people of other races or a tepid cultural tolerance for hearing or acting on such voices. I was also raised not to suffer seriously from anything that darker-skinned people might say about my group, "protected," though perhaps I should more accurately say *prohibited*, through the habits of my economic class and social group, from living in racially mixed groups or being reflective about interactions between people of differing races.

In proportion as my racial group was being made confident, comfortable, and oblivious, other groups were likely being made unconfident, uncomfortable, and alienated. Whiteness protected me from many kinds of hostility, distress, and violence, which I was being subtly trained to visit in turn upon people of color.

For this reason, the word "privilege" now seems to me misleading. Its connotations are too positive to fit the conditions and behaviors which "privilege systems" produce. We usually think of privilege as being a favored state, whether earned, or conferred by birth or luck. School graduates are reminded they are privileged and urged to use their (enviable) assets well. The word "privilege" carries the connotation of being something everyone must want. Yet some of the conditions I have described here work to systemically overempower certain groups. Such privilege simply *confers dominance*, gives permission to control, because of one's race or sex. The kind of privilege that gives license to some people to be, at best, thoughtless and, at worst, murderous should not continue to be referred to as a desirable attribute. Such "privilege" may be widely desired without being in any way beneficial to the whole society.

Moreover, though "privilege" may confer power, it does not confer moral strength. Those who do not depend on conferred dominance have traits and qualities that may never develop in those who do. Just as Women's Studies courses indicate that women survive their political circumstances to lead lives that hold the human race together, so "underprivileged" people of color who are the world's majority have survived their oppression and lived survivors' lives from which the white global minority can and must learn. In some groups, those dominated have actually become strong through *not* having all of these unearned advantages, and this gives them a great deal to teach the others. Members of so-called privileged groups can seem foolish, ridiculous, infantile, or dangerous by contrast.

I want, then, to distinguish between earned strength and unearned power conferred systemically. Power from unearned privilege can look like strength when it is, in fact, permission to escape or to dominate. But not all of the privileges on my list are inevitably damaging. Some, like the expectation that neighbors will be decent to you, or that your race will not count against you in court, should be the norm in a just society and should be considered as the entitlement of everyone. Others, like the privilege not to listen to less powerful people, distort the humanity of the holders as well as the ignored groups. Still others, like finding one's staple foods everywhere, may be a function of being a member of a numerical majority in the population. Others have to do with not having to labor under pervasive negative stereotyping and mythology.

We might at least start by distinguishing between positive advantages that we can work to spread, to the point where they are not advantages at all but simply part of the normal civic and social fabric, and negative types of advantage that unless rejected will always reinforce our present hierarchies. For example, the positive "privilege" of belonging, the feeling that one belongs within the human circle, as Native Americans say, fosters development and should not be seen as privilege for a few. It is, let us say, an entitlement that none of us should have to earn; ideally it is an *unearned entitlement*. At present, since only a few have it, it is an *unearned advantage* for them. The negative "privilege" that gave me cultural permission not to take darker-skinned Others seriously can be seen as arbitrarily conferred dominance and should not be desirable for anyone. This paper results from a process of coming to see that some of the power that I originally saw as attendant on being a human being in the United States consisted in *unearned advantage* and *conferred dominance*, as well as other kinds of special circumstance not universally taken for granted.

In writing this paper I have also realized that white identity and status (as well as class identity and status) give me considerable power to choose whether to broach this subject and its trouble. I can pretty well decide whether to disappear and avoid and not listen and escape the dislike I may engender in other people through this essay, or interrupt, answer, interpret, preach, correct, criticize, and control to some extent what goes on in reaction to it. Being white, I am given considerable power to escape many kinds of danger or penalty as well as to choose which risks I want to take.

There is an analogy here, once again, with Women's Studies. Our male colleagues do not have a great deal to lose in supporting Women's Studies, but they do not have a great deal to lose if they oppose it either. They simply have the power to decide whether to commit themselves to more equitable distributions of power. They will probably feel few penalties whatever choice they make; they do not seem, in any obvious short-term sense, the ones at risk, though they and we are all at risk because of the behaviors that have been rewarded in them.

Through Women's Studies work I have met very few men who are truly distressed about systemic, unearned male advantage and conferred dominance. And so one question for me and others like me is whether we will be like them, or whether we will get truly distressed, even outraged, about unearned race advantage and conferred dominance and if so, what we will do to lessen them. In any case, we need to do more work in identifying how they actually affect our daily lives. We need more down-to-earth writing by people about these taboo subjects. We need more understanding of the ways in which white "privilege" damages white people, for these are not the same ways in which it damages the victimized. Skewed white psyches are an inseparable part of the picture, though I do not want to confuse the kinds of damage done to the holders of special assets and to those who suffer the deficits. Many, perhaps most, of our white students in the United States think that racism doesn't affect them because they are not people of color; they do not see "whiteness" as a racial identity. Many men likewise think that Women's Studies does not bear on their own existences because they are not female; they do not see themselves as having gendered identities. Insisting on the universal "effects" of "privilege" systems, then, becomes one of our chief tasks, and being more explicit about the *particular* effects in particular contexts is another. Men need to join us in this work.

In addition, since race and sex are not the only advantaging systems at work, we need to similarly examine the daily experience of having age advantage, or ethnic advantage, or physical ability, or advantage related to nationality, religion, or sexual orientation. Professor Marnie Evans suggested to me that in many ways the list I made also applies directly to heterosexual privilege. This is a still more taboo subject than race privilege: the daily ways in which heterosexual privilege makes some persons comfortable or powerful, providing supports, assets, approvals, and rewards to those who live or expect to live in heterosexual pairs. Unpacking that content is still more difficult, owing to the deeper imbeddedness of heterosexual advantage and dominance and stricter taboos surrounding these.

But to start such an analysis I would put this observation from my own experience: the fact that I live under the same roof with a man triggers all kinds of societal assumptions about my worth, politics, life, and values and triggers a host of unearned advantages and powers. After recasting many elements from the original list I would add further observations like these:

1. My children do not have to answer questions about why I live with my partner (my husband).

2. I have no difficulty finding neighborhoods where people approve of our household.

3. Our children are given texts and classes that implicitly support our kind of family unit and do not turn them against my choice of domestic partnership.

4. I can travel alone or with my husband without expecting embarrassment or hostility in those who deal with us.

5. Most people I meet will see my marital arrangements as an asset to my life or as a favorable comment on my likability, my competence, or my mental health.

6. I can talk about the social events of a weekend without fearing most listeners' reactions.

7. I will feel welcomed and "normal" in the usual walks of public life, institutional and social.

8. In many contexts, I am seen as "all right" in daily work on women because I do not live chiefly with women.

Difficulties and dangers surrounding the task of finding parallels are many. Since racism, sexism, and heterosexism are not the same, the advantages associated with them should not be seen as the same. In addition, it is hard to isolate aspects of unearned advantage that derive chiefly from social class, economic class, race, religion, region, sex, or ethnic identity. The oppressions are both distinct and interlocking, as the Combahee River Collective statement of 1977 continues to remind us eloquently.[3]

One factor seems clear about all of the interlocking oppressions. They take both active forms that we can see and embedded forms that members of the dominant group are taught not to see. In my class and place, I did not see myself as racist because I was taught to recognize racism only in individual acts of meanness by members of my group, never in invisible systems conferring racial dominance on my group from birth. Likewise, we are taught to think that sexism or heterosexism is carried on only through intentional, individual acts of discrimination, meanness, or cruelty, rather than in invisible systems conferring unsought dominance on certain groups. Disapproving of the systems won't be enough to change them. I was taught to think that racism could end if white individuals changed their attitudes; many men think sexism can be ended by individual changes in daily behavior toward women. But a man's sex provides advantage for him whether or not he approves of the way in which dominance has been conferred on his group. A "white" skin in the United States opens many doors for whites whether or not we approve of the way dominance has been conferred on us. Individual acts can palliate, but cannot end, these problems. To redesign social systems, we need first to acknowledge their colossal unseen dimensions. The silences and denials surrounding privilege are the key political tool here. They keep the thinking about equality or equity incomplete, protecting unearned advantage and conferred dominance by making these taboo subjects. Most talk by whites about equal opportunity seems to me now to be about equal opportunity to try to get into a position of dominance while denying that *systems* of dominance exist.

Obliviousness about white advantage, like obliviousness about male advantage, is kept strongly inculturated in the United States so as to maintain the myth of meritocracy, the myth that democratic choice is equally available to all. Keeping most people unaware that freedom of confident action is there for just a small number of people props up those in power and serves to keep power in the hands of the same groups that have most of it already. Though systemic change takes many decades, there are pressing questions for me and I imagine for some others like me if we raise our daily consciousness on the perquisites of being light-skinned. What will we do with such knowledge? As we know from watching men, it is an open question whether we will choose to use unearned advantage to weaken invisible privilege systems and whether we will use any of our arbitrarily awarded power to try to reconstruct power systems on a broader base.

Notes

[1] This paper was presented at the Virginia Women's Studies Association conference in Richmond in April, 1986, and the American Educational Research Association conference in Boston in October, 1986, and discussed with two groups of participants in the Dodge seminars for Secondary School Teachers in New York and Boston in the spring of 1987.

[2] Andersen, Margaret, "Race and the Social Science Curriculum: A Teaching and Learning Discussion." *Radical Teacher*, November, 1984, pp. 17–20. Smith, Lillian, *Killers of the Dream*, New York: W. W. Norton, 1949.

[3] "A Black Feminist Statement," The Combahee River Collective, pp. 13–22 in G. Hull, P. Scott, B. Smith, Eds., *All the Women Are White, All the Blacks Are Men, But Some of Us Are Brave: Black Women's Studies*, Old Westbury, NY: The Feminist Press, 1982.

Pamela Fletcher is a writer, editor, critic, and educator. Currently, she is a member of the English faculty at the College of St. Catherine where she teaches creative and expository writing and literature. Her story, "A Dream Deferred," appeared in Do You Know Me Now? An Anthology of Minnesota Multicultural Writings *(1993). It poignantly addresses issues of race, identity, self-knowledge, betrayal, and loss of innocence. What "dream" does her title refer to? What characterizes the loss of innocence she describes? How does her narrative express the complexity of the relationship between individual and community? In what ways does it compel us to consider issues of truth and justice? How does it relate to Peggy McIntosh's essay about white privilege?*

A Dream Deferred[1]

Pamela Fletcher

Prancing on Seal Beach waves atop our slippery surfboards, we wiped out and choked on the foamy, pickled sea and giggled and pranced and wiped out and choked and giggled and pranced under a hot sun that browned B.K. like a chicken breast in a pan of sweet butter and blackened me like a filet of red snapper dusted with savory spices and fried over a high blue flame.

Occasionally B.K. and I took breaks to replenish our energy, eating sandwiches Mama Bindels made so lovingly with Wonder bread, margarine, and chocolate sprinkles. We also munched juicy black plums that Mama Bindels had picked from the plum tree in their backyard. To cool down, we drank enormous bottles of RC cola that I could barely swallow because the bubbly syrup stung my throat. B.K. and her older sisters glugged the liquid in large gulps and were instantly revived.

Mama and Papa Bindels waved at us with dark-shaded eyes and sun-lightened grins. Every now and then Papa Bindels swam quickly behind us, squealing and splashing and breaking our concentration when it appeared that we were about to ascend a giant wave. I adored him and his mischievous manner. He loved to tease and do pranks. Whenever I saw him, he gave me wholesome, warm hugs and tenderly patted my head. Most of the time I didn't completely understand his words when he talked to me because he spoke in a melodious Dutch accent that confused and delighted me. Yet I understood that he thought of me as his daughter and I felt quite special to have both him and my father care about me. I often wondered how it would feel to really be Mr. Bindels' daughter. He and my father were very different men, separated by age, color, and opportunity. I knew they were different, but at nine years old I had no idea just how different their lives were. I wonder now just what it's like to be the daughter of a man who is not routinely beaten with a thick switch broken from a branch of the lynching tree.

B.K., blonde, tall, and Canadian, and I, dark, tall, and American, loved each other more than we loved our own sisters. In the summer of 1965, as in the previous two years, this love kept me afloat in the hostile suburban community of La Puente, located approximately thirty miles east of Watts where rebellion would soon erupt. I had no knowledge of what racism and discrimination meant; I never had heard the words before. But I was familiar with the slur "nigger" that the white and Mexican children fired like poison gas in my face and in the faces of my siblings. I vaguely remember hearing that Malcolm X was shot to death that year on February 21, the day of my brother's eighth birthday, but I didn't know who Malcolm X was and didn't know that I should even care. I also didn't understand the significance of the civil rights march that King and some thirty-five thousand national supporters had recently accomplished in Alabama. As far as I knew, Watts and Alabama were strange lands with voting rights violations, unfair housing, segregated schools, separate public accommodations, and police brutality that had nothing, whatsoever, to do with my life. Living in La Puente at nine years old, I had no idea what those problems meant at all. Besides, Mama and Daddy never mentioned them nor commented on the news. They moved us to San Gabriel Valley so we wouldn't have to worry about such things.

The Fletchers and the Bindels were oblivious to what was happening outside our suburban cocoon. All I cared about was how often B.K. and I would play together and how soon we would make up after a fight. About once a month we underwent a power struggle about some petty thing, nothing memorable. We had it down to a science: we screamed at each other, stomped our feet, and cried; then she ran away and I nervously awaited her return (sometimes it took a day or two), and then we hugged, laughed, and began anew. Our families did not understand our combative interaction, but these theatrics simply became our ritual for emotional adventure.

B.K. ran wild and barefooted, her straight hair swinging every which way. I didn't like getting my feet dirty so I wore tennis shoes, and since it was not proper for a colored girl to let her hair go its own direction, I captured its unruly nature in a ponytail. Once, while we played house, Valerie, my baby sister, attempted to braid B.K.'s hair but the ends would not stay. "It just won't act right," Valerie sighed, trying to braid B.K.'s hair as tightly as possible. As the braid unraveled, B.K. hunched her shoulders and we giggled, and left it up to God. This difference between our hair and hers mystified us sometimes. It struck me that while Mama permed our hair to straighten it, B.K.'s big sister, Bianca, permed her hair to curl it. I began to realize that girls spent a lot of time worrying about their hair, especially as they grew older. Bianca and her friends regularly changed their hair color and hair styles. B.K., though, liked her hair plain and natural. Once in a while she wore a ponytail, but she never wore braids. We colored girls kept our hair in bondage. Braiding it seemed to be the easiest way to create a presentable colored appearance. I envied B.K.'s nonchalance about hair; she never worried about being presentable. This child of Dutch ancestry, named after Queen Beatrix of Holland, had such confidence and spunk. I envied her rebellious spirit. She had the audacity to defy everyone, including her parents, especially Papa Bindels, who grounded her at every turn. But he never forbade us to see each other; somehow he knew that it would be cruel and unusual punishment. When he banished her to her room, I just moved in, and we often spent hours planning or replanning our next beach trip and laughing about the silly things we did the last time we went surfing.

In 1968 our elementary school years came to an abrupt end. One day, when we weren't looking, our bodies abandoned us and moved to some foreign land while our minds had yet to venture beyond the fifth grade. Feeling awkward and insecure, we began to experience things that we could not or would not mention to each other. For instance, although we didn't tell each other when we began to menstruate, I could tell her time had come because she acted guilty just like I acted once I began menstruating. Suddenly we discovered a horrible secret we didn't want anyone else to know. We no longer laughed easily. We walked with constraint and held our bodies close. We stopped wrestling, climbing trees, and playing house. We began to see through wide eyes that there was a direct correlation between our new external selves and how the world reacted to us. "Keep your legs shut!" Daddy said. "Stop rolling around out there on that grass like you somebody wild," Mama said. Men leered at us when we walked around the shopping center.

Yet, initially, I didn't see everything so clearly. I didn't see how much the world's reaction to our friendship would change our lives forever—until one certain day. That day we walked home from school together, talking and laughing just like our old selves. Suddenly B.K. startled me with a tone of voice that I hadn't heard before. It wasn't her angry I-will-never-speak-to-you-again voice; it was a voice that no longer recognized me.

"Quick! Get behind me. Walk behind me."

"Huh?" I said. "What do you mean?"

"Walk behind me," she repeated. But then she rushed ahead of me and walked away fast as if we weren't walking together. As she walked ahead, a car slowed, approaching us.

"Hey, B.K.! What cha doing?" a blonde girl yelled out of the car window.

"Hey, Cathy! You coming over later?"

"My mom says she might drop me off while she goes shopping. I'll call ya."

"Okay. See you guys later," B.K. waved as the car gained speed.

She maintained a safe distance from me until the car turned the corner and then she stopped and waited for me to catch up. B.K. resumed the conversation as if nothing had happened and I forced myself to withhold my riotous and jealous rage, though I did not know why. I may have been afraid of what I would have done if I released my fury; after all, I was not supposed to be <u>this</u> angry, so angry I could have killed her. Unlike most colored people, I was living the integrated dream of the late Martin Luther King and it was supposed to be good and equal, but over time I began to realize that it wasn't what my parents had expected and what they had led me to believe it would be. As we walked along that wide street together, I found that it didn't matter that for years B.K. and I lived in the same neighborhood on the same side of the street, one house away from each other, that we ate and slept in each other's homes, that we shared silly secrets and protected each other, that we went to the same schools and shopped in the same stores. Together. The fact that we were different colors still separated us.

King's recent death had touched so many people, including my family, and I began to pay close attention to what was happening around the country and what was happening to me as I was growing into someone brand new. The world exploded with talk about race and violence and civil rights, and I ascertained that society was forcing me to choose between being a person and being a "black" person. When I looked at B.K. then, she was no longer B.K.; she was now a "white" girl, representative of all the whites who had rejected and oppressed me. Although she walked beside me now, I realized that she had just relegated me to that "place" where black people are meant to placate or perish. As she assumed her privileged position in the white world, we were torn asunder. My best friend whom I considered my sister died right in front of my very eyes. And a piece of me died right along with her. Yet, my rage gave birth to an awareness that Watts and Alabama were not so distant from La Puente after all. It occurred to me that no matter where we lived, black people still had so much to overcome. While B.K. talked, I nodded my head for fear that if I opened my mouth, I would flood her with murderous grief. When we reached Barrydale Street, instead of stopping at her corner house as usual, I said good-bye with averted, teary eyes and walked away.

That afternoon I buried B.K. along with my innocent belief that love is a protective shield that saves one from being devoured by a world that eats the hearts of those who dare to be human and who dare to accept the humanity of someone else. B.K. and I had never discussed our blatant difference so I naively thought that for once it didn't matter. After having suffered loneliness for so long in La Puente, I thought I finally had found a friend who loved me regardless of how I looked, who loved me for my "character." Forever. I had never imagined that once we reached Edgewood Junior High our emotional points would no longer intersect simply because I was black and she was white. Although I had willed myself to forget that day, deep in my heart I was afraid I would never recover; I was afraid that I would continue to mourn the loss of the dream.

Yet, like the living dead who didn't die a timely death or get a proper burial, the dream can't rest. It's as alive as my vivid memory of B.K. and me prancing on those waves. Together.

Note

[1] Taken from a line in Langston Hughes' poem, "Dream Boogie."

UNIT 2

Searching for Truths

Every day, in countless ways, you and I convince ourselves about our-selves. True art, when it happens to us, challenges the "I" that we are.

Jeannette Winterson

Introduction to Searching for Truths

A key value in liberal education is to engage in life-long learning, never to rest complacently on what we think is true about ourselves or others, but always to challenge ourselves, remain open to new ways of thinking, and hone skills in evaluating the assertions of those around us. The primary goal of this unit is to improve your skills as a critical thinker and to develop your awareness of the variety of disciplinary approaches for exploring truths. We will ask, "What is truth? How do we recognize it?" And we will ask those questions from different angles—philosophical, aesthetic, theological, and scientific. We will also consider the differences between opinion and evidence and how we construct a reasoned argument. There are fewer personal narratives in this section and more essays written for an academic audience—these are not so much telling a story as making a claim and supporting it with logic and evidence.

Some skills you might polish in this unit include how to: read academic essays; learn collaboratively; communicate orally and visually; structure an argument; question objectively; sift through perceived truths; develop an opinion from knowledge, not just habit; agree to disagree; recognize stakeholders and claims to power in arguments; and argue not to "win" but to listen, learn, and understand. We will also approach the question of how to know truth in a practical way in the context of library research. In other words, how do you find different types of information and distinguish between reliable and not-so-reliable sources?

By way of the "Structured Controversy" project, you will have a chance to increase your capacity for reflective judgment on matters of fact and conflicting ideas, and to connect that capacity to your education, aesthetic, and spiritual experiences. In the end, this unit aims to help you clarify the relationship between self-knowledge and academic learning.

Anita Ho (b. 1971) is a philosopher who joined the faculty of the College of St. Catherine in the fall of 2000. In this piece written in 2002 for the TRW Reader, Ho asks us to consider the philosophical nature of moral truth. Are there any absolute or universal moral standards? What are the ramifications of thinking there are or are not? Raised in Hong Kong, educated in Canada, and teaching in the U.S., Ho is well positioned to address both cultural and individual differences in customs and beliefs. She critically evaluates arguments for and against ethical relativism and subjectivism. Does this help you to clarify your own values? In the end, do you agree with Ho that a universal approach to morality does not imply ethnocentrism?

"It's So Judgmental!"
A Lesson on Subjectivity and Relativism

Anita Ho

"I wouldn't do it, but how can I tell you that you can't do it either?" one of my students comments on the issue of slavery. "I believe in equality, and I think it is wrong for me to own slaves. But who am I to tell you that you shouldn't own slaves? That's your decision to make, not mine!" Other students from the class start to get into the discussion. One of them says, "I agree. We should just mind our own business. How can we tell others what to do and what not to do? It's so judgmental!"

Yes, we are talking about relativism and subjectivism. We are trying to figure out if there are any absolute or universal moral standards that each and every one of us should follow. We are wondering if there are certain things that people should simply never do to another human being. Almost all my students say that there is no such universal moral standard. Each culture has its own custom, and people outside of that culture should not interfere. As a matter of fact, some students believe that each person has his or her own moral beliefs, and people should not tell others that they are wrong.

Our discussion moves from slavery to the Holocaust. I ask, "What about the Nazis? Can't we say that it was absolutely wrong for them to kill six million Jews?"

Everyone looks at each other. A couple of them gently nod, but still say that they cannot tell the Nazis what to do. One of them says that it was horrible that the Nazis killed these people. She says she hopes that nobody would ever do this again. However, she understands why they did it. She says, "These people were taught to believe that the Jewish people were subhuman. Obviously, I don't believe in that. But it is easy for me to say that, because we don't have Hitler here. But if these people were brought up in that environment, it is unfair for outsiders to judge them."

Other students make similar remarks. They say that the concentration camps were terrible, but they refuse to say that it was morally wrong for the Nazi Germans to kill all those people.

What's happening here? Really, can we not say that ethnic cleansing and slavery are absolutely wrong, no matter who you are, where you live, and when you live? Do these students really believe that we should not judge these actions, even though they also think that they themselves should not engage in these practices? Is it really so bad to be judgmental on some issues? I know some of these students are working in various volunteering projects to promote social justice, so why do they somehow deny that there is fundamental injustice in some practices? Are they simply confused about what they believe in?

Students often say that there is no such thing as a "universal moral standard." They insist that morality is simply a matter of one's own personal opinion. You have your opinion, and I have mine. You cannot tell me that I am wrong, and I also cannot tell you that you are wrong. They worry that believing in universal moral standards means that they are arrogant and are trying to impose their viewpoints on others. As Robert Simon says, students often think that any criticism of another culture's practices or ideologies is a kind of cultural imperialism.[1] There is the belief that if a practice is part of some people's cultural or moral belief, and if it has worked for them, then others should not pass judgment or interfere.

Worrying about being called judgmental and arrogant, many students say that they are *relativists*. They use the word in many different ways, but in general, they think that ethical beliefs or viewpoints are relative to societies and cultures. If your culture believes in footbinding, it is correct for your culture. If it does not, it is incorrect for your culture. Other cultures may have different ideas than your culture, and they can judge the rightness of this practice according to their own cultural beliefs. However, they cannot judge *your* culture's ideology, but can only determine for *themselves* what is right and wrong. If the Nazi Germans believe that ethnic cleansing was acceptable in their culture, contemporary Americans like my students simply cannot judge them, even if my students would not want that to happen here.

What is interesting in our discussion about relativism is that, students seem to believe that not only are cultures entitled to their traditions and beliefs, but so are individuals. When we start talking about whether it is absolutely wrong for an American today to own slaves, most students are still reluctant to say yes. I ask, "If you find out that your neighbor has a slave, you still don't think that is wrong?" One student says, "Well, I don't think I can tell anyone what to do. Of course I wouldn't own slaves, but what he does is not my business." In other words, it seems that my students believe that each and every individual is the only one who can decide what is right for himself or herself.

Surprised by the unanimous agreement among my students who almost never agree on anything, I proceed with the most awful and shocking example I can think of: "Suppose there is a group of people who believe that burning babies just for fun is acceptable." One student whispers, "Oh my god!" Another student quietly says, "Yuck!" Almost all of them give me a big, long, and disgusted stare. I realize that I am on dangerous ground, but I am hoping that a shocking and extreme example can get my students to rethink their position. I cautiously ask, "Can we tell them that it is absolutely wrong for them to do that? Can we say that it does not matter what their preference of entertainment may be, it is simply wrong for anyone to burn babies for fun?"

By the look of disbelief and shock on my students' faces, I start to think that they may be seriously questioning their position.

A few seconds lapse, and then I hear a quiet voice, "I guess it is awful for anyone to do that." A couple other nods follow.

I secretly think, *I am getting somewhere.*

Then, I hear a voice, "Yeah, but I still don't think we can make such a blank statement to say that it is wrong for anyone to do this. Sure, I think it is gross and everything, and like I said about slavery, I wouldn't do this myself. But again, I don't think I can tell these people what to do. I don't think we should be judgmental about what others do. I am not God. I can't tell others what is right and what is wrong."

Another voice follows, "I agree. I'm sitting here thinking, would I want others to tell me that what I do in my private life is wrong? No! I should be allowed to do whatever I believe in. I don't need to explain anything to other people. It's my life!"

Do students really believe that? Why do even the best students think that we can never say that there are things that are simply wrong?

When I probe the matter further, I realize that these students seem not only to be ethical relativists, but also subjectivists. They say that whether something is right or wrong depends solely on what you subjectively believe. For example, if I believe burning babies is a cruel and illegitimate way to derive pleasure, then it is wrong for me. If you believe it is the best form of entertainment, then it is right for you. People have different perspectives, and no one can say that one perspective is objectively better than another.

This is a worrying position. If everything is "free for all" and people can do whatever they want, wouldn't we have chaos? Why would our students believe in such a position?

Arguments for Ethical Relativism and Subjectivism

There are a few reasons why students are or at least think they are ethical relativists and subjectivists. "Evidence" of diversity is overwhelming. People of different times and places have vastly different or even conflicting ideologies and experiences. Anthropologists such as Ruth Benedict have given us numerous examples to show that it is not unusual for one society to approve of an act that is held to be abnormal or immoral by another.[2] When people around the world have vastly different customs and beliefs, it is unclear how we can evaluate them objectively. Some cultures avoid eating certain types of animals, while others use different kinds of animals for celebration. Some cultures avoid using certain numbers (e.g., "7" in the Chinese culture), while other societies think of the same number as lucky. Certain societies believe that female circumcision is an important element of cultural identity, while others believe that such practice is oppressive and barbaric. Some cultures require women to wear head-to-toe burkas, while other societies allow women to wear bikinis or even go to nude beaches.

On an individual level, there are also different ideas of the morality of practices such as abortion, capital punishment, and cloning. In the face of diversity, it is doubtful that we have any one custom or practice that is embraced by all. It is also unclear if anyone has a legitimate basis for interfering with customs and practices that are different from their own.

Ethical relativism and subjectivism also seem more plausible when we consider how there are various perspectives even among academics who are supposedly "experts" on ethics. They disagree on all the aforementioned ethical issues. If there is disagreement even among experts on the morality of various practices, it seems unlikely that there can be any absolute moral standard governing everyone. As one of my students says, "If these so-called experts can't straighten everything out for us, I doubt we can ever come to agreement anywhere else."

Another reason why many embrace ethical relativism and subjectivism is that they are uncertain if any culture or person should have the authority to determine for everyone else what is moral and immoral. As my students ask, who can be the judge, and how can we force others who have different ideologies to adopt our values? They claim that people of various societies should respect each other and not interfere with their culture and customs. They sometimes also say that whatever happens within a culture or society, it is a "domestic" or "private" matter of that society, and people outside of that society have no right to criticize its "domestic affairs." If certain societies require their women to wear a burka, we should simply respect their custom.

Foreign diplomats have said similar things. Chinese officials, for example, have repeatedly criticized the United States and other countries for trying to interfere with their domestic policies, such as how they deal with dissidents and criminal defendants. They argue that other countries have no right to impose their values on China. They insist that other countries that try to interfere with their internal affairs are claiming moral superiority and are therefore ethnocentric. In a speech regarding the China–U. S. relationship, President Jiang Zemin of The Republic of China argues that friendly relations and cooperation can only exist on the principles of "mutual non aggression" and "non interference in each other's internal affairs."[3] He insists that the United States cannot legitimately ask all countries to institute the same political system or to judge the various choices made by people of other countries according to their own values.

Many people also think that we can only have a harmonious society if we respect different ideologies. They worry that allowing some people to make decisions for everyone else will inevitably lead to an oppressive and totalitarian regime. This is especially an important concern for democratic societies like the United States, since we cannot consistently argue for democracy and at the same time impose certain beliefs on other cultures or even our own citizens. After all, democracy requires that all rational human beings be allowed to determine for themselves their way of life and personal values. It requires that others do not authoritatively impose their view as absolute and coerce everyone else to follow it. When there are different moral standards, we cannot simply ignore the perspectives of certain individuals. Imposing one's moral standard on others ignores people's ability to make decisions for themselves and violates their autonomy. As some of my students say, it seems to be pure arrogance for us to exalt our own morality as the only true one and dismiss all other ideas as false or inferior.

Responses to Ethical Relativists and Subjectivists

It is admirable that students want to respect different perspectives. But does respect require that we can never say that certain practices are illegitimate? Students are correct that there are many different beliefs in the world, and it is often difficult to find one right answer for any ethical dilemma. There are usually many complex issues involved in each case, and sometimes there is no simple way to reach an answer. In many instances, even after reflecting on various possible perspectives, we may still not know which perspective is the best one.

However, admitting the difficulty to determine which of the various per-spectives is best is different from claiming that each perspective is equally valid, or that we cannot critically evaluate them. Just because there are numerous perspectives or ethical positions does not mean that every-thing reduces to cultural or personal opinions, or that there is no right or wrong answer to anything. While it is often difficult to find the right answer, we do not have to immediately reject the possibility that some perspectives have *more* validity than others. Although it is difficult to find *one* idea that will be agreeable for all, it is often possible for us to find out which viewpoints are at least more plausible than others. Sometimes even when we do not know what the best answer may be, we can still say that there are certain perspectives that are clearly objectionable. For example, although it is difficult to find a simple answer to the question of how we should treat other human beings, it is clear that there are good reasons to reject the idea that we can kill others whenever we want. Killing each other is a less plausible perspective *in any society* partly because life will become "nasty, brutish, and short," to use the philoso-pher Thomas Hobbes' phrase.[4]

It is admirable that students want to listen to and respect different per-spectives. I agree that we need to refrain from assuming that there is always only one answer to each problem. There are times when there may be various plausible approaches to deal with an ethical issue. I also agree that we should not assume that we are always correct, and that dissenting viewpoints are automatically inferior or wrong. However, the argument that some perspectives are objectively better than others does not imply that one is presuming her moral superiority. Rather, the universal approach to morality only says that there are certain perspectives that are objectively more valid than others, and that these perspectives should apply to every-one. Our job is to *consider various perspectives carefully*, and then find out which ones are better than the rest, and why they are better. It is consistent for one to argue that some perspectives are better and deny that one actu-ally is holding the better perspective. When we question the legitimacy of relativistic positions, we are not saying that we have to condemn *other* peo-ple's values. What we are saying is that we need to critically evaluate every perspective, *including our own*. Such a task acknowledges the possibility that we may be holding the wrong perspective.

In other words, it is a mistake to think that a universal approach to moral-ity implies ethnocentrism. It is also a mistake to think that relativistic positions only ask us to withhold judgment of other people's cultural and personal beliefs. Relativism and subjectivism actually permit us to not even judge or evaluate our own beliefs. After all, under these relativistic positions, you do not need to question your beliefs. As one of my stu-dents says, she does not want anyone to tell her that she may be wrong, because she thinks she should be allowed to do whatever she believes in. Her idea is that, whatever you believe in is right for you. You do not have to explain or justify to others why you believe in certain things, and others have no right to impose their standard on you. In other words, there is no need for you to give reasons for your actions.

In this way, it is not the universal approach to morality that leads to ethnocentrism and unwillingness to question one's own beliefs. Rather, it is when we adopt a relativistic approach that we may fall into the idea that we are always correct in holding our own beliefs, so that we do not need to critically examine or correct our own belief. After all, if we are all correct in our opinions, we never have to question whether our sense of morality is distorted. Ironically, it seems that by adopting the universal approach to morality, we can have a better chance of questioning our own beliefs.

It is admirable that students want to withhold judgment of other cultures and people. Certainly, people from different cultural and social backgrounds may not understand each other's viewpoint, and without such understanding it is arrogant to impose our views on others. Some societies have long-established traditions, and it may be difficult and traumatic to make them change their ways of life, since people may feel that they are losing their cultural identity. When we are non-judgmental, we can learn from each other and improve our understanding of others' viewpoints. Such a tolerant attitude can help us to live harmoniously in a morally and culturally diverse society.

Moreover, it is only when we all respect others and remain tolerant that those of minority opinions have a fair chance to express their views. One of the reasons why democratic societies are appealing is that everyone has a legal right to express his or her ideas, even when his or her views are in the minority.[5] Maintaining such a tolerant attitude ensures that unpopular views are not being unfairly suppressed.

While these are all good reasons for us to keep an open mind, commitments to respect others and keep an open mind do not imply that ethical relativism and subjectivism are correct. While some customs and practices are relatively innocent and people should have a right to engage in them, not all practices fall into this category. Certainly, worshipping, burning incense, or not eating certain animals do not negatively affect the lives of others, and there is little reason to reject such practices even if we do not agree with them. However, it seems that there are limits on what people can do in the name of customs or personal beliefs. When one's action harms another person, as in the examples of ethnic cleansing and slavery, it is unclear if one can justify it simply by claiming that it is one's cultural or personal belief. It is also unclear if people can deny the legitimacy of criticism or interference in the convenient name of "internal affairs" or "private matters."

John Stuart Mill's idea of liberty may be helpful here. As a moral philosopher who values liberty, Mill argues that the only justification for interfering with liberty is to prevent harm to others.[6] Mill acknowledges that people have different beliefs, and we need to have open dialogues to discuss such beliefs. He argues that freedom of expression should be allowed, since it is only when we have such freedom that we can fairly evaluate various perspectives and get closer to the truth. Mill also values diversity and originality. He argues that we should not try to shape people after one model, but should allow them to develop in their own ways. He argues that we should resist "forcing improvements on an unwilling people," since "the only unfailing and permanent source of improvement is liberty."[7] Mill argues that even when we disagree with each other's choices, *if such choices do not harm others*, we cannot interfere.

This last point is important. Mill treasures liberty and autonomy, and he thinks that we need to allow rational adults to express their own views and act on their own ideologies. However, he does not think that respect for others implies that we have to allow absolute freedom. There can still be limits to what people can do. As Mill says, "the fact of living in society renders it indispensable that each should be bound to observe a certain line of conduct towards the rest."[8] For example, people cannot injure the interests of another. After all, one cannot consistently argue for one's own freedom but harm another. In this way, respect for freedom does not imply that people should never be accountable for their actions. We can argue that people can engage in various activities in accordance with their cultural and personal ideology, *so long as their actions do not harm another human being's well being or violate another's freedom.* For example, ethnic cleansing and killing infants for entertainment purposes cannot be justified by cultural and personal ideologies, because they harm other people.

More Problems for Ethical Relativists and Subjectivists

Mill's "harm principle" brings out another inadequacy of ethical relativism and subjectivism. When pushed to the extreme, relativistic views run into trouble. Their view that morality is relative to one's cultural or individual beliefs makes it impossible for anyone to condemn or correct even the most atrocious practices. Ethical relativists and subjectivists do not distinguish between innocent customs and unethical practices. They seem to think that they are morally equivalent, i.e., they are all correct if you believe in them. Their failure to see the distinction may have led them to deny the legitimacy of condemning practices that are harmful to others. This is perhaps why many students refuse to say that the Nazi

Germans were absolutely wrong in killing six million Jews. After all, we cannot condemn ethnic cleansing unless we accept the view that these practices are not "simply domestic affairs," and that they are wrong regardless of people's personal or cultural beliefs.

One may ask, does it matter whether one believes in relativism or subjectivism? What is the big deal? If we simply allow people to do what they believe in, can't we get along better?

No. I don't think we can get along better by being relativists. Yes. It is a big deal if people believe in relativism. It has enormous implications for social policies and justice issues. After all, we cannot do anything to "correct" injustice unless we can truly say that certain things that happened to people in the past were wrong. If we adopt a relativistic approach, we will be rejecting some of the most important ideas, such as the notion of human rights. Human rights are supposed to apply to all human beings regardless of who they are, where they live, and when they are born. No society or individual is allowed to violate these rights, regardless of their cultural or personal beliefs.

What will happen if we all become relativists? As shown in my class discussion, we will not be able to say that people were wrong in owning slaves, because they lived in a different time in which such practice was allowed. We also will not be able to talk intelligently about international tribunals prosecuting war crimes. If the Nazi Germans believed that it was morally legitimate to kill Jewish people, then according to ethical relativism, it was right for them to do so. It makes no difference that other societies thought or continue to think that it was wrong for the Nazis to kill innocent people. We also cannot criticize the Taliban regime in Afghanistan, even though they publicly kill women who go outside without a male relative or a burka. If we accept relativism, we will have to say that all these actions are morally right for those who believe in them. If we disagree with such actions, all that means is that we will not condone it in our own society. However, acceptance of ethical relativism implies that we cannot interfere with or even intelligently criticize the Taliban's policies.

In the end, we will not act against injustice. If we cannot even say that certain things are morally wrong, of course we will not do anything to prevent or correct the wrong. We also do not need to strive for better societies. If the belief that we are entitled to our opinions implies that we are all correct in holding our opinions, then there is no point of questioning or improving ourselves. We will always be right! Ethical relativism and subjectivism seem to give us a convenient justification never to question our own viewpoints. It also provides justification for us to sit by and do nothing even when we have fundamental disagreement on moral matters.

It is no surprise that many proponents of ethical relativism, such as China and other regimes in the Middle East, have been the most flagrant violators of human rights. After all, if various cultures are entitled to their own moral standard and call their practices "domestic policies," other cultures cannot judge them or interfere with their policies. They are automatically immune from scrutiny. Feminists have criticized how many abuses of women are tolerated in the name of privacy and family autonomy. Women who suffer from abuse and other forms of inequality and violence often are not protected under relativistic positions, because what happens in a household or society is considered a private or domestic matter. Such matters cannot be interfered with, even if others may not agree with them. After all, under ethical relativism and subjectivism, whatever people believe is right for them.

What is most startling about ethical relativism and subjectivism is that, according to these doctrines, we can hold contradictory views and all be correct at the same time! According to relativism and subjectivism, part of the reason why we cannot criticize and interfere with each other's position is that we are each correct in holding our individual views! If I believe that physical assault is the right way to teach my spouse about his household duties, it is right for me to do so. If you are against such practice, your view is right for you. In the end, we are both right![9] This means that it is impossible for any culture to condone the wrong practice, or for any individual to believe in the wrong thing.

This is certainly a convenient but troubling position. If we accept the subjectivist idea and believe that we are each correct in believing contradicting positions, it is unclear if any society can legitimately have laws. It appears that under subjectivism, laws are inherently discriminatory, since they treat certain moral beliefs unfavorably. After all, laws that prohibit people from killing others or beating their spouses impose a standard on those who may have different beliefs. They prohibit these people to act on their beliefs.

Certainly, ethical relativists may argue that we need laws for practical reasons, since chaos will result if people can do anything that they "believe" in. However, the fact that we need laws to prevent chaos already shows that ethical relativists and subjectivists are mistaken. Contrary to what they believe, we simply cannot have a harmonious world or safe society if we take these relativistic positions seriously and allow people to do whatever they believe.

Putting aside the problem of chaos in accepting ethical relativism and subjectivism, it seems absurd that the correctness of a position depends on whether one believes in it. My students seem to think that whether slavery is wrong depends on whether people who own slaves believe in such a practice. (Of course, these students are not thinking about whether the slaves agree with such a practice!) But this makes all moral judgments arbitrary. If a culture or an individual happens to believe that owning slaves is wrong, it is wrong. However, if this culture or individual happens to hold the opposite belief, then owning slaves is moral. It does not ask *why* a certain culture or individual believes in various practices. It only asks *if* this culture or individual believes them.

However, it is unclear how my believing in certain things automatically makes it right. Relativistic positions do not require us to give independent reasons or logical arguments for holding such beliefs. They seem to believe that what we *think* is right is the same with what *is* right. The fact that some people believe in ethnic cleansing is sufficient to make it right for them. They do not need to provide any other supporting arguments to show *why* they believe such a practice is right. If another group of people believe the opposite, they also do not need to explain why they hold such position.

If ethical relativism and subjectivism are true, moral dialogues or arguments will be meaningless. As I ask my students who are reluctant to say that anything is morally wrong, what is the point of studying ethics, if we are all correct in believing in whatever opinion we happen to hold? There is no point of evaluating different moral positions. And what is the point of trying to teach our children to become "moral citizens"? They can simply do whatever they want, and they will automatically be right! Moreover, what is the point of convincing others or even ourselves that our point of view may have merits? After all, others are also equally correct in holding their viewpoints.

When everyone is automatically right at all times, the whole notion of moral progress is also meaningless. Moral progress means an improvement from worse to better, and it implies an acknowledgement that certain ideologies are better than others. According to relativistic positions, however, we cannot say that the society we are living in right now is better than the one that allowed slavery. We cannot say that various anti-discriminatory practices enforced in the United States today are better than the discriminatory ones that resulted in the deaths of millions in Germany in the 1940s.

It is difficult to balance tolerance and a critical perception of various cultural and individual ideologies. On the one hand, we need to be open-minded and allow other rational beings to reach moral judgements on their own. On the other hand, we also need to keep in mind that being open-minded does not mean that we cannot be critical of various ideas, or that every idea is equally valid. In other words, while we need to keep an open mind, we can still reject ethical relativism or subjectivism. Certainly, we need to be extremely careful in evaluating various views and imposing our views on others. We may be wrong, or there may be practical difficulties in imposing our views on others. However, a commitment to respect others and to keep an open mind does not imply that we can never make judgments about right and wrong. When we keep an open mind, we have a greater chance of understanding each other's viewpoints. At the same time, we will also be more equipped in critically evaluating various positions, including our own. Respect of others only requires that we carefully evaluate different perspectives, and give people of different ideologies an equal chance to explain and defend their respective positions. It requires that we do not assume authority on moral matters and automatically judge others' perspectives as inferior to ours. However, ethical relativism and subjectivism are not the best ways to keep us open-minded and respectful of others. In fact, they prevent us from understanding different viewpoints. The idea that there are universal moral standards may give us a better chance to evaluate critically various ideologies. The universal approach to morality does not argue that we are the ones who always have the right answer, and that others who have different ideologies are inferior. Rather, it requires that we all accept the possibility that everyone is susceptible to mistakes, and we all have to be patient and careful in investigating various moral positions.

I discuss all these issues with my students. Are they convinced? One of them says, "I guess I was wrong in thinking that I am a relativist. I am still not sure when we can impose our ideas on others, but I do think our laws prohibiting slavery and killing are right, and those who commit these acts should be punished." Another says, "I never thought that relativism might give people the perfect reason to sit by and watch injustice happening in the world, but I guess it inevitably leads to that." A few more students nod. As we are ready to leave the class, one student says, "Well, I guess that's your opinion. I still don't buy it." I respond, "And you can't tell me I am wrong."

Notes

[1] Robert Simon, "The Paralysis of Absolutophobia," *The Chronicle of Higher Education*, 27 June 1997, 85–86.

[2] Ruth Benedict, "Ethics Are Relative," in *Classical Philosophical Questions* 9th ed., ed. J. A. Gould (Upper Saddle River, NJ: Prentice Hall, 1998), 159–167.

[3] For the complete speech made by President Jiang, please see http://www.ncuscr.org/articles%20and%20speeches/jiang.speech.htmI

[4] Thomas Hobbes, *Leviathan* (1651; reprint, Harmondsworth, Middlesex: Penguin Books, 1975), 186.

[5] There are often other barriers to minorities actually voicing their opinions, even when they have the legal right to do so. For example, minorities may worry about the "tyranny of the majority." They may worry that even when they have

the "right" to voice their opinions, their unpopular views will still go unnoticed or be intentionally ignored. However, for the purpose of this essay, I will put aside this issue.

6 John Stuart Mill, *On Liberty* (1859; reprint, London: Penguin Books, 1985).

7 Mill, 136.

8 Mill, 141.

9 The ironic result of ethical relativism and subjectivism is that their proponents cannot prove that I am wrong. They cannot even try to convince me that they are correct. If I believe that there are universal moral standards, according to subjectivism, I am automatically correct! In the end, ethical relativism, subjectivism, and a universal approach to morality are all correct!

Nancy A. Heitzeg teaches sociology and is the co-director of the interdisciplinary program in Critical Studies of Race and Ethnicity at the College of St. Catherine. As a sociologist, Heitzeg has long been interested in issues of inequality and their intersection. In this essay, she presents us with certain facts about human society and asks us if they are justice issues. It is not enough to know what is, but we must also decide on what is right or just. How do we decide? We don't often consciously recognize the sources of our belief system or the assumptions we are making. Heitzeg's analysis of the sources, standards, and scope of justice frameworks helps us to see how different disciplinary approaches to justice reflect their approaches to truth. What would you say are the sources of your sense of justice? What does it mean to be anthropocentric vs. ecocentric? Can we say that differences in "opinion" can come honestly through differences in approach, assumptions, and method of study?

Searching for Truths, Searching for Justice

Nancy A. Heitzeg

Facts, Values, Truths, and Justice

> the earthen vessel may hold the sweet wine
> the handwrought silver goblet—gall
> the tattered cover—words of wisdom
> the gold-edged leaf—the cruelest lie
> stumbling words—love's true oath
> the silver tongue—a razor's edge
> the truth arrives disguised,
> therein the sorrow lies

—Jimmy Glass, 1984
Executed in Louisiana 1987[1]

Consider the following points:

- The richest 400 Americans—all billionaires—have a net worth of over $1.5 trillion, which is 1,000 times greater than the net worth of the 40 million poorest Americans. (*Forbes*, 2007; DeNavas-Walt, et al, 2006)

- Only 39 women are listed among the 400 richest Americans. Of those, 35 directly inherited their wealth. Oprah Winfrey is one of two African Americans on the list and the only "rags to riches" story of the *Forbes* 400. (*Forbes*, 2007)

- Nearly 37 million Americans live in official poverty (i.e., annual income of approximately $9,000 for a single person, $13,000 for a two-person household, and $19,000 for a family of four). A more accurate indicator

124

(i.e., relative poverty) would count over 50 million Americans as poor. (DeNavas-Walt, et al., 2006)

- People of color, women, and children are disproportionately in poverty. Female-headed single-parent households represent 60% of the poor, and one-third of all female-headed households, one-fourth of racial/ethnic minorities, over 50% of children of color, and nearly 20% of all children in the U.S. live in official poverty. (DeNavas-Walt, et al., 2006)

- The U.S. has the highest rate of child poverty, and the greatest extremes of income/wealth inequality, of any First World country. (Shah 2007; United Nations Statistics Division, 2007)

- One to two million Americans are homeless at some point during the course of a year. Over 50% percent are families with children; 10 percent are over 65 years of age. (National Coalition for the Homeless, 2007)

- Over 50% of the U.S. poor are working. Federal minimum wage is $5.85 an hour, although most independent estimates suggest that a living wage is $13 per hour. (U.S. Department of Labor, 2006)

- Women still earn only 78 cents for every dollar men make. Women and people of color remain under represented in the professions and over represented in blue- and "pink-"collar occupations. (Goldberg Day and Hill, 2007)

- The typical woman with a Ph.D. degree earns less than the typical male with a B.A. degree. (Goldberg Day and Hill, 2007)

- There are no Federal Civil Rights protections in the U.S. for GLBT persons and only 15 states offer full protection against discrimination based on sexual orientation. American Civil Liberties Union [ACLU], 2007; Human Rights Campaign [HRC], 2007)

- The U.S. has more than 2 million persons in prison; this is the highest incarceration rate in the world. The majority of inmates are serving time for non-violent property and drug offenses. (Bureau of Justice Statistics, 2007)

- Corporate crime results in 5 times more deaths and at least 10 times more economic loss every year than "street crime". (Simon, 2006; Federal Bureau of Investigation [FBI], 2007)

- Although there are no racial differences in participation in crime, African Americans and Latinos are approximately 10 times more likely to be arrested and 7 times more likely to be incarcerated than whites. (Walker, et al., 2007)

- There are nearly 4,000 prisoners on death rows federally and in the 37 states that allow for capital punishment. African Americans and Latinos comprise 25% of the U.S. population, but account for nearly 70% of death row inmates. (Bureau of Justice Statistics, 2007; Walker, et al., 2007)

- Women do nearly 70% of the world's unpaid labor. (Mather, 2007)

- Nearly a billion people entered the 21st century unable to read a book or sign their names. Two of every three of these illiterate people are women. (United Nations Statistics Division, 2007)

- One half of the world's 6 billion people live on the equivalent of $2 per day. (United Nations Statistics Division, 2007)

- Every 3.6 seconds, someone dies of hunger. (United Nations Statistics Division, 2007)

- 80% of the grain produced in the U.S. each year is fed to livestock and 70% of all antibiotics produced annually are used for the production of meat. (Tansey and D'Silva, 2000; Humane Farming Association, 2007; Farm Sanctuary, 2007)

- Over 25 billion animals are killed in the U.S. each year for food, fur, laboratory research or in the course of providing entertainment. (Schlosser, 2001; Patterson, 2002; Newkirk, 2005; People for the Ethical Treatment of Animals, 2007)

- The U.S. represents 5% of the world's population and consumes over 25% of all fossil fuels, 20% of metals and 33% of paper. The U.S. is responsible for the creation of nearly 75% of the world's hazardous waste every year. (Shah 2007; World Resources Institute, 2006)

- Although scientists have identified only a fraction of the world's life forms, it is estimated that anywhere from 15 to 150 plant, animal, aquatic, or insect species become extinct every year. (Shah, 2007; World Wildlife Federation, 2006)

- Humans have destroyed more than 30 percent of the natural world since 1970. (Shah, 2006; World Wildlife Federation, 2006)

All of the preceding points are "facts"; they are empirically measurable by scientists and social scientists using multiple methods, both quantitative and qualitative. Many of these facts are also long-standing; for example, extremes of wealth and poverty in the U.S. and the world represent patterns that have remained relatively unchanged for hundreds of years. There are minor fluctuations, some small movement and minor change over time, but the general pattern remains. Consequently, these statistics are widely accepted as accurate, as factual, as "true."

Unlike the truths of the natural world, however, these truths are socially constructed, i.e., they are the result of human activity, of social interaction, of institutional and organizational arrangements, of social structures and status inequality, of public policy, political decisions and economic endeavors. These "truths" are created by social action and, as such, they can also be changed by social action. And unlike the truths of the natural and mathematical sciences, these social facts of poverty and racism and sexism and more evoke an evaluative response. It is unlikely that "e=mc²" or the Pythagorean Theorem calls us to an emotional response, or to a judgment. We do not assess them as morally "right" or "wrong," "fair" or "unfair"—they simply are. But the social truths cited above raise these very questions for us—we are left asking about fairness, about equity, about values. We are left asking about justice.

And are these justice issues? It is likely that most of us would answer yes. When pressed, however, to elaborate as to why, and how, and for what reasons, we may have more difficulty responding. Justice, it seems, is easy to acknowledge intuitively, but more difficult to articulate. Justice for whom? By what standards? According to which perspectives—social, economic, political, legal, theological, philosophical, ecological? To what end? What exactly do fairness, equality and freedom mean? What rights do we have? What rights should we have? And what are our obligations?

Fortunately we are not alone in our questioning or our search for answers. Debates over justice are timeless and as varied as historical experience. Questions of justice have been raised and disputed, asked, answered and re-asked by theologians, philosophers, political theorists, economists, sociologists, biologists and grassroots activists as well. All of the disciplines of the Liberal Arts and Sciences offer us either explicit or implicit perspectives on justice, and offer us some guidance in discussing justice and action. (See Appendix A.) Poets and artists, philosophers and theologians, social and natural scientists have all explored the truths of human society and the human experience in the socially constructed and perhaps, unjust, world.

Often these discussions are explicit, expressly directed towards defining justice. Such is the case with many religious tracts, political treatises, and philosophical essays. Similarly, analyses of justice are also found in the writings of sociologists, anthropologists, historians and political scientists, among others. Issues of justice also form the foundation for many areas of interdisciplinary studies, which emphasize the vantage point of disenfranchised groups. Women's Studies, GLBT Studies, Racial/Ethnic Studies and Post-Colonial Studies are all cases in point. In all of these areas, issues of justice are at the fore; indeed, a primary goal of the discipline is to advance discourse on issues of justice.

On other occasions, perspectives on justice are emergent, less overtly articulated, but present nonetheless. Some of these are implicit in the theoretical perspectives and applications of various disciplines of the humanities— literature, art, music, and theater, and in the social and natural sciences as well. Here, notions of equity, of balance, of resource allocation provide a seminal justice/action framework. Other emergent views of justice and action emanate from the grassroots, from everyday understandings of the world, from patterns of interaction with others, nature and the unseen. These are worldviews, ways of life which are based on a taken for granted notion of what constitutes justice and right action. Grassroots perspectives on justice and action also arise under duress, from sponta-neous collective responses (e.g., demonstrations, riots, and revolt) to per-ceived injustice. These latent definitions of justice may become manifest in the face of oppression, and what was unclear becomes certain as the people respond. In other words, notions of justice and also, of action, may be embedded in ways of thinking and being; these are implied rather than explicitly stated, but become apparent under closer examination.

Questions of truth, questions of justice are complex. Their exploration requires a critical examination of our values and those of the societies we live in. This exploration also requires critical analysis of evidence and argument and ultimately, it calls us to decide. What follows is an overview of general themes and considerations that can guide our analy-sis and our understanding.

Justice Frameworks

The arc of the moral universe is long, but it bends towards justice . . .

—Rev. Dr. Martin Luther King Jr., 1968[2]

While justice has been approached from many disciplinary perspectives, there are common themes. These themes serve as a framework for ana-lyzing issues of justice and comparing possible responses; they offer a way of organizing and evaluating the common threads that are woven through most considerations of justice.

First of all, justice is ultimately a collective, rather than individual concern. Justice issues are issues of community, accountability, and right relationship. Justice issues have a broad impact, and even seemingly isolated incidents often have global connections. Many grassroots actions for justice emerge at the local level only to uncover links with global goals. Consider Lois Gibbs and Love Canal. In 1978, Lois Gibbs was a lower-middle-class housewife in Niagara Falls, who, with other women in her neighborhood, "became politi-cized by the life and death issues directly affecting their children and their homes" (Merchant, 2005, pp. 192–3). Gibbs and other members of the Love Canal Homeowners Association conducted studies documenting the health problems associated with the Hooker Chemical and Plastic waste site and succeeded in obtaining redress from the state of New York. As the involvement of these women deepened, they came to realize that the haz-ardous waste was not an isolated local problem. Similar action by women globally linked them together as eco-feminists—i.e., women who connect the liberation of women with that of nature. As Carolyn Merchant (2005) writes, "From initial Not In My Back Yard (NIMBY) concerns, the movement has changed to Not In Anybody's Back Yard (NIABY) to Not On Planet Earth (NOPE)" (p. 193).

Secondly, justice issues are often systemic issues, i.e., they reflect larger structural patterns of inequality and disparity. All of the aforementioned statistics reveal structured inequality both globally and nationally. They all represent the consequences of systemic and institutionalized classism, racism, sexism, heterosexism, ageism, ableism, speciesism, and anthropocentrism. Consideration of justice issues as systemic requires distinguishing between what sociologist C. Wright Mills (1959) calls "personal troubles and social issues" (p. 45). If, for example, someone becomes poor due to laziness, bad habits, and inertia, that is a personal trouble. When, however, more than 36 million people (most of them women, children, persons of color, and senior citizens) live in absolute poverty in the richest nation in the world, this can no longer be attributed to personal failing. That is an issue of structured inequality, an issue of justice.

Thirdly, justice issues imply, indeed, impel action. Justice and action are inextricably linked. In fact some such as Gandhi (Murton, 1964) argue that questions of justice and action are inseparable; "I would say means are after all everything. As the means, so the end" (p. 28). While our primary concern here is the analysis of justice issues, justice claims are more often than not, accompanied by calls to action. Conversely, spontaneous action is often later linked to broader justice issues. The Stonewall riots provide an example. On the fringes of the emerging gay liberation movement, the gay men, lesbians and transgender patrons who frequented the Stonewall Inn (a Greenwich Village bar) wanted merely to dance and socialize. But a night in late June 1969 changed all that. Fed up with perpetual police harassment and arrests, the patrons fought back as yet another police raid unfolded. The officers were outnumbered, and three days of street fights and skirmishes ensued. The event, now referred to as the Stonewall Riots, is widely regarded as the symbolic beginning of the gay liberation movement. Action led to activism (out of the closets and into the streets . . .) and many disenfranchised Stonewall patrons became part of the general movement for GLBT rights (Duberman, 1993). What was initially a very specific response to perceived injustice became linked with general justice issues and broader goals, and in many respects, became a symbolic rallying point.

Finally, justice and action, despite their complexities and often, emotional overtones, can be critically analyzed. That is our primary objective here, to identify general themes and common threads that link the wide range of perspectives on justice and eventually lead us to imagine corresponding action. In general, discussions of justice share also these central features: all emerge from specific sources that frame the nature of the discussion and the criterion for evaluating justice; all identify standards by which justice/injustice is measured and meted out, and all, in varying degree, address the scope of justice—the range of beings to which the standards apply. And finally, all, directly or indirectly suggest actions appropriate for achieving justice. Each will be considered in turn.

Sources

> The white fathers told us: I think, therefore I am. The Black mother within each of us—the poet—whispers in our dreams: I feel therefore I can be free. . . . For there are no new ideas. There are only new ways of making them felt. . . .
>
> —Audre Lorde, 1977[3]

Justice frameworks may be most immediately analyzed with reference to their inspirational sources. Perspectives on justice or conversely, injustice began with a particular worldview, a vantage point from which to gauge and assess. One of the most important steps in searching for truths and justice involves the identification of the source of the claims. The source reveals the types of arguments and evidence offered as well as the methods for arriving at an understanding of justice.

Historically and currently, justice has been defined from several perspectives: religious/spiritual, philosophical, political, and scientific—both natural and social. These sources continue to frame most discussions of justice.

The world's religions provide some of the oldest and most diverse perspectives on justice. Here justice is divinely revealed as absolute. All of the major world religions as well as nature-based perspectives of indigenous peoples include notions of duties, rights, and standards of conduct. These outline just relationships between humans, the divine, and nature. Often, religious perspectives on justice have both sacred and secular implications. Divinely inspired justice should pervade this world as well as the next. Indeed, for much of human history, sacred justice was synonymous with secular justice; it was "on Earth as it is in Heaven." (Connors, 2000; Ishay, 1997, 2004; Klass, 1995)

Of course, philosophy is an equally significant source regarding justice. From the early Greeks to the present day, explicit discussions of justice remain a central topic of philosophical debate. Philosophical views of the common good, universal rights and ethics, just distribution, and retribution have shaped both political and scientific views of justice. (Ishay, 1997, 2000; Shute and Hurley, 1993)

Political theorists, governmental legal systems and international bodies offer secular views of justice in treaties, constitutions, documents, and

Justice Frameworks

Sources

- Theological/spiritual
  (e.g., Catholic, Protestant, Judaic, Islamic, Eastern, Native American spirituality, feminist theology, revitalization)

- Political
  (e.g., Nationalist, Democratic/Pluralist, Socialist/Communist, Anarchist, international accords)

- Philosophical/Cosmological
  (e.g., idealism, materialism, utilitarianism, libertarian, communitarian, existentialism, feminist philosophy, post-modernism, Eastern philosophies, indigenous worldviews)

- Natural/Social Scientific
  (e.g., ecological, biological, psychological, anthropological, sociological, economic, demographic)

Standards

- universalism/absolutism
- relativism/particularism

- distributive
- commutative
- retributive
- restorative

- merit or need
- liberty or equality

Scope

- human-centered
  (e.g., exclusion/inclusion based on class, race/ethnicity, gender, sexual orientation, age, ability, religion, and nationality)

- eco-centered
  (e.g., earth-based religious/political movements, animal rights and green movements, Gaia hypothesis)

Figure 1. Justice Frameworks

accords. The common sense understandings that many hold regarding justice and the relationship between citizens and the state, civil rights and liberties, access to resources, and just law and punishment derive from these legal/political documents. Originally, political notions of justice were most often discussed relative to the nation state. Many current political discussions of justice, however, are global; these emerge from international bodies such as the United Nations or transnational non-governmental organizations (NGO's) such as Amnesty International and Human Rights Watch.

The sciences, both natural and social, are less explicit sources on the topic of justice. Like political sources, earlier philosophical perspectives often inform these views. Although the term "justice" itself is rarely used, perspectives on justice are embedded in analyses of the social institutions and arrangements, the psyche and the natural world. The conflict paradigm in sociology for example, presents a clear commentary on structured inequality and its correlation with classism, racism, sexism, heterosexism, and ageism. (Collins, 1994) Similarly, ecology incorporates mechanistic models of science into a holistic view that emphasizes balance, biodiversity, and sustainability (Merchant, 2005). All the previous justice questions regarding distribution, rights, responsibilities, and equity are implicit in these approaches.

It is crucial to note that these sources do not provide unified perspectives on justice. These sources of justice, in fact, are neither internally consistent nor mutually exclusive. There are vast disagreements within categories as well as points of congruence between them. Philosophers, for example, have debated for centuries over the nature of justice—is it an absolute ideal or a construct relative to socio-cultural circumstances? Is justice best represented by "the greatest good for the greatest number" or "from each according to his/her ability to each according to his/her need"? Is liberty, equal treatment, or equal opportunity the standard? (Ishay, 1997, 2004; Lebacqz, 1986) Such is also the case with religious, political, and scientific sources; they share a certain starting point for framing justice, but diverge on its precise meaning.

There are, on the other hand, many similarities that exist between the different sources. Indeed some of the most compelling justice arguments are made by relying on multiple sources to make the same central case. Perhaps one of the most striking examples of this congruency can be found in the life and work of Dr. Martin Luther King, Jr. As a minister, president of the Southern Christian Leadership Conference, and a leader in the struggle for civil rights, he moved with ease from framing justice religiously to framing it politically. Full civil rights for African Americans, he argued, must be granted for moral and political reasons. Legal segregation on the basis of race was both a sin and an affront to the Constitution of the United States. The Bible and the Bill of Rights both spoke to the issue, and, for

King, were completely compatible sources on justice (Carson, et al. 1991; Washington, 1992).

Sister Helen Prejean, CSJ, provides another excellent example of drawing upon the congruencies among justice frameworks. The author of *Dead Man Walking* (1993), *The Death of Innocents* (2005), and presenter at a CSC Core convocation in the fall of 1999, Sister Helen opposes the death penalty on several grounds: moral/theological, philosophical, and political. As honorary chair of Moratorium 2000, a global grassroots campaign that aims towards the ultimate abolition of capital punishment, Sister Helen Prejean eloquently opposes the death penalty, first on the basis of Catholic social teaching on life. She also notes high financial and political costs, the issue of incompetent legal representation for poor defendants, the question of error and the execution of innocents, the question of cruelty in method of execution, and the race and class disparities in prosecution and conviction. All suggest U.S. constitutional violations of due process and equal protection as well as violations of standards set by the U.N. Commission on Human Rights.

These interconnections among seemingly disparate sources are closely related to questions of justice standards and scope. What constitutes justice? Who is justice for?

Standards

> What would the coal in the mines be worth if you did not work to take it out?? You create its wealth, so I say let the fight go on . . .
>
> —Mary Harris "Mother" Jones, 1914[4]

The sources for framing justice arguments are only a starting point. The issue of how justice might be measured—what are the standards for justice—is at the heart of all discussions. Again, there are many questions and no definitive answers.

Three general dimensions of justice standards will be considered here. First of all, justice standards may be construed as universal or relative. Are there universal standards of justice that apply to everyone at all times and places? As Ho (2004) notes, the relativists and subjectivists would say no. They argue that justice standards emanate from particular historical circumstances, perspectives, or cultures. We cannot judge what works for others in the context of their culture, their time, their experience. This perspective is often rooted in a critique of supposedly universal standards as non-inclusive, and proceeds from the perspective of excluded groups. Relativistic standards of justice are explicitly expressed in strands of existential and feminist philosophy, in some variations of identity politics of racial/ethnic minorities, women, GLBT persons, and Third World nationalists; in the standpoint critiques of theory in the social sciences, the interdisciplinary approaches of women's, multicultural, and GLBT studies and in the religious/political agendas of liberation movements (Ishay, 1997, 2004; Hill Collins, 1990; hooks 1984; Cruikshank, 1992). Perhaps the anthropological debate over "cultural relativism" represents one of the clearest discussions of relativistic views of justice in the social sciences. From this perspective, cultures can only be observed and described—they cannot be judged by any standards outside their own particular context (Ward, 1999; Walker, A., 1992).

Proponents of the universalist position argue that justice standards are universally applicable, transcending time, culture, and social context—and often absolute. Until recently, the universalist approach has characterized most theological, philosophical, political, and scientific views of justice. Discussions of divine and natural law, "the inalienable rights of citizens," and universal human rights as set forth by the United Nations all suggest universal standards (Declaration of Independence, 1995; United Nations, 1999). The majority of explicit theological, philosophical, and political justice tracts are grounded in universal standards. So, too, are many of the more implicit justice perspectives that emerge from the sciences and the humanities as well as indigenous religions and grassroots social movements.

One of the most heated debates over universal/relative justice standards is centered on the practice of female genital mutilation (FGM), which involves the removal of all or part of the external female genitalia without anesthetic. While FGM is practiced in other regions of the world, it is most widely practiced in Northern Africa, where over 100 million women have undergone the procedure. First brought to Western attention in the work of Alice Walker (i.e. *Possessing the Secret of Joy*, 1992 and *Warrior Marks*, 1999), FGM clearly illustrates the tension between universal and relative views of justice. Proponents contend that it is a cultural tradition that can only be understood and addressed from within (Cohn, 2007). Opponents cite a long list of physical complications (e.g., infection, pain-induced shock, urine and menstrual retention, damage to the urethra, painful intercourse, greater risk of STD infection, and obstructed labor) and maintain that FGM is a civil rights issue for women, human rights violation, and grounds for political asylum (Cohn, 2007; Seager, 1997, p. 52–53). As a result, the practice is increasingly banned in many regions of the world. The universal perspective on rights has largely prevailed here; Alice Walker (Walker and Parmar, 1999) so succinctly puts it, "Torture is not culture" (p. 95).

Secondly, discussions of the general or specific applicability of justice standards are closely intertwined with the universalism/relativism debate. Here, the debate centers on the extent to which justice standards apply to all areas of social life or are limited to certain select concerns. Philosophers and political theorists have provided most of the explicit discourse, here often dividing justice into four areas: distributive (i.e., distribution of rewards and resources), commutative (i.e., justice in exchange), retributive (i.e., justice in punishment), and restorative (i.e., justice in compensation) (LeBacqz, 1986). Perspectives on justice may encompass some or all of these. Many theological and political perspectives often encompass all four, as part of divinely sacred and secular justice (Ishay, 2004).

Certain political perspectives and grassroots movements, on the other hand, narrow the focus. Libertarians, for example, emphasize commutative justice in exchange, arguing that the only just government intervention involves minimal regulation of the economy to insure equitable exchange (Lebacqz, 1986; Ishay, 1997). In contrast, civil rights movements of disenfranchised groups often argue for distributive justice. Globally, for example, women perform over 65% of the world's unpaid labor, are more likely than men to live in poverty, and earn less than 80% of what men make for comparable work. Women are over-represented in the lower wage sectors of economies, and are disproportionately employed in the unprotected enterprise zones of the global economy. (Mather, 2007; Seager, 1997). These are clearly issues of distributive justice.

Retributive and restorative justice are concerns for groups who focus on issues related to the criminal, civil, and administrative law, such as racial profiling, incarceration, capital punishment, political prisoners, calls for compensation and reparations (Davis, 2003; Magnani and Wray, 2006; Walker, et al., 2007). Supporters of retribution make the claim that it is just to punish and often to punish harshly with long imprisonment or death. Others argue that justice requires a restored balance—the righting of a wrong—whether to a victim of crime or a group that has been harmed by practices of the past. Victim-offender mediation programs, restitution, and the call for reparations—to the descendants of slaves, the survivors of the Holocaust or Native Americans who have been robbed of lands— are all examples of restitutive or restorative justice (Winsbush, 2003; Robinson, 2000).

The final dimension relative to justice standards is the hallmark, the ultimate measure of justice. How should we measure justice? What is the central feature? This is the subject of much debate within and between all the perspectives on justice and is at the heart of much theological, philosophical, and political literature on justice. In general, discussions of justice often make reference to key concepts such as merit and/or need, liberty and/or equality. Again, these are elusive concepts, which are variously defined in religious documents, philosophical tracts, and the constitutions of nation states (Ishtay, 1997, 2004; Shute and Hurley, 1993).

Most national constitutions for example, enumerate the rights and free-doms available to all or particular groups of citizens. The United Nations Universal Declaration of Human Rights, however, lists rights that seem applicable to everyone regardless of nationality; ". . . recognition of the inherent dignity and of the equal and inalienable rights of all members of the human family is the foundation of freedom, justice, and peace in the world." (United Nations, 1999, p. 21) (See Appendix B).

More importantly, however, is the prioritizing of these standards. Liber-als, particularly in capitalist Western democracies, tend to hold freedom and liberty central to justice. This often refers to a "free-market" where there are limited governmental interventions in the economy. The rights of individuals, then, especially those safeguarding freedoms, take prece-dence over equality. The rights of free speech, to keep and bear arms, to own/accumulate private property, to pursue happiness, are supposedly universal standards of justice. In the U.S. however, the emphasis on lib-erty in law and public opinion, however, leads to a limited definition of equality. Equal access to all social resources, in most liberal analyses of justice, is a lesser hallmark of justice that is limited by individual merit, rights, and liberties (LeBacqz, 1986; Ishay, 2004). Equality, then, is fre-quently defined in the most minimal of terms, as equal protection under the law. It has, rarely meant equal access to rewards and resources, a point that is painfully clear to the poor, people of color, and women. This prioritizing of liberty over equality helps us understand the high rates of poverty and homelessness in the richest nation on earth.

Socialists and Marxists, on the other hand, regard economic equality and freedom from economic oppression as the precondition for justice. Need, not merit, is the measure; the famed Marxian dictum speaks directly to this point—"from each according to their ability to each according to their need" (Tucker, 1972. p. 383). Further, individual freedoms, especially those related to material accumulation, are defined as lesser considerations sub-ject to restraint in pursuit of the higher standard and the communal good (Marx and Engels, 1948; Tucker, 1972; Shiva, 1997, 2000). Consequently, the socialist democracies of Western Europe and elsewhere take for granted that citizens will have the right to free education, adequate housing, multi-ple employment benefits and universal health care—issues that are often highly contested in the U.S. Indeed, much historical conflict over the ide-ologies of capitalism and socialism/communism revolve around the stan-dards of justice and the value of freedom vs. equality, merit vs. need, the right to accumulate wealth vs. the right to basic necessities of survival.

Finally, the definitions of justice standards such as freedom, equality, and rights are shaped by considerations of the scope of justice, i.e., justice for whom and why? To whom do these standards apply? Who has standing to receive justice?

Scope

> I saw the whole globe symbolized at Auschwitz, and it was covered in blood: people being manipulated and used; animals tortured in useless experiments; men hunting helpless, vulnerable creatures for 'thrill'; human beings ground down by inadequate housing and medical care and by not having enough to eat; men abusing women and children; people polluting the earth, filling it with poisons that foul the air, the soil, and the water; the imprisonment of dissident voices; the elimination of people of opposing political views; the oppression of those who look, act or feel differently.
>
> —Judy Chicago, 1993[5]

The scope of justice is one of the most significant elements that shape justice perspectives. Scope, here, refers to the range of persons and/or beings to whom justice standards apply. It refers to considerations of inclusion and, conversely, discrimination, as well as human-centered and eco-centered claims.

Perspectives on justice—from all sources—have long held that justice was a concept applicable and available to humans. On closer examination, however, it is clear that historical and contemporary perspectives have frequently narrowed the concept of justice, which permits the exclusion of certain categories of persons.

Prior to the twentieth century, the classical philosophical, theological, and political perspectives of the West have limited justice to those who were deemed "deserving" by nature or "reason," or nationality or "morality." Almost invariably, this led to the dehumanization and subsequent oppression of persons who allegedly failed to meet these standards. As Richard Rorty (1993) notes, "For most white people, until very recently, black people did not so count. For most Christians, up until the seventeenth century or so, most heathens did not so count. For the Nazis, Jews did not so count. For most males, in countries where the average annual income is under $4000, most females still do not so count. Whenever tribal and national rivalries become important, members of rival tribes and nations will not so count" (p. 263).

Philosophically and theologically, such a narrow scope of justice allowed seemingly "righteous" and "reasonable" men to endorse slavery, conduct inquisitions, colonize and exterminate indigenous peoples globally, brutalize women and children in the name of discipline and property rights, and execute anyone who deviated from proscribed norms of sexual conduct (Golden, et al., 1991).

Politically, this constricted view of personhood allowed even the "enlightened" Western democracies to limit those so-called universal and "inalienable" rights to white men who owned property. At the time of its writing, the rights and freedoms enumerated in the U.S. Constitution were only available to white, adult, property owning males. Native Americans—the only indigenous Americans—are mentioned in the Declaration of Independence as the "merciless Indian savages, whose known rule of warfare, is an undistinguished destruction of all ages, sexes, and conditions" (Declaration of Independence, 1995, p. 7). African Americans, then enslaved, were counted as three-fifths of a person for purposes of determining state population size and subsequent representation. They remained property (a point reinforced by several Supreme Court decisions) until the ratification of the Thirteenth Amendment in 1865 (Constitution of the United States, 1995, p. 14, 42). Women, of course, were not citizens either and were, for all intents and purposes, the property of their parents or husbands. Full Constitutional rights were finally extended to women with the passage of the Nineteenth Amendment in 1920 (Ibid, p. 48).

Constricted views of personhood and consequently justice are not limited to the past. In the U.S., federal law did not prohibit discrimination against racial/ethnic minorities, women, the differently abled, and senior citizens until the mid-1960s. GLBT persons and those under eighteen still do not have the full rights of citizenship here, and GLBT persons, in particular, are denied federal civil rights protections against discrimination in several areas including employment, housing, family relationships, the military, security clearances, and matters of the criminal law (ALCU, 2007; HRC, 2007). In addition, many contend that the theoretical inclusion of formerly disenfranchised groups in constitutional claims of justice does not necessarily translate into justice in practice. As noted before, equal protection under the law does not translate into equal access to social resources. The persistence of institutionalized classism, racism, sexism, heterosexism, and ageism is well documented and continues to be regarded as just by certain groups of religious and political conservatives (Feagin, 2000; Bonilla-Silva, 2005).

Globally, the scope of justice also continues to be narrowly construed. Despite the broadly based universal human rights outlined in a series of international accords, a variety of explicit and implicit theological, philosophical, and socio-political perspectives exclude certain persons from the purview of justice. Race/ethnicity, gender, sexual orientation, age, and religion remain the source of devalued status in many regions of the world. For example, the system of apartheid in South Africa remained legal until 1992, and the ill effects are still felt by the black majority (Bratton, 1998). Similarly, post-colonial religious and ethnic conflict rages from Bosnia to Iraq, throughout the continent of Africa to Indonesia to beyond. Women are still denied social and legal rights in many areas of the world. They remain the property of men, are denied access to education, restricted in their movements, are bought, sold, beaten, mutilated, forced to labor, raped, and killed at will. In many of the Middle Eastern Islamic theocracies, the movement and dress of women is also restricted (Mather, 2007; Seager,

1997). Prior to its collapse in 2002, the Taliban in Afghanistan banned employment for women, halted formal female education pending the development of an 'appropriate' curriculum, imposed strict dress codes, and introduced strict controls on the movement of women outside the home (Rashid, 2000).

So, too, in most of the world, GLBT persons and children are often excluded from the scope of justice. Same-sex activity is still illegal in most nations of the world, and GLBT persons continue to be religiously and politically persecuted. Children are parental property and, in spite of international standards to the contrary, over 75 million children under fifteen labor, often in sweatshop conditions. Female children, particularly in areas of Central and East Asia, are viewed as economic and social liabilities and are disproportionately subject to abortion, infanticide, enslavement, and abandonment (Seager, 1997; Population Reference Bureau [PRB], 2006).

The scope of justice is not always so narrow. More inclusive perspectives flourish as well. Historically, these can be found in some strands of early Greek philosophy, and the nature-based religions of many indigenous peoples, the universal tenets of Buddhism, which extend to all sentient beings; and the informal, non-stratified political arrangements of foraging bands (Ishtay, 2004; LaDuke, 1999; Ward, 1999). Some of these perspectives are supported by extensive writings; others are reported in the anthropological and historical literature. All, however, limit social differentiation and inequality and extend the scope of justice at minimum, to all humans.

Several Western-based theological, philosophical, and political perspectives also broaden the scope. Progressive interpretations of Christianity include all people and often advocate for secular justice for all, as well. Many Catholic and Protestant theologians have been involved in the struggle for civil rights, economic justice, and women's rights on religious as well as political grounds. Catholic social teaching holds up the dignity of every person and the preference for the poor as key tenets (Connors, 2000; Hennelly, 1990). Feminist theology has also expanded traditional interpretations of Christianity to be more inclusive of the role(s) of women, both spiritually, and in institutional roles in the church (Johnson, 1993).

In the past 150 years, the identity politics of disenfranchised groups have staked both explicit and implicit claims for inclusion within justice frameworks. The poor, racial/ethnic minorities, women, religious sects, senior citizens, the differently abled, and GLBT persons through social action and interdisciplinary writings have continued to push the margins of justice debates. Much of this work is rooted in a critique of the narrow Eurocentric patriarchal view of justice held by many Western political and philosophical frameworks. A vast array of work is included here: socialist critique of capitalism ranging from Marx to the present; feminist and post-colonial philosophy; political theory; critical, conflict, and standpoint theory in sociology; multicultural and feminist perspectives in a variety of disciplines; and political demands for inclusion that range from abolition and Seneca Falls, to the Civil Rights era and beyond (Ishay, 1997; 2004; Tucker, 1972; Burns, 1990). The common feature of all is a broad-based scope of justice that seeks to include all persons within existing socio-political parameters of justice or abandon them in favor of non-discriminatory alternatives.

At the heart of all these claims are several key points. Oppressions intersect; class, race, gender, sexual orientation, and age are sources of inter-related disadvantages and subsequent injustice. Further, justice is not a commodity that can be parceled out to some and not all. It is an all or nothing proposition. As Martin Luther King, Jr. (Washington, 1992) so aptly noted in "Letter From a Birmingham Jail": "Injustice anywhere is a threat to justice everywhere. We are caught in an inescapable network of mutuality tied in a single garment of destiny" (p. 85). Whatever affects one directly affects all indirectly.

Finally, the scope of justice may be extended to non-human species and, in fact, the entire planet. Eco-centered perspectives on justice contend that the classical Western views of justice limit the scope to human centered concerns, thus overlooking a range of beings who may also be entitled to rights, freedoms, and equality. While some eco-centered justice arguments are centuries old, many have emerged in the late 20th century in conjunction with the ecology and animal rights movements (Merchant, 2005; Finsen and Finsen, 1994).

Historically, eco-centric views of justice are found in non-Western religions such as Buddhism, Hinduism, and Native American spirituality. In fact, according to anthropological evidence indigenous animistic religions are the oldest in the world. Many still persist and, in the U.S., Native American spirituality continues to inform both the religious and ecological positions of many Native Americans. In *All Our Relations*, Winona LaDuke (1999) makes this observation, "Native American teachings describe the relations all around—animals, fish, trees, and rocks—as our brothers, sisters, uncles, and grandpas . . . Our relations to each other, our prayers whispered across generations to our relatives, are what bind our cultures together. These relations are honored in ceremony, song, story, and life that keeps the relations close—to buffalo, sturgeon, salmon, turtles, bears, wolves, and panthers. These are our elder relations—the ones that came before and taught us how to live" (p. 2).

More recently, eco-centered conceptions of justice have begun to be included in Western theological thought. Feminist theology in particular, is a key contributor here. Elizabeth Johnson, CSJ, in *Women, Earth, and Creator Spirit* (1993), argues for an ecofeminist reconsideration of "hierarchical dualism" which has relationships between God/Man, Man/Woman, and Man/Nature. Johnson writes, "Hierarchical dualism . . . places the privileged, so-called rational man apart from and above other persons such as the poor and people of color . . . Feminist analysis insists that the devastating ecological consequences of this two-tiered vision cannot be fully addressed until we face it as a whole . . . We need to realize that the natural environment is oppressed, manipulated, and abused in ways analogous to the patriarchal use of women" (pp. 11–12).

Eco-inclusive perspectives on justice extend beyond theology. Philosophy has made significant contributions including further development of eco-feminist ideas. Perhaps, most importantly, philosophy paved the way for continued challenges to human-centered views of justice on several fronts. From the "land ethic" of Aldo Leopold (1966) to the "deep ecology" of Norwegian philosopher Arne Naess (1989), philosophers have extended claims of justice to the natural environment—"that land is a community is the basic concept of ecology, but that land is to be loved and respected is an extension of ethics" (Leopold, 1966, p. 239). The Philosophers were also among the first to critique speciesism and make the case for animal rights. In particular, Peter Singer (drawing on the classical writings of Jeremy Bentham) and Tom Regan inspired the contemporary animal rights movement with their respective works, *Animal Liberation* (1975), and *The Case for Animal Liberation* (1985).

Several perspectives found in the natural and social sciences comparably widen the scope of justice. Physicists, biologists, and chemists have begun to question the predominance of the Western mechanistic view of science (Merchant, 2005; Sheldrake, 1981; Sheldrake, et al., 1992; Shiva, 1997, 2000). Holistic approaches, which view the earth as an ecosystem or a complex organism, itself, imply that balance, equality, and in fact, justice, require a consideration of non-human nature. In fact, one scientific approach—the Gaia hypothesis—contends that the entire earth itself is a complex organism that should receive consideration as such (Lovelock, 1979).

The social sciences and interdisciplinary areas of study have also begun to expand their scope of inquiry to the environment and other species. Increasingly, sociology, psychology, women's studies, and racial/ethnic studies have considered the relationship between social and environmental inequality. The sociological interest in the green and animal rights movements, eco-psychology, and the study of environmental racism, sexism, and classism are all cases in point (Bullard, 1993, 2005; Roszak, 1992; Finsen and Finsen, 1994; Patterson, 2001).

Finally, more inclusive, eco-centered views of justice have emerged from political thought and practice. Rudimentary notions of eco-justice can be found in the socialist writings of Marx and Engels, as well as the early anarchists (Merchant, 2005). Both critique economic and political relations as oppressive and exploitative to humans as well as the environment. These perspectives have informed much of the green movement in the U.S. as well as indigenous efforts globally to maintain ecologically sound practices (LaDuke, 1999; Shiva, 2000).

National legislation and international treaties have also begun to reflect more expansive views of justice. Animals and the environment have limited legal protection here, and there is continued lobbying and political pressure to expand our legal notions of animal and environmental rights. Political proponents are for a variety of changes in our legal system including enhanced penalties for animal cruelty, the abolition of animal experimentation and factory farming, and moratoria on nuclear energy, urban sprawl, and the use of fossil fuels (Bullard, 1993, 2005; Merchant, 2005; Newkirk, 2005). In addition, international bodies and agencies are increasingly called upon to consider the environment and other species in political treaties and agreements. Pressures from indigenous peoples and environmental groups globally have led to agreements on sustainable development, pollution reduction, responses to the climate crisis, and endangered species protection. Examples include the inaugural Earth Summit held in Rio de Janeiro in 1992, the United Nations Declaration of Indigenous People's Rights, and the international climate meetings from Kyoto 1992 to Bali 2007 (Merchant, 2005). While many such documents are motivated by human-based concerns, they do nonetheless extend the concept of justice, rights, and protections to non-humans as well.

Truths, Justice, and Action

> The philosophers have only interpreted the world in various ways—the point, however, is to change it.
>
> —Karl Marx, 1845[6]

The truths created by the social world call out for evaluation, for critical analysis, for judgment. They call for the consideration of justice. Justice frameworks—those common threads among a multiplicity of experiences and perspectives—provide this analytical basis from which to identify and evaluate justice arguments. Justice frameworks may be characterized by their implicit or explicit definitions of justice—its source, standards, and scope. As the all of foregoing suggests, even this rudimentary classification scheme quickly becomes complicated with both comparisons and caveats, and, at best, serves as a rough guide to the intricacies of justice.

And yet, this is only half the story. The rest will be fully explored another day. For now, know that this is just the start of the journey—issues of justice are also calls to action. Once justice has been conceptualized, its realization inevitably comes into question. Justice without action is mere intellectual exercise; the circumstances of everyday, our inevitable connection to community, and our obligation as engaged citizens demand much more.

Epilogue/The Past Is Prologue

First they came for the Socialists, and I did not speak out—
because I was not a Socialist.
Then they came for the Trade Unionists, and I did not speak out—
because I was not a Trade Unionist.
Then they came for the Jews, and I did not speak out—
because I was not a Jew.
Then they came for me—and there was no one left to speak for me."

—Pastor Niemöller, 1955[7]

Notes

[1] Jimmy Lee Glass (1962–1987) quoted on the inscription page of Prejean, H. (2005). *The Death of Innocents: An Eyewitness Account of Wrongful Executions*. NY: Random House. Glass, along with co-defendant Jimmy Wingo, was executed in the Louisiana electric chair (aka "Gruesome Gertie") for two murders committed during a prison escape. Glass is best known for his writ of certiorari to the U.S. Supreme Court. In *Glass v. Louisiana*, 471 U.S. 1080 (1985), he argued that the use of the electric chair constituted "cruel and unusual" punishment in violation of the 8th Amendment. His petition was denied despite strong dissent from Justices Brennan and Marshall.—"For the reasons set forth above, there is an ever-more urgent question whether electrocution in fact is a 'humane' method for extinguishing human life or is, instead, nothing less than the contemporary technological equivalent of burning people at the stake." Louisiana —and most states that retain capital punishment—abandoned the use of the electric chair in 1993 in favor of lethal injection. Ironically, this method of execution is under similar 8th Amendment constitutional challenges at the time of this writing.

[2] Reverend Dr. Martin Luther King, Jr. (1929–1968) from the speech delivered at the National Cathedral, Washington, DC, on 31 March 1968—"Remaining Awake through a Great Revolution." Retrieved January 15, 2008 from http://www.africanamericans.com/MLKRemainingAwakeThroughGreatRevolution.htm. King is unarguably the most famous of a series of great 20th century Civil Rights leaders—Ella Baker, Fannie Lou Hamer, Malcolm X, Rev. Ralph Abernathy, Rosa Parks, Huey P. Newton, many more. King was the youngest recipient of the Nobel Peace Prize, and is the only U.S. citizen who was not a President to have a National Holiday declared in his honor. Following the passage of the Civil Rights Act of 1964 and the Voting Rights Act of 1965, Dr. King turned his attention to combating issues of poverty via The Poor People's Campaign, and questioning the U.S. role in Vietnam. He was assassinated in Memphis on April 4, 1968, while working to end a sanitation workers strike.

[3] Audre Lorde (1934–1992) quotation from "Poetry Is Not a Luxury" in Lorde, A. (1984) *Sister Outsider: Essays and Speeches*. Freedom, CA: Crossing Press. Black, woman, lesbian, immigrant, mother, survivor, warrior poet, Audre Lorde is widely credited with ushering in the Third Wave of feminism. Her attention to intersecting oppressions, the voices of marginalized women, and her call to speak out and to make our differences strengths were all ground-breaking contributions to both the women's movement and scholarly feminist analysis.

[4] Mary Harris "Mother" Jones (1837–1930) from a speech to striking coal miners following the Ludlow Massacre (Colorado) of 1914, quoted in Zinn, H. (2004). *Let the People Speak*. New York: Perennial. Jones was 82 at the time she was a prominent U.S. labor organizer, Socialist, and member of the United Mine Workers and I.W.W. The progressive magazine *Mother Jones* is named as a tribute to her tireless efforts for the workers. Her most famous quote is this: "Pray for the dead—but fight like hell for the living."

[5] Judy Chicago (1939—) quoted in commentary about the *Holocaust Project: From Darkness into Light*, http://www.throughtheflower.org/page.php?p=13&n=2. Judy Chicago is a feminist artist, educator, and author who is best known for her art installation projects including *The Dinner Party* (1974–79) (an homage via a place setting for 39 famous women of history), *The Birth Project* (1980–85), and the *Holocaust Project* (1993). In 1978, Chicago founded Through the Flower, a non-profit feminist art organization devoted to education, collaboration, and change.

[6] Karl Marx (1818–1883) the last line from the "Thesis on Feuerbach" quoted in Tucker, R., (1972). *The Marx–Engels Reader*. NY: W. W. Norton. These words are also inscribed on his tombstone at Highgate Cemetery in London. A philosopher, political theorist, economist, sociologist, founder of the Communist Party and revolutionary, Marx was one of the most influential thinkers of all time. The opening line of *The Communist Manifesto* (1948)—"The history of all hitherto existing society is the history of class struggle"—sums up the central theme of his voluminous body of work. His epitaph illustrates his life-long commitment to praxis—the union of theory and action—to seek justice in an unequal world.

[7] Pastor Martin Niemöller (1892–1984) credited to post-War writings and speeches. There are various versions of this poem—the version cited is inscribed at the U.S. Holocaust Museum in Washington, DC, http://www.ushmm.org/. Niemöller was a Lutheran Minster, and an early supporter of Hitler who became a vocal critic of the Nazi regime. He spent seven years in concentration camps, and survived to be a leader of reconciliation in post-war Germany. This quote is often cited as a reminder of the dangers of apathy as well as the deep connections between justice issues and situations of oppression.

Appendix A

Liberal Arts: Disciplines, Subject Matter, and Methods

Humanities	Social Sciences	Natural Sciences
• The Fine Arts, Foreign Languages, History, Literature in English, Philosophy, Theology	• Anthropology, Economics, Geography, Political Science, Psychology, Sociology	• Biology, Chemistry, Physics, Mathematics and all related sub-fields of study
• Emphasis on symbolic communication and expression, interpretation, and questions of meaning, experience, existence, metaphysics, and cosmology	• Emphasis on empirical examination of human interaction with the environment, culture, economic and political arrangements and activity, the self and society	• Emphasis on the observable, empirical underpinnings, and unchanging principles of the physical world, including human existence
• Rules and norms of grammar, logic and composition/Multiple paradigms, and schools of theory and practice/Qualitative methods—reliance on critical thinking and a degree of methodological "subjectivity" in interpretation of historical, philosophical and religious texts, works of art, literature, and music	• Standard methodologies that span disciplines/Multiple paradigms within disciplines with common historical and theoretical roots/Use of both qualitative and quantitative methods—emphasis on empirically measurable variables, correlation, and a degree of "objectivity" in examining human activity	• Standard methodologies that span disciplines/Tendencies towards single paradigms that stand until "disproved"/Use of quantitative methods—emphasis on mathematical formulas, theorems, the experiment, causation, "proof," and "objectivity" in the examination of empirical data

Appendix B

Universal Declaration of Human Rights

Adopted and proclaimed by General Assembly
Resolution 217 A (III) of 10 December 1948

On December 10, 1948, the General Assembly of the United Nations adopted and proclaimed the Universal Declaration of Human Rights the full text of which appears in the following pages. Following this historic act the Assembly called upon all Member countries to publicize the text of the Declaration and "to cause it to be disseminated, displayed, read, and expounded principally in schools and other educational institutions, without distinction based on the political status of countries or territories."

Article 1.

All human beings are born free and equal in dignity and rights. They are endowed with reason and conscience and should act towards one another in a spirit of brotherhood.

Article 2.

Everyone is entitled to all the rights and freedoms set forth in this Declaration, without distinction of any kind, such as race, colour, sex, language, religion, political or other opinion, national or social origin, property, birth, or other status. Furthermore, no distinction shall be made on the basis of the political, jurisdictional or international status of the country or territory to which a person belongs, whether it be independent, trust, non-self-governing or under any other limitation of sovereignty.

Article 3.

Everyone has the right to life, liberty and security of person.

Article 4.

No one shall be held in slavery or servitude; slavery and the slave trade shall be prohibited in all their forms.

Article 5.

No one shall be subjected to torture or to cruel, inhuman or degrading treatment or punishment.

Article 6.

Everyone has the right to recognition everywhere as a person before the law.

Article 7.

All are equal before the law and are entitled without any discrimination to equal protection of the law. All are entitled to equal protection against any discrimination in violation of this Declaration and against any incitement to such discrimination.

Article 8.

Everyone has the right to an effective remedy by the competent national tribunals for acts violating the fundamental rights granted him by the constitution or by law.

Article 9.

No one shall be subjected to arbitrary arrest, detention or exile.

Article 10.

Everyone is entitled in full equality to a fair and public hearing by an independent and impartial tribunal, in the determination of his rights and obligations and of any criminal charge against him.

Article 11.

(1) Everyone charged with a penal offence has the right to be presumed innocent until proved guilty according to law in a public trial at which he has had all the guarantees necessary for his defence.

(2) No one shall be held guilty of any penal offence on account of any act or omission which did not constitute a penal offence, under national or international law, at the time when it was committed. Nor shall a heavier penalty be imposed than the one that was applicable at the time the penal offence was committed.

Article 12.

No one shall be subjected to arbitrary interference with his privacy, family, home or correspondence, nor to attacks upon his honour and reputation. Everyone has the right to the protection of the law against such interference or attacks.

Article 13.

(1) Everyone has the right to freedom of movement and residence within the borders of each state.

(2) Everyone has the right to leave any country, including his own, and to return to his country.

Article 14.

(1) Everyone has the right to seek and to enjoy in other countries asylum from persecution.

(2) This right may not be invoked in the case of prosecutions genuinely arising from non-political crimes or from acts contrary to the purposes and principles of the United Nations.

Article 15.

(1) Everyone has the right to a nationality.

(2) No one shall be arbitrarily deprived of his nationality nor denied the right to change his nationality.

Article 16.

(1) Men and women of full age, without any limitation due to race, nationality or religion, have the right to marry and to found a family. They are entitled to equal rights as to marriage, during marriage and at its dissolution.

(2) Marriage shall be entered into only with the free and full consent of the intending spouses.

(3) The family is the natural and fundamental group unit of society and is entitled to protection by society and the State.

Article 17.

(1) Everyone has the right to own property alone as well as in association with others.

(2) No one shall be arbitrarily deprived of his property.

Article 18.

Everyone has the right to freedom of thought, conscience and religion; this right includes freedom to change his religion or belief, and freedom, either alone or in community with others and in public or private, to manifest his religion or belief in teaching, practice, worship and observance.

Article 19.

Everyone has the right to freedom of opinion and expression; this right includes freedom to hold opinions without interference and to seek, receive and impart information and ideas through any media and regard-less of frontiers.

Article 20.

(1) Everyone has the right to freedom of peaceful assembly and association.

(2) No one may be compelled to belong to an association.

Article 21.

(1) Everyone has the right to take part in the government of his country, directly or through freely chosen representatives.

(2) Everyone has the right of equal access to public service in his country.

(3) The will of the people shall be the basis of the authority of government; this will shall be expressed in periodic and genuine elections which shall be by universal and equal suffrage and shall be held by secret vote or by equivalent free voting procedures.

Article 22.

Everyone, as a member of society, has the right to social security and is entitled to realization, through national effort and international co-operation and in accordance with the organization and resources of each State, of the economic, social and cultural rights indispensable for his dignity and the free development of his personality.

Article 23.

(1) Everyone has the right to work, to free choice of employment, to just and favourable conditions of work and to protection against unemployment.

(2) Everyone, without any discrimination, has the right to equal pay for equal work.

(3) Everyone who works has the right to just and favourable remuneration ensuring for himself and his family an existence worthy of human dignity, and supplemented, if necessary, by other means of social protection.

(4) Everyone has the right to form and to join trade unions for the protection of his interests.

Article 24.

Everyone has the right to rest and leisure, including reasonable limitation of working hours and periodic holidays with pay.

Article 25.

(1) Everyone has the right to a standard of living adequate for the health and well-being of himself and of his family, including food, clothing, housing and medical care and necessary social services, and the right to security in the event of unemployment, sickness, disability, widowhood, old age or other lack of livelihood in circumstances beyond his control.

(2) Motherhood and childhood are entitled to special care and assistance. All children, whether born in or out of wedlock, shall enjoy the same social protection.

Article 26.

(1) Everyone has the right to education. Education shall be free, at least in the elementary and fundamental stages. Elementary education shall be compulsory. Technical and professional education shall be made generally available and higher education shall be equally accessible to all on the basis of merit.

(2) Education shall be directed to the full development of the human personality and to the strengthening of respect for human rights and fundamental freedoms. It shall promote understanding, tolerance and friendship among all nations, racial or religious groups, and shall further the activities of the United Nations for the maintenance of peace.

(3) Parents have a prior right to choose the kind of education that shall be given to their children.

Article 27.

(1) Everyone has the right freely to participate in the cultural life of the community, to enjoy the arts and to share in scientific advancement and its benefits.

(2) Everyone has the right to the protection of the moral and material interests resulting from any scientific, literary or artistic production of which he is the author.

Article 28.

Everyone is entitled to a social and international order in which the rights and freedoms set forth in this Declaration can be fully realized.

Article 29.

(1) Everyone has duties to the community in which alone the free and full development of his personality is possible.

(2) In the exercise of his rights and freedoms, everyone shall be subject only to such limitations as are determined by law solely for the purpose of securing due recognition and respect for the rights and freedoms of others and of meeting the just requirements of morality, public order and the general welfare in a democratic society.

(3) These rights and freedoms may in no case be exercised contrary to the purposes and principles of the United Nations.

Article 30.

Nothing in this Declaration may be interpreted as implying for any State, group or person any right to engage in any activity or to perform any act aimed at the destruction of any of the rights and freedoms set forth herein.

References

American Civil Liberties Union [ACLU] (2007). Lesbian-Gay Rights. Retreived January 14, 2008 from http://www.aclu.org/lgbt/relatedinformation_fact_sheets.html.

Amnesty International. (1998). *United States of America: Rights For All.* NY: Amnesty International.

Amnesty International. (2006). *Amnesty Report 2006.* NY: Amnesty International.

Bonilla-Silva, E. (2006). *Racism without racist: Color-blind racism and the persistence of racial inequality in the United States.* New York: Rowman and Littlefield.

Bratton, M. (1998). After Mandela's Miracle in South Africa. *Current History* 97: 214–219.

Bullard, R. (2005). Environmental Justice in the 21st Century. Retrieved December 15, 2007 from http://www.ejrc.cau.edu/ejinthe21century.htm at The Environmental Justice Resource Center.

Bullard, R. (1993). *Confronting Environmental Racism: Voices from the Grass-roots.* Boston, MA: South End Press.

Bureau of Justice Statistics. (2007). Prison Statistics. Retreived January 8, 2008 from http://www.ojp.usdoj.gov/bjs/prisons.htm.

Burns, S. (1990). *Social Movements of the 1960s: Searching for Democracy.* New York, NY: Twayne.

Carson, C; Jarnow, D. J.; Gill, G.; Hardy, V., & Hine, D. C. (Eds.) (1991). *The Eyes on the Prize Civil Rights Reader: Documents, Speeches and Firsthand Accounts from the Black Freedom Struggle.* New York, NY: Penguin Books.

Collins, R. (1994). *Four Sociological Traditions*. New York, NY: Oxford University Press.

Connors, R. (2000). Catholic Social Teaching—Convictions and Connections. In College of St Catherine (2004). *Global Search for Justice Reader* 2E. Acton, MA: Copley Custom Textbooks: 58–88.

Cohn, D. (2007) The Campaign Against Female Genital Cutting: New Hope, New Challenges. *Population Reference Bureau*. Retrieved January 5, 2008 from http://www.prb.org/Articles/2007/CampaignAgainstFemaleGenitalCutting.aspx.

Cruikshank, M. (1992). *The Gay and Lesbian Liberation Movement*. New York, NY: Routledge, Chapman and Hall.

Declaration of Independence and the Constitution of the United States, The. (1995). New York, NY: Penguin.

Davis, A. (2003). *Are prisons obsolete?* New York, NY: Seven Stories Press.

DeNavas-Walt, C., Proctor, B. D., and Smith, J. (2007). Income, Poverty, and Health Insurance Coverage in the United States: (2006), *U.S. Census Bureau. Current Population Reports, P60–233*. Washington, DC.: U.S. Government Printing Office.

Duberman, M. (1993). *Stonewall*. New York, NY: Plume.

Feagin, J. R. (2000). *Racist America: Roots, realities, and future reparations*. New York: Routledge.

Farm Sanctuary. (2007). Factory Farming:The Issues. Retrieved December 17, 2007 from http://www.farmsanctuary.org/issues/factoryfarming/.

Federal Bureau of Investigation [FBI] and U.S. Department of Justice (2006). *Crime in the United States 2006*. Retrieved December 20, 2007 from http://www.fbi.gov/ucr/cius2006/index.html.

Finsen, L. and Finsen, S. (1994). *The Animal Rights Movement in the United States*. New York, NY: Twayne.

Forbes. (2007). The Forbes 400: Rich Lists. Retrieved January 12, 2008 from http://www.forbes.com/lists/2007/09/19/richest-americans-forbes-lists-richlist07-cx_mm_0920rich_land.html.

Glass v. Louisiana, 471 U.S. 1080 (1985).

Golden, R.; McConnell, M.; Mueller, P.; Popper, C.; and Turkovic, M. (1991). *Dangerous Memories: Invasion and Resistance Since 1492*. Chicago, IL: Chicago Religions Task Force on Central America.

Goldberg Day, J. and Hill, C. (2007). *Behind the Wage Gap*. Washington DC: AAUW.

Hennelly, A., (Ed.) (1990). *Liberation Theology: A Documentary History.* Maryknoll, NY: Orbis.

Hill Collins, P. (1990). *Black Feminist Thought: Knowledge, Consciousness and the Politics of Empowerment.* Boston, MA: Unwin Hyman.

Ho, A. (2000). "It's So Judgmental!" in College of St. Catherine (2004). *The Reflective Woman Reader.* 6e. Acton MA: Copley Custom Textbooks: 222–234.

hooks, b. (1984). *Feminist Theory from Margin to Center.* Boston, MA: South End Press.

Human Rights Campaign [HRC] (2007). GLBT Issues. Retrieved January 5, 2008 from http://www.hrc.org/issues/index.htm.

Human Rights Watch [HRW] (2007) Defending Human Rights Worldwide. Retreived January 12, 2008 from http://www.hrw.org/.

Ishay, M., (Ed.) (1997). *The Human Rights Reader: Major Political Essays, Speeches and Documents from the Bible to the Present.* New York, NY: Routledge.

Ishay, M. (2004). *The History of Human Rights.* Berkeley: University of California Press.

Johnson, Elizabeth A., CSJ. (1993). *Women, Earth, and Creator Spirit.* Mahwah, NJ: Paulist Press.

Klass, M. (1995). *Ordered Universes: Approaches to the Anthropology of Religion.* Boulder, CO: Westview.

King, M. L., Jr. (1968, March 31). Remaining Awake through a Great Revolution. Retrieved January 15, 2008 from http://www.africanamericans.com/MLKRemainingAwakeThrough GreatRevolution.htm.

King, M. L., Jr. (1963). Letter from a Birmingham Jail. In J. Washington (Ed.) (1992). *I Have a Dream: Writing and Speeches That Changed the World/Martin Luther King Jr.* New York, NY: Harper Collins.

LaDuke, W. (1999). *All Our Relations: Native Struggles for Land and Life.* Cambridge, MA: South End Press.

Lebacqz, K. (1986). *Six Theories of Justice.* Minneapolis, MN: Augsburg Publishing House.

Leopold, A. (1966). *A Sand County Almanac.* New York, NY: Ballantine.

Lorde, Audre. (1984). *Sister Outsider: Essays and Speeches.* Freedom, CA: Crossing Press.

Lovelock, J. (1979). *Gaia: A New Look at Life on Earth.* New York, NY: Oxford University Press.

Magnani, L.and Wray, H. (2006). *Beyond Prisons*. Minneapolis, MN: Fortress Press.

Marx, K. and Engels, F. (1948). *The Communist Manifesto*. London: International Publishers.

Mather, M. (March 2007). Closing the Male-Female Labor Force *Gap Population Reference Bureau*. Retrieved January 5, 2008 from http://www.prb.org/Articles/2007/ClosingtheMaleFemaleLaborForce Gap.aspx.

Merchant, C. (2005). *Radical Ecology*. 2e. New York, NY: Routledge.

Mills, C. W. (1959). *The Sociological Imagination*. New York, NY: Oxford University Press.

Murton, T. (1965). *Gandhi on Non-Violence*. New York, NY: New Directions.

Naess, A. (1989). *Ecology, Community, and Lifestyle*. Cambridge: Cambridge University Press.

National Coalition for Homeless.(August 2007). Factsheets on the Homeless. Retrieved January 15, 2009 from http://www.nationalhomeless.org/publications/facts.html.

Newkirk, I. (2005). Making Kind Choices. New York, NY: St. Martins Griffin.

Patterson, C. (2001). *Eternal Treblinka: The Holocaust and Our Treatment of Animals*. New York, NY: Lantern.

People for the Ethical Treatment of Animals. [PeTA] (2007). Why Animal Rights? Retrieved January 10, 2008 from http://www.peta.org/about/WhyAnimalRights.asp.

Population Reference Bureau [PRB] (February 2007) Worlds' Youth Data Sheet. Retrieved January 10, 2007 from http://www.prb.org/pdf06/WorldsYouth2006DataSheet.pdf.

Prejean, H. (1999). *Dead Man Walking*. New York, NY: Vintage.

Prejean, H. (2005). *The Death of Innocents: An Eyewitness Account of Wrongful Executions*. New York, NY: Random House.

Rashid, A. (2000). *Taliban: Militant Islam, Oil, and Fundamentalism in Central Asia*. New Haven, CT: Yale University Press.

Regan, T. (1985). *The Case for Animal Rights*. Berkeley, CA: University of California Press.

Robinson, R. (2000). *The Debt*. New York, NY: Plume.

Rorty, R. (1993). Human rights, rationality, and sentimentality. In M. Ishay (ed.) (1997). *The Human Rights Reader: Major Political Essays, Speeches and Documents from the Bible to the Present*. New York, NY: Routledge: 253–265.

Roszak, T. (Ed.) (1992). *The Voice of the Earth*. New York, NY: Touchstone.

Schlosser, E. (2001). *Fast Food Nation*. Boston, MA: Houghton Mifflin.

Seager, J. (1997). *The State of Women in the World Atlas*. New York, NY: Penguin.

Shah, A. (2007). Global Issues. Social, Political, Economic and Environmental Issues That Affect Us All. Retrieved January 12, 2008 from http://www.globalissues.org/.

Sheldrake, R., (1981). *A New Science of Life*. Los Angeles, CA: Jeremy P. Tarcher.

Sheldrake, R., McKenna, T. and Abraham, R. (1992). *Chaos, Creativity and Consciousness*. Rochester, VT: Park Street Press.

Shiva, V. (1997). Staying Alive: Development, Ecology and Women. In *The Human Rights Reader: Major Political Essays, Speeches and Documents from the Bible to the Present*. In M. Ishay. (Ed.) New York, NY: Routledge. 253–263.

Shiva, V. (2000). *Stolen Harvest*. Boston, MA: South End Press.

Shute, S. and Hurley, S. (Eds.) (1993). *On Human Rights: Oxford Amnesty Lectures*. New York, NY: Basic Books

Simon, D. (2006). *Elite Deviance*. 7e. Boston MA: Allyn and Bacon.

Singer, P. (1975). *Animal Liberation*. Berkeley, CA: University of California Press.

Tucker, R, (1972). *The Marx–Engels Reader*. New York, NY: W. W. Norton.

United Nations. (1999). *Human Rights: A Compilation of International Instruments*. Vol. 1. New York, NY: United Nations Publications.

United Nations Statistical Division (2007). *Statistical Annex: Millennium Development Goals, Targets and Indicators*. Retrieved December 20, 2007 from http://unstats.un.org/unsd/mdg/Host.aspx?Content=Data/Trends.htm.

U.S. Census Bureau. Current Population Survey (2007). *2007 Annual Social and Economic Supplement* (POV 10). Washington DC: U.S. Government Printing Office.

U.S. Department of Labor, (May 2006).U.S. Bureau of Labor Statistics. *A Profile of the Working Poor, 2004*. Washington, DC: U.S. Government Printing Office.

Walker, A. (1992). *Possessing the Secret of Joy.* New York, NY: Harcourt Brace Jovanovich.

Walker, A. and Parmar, A. (1993). *Warrior Marks: Female Genital Mutilation and the Sexual Blinding of Women.* New York, NY: Harcourt Brace Jovanovich.

Walker, S., Spohn, C., & DeLone, M. (2007). *The color of justice: Race, ethnicity and crime in America.* 4th ed. Belmont, CA: Wadsworth.

Ward, M.C. (1999). *A World Full of Women.* 2nd ed. Boston, MA: Allyn and Bacon.

Washington, J., (Ed.) (1992). *I Have a Dream: Writing and Speeches That Changed the World/Martin Luther King Jr.* New York, NY: Harper Collins.

Winbush, R. (2003). *Should America Pay? Slavery and the Raging Debate on Reparations.* New York, NY: Amistad.

World Resources Institute (2007) *Climate Change and Developing Countries.* Retrieved January 11, 2008 from http://archive.wri.org/item_detail.cfm?id=1284&section=climate&page=project_content_text&z=?.

World Wildlife Federation (2006) *The Living Planet Report 2006.* Retrieved January 2, 2008 from http://assets.panda.org/downloads/living_planet_report.pdf.

Zinn, H. (2004). *Let the people speak.* New York, NY: Perennial.

William Andrew Myers (b. 1944) is a philosopher who has taught at CSC since 1980. Most of his courses have been in ethics, political philosophy, history of philosophy, philosophy of science, and philosophy of the arts. He also is a printmaker and book artist on the faculties of Minnesota Center for Book Arts and the Grand Marais Art Colony. In this essay Myers describes the standards that govern modern scientific practices and shows why examples of three other belief systems are not scientific. What reasons can you give for accepting the results of a scientific research project? Does the fact that a belief is not supportable scientifically make it false? What position is he taking when Myers says that he does not know if the claims of astrology are true or false?

Evidence and the Projects of Rationality

William Andrew Myers

The ideal of rational objectivity used as a standard to guide inquiries into truth is one of the hallmarks of Western Civilization. Our sciences, medical practices, legal processes, and many academic fields of study depend for their credibility and practical success on some version of this standard. Critics of the concepts of rationality and of objectivity have in general complained that these are fictional standpoints, culturally relative and no different in principle from other perspectives on truth. But to understand such criticisms we have to know something of the history and practice of rational objectivity. This essay will provide a sketch of the standpoint as it is expressed in the sciences and show its applications in a few selected areas.

I. The Fixation of Belief

The American philosopher Charles Sanders Peirce (1839–1914) wrote an important essay called "The Fixation of Belief" (1887) in which he discusses the ways in which people typically form their own beliefs. "Fixation" here means taking an idea to be settled and adopting it as your own. Peirce (note the spelling—it is pronounced "purse") observes that people tend to engage in thinking when they are prodded by doubt or uncertainty about some issue. Doubt is uncomfortable, and when we encounter it we "struggle to free ourselves and pass into the state of belief."[1] He then describes four ways in which people typically settle on their beliefs.

First, some people deal with the discomfort of uncertainty by walling it off from their sight. They concentrate on all the ideas that seem to support their view, and they treat with contempt or just ignore anything that might look like a contrary idea. Their minds are made up, and their minds are closed. Peirce calls this the *method of tenacity*.[2] It has the advantage that employing this method will insulate you from the discomfort of uncertainly and enable you to avoid the hard work of research, actual thinking. But, he says, it has the disadvantages that unless you are a hermit you will encounter alternative beliefs which can be just as well supported as your own, and unless you simply refuse to discuss anything or read or listen to anything that might challenge your belief, doubt is going to creep in at some point.

Second, opinions might be established for the community as a whole by government, religious authority, or a political party. For some people it is very comforting to accept what others have established as the true belief. Peirce calls this the *method of authority*.[3] Once again it has the advantage that it helps avoid the discomfort of uncertainty and the labor of investigation. But it has the disadvantage that if you look at others' beliefs, for example those of citizens of other countries, you might conclude that your beliefs established by authority are rather arbitrary, an accident of where you grew up. And if you dwell on that fact, doubt can slip in and you can lose the comfort of established opinions.

Third, we might accept only beliefs that fit in with what we already do believe. He calls this the *a priori method*[4] of establishing belief. This is a way of avoiding the arbitrariness of the first two methods and it has the advantage that, if we think logically, we will avoid any contradictions in our thought, and we will have a coherent system of beliefs. But in fact, Peirce says, this method does not differ much from the method of authority; it simply trades the authority of the government or the church for the authority of whatever happens to be in our minds that new knowledge must conform to. It makes the establishment of belief rather like the establishment of taste in fashions or the like.

Notice that for all three of the methods Peirce has described so far one's beliefs may be true, or they may be false. The problem with them is not just the psychological one that they ultimately fail to make your beliefs stand still, but that as methods they have nothing to do with establishing the actual truth of an idea. That, he thinks, comes with the fourth method, which he calls the *method of science*.[5]

Now Peirce regards scientific method not merely as a set of formal procedures used in a laboratory or observatory, but as what we all do when we pay proper attention to reality and investigate it. Starting from what we know to be true we can investigate and reason to new knowledge that is grounded in evidence. Peirce, as a philosopher of science, knew that scientific investigation was always fallible—further investigation might overturn the settled beliefs of today. But he says that, of the four methods he describes, this is the only one that pays proper attention to whether a belief conforms to observations repeatable by members of a community investigating the same questions.

I take the importance of Peirce's article to be the propositions that, (1) though there are a number of ways of creating opinions, most of them boil down to arbitrary or ideological ways to block inquiry. This is the closed mind, and on a larger scale the closed society. And (2) an openness to new evidence and new thinking, the willingness to rethink our opinions while looking for better ways to support them, is the practice of the reasonable person who cares more about finding out what is true than about being comfortable.

II. The Methods of Science

Ancient Greek thinkers had considerable success understanding and manipulating the physical world. Thales, credited with being the first philosopher, accurately predicted the year (585 B.C.E.) of a solar eclipse and engineered a way to split the course of a large river so that an army could cross the resulting shallower streams. Aristarchus of Samos taught that the sun was the center of the universe with the earth orbiting it, and he and other natural philosophers made reasonable estimates of the size (and shape) of the earth and the distance to the moon. The Hippocratean school of medicine developed the first systematic observations of diseases in the West. The Greek physician, or *iatros*, used most of his senses in examining a patient, and most important for developing medicine as a science in our modern sense, he kept careful records of those observations. These records formed a body of case studies that showed that symptoms and diseases followed regular patterns. Getting sick wasn't just a visitation of some angry god, but a rationally understandable process. Through the concepts of *diagnosis* (literally, "knowing-through") and *prognosis* ("knowing ahead") the Greek physician could identify what was wrong with a patient and predict what was likely to happen.

Greek science was certainly limited. It never developed an idea of systematic experiment to go along with observations, and medicine was shackled to an unfortunate belief system about the human body—the doctrine of the four humors—that still held sway as late as the nineteenth century. And there wasn't much the *iatros* could do by way of intervention; diseases like tetanus and diabetes, for instance, were common and invariably fatal. Yet the recognition of common patterns to disease that could be understood rationally is one of the foundations of a more general Western approach to nature that we today have inherited. That approach holds as its basic tenet the belief that the universe is rational, and that since human beings are rational, we can understand it. Close observation of physical evidence is the basic practice that gives life to this belief.

III. The Beginnings of Modern Scientific Practice

Science as we know it is a product of European philosophers and scientists who worked to build a system for investigating nature that would be rational, independent of dogma, especially religious dogma, and reliable—they wanted it to work. In the landmark year 1543 Nicolaus Copernicus, a Polish mathematician and monk, published a book hypothesizing that the planets orbited the sun, not the earth, thus threatening the entrenched Medieval belief in the cosmology of Aristotle, which located earth at the center. And in the same year Andreas Vesalius published an anatomy textbook with woodcuts showing with unprecedented detail and accuracy the workings of the human body. Both works inspired a tremendous amount of scientific observation and experiment. In the following century, Galileo's use of the newly invented telescope to support the Copernican world view and Van Leuwenhoek's use of his invention, the microscope, to discover a previously unsuspected world of microbes, continued what the works of Copernicus and Vesalius started: what we now call the Scientific Revolution.

As is well known, Galileo also discovered the principle of the pendulum and rolled balls down ramps to measure the force of gravity. (It is not actually certain that he ever dropped balls off the Leaning Tower in Pisa.) Although his publications led to his trial for heresy and a sentence of perpetual house arrest, he probably did more than any single person to create the standards of the new science. Three major principles have animated the physical sciences from Galileo's time until ours.

First, hypotheses—those initial guesses we make about how to explain something—must be *testable*. Sir Karl Popper, a major Twentieth Century philosopher of science, says that "the criterion of the scientific status of a theory is its falsifiability, or refutability, or testability."[6] If no evidence in principle will count against a theory, then the theory is not scientific. The search for life on Mars can be a scientific quest because the hypothesis that life once existed there is testable (though with difficulty and at great expense). Given certain definitions of what counts as a living organism and theories about how such organisms might show up even if long dead, we can send space craft equipped to look for evidence of life. However, to revive an old cliché about arguments in Medieval philosophy, a hypothesis about the number of angels that will fit on the head of a pin is untestable because current methods of investigation give us no way to observe and count angels. Ideological commitments and religious beliefs tend to be untestable by observation or experiment. If evidence or observation would count as a disproof of a hypothesis, then the hypothesis is outside the range of application of scientific method. That does not in itself mean the hypothesis is false. It simply means that if it is worth believing, the grounds for that belief will not be scientific.

Second, the phenomena under study must be *measurable*. Galileo once wrote, "The Book of Nature is written in the language of mathematics." The lack of accurate clocks (let alone stopwatches!) in his time hampered Galileo's own measurements, but he used ingenious methods to get around this barrier. The ramps he rolled balls down had the effect of slowing their fall so it could be observed more precisely (watching something fall through the air, it is quite difficult to say just exactly when it passes a certain point). And he is said to have used his own pulse as a clock to measure the swing of a lamp (or perhaps an incense sensor—stories conflict) in the cathedral in Pisa. However he did his work, Galileo's belief in measuring the phenomena as precisely as possible became a foundation stone for modern scientific practice.

The third major principle is that observations and experiments must be *repeatable by others*. It is all well and good for Galileo to point his telescope at Jupiter and claim he saw "little stars" orbiting close to the planet. But only if others could see them too could it be known that Galileo was observing something real in the sky, and not dirt on the lens or some apparition inside the tube. (With low power binoculars on a clear night you can make the same observations he did. The "little stars" he saw are now called the Galilean moons of Jupiter.)

These ideas, *testability, exact measurement*, and *repeatability of observations*, are the basis for scientific practice in our time. A fourth important idea, *peer review*, operates in a practical way for scientists today to connect their work to a community of practice—other scientists pursuing the same or similar questions. The old film stereotype of the solitary genius in a private laboratory discovering "breakthroughs" is quite contrary to the communal nature of actual scientific practice. Up front, applications for research grants are reviewed and critiqued by others in the field before funding is approved. For research involving human subjects, for instance in psychology, groups usually called Institutional Review Boards (there's one at St. Kate's) examine the research design for ethical problems. And then, before results can be published in scientific journals they are reviewed by peers as well. Though the process of peer review is not without problems (we are talking about the activities of actual human beings, after all), it does help to ensure that scientific results are reliable and conform to the basic standards of experimentation in that field.

As criteria, testability, measurement, repeatability, and peer review provide a way of separating practices and beliefs that are scientific from those that are not. But how are they applied in actual research work? How do peer reviewers know—in detail—that a study fits the criteria for research in its specific field?

IV. The Paradigm of Science

One of the most influential answers to these questions was provided by Thomas Kuhn in his 1962 book *The Structure of Scientific Revolutions*.[7] This thin little volume is one of the landmarks of twentieth century philosophy. Kuhn studied the Copernican Revolution and the tortuous evolution of chemistry out of Medieval alchemy, and he proposed that the contents and methods of individual sciences like astronomy and chemistry are the result of the formation of *paradigms*. He argued that most of the time a science has a settled content and methodology that guides its practitioners in their work. He called these periods of stability *normal science*. Scientific progress is not a matter of adding more and more facts to a body of learning. Instead, it takes the form of occasional radical changes in the understanding of what questions to ask of Nature and how to attempt to answer them. When a revolution in scientific understanding occurs, Kuhn said, it looks like a thorough revision of what counts as doing science at all. He called these events paradigm shifts.

Unfortunately for our understanding of Kuhn, the phrase "paradigm shift" has entered the common vocabulary, becoming a piece of organizational jargon. It has been watered down to mean any change of thinking. But Kuhn was referring to something momentous. After the discovery of electricity, of x-rays, of oxygen, the relevant sciences were changed from top to bottom. Take the theory of combustion: right down to the eighteenth century people had only a sketchy sense of what actually happened when something burned. They had invented an explanation based on a substance called phlogiston. The presence of this substance in a material such as wood or coal is what made it flammable. The process of combustion was thought to be simply the process of *phlogiston* leaving the substance. Wood and coal were claimed to be mostly phlogiston, so when they were, in the term of the time, dephlogisticated, they mostly disappeared. An elaborate set of theories developed around the hypothesis of phlogiston, and they went along with another idea common in that era, that heat was a substance that flowed through materials. That substance was called *caloric*. Chemists of the time (this would be the mid-1700s) were thus working within a paradigm that included phlogiston and caloric as part of their basic understanding, a paradigm that guided them in designing experiments and thinking up what questions they wanted their experiments to answer. All this changed, over the course of a couple of years, when a number of scientists independently in Sweden, England, and France isolated a gas that came to be called *oxygen* and figured out that it was one of the main constituents of air. Antoine Lavoisier through carefully quantified experiments (precise weighing of samples before and after combustion) showed that combustion was the process of oxygen combining with other substances. In time the new theory of combustion based on oxygen generated completely new questions and experimental designs. Phlogiston disappeared from the scientific vocabulary, only to be referred to henceforth by historians and philosophers of science who like the feel of the word on the tongue.

From phlogiston to oxygen was such a fruitful shift in understanding, uniting disparate phenomena—it wasn't long before scientists figured out that oxygen had an essential role to play in supporting life—that it changed the very meaning of doing chemistry. Questions that had been asked before were no longer relevant to anything, and brand new questions that were unimaginable before became the basis for normal science. A paradigm shift had occurred. And a young student learning how to be a chemist would be introduced to a completely different science than had existed before. This is one example among many of fundamental changes in scientific understanding during the last 250 years that confirm Kuhn's approach. There are numerous other examples: relativity theory and quantum mechanics did not merely add to the sum of knowledge in physics, but changed what it meant to be doing physics at all.

Kuhn's book generated a lot of critique, especially as he was initially not as clear as he might have been about the definition of a paradigm. We might generalize Kuhn's refinement of the concept in later essays in this way: a scientific paradigm is a shared communal understanding of the meaning of a certain kind of research. It contains rules of methodology—including the symbolic language practitioners use, such as chemical formulas and statistical charts; basic ideas about what questions should be investigated; and, most important, a definition of the boundaries that define the discipline.[8] One of the strengths of Kuhn's work is that it locates the paradigm within the practices and shared understandings of scientists themselves. Thus paradigms are always relative to a community of practice in a given era. In this discussion I have emphasized physics, chemistry, and biology, because Kuhn takes his examples from those fields. But exactly the same points can be made about the social sciences as well. Psychology, sociology, political science, etc., likewise operate on shared paradigms imbedded in the practices of their respective fields.

This leads to a major point of this essay. Though Kuhn emphasizes the existence of discipline-specific paradigms, the ones that guide individual sciences, he recognized that there is a large scale paradigm of what counts as scientific research in general.[9] This large scale paradigm of scientific research is what I was describing when I talked about testability, measurement, repeatability of observations, and peer review.

V. Science and Non-Science

The large scale paradigm expresses the scientific community's under-standing of its work today. This matters because the role of scientific knowing in contemporary American society is a contested issue. To illustrate I will consider three areas: astrology; the New Age belief in ley lines; and creationism. In selecting these examples from among many possibilities I looked for areas that have many adherents and that clearly do not fit the general paradigm of science as it stands today.

A. The Persistence of Astrology

Astrology is a system of understanding that connects human lives to astronomical phenomena, chiefly the motions of the planets. It is very ancient: archeologists have found horoscopes scratched on buried walls in Greece, and there are astrological texts in every major civilization we know of, from ancient Babylon and China to the pre-conquest people of Mesoamerica. There are basically two sides to the astrological under-standing: first there is the calculation of the positions of the sun, earth's moon, and the planets measured against the background of the constella-tions lying along the ecliptic, for a particular time, normally a person's time of birth.* This information is really astronomical in the sense that it depends on observation and measurement of the skies, and it is what ancient systems of astrology had in common; that is, Greek and Arab and Chinese systems tended to agree on where things were in the skies (within broad limits, given the lack of precise measuring tools) because they were seeing the same motions. The second part of astrological understanding is the interpretation of the meaning of these motions for the formation of individual personality and fate. These interpretations are the part of astrology that is handed down as a system of traditional lore. An astrologer casting an individual's horoscope uses many calculations of positions of planets and the angles between them; these measurements and their interpretations for a person's life are quite complex and detailed. (It should be clear from this that the fanciful astrology columns in the newspapers have little to do with the serious practice of casting horo-scopes. That's why they typically are printed on the comics pages!)

---

* The ecliptic is an imaginary line across the sky near which most of the planets in the solar system appear. It is a line because most of the planets orbit the sun in the same plane, so throughout the year we always see them against the back-ground of the same constellations. The ecliptic passes through twelve ancient constellations, known as the zodiac.

Though some advocates of astrology attempt to compare it favorably with scientific method, these efforts tend to be based on faulty analogies. For instance, in his *Encyclopedia of Astrology* James R. Lewis says,

> We cannot touch, taste, or see astrological forces, but neither can we touch, taste, or see gravity. Gravity is perceived only indirectly—in terms of its effects. Astrological forces are also perceived indirectly—in terms of their impact on human beings and worldly events.

He goes on to note that statistical studies have been done "which have yielded significant correlations between career choices and the prominence of certain planets in the natal chart."[10] Now it may well be that well-designed research programs in psychology will come to verify statistically some of the findings of astrology. But that is beside the point. Psychological research operates from a scientific paradigm in which careful measurement and repeatability of observations are basic. Astrologers cast horoscopes using interpretive methods and a complex system of meanings which are not the result of application of scientific methods. And the analogy between astrological forces and gravity is weak, though certainly there are plenty of forces and entities studied by physicists, chemists, etc., that are known only through their effects. The point is not whether what is studied is effects of unobserved forces, but the *methods* by which those effects are studied.

It makes perfect sense for someone like Lewis, writing a comprehensive encyclopedia of his field, to be somewhat defensive about the place of astrology in contemporary culture. As he says,

> Since the Enlightenment, the Western world has been home to a vocal group of scientists and science believers who have railed against religion and anything else that dared suggest the human being is anything more than a physical-chemical organism. Astrology has been lumped in the category of irrational superstition, along with anything else that does not fall within a narrow definition of science.[11]

He is correct that there are many people who regard astrology as irrational superstition. But the counter to that misconception is not to try to pretend that astrology is more scientific than it actually is, but to recognize that it is a body of self-consistent traditional lore, with its own methods and practices. It may not be stretching Kuhn's meaning too much to say that astrology has its own paradigm of practice. Indeed, Lewis's encyclopedia attempts to be a comprehensive account of this paradigm and to serve as a textbook as well. Still, the extensive body of knowledge that forms the system of astrological interpretation was not developed from within a paradigm of *scientific* research. Contemporary astrology still relies on astronomy—more precisely, celestial mechanics—in calculating positions of planets, moon, and sun, and it is interesting that various asteroids, which were not known to ancient observers, have now been incorporated in the calculations. But it is the system of interpretation that makes these calculations applicable to human lives, and these, again, have not been developed via scientific methodology. Take this example, again from Lewis:

> Of particular importance are the four elements—earth, water, air, and fire—which represent certain basic personality orientations. Earth represents practicality; water, emotional sensitivity; air, a mental orientation; and fire, activity. So for people whose charts are comprised primarily of water signs (Cancer, Scorpio, and Pisces), feelings are what are most *real* in life; for a predominance of air signs (Gemini, Libra, and Aquarius), ideas are most valued; for earth (Taurus, Virgo, and Capricorn), practical concerns; and for fire (Aries, Leo, and Sagittarius), activity.[12]

We can perhaps imagine an experimental design that would test these correlations, but *they themselves are not the result of scientific experiment.* They have been handed down through ages of tradition. To the extent that the system is self-coherent, that is, does not contain within itself any contradictions, it is not irrational. I do not know whether the central claim of astrology, that the positions of the planets, moon and sun at the time of one's birth influence one's personality and life's path, is true. But I do know that this claim is not a scientific one.*

B. Ley Lines

In 1922 Alfred Watkins (1855–1935) published a book in which he described a number of straight lines linking ancient sites on a map of Blackwardine, England.[13] He thought they represented trade routes constructed by prehistoric Britons. In his second book on his discovery, he said

> Imagine a fairy chain stretched from mountain peak to mountain peak, as far as the eye could reach, and paid out until it reached the 'high places' of the earth at a number of ridges, banks, and knowls [sic]. Then visualize a mound, circular earthwork, or clump of trees, planted on these high points, and in low points in the valley other mounds ringed around with water to be seen from a distance. Then great standing stones brought to mark the way at intervals, . . .[14]

Watkins extended his search for straight lines on maps to other parts of Great Britain and Europe, and named the lines he could draw between

---

* The basic belief of astrology, that human lives are influenced by the positions of planets, etc., at the time of birth, also raises the issue of determinism, that is, it calls into question the degree to which people have free will and can choose their own destiny. This consequence of the system may lead it into conflict with other systems of belief, for instance some forms of Christianity, but that in itself does not bear on whether the claim is true or not.

sites "Ley lines," apparently because a number of them passed through present day places with names ending in –ley, a common British place name ending. It wasn't long before Watkins's readers noted that some of the supposed trade routes would have required travelers to ascend vertical cliffs, and another explanation for the lines emerged, one that enjoys considerable popularity today. This is the thesis that the lines are "sources of power or energy," and by some accounts are used as navigational guides by UFOs.

> New Age occultists believe that there are certain sites on the earth which are filled with special "energy." Stonehenge, Mt. Everest, Ayers Rock in Australia, Nazca in Peru, the Great Pyramid at Giza, Sedona (Arizona), Mutiny Bay, among other places, are believed to be places of special energy.[15]

I can add to this list Machu Picchu in Peru and the cathedral in Kracow, Poland, where so many people came to put their hands on a particular outside wall of the building to feel the energy alleged to be emanating from a sacred stone underneath the cathedral that the Bishop of Kracow had that section of wall roped off, and posted a sign there debunking the belief.[16]

In 1987 in Seattle an environmental art organization called the Geo Group received funding from the city's Arts Commission to produce a ley line map of the city. The method of creating the map was described by Chuck Pettis.

> I created the map by using a brass pendulum to map dowse a large four-by-eight foot Seattle road map for ley lines. Then, we verified the ley-line power centers by visiting the sites and dowsing the exact location of the power center.[17]

Dowsing is the process by which some people are able, using forked sticks or other tools, to discover subterranean water or, in this case, "electromagnetic energy fields emanating from the Earth."[18] Pettis describes the results of this process:

> 60 ley lines and 44 power centers were identified within Seattle city limits. Ley lines are a network of energy lines that crisscross the Earth. Ley lines originate at power centers. Ancient monuments such as pyramids, stone circles, medicine wheels, shrines, cathedrals and other sacred architectural structures have traditionally been located on power centers. Power centers are significant because they can affect consciousness and uplift the human condition, the time-honored missions of art.[19]

As an artwork the resulting map is quite intriguing, a satellite image with a network of lines superimposed. But what is behind the whole concept of the map is a belief system that has at its center a concept that cannot be verified within the methodologies of the physical sciences. Though people like Chuck Pettis use terms like "electromagnetic energy," if the power centers actually emanated *electromagnetic* energy, one would not need to dowse to detect it: there are any number of actual measuring devices that could do the job. The uses of the word "energy" in New Age beliefs would make an interesting scholarly study on its own, but for my purposes here, suffice it to say that energy for a practitioner of New Age spirituality is most likely not the same thing as energy for a physicist.

This point is one basis for my conclusions about belief in ley lines. First, it is not impossible that mapped ley lines represent a real phenomenon that our scientific methods are at present unable to detect. After all, at the time of their discovery x-rays, "energy" that could pass through walls and metal cabinets to fog photographic plates, were quite incredible. But second, belief in ley lines remains unscientific, for the straightforward reason that the methods of detecting them do not fit the current paradigm of scientific research. I conclude that ley lines may be perfectly real (I don't know), but if you believe in them you are doing so outside the paradigm of scientific investigation that prevails at this time.

C. Creationism

In an essay of the scope of this one I cannot hope to give more than a cursory account of the anti-evolution controversy in the United States. But I think it is worth risking oversimplification in order to put in front of you an important debate about the place of the sciences in contemporary society. Recently, the paradigm of scientific research in biology itself has been challenged as creationists attempted to borrow some of the prestige of the word "science" by asserting a new model of research called "creation science." Along with the doctrine of intelligent design, proponents of creation science have tried to shift the grounds of the debate about evolution. In no other area is the line between science and non-science more important. First, some background.

In the nineteenth century two major and interrelated scientific revolutions took place, one in geology and one in biology. Naturalists of the period had for a long time puzzled over the fossil remains of fish found in landlocked limestone quarries in England. Many people interpreted these as accidental freaks of nature. But in 1830 Charles Lyell published the first volume of his *Principles of Geology*, in which he established the science of paleontology based on analysis of rock strata. On the basis of Lyell's work it became possible to interpret fossils as evidence of ancient seas. Real fish had died and their shapes had been preserved in sedimentary deposits that later hardened to stone. If that was correct, then the processes of fossilization required lots more time than the prevailing opinion allowed. That opinion held that the universe, including the earth and all its species of life, was created complete and whole on Sunday, October 23, in the year 4004 B.C.E. This rather precise calculation came from an intrepid Biblical and Near Eastern scholar named James Ussher, an Irish archbishop, who in 1650 published a book called *The Annals of the World*. He used evidence within the text of the Bible correlated with other accounts of the history of the ancient Near East in calculating his chronology. In 1701 Ussher's dating of the creation and many other events was included in an authorized printing of the Bible, and thereafter came to be regarded as being nearly as authoritative as the scriptures themselves. The tradition of printing Ussher's dates alongside scripture has continued well into our own time, though more contemporary translations of the Bible omit it. Ussher's book lives on: an English translation of the *Annals* published in 2003 has been praised as a major support for present day creationists.[20] But Lyell's work provided the evidence for dating the earth as much older than Ussher's chronology allowed, and provided an essential framework for the work of Lyell's friend, Charles Darwin.

Darwin published *On the Origin of Species* in 1859. In it he advanced two ideas to explain observations he made as a naturalist voyaging in the southern hemisphere in the early 1830s on a British naval vessel, the Beagle. Attempting to explain differences in the weight and shape of the beaks of Galapagos Finches on different islands, he noted that the food available to them differed in a way that correlated exactly with beak shape. Darwin hypothesized that these variations were adaptations to local conditions, changes that allowed the birds to be more successful in feeding, and therefore more successful in reproducing. Chance mutation in the genetic makeup of the birds met with a favorable environment and so was passed on to progeny who were similarly successful in that environment. Darwin called this process natural selection. He began to find examples of it in other species. And he further hypothesized that species themselves are the product of the age-long working out of these two principles: chance mutation and natural selection.

Darwin knew his work would be controversial, and it was, especially as the new explanation of how members of biological species come to have the form they do began to be applied to human beings. From ancient times to Darwin's there were powerful traditions regarding humans as unique in the universe. For Aristotle, we were the only reasoning beings, the only ones with language. For Medieval thinkers, we were the only beings with souls, placed by God just below the angels in the Great Chain of Being. The Darwinian revolution in biology seemed to challenge the imbedded idea of the uniqueness of humans, particularly our distinctness from other primates, and it is that challenge today to which creationists respond.

Creationist beliefs have themselves changed over time. Followers of Archbishop Ussher's chronology or similar calculations of the age of the earth are called Young Earth Creationists, and they typically hold that the earth is between 6,000 and 10,000 years old.[21] This belief requires denying multiple independent sources of evidence for a very much older earth and universe. Logically, one cannot disprove the hypothesis that God created the earth in 4004 B.C., created it complete with the fossil record and all the other evidence of much longer existence. I think it was Bertrand Russell who pointed out that you cannot positively disprove the hypothesis that the whole universe and everything in it, including us, was created five minutes ago, complete with all our memories, etc. His point was that though it cannot be positively disproved, no reasonable person would believe it, because all the evidence is against it. The same logic applies to the major belief of Young Earth Creationists, except that a lot of people do seem to believe it. Still, divine creation (at any time) is not a scientifically testable belief.

Recently some creationists have shown a willingness to accept a much older age for the earth. A new orientation to creationism has emerged with two facets to it: one, called creation science, applies scientific methodology to the project of critiquing the findings of evolutionary biology and the methods used to date the earth. The other, called the theory of intelligent design, uses the fact of the orderliness of life to argue for a designer, that is, an intelligence who created it. Intelligent design theory is a contemporary version of one of the classic arguments for the existence of God, the Argument from Design, and it suffers some of the same problems that argument has. One of them is that though it may be difficult to comprehend how the apparent orderliness of the world could have arisen entirely by chance, nothing *logically* prohibits chance from being the true origin of our observed world. Improbability is not the same as impossibility. But second, even if we accept the argument as proving the existence of a designer, nothing in the argument requires us to conclude that the designer is of divine origin. In fact, there is an international group of people, the Raëlian Movement, who believe that life on earth is the product of the intervention of extraterrestrial beings who are the intelligent designers. The Raëlians are a religious movement and, like creationists, oppose evolution. They accept the thesis of intelligent design, but they hold "that intelligent aliens landed here millennia ago in spaceships and formed all of life on earth, including human beings, using highly advanced genetic engineering."[22]

A counter to the thesis of alien intelligent designers might be that the orderliness of things extends to the structures of the universe itself and its natural laws. It isn't just the presence of *life* on earth that is to be explained, but the presence of order itself in the cosmos. Still, as the philosopher David Hume pointed out in the eighteenth century, even if the argument works to establish that the apparent orderliness of the cosmos is the product of a intelligent designer, it does not establish that the designer has the characteristics, such as perfection, typically attributed to the Christian

God.[23] As a result, the Argument from Design has been regarded by many as giving only probable grounds for its conclusion. Many people accept the argument as giving a measure of rational support to their belief in the existence of God, but their belief is actually grounded on faith. Creationists, because they want to challenge evolution as the basis for the prevailing paradigm of research in the sciences, attempt to go beyond faith in the field called creation science.

The Institute for Creation Research (ICR) is one of a number of organizations whose work is to foster research supporting a creationist conception of the world and human life. Under "Creation Scientists" its website says,

> Scientists who are creationists repudiate any form of molecules-to-man evolution in their analysis and use of scientific data. Creation scientists and the work they conduct are at the heart of ICR's mission to defend biblical truth with scientific evidences, particularly on the issue of origins.[24]

To explain why this approach to science fails to fit the current general paradigm of research, I'll return to some ideas of Karl Popper. Opponents of evolution often say, "It's just a theory—it hasn't been proven." This comment reveals a mistake about the way the sciences work. First, every scientific claim is a theory, or more precisely a hypothesis. The word "theory" in science does not carry the connotation that it has in common language, of being uncertain or unsure. A theory is simply a hypothesis offered for testing. At first, the truth of a hypothesis is unknown. If it were known, there would be no reason to test it. Over time, some theories come to be more thoroughly tested than others. Popper wrote that a good experiment does not attempt to prove that a theory is true—in most cases that is nearly impossible. It attempts to prove that the theory is false. If an experiment does not prove the theory to be false, then belief in its truth is just that little bit more justified. But you should keep trying to *dis*prove it. If you succeed, then you know the claim is false and you can move on. And you have learned something. Each time a serious program of research *fails* to *dis*prove a hypothesis, belief in the truth of the theory is that much more justified. That's Popper's idea of scientific progress. It takes a lot of time and the work of many people experimenting, observing, and measuring to arrive at a consensus that a theory is well established, worthy of belief.[25]

Evolution by natural selection is one of those now well established theories. Natural selection has been observed in birds, fruit flies, and bacteria.* Chance mutation plus natural selection has proved such a fruitful framework for understanding biological phenomena that that it has become part of the paradigm for research in the biological sciences, tested over

---

* Indeed, the present day problem of antibiotic resistant strains of microbes is an eloquent demonstration of natural selection at work.

and over again in multiple, independent research programs. We have abundant good reasons to accept evolution as explaining the phenomena it applies to. By contrast, creation science starts from a standpoint that is essentially religious and political, and attempts not to disprove its hypotheses but to find evidence that can be described as proving their point of view. To propose a hypothesis explaining some observed phenomena and then to design rigorous research to test that hypothesis is the essence of scientific practice. Scientists have to follow the evidence where it leads and have to be willing to accept that their hypotheses may be wrong. On the other hand, to engage in research to prove a thesis one has already arrived at through other means, especially the religious thesis of creationism, is to engage in the pretense of doing science without the necessary commitment to the openness of scientific methods, acceptance of the possibility of completely new insights and surprise endings.

The mark of an ideology is that people who hold it regard it as impervious to critique; no evidence is allowed to count against it. That is Peirce's Method of Tenacity in action. Could the paradigm of evolutionary biology ever change or be replaced? Certainly. For one thing there are disputes among biologists and paleontologists about different models of evolution, and it is probable that one or another of these will stand up to testing better than the others.[26] Also, a follower of Popper would say that *no* theory is ever provable beyond any possibility of refutation. And it is possible that an entirely different understanding of biological species and the prehistory of human life will emerge in time from the work of scientists. We cannot predict what that new understanding might look like any more than an early nineteenth century thinker could have predicted quantum physics. But if there is such a paradigm shift, it will almost certainly emerge from work being done within the prevailing scientific paradigm, not from the work of religious ideologues.

The paleontologist and historian of science, Stephen Jay Gould, one of the major figures in the development of contemporary evolutionary theory, wrote a book toward the end of his too-short life in which he argued that science and religion should never come into conflict. His idea was that the domains of the two areas were so different that though they might illuminate each other they cannot "be unified, or even synthesized, under any common scheme of explanation or analysis."[27] He hoped for something called "respectful noninterference":

> Science tries to document the factual character of the natural world, and to develop theories that coordinate and explain these facts. Religion, on the other hand, operates in the equally important, but utterly different, realm of human purposes, meanings, and values—subjects that the factual domain of science might illuminate, but can never resolve. Similarly, while scientists must operate with ethical principles, some specific to their practice, the validity of these principles can never be inferred from the factual discoveries of science.[28]

I agree with Gould that in principle there should not be a conflict: science does not do its work *versus* religion, and religious believers should not be threatened by the findings of the sciences. The debate about evolution in the U.S., which is essentially political, does try to set up a rigid dichotomy between the two, which is unfortunate. Paying attention to the demarcation between the sciences and areas whose truths have a non-scientific basis should help us understand the grounds for inquiry and belief in different fields.

The sciences have fostered important human goods, both in terms of individual life expectancy and in terms of the quality of lives lived. Examples are abundant: organ transplants, antibiotics, and synthetic human insulin harvested from genetically engineered *e. coli* bacteria quickly come to mind. Millions of people have benefited from these products of scientific method. Still, there are many criticisms of our dependency on the technologies that have resulted from applications of scientific research. Antibiotics have been overused, so that we may be facing a time when they will no longer be as effective as they have been in controlling infections. Distribution of medicines is controlled by large for-profit corporations, so that many in the world cannot afford the benefits of current medical understanding. And much scientific work throughout history has been devoted not to fostering the quality of human life but to technologies of warfare. Yet these are criticisms not of the paradigms of scientific research itself, but of the societies in which scientific practice is imbedded.

Conclusion

The English mystery novelist Josephine Tey, active in the 1940s and '50s, once wrote,

> There is a little phrase commonly used in police work that says, 'in accordance with the evidence.' You say that over six times a day as a grace before and after meals, and perhaps it will keep your feet on the ground and stop you ending up thinking you're Frederick the Great or a hedgehog or something.

I think this succinctly expresses an attitude that is basic to the rationalist orientation. You can of course believe anything you want to and you can use any method you wish—or no method at all—to establish your beliefs. But paying scrupulous attention to evidence and its analysis has proved to provide a fruitful standpoint for inquiry in areas where beliefs can be fixed by such methods.

There is a dogma called "scientism" according to which it is irrational to believe anything that has not been established by the empirical methods of the sciences. I hope this essay is not read as an exercise in scientism. There are a few useful guide dogmas, but scientism is not one of them. My purpose has been to show in a general way where the line is drawn between the paradigms of scientific inquiry and other ways of establishing beliefs. Like Peirce, I do think that some methods of fixing belief are better than others in the long run in getting us the truths we can live by. But I am also convinced that no single orientation to truth seeking will completely satisfy our human drive to understand the world and ourselves in it.

Notes

[1] Charles Sanders Peirce, "The Fixation of Belief," in *Philosophical Writings of Peirce*, ed. Justus Buchler (New York: Dover, 1955), 10.

[2] Ibid., 12.

[3] Ibid., 14.

[4] Ibid., 17.

[5] Ibid., 18.

[6] Karl R. Popper, *Conjectures and Refutations* (New York: Basic Books, 1962), 37.

[7] Thomas S. Kuhn, *The Structure of Scientific Revolutions* (2d. ed. Chicago: University of Chicago Press, 1970).

[8] Ibid., "Postscript," 174–210.

[9] Ibid., 42.

[10] James R. Lewis, *Encyclopedia of Astrology* (Detroit: Gale Research, 1994), xvi.

[11] Ibid.

[12] Ibid., xxii.

[13] Alfred Watkins, *Early English Trackways*, (1922).

[14] Ibid., *The Old Straight Track* (1925), quoted in http://whitcomb.sbc.edu/earthmysteries/EMLeyLines.html (Jan. 15, 2008).

[15] http://skepdic.com/leylines.html (Jan. 15, 2008).

[16] This was as of my visit there in 2001.

[17] http://geo.org/qa.htm#tof (revised Feb. 14, 2000, accessed Jan. 15, 2008).

[18] Ibid.

[19] Ibid.

[20] James Ussher, *Annals of the World: James Ussher's Classic Survey of World History*, Larry Pierce and Marion Pierce, eds. (Master Books, 2003).

[21] Robert T. Pennock, *Tower of Babel: The Evidence Against the New Creationism* (Cambridge, MA: MIT Press, 1999), 216 ff.

[22] Ibid., 234.

[23] David Hume, *Dialogues Concerning Natural Religion* (1779).

[24] http://www.icr.org/research (accessed January 25, 2008).

[25] Popper, Ch. 1.

[26] See, for instance, Stephen Jay Gould, "Bushes and Ladders in Human Evolution," in *Ever Since Darwin* (New York: W.W. Norton, 1977) 56–62.

[27] Stephen Jay Gould, *Rocks of Ages; Science and Religion in the Fullness of Life* (New York: Ballantine, 1999), 4.

[28] Ibid., 4–5.

Brian E. Fogarty (b. 1950) came of age during the turbulent '60s—amid the Cold War, Beatlemania, and Vietnam. Born to a solidly working-class family, his college education opened up a world of ideas and interests that had previously been unknown or unappreciated. Besides teaching sociology at the College of St. Catherine, he is a writer of opera and a supporter of the arts. Fogarty asks us "Why learn about the arts?" and gives us compelling reasons why we should. Do you agree with Fogarty's reasoning that art matters? He says artistic expression both conveys truths and is a way to explore truths. Can art do what words cannot? Do you agree or disagree that "to reject 'difficult' art in favor of what we like and are comfortable with is to reject a message"?

Art Matters

Brian E. Fogarty

The study of the arts is not new to any of us. We have taken "art class" since kindergarten, starting with finger painting and flower-pressing activities, and gradually gaining artistic sophistication through our school years. But one thing has remained consistent throughout our academic experience with art: for most of us, it has always been a less serious, non-academic class. Art class is fun; a break from books and tests. It's a chance for self-expression, unfettered by too much thinking or scholarly principles. In fact, one might argue that art is the course taken least seriously by students and school authorities alike. Even physical education classes involve a certain amount of exertion at least, and the importance placed in American society on fitness and competition is surely reflected in the authority of the PE coach. By the time we are in high school, only art retains its playful, non-serious status among our classes.

It's no wonder, then, that by the time we enter college, we might question the importance of art to the serious education we seek. Although our previous experience of the arts has been a break from the more serious routine of learning things, at least that education was free for most of us. We could afford the luxury of dabbling in something we had no real need to learn about, and besides, our younger years were less serious anyway. Today the stakes are higher: as college students we are motivated to learn something useful; we may even have specific career goals in mind—and college is expensive. In the end, it seems worthwhile to ask: why should we commit this kind of money and effort to something that seems recreational? Why *learn* about the arts?

I'd like to make the case that learning about the arts and about aesthetics in general is as important and as worthwhile as the learning you'll do about biology or literature or political science. Nor do I mean that it is important in some unspecified, vague way, perhaps because it will make you a better citizen, or because it will enrich your middle age when the pursuits of youth become less interesting. On the contrary, the study of aesthetics will make you a more skilled, more perceptive student right away, and it will make you a better qualified graduate. Whether you aspire to become a business executive, nurse, physicist, sociologist, or something else, the study of aesthetics will better qualify you for a career, and it will help that career advance more rapidly than it otherwise would. In short, *art matters*, and the study of art matters is an important part of serious higher education.

I don't mean to suggest that thinking a little about aesthetic values in *The Reflective Woman* or taking a course in art history or jewelry design will turn you from an intellectual ugly duckling into a magnificent swan. No single course or body of knowledge does that. I do believe, though, that learning about the arts is at least as useful as learning any other body of knowledge; say, chemistry or history or accounting. Here are some reasons why.

1. Art is another form of communication. We know that college work (and, by the way, the work of most professions as well) involves communicating ideas to people and understanding communications from others, usually through writing or speaking. And many of the ideas we deal with are fairly mundane ones. Ordinary words, in the form of essays, research reports, memos, and letters are usually good enough communications devices in these instances. But what happens when you need to express some subtle and complex idea about love, or faith, or freedom, or oppression? How many pages would it take for your essay to describe a strong feeling or passion about one of these ideas? At some point, you might depart from prose and write a poem, or perhaps words would simply fail altogether.

Yet music, film, painting, dance, even architecture—all the arts are exactly geared to expressing those very ideas and values that words fail to express. We are often "left speechless" by a work of art or music for precisely that reason—the work expresses something for which words are inadequate. After all, if words could be used to describe the ideas conveyed, we wouldn't need the art in the first place.

This is hardly a twentieth-century discovery, by the way. I once heard a lecture by an expert on Chartres cathedral, in which he demonstrated how its stained-glass windows were used to express the metaphorical subtleties of holy scripture. Each main window, it turns out, is actually a pair of windows: one side tells a New Testament story, while the other side shows the Old Testament parallel to it. The "language" of the images is capable of expressing the thematic similarities and contrasts between the two sources far more subtly and more efficiently than words could do—and this was just as well, since almost no one could read in the thirteenth century anyway. What an irony that the lowest serf of the middle ages may have understood the Bible in a more subtle way than we literate moderns do!

Art also has the advantage of speaking "below the surface" of consciousness. One doesn't always have to be trying to "read" a piece of art in order for it to communicate to us. For example, the U.S. Capitol building probably expresses both majesty and democracy, even to the casual visitor, better than reams of written material or lofty speeches. Try imagining a modern steel-and-glass capitol instead, or a gothic one, or a square one of red brick, and the impact of architecture becomes clear. And speaking of Washington, doesn't the starkness of the Vietnam memorial speak as clearly about the legacy of that war than all the heroic statuary we see commemorating World War II?

The trouble is, art is by nature subtle and it requires some effort to understand. Thus, our previous non-serious training in the arts—not only in school but throughout our experience—encourages us to reject a lot of difficult art, because it doesn't give pleasure right away, or sometimes not at all. This has a serious implication for our intellectual and professional development: that to reject "difficult" art in favor of what we like and are comfortable with is to reject a message. It's a little like deciding to read at only a fifth-grade level because all the stories are easy, happy ones. And this, of course, is nothing more than opting for ignorance. Shouldn't the task of higher education be to discourage this?

People are trying to communicate with us; to tell us things we can't understand any other way. They are artists, musicians, dancers, playwrites, poets, architects. And in fact, the more complex and subtle the idea being communicated, the more "difficult" the art is. The ability to participate in this sort of communication may not be very important to those in careers that don't involve subtleties. But people who make decisions for a living, who work at non-routine and complex jobs, are at a serious disadvantage if they haven't developed the skill to get something from a poem or painting or dance.

2. Art provides an analytical workout. I was a teenager in the summer of 1964 when the "British invasion" of rock music arrived on American shores. Literally dozens of recordings would be released by these new English groups every week. I remember a promotional contest that my local radio station ran at the time: they would play a new release from one of the new groups, and you would have to guess whether or not it was the Beatles. Sometimes it was, but often it was the Dave Clark Five, or Jerry and the Pacemakers or the Zombies or somebody else. Since nobody had heard the new release before, there was an interesting analytical task involved: you had to develop some concepts for determining whether the new song had the *sound* of the Beatles, or whether it was some other group. What made up the Beatles' sound? Were there certain characteristics of the melodies, or the lyrics, or the arrangements, that made them Beatles songs? I became very good at this by the end of the summer—though I can't put into words what rules or concepts or theories I used to distinguish the Beatles from the others.

A few years later I found myself in a large college lecture hall, trying to do the same thing with Beethoven and Mozart. As a matter of fact, the "game" hadn't changed much: the final exam consisted of listening to short recorded musical passages; we'd have to write down the composer's name for each one. Now, the hard way to approach this was to try to memorize which composer went with which recording. They were all on reserve at the library and we were to spend our evenings there drumming into our brains various tricks for linking them together ("It's a bird, it's a plane, it's a Mozart," sung to the tune of the Mozart piece that would be on the quiz, was one device). The smart students figured out the better tactic: to try to develop some analytic concepts for distinguishing Beethoven's sound from Mozart's—and Stravinsky's, Prokofiev's and Britten's and all the others.

The funny things is, while I had become adept at distinguishing very readily the Stones from the Beatles, I had great difficulty distinguishing the various symphonic composers from one another. And this was remarkable, since I'm sure that Beethoven's music was in its day considered as great a departure from Mozart as Pearl Jam is from Frank Sinatra. But to an eighteen-year-old whose experience had included little of this, it all sounded the same—the way that, say, traditional Japanese music still does to my unschooled ear.

The study of aesthetics thus affords us an opportunity to exercise our analytical powers in ways that are not always tapped by other academic work, and this is probably a worthwhile thing in itself. But still, what reason do we have to believe this exercise to be beneficial in a pragmatic way? Put bluntly, how will it make one a better physical therapist, or lawyer, or insurance underwriter? The answer is that these same analytical skills are the ones that professional people put to use every day. They are the mental faculties by which we make subtle decisions based on scanty information. The care of a patient, the handling of a personnel dispute, the tone of a memo, the design of a lesson plan—they all involve reading the subtle cues of a situation, forming categories and concepts, and applying them to a decision. They are the kind of skills that people might say "can't be taught" but rather are innate or acquired through long experience. People who possess these skills are simply considered "smart" people. But the fact is, they *can* be taught—you can learn them through study of the arts.

3. Art expresses political realities that must be reckoned with. The arts have a curious and ambivalent character regarding politics and morals. On the one hand, the arts tend to be at the forefront of avant-garde thinking, and seem to endorse and celebrate new lifestyles, challenge traditional values, and elevate the bohemian to the artistic elite. But on the other hand, the arts also express the traditions of a society, not only in what is portrayed but in who portrays it. A walk through your local art museum or a visit to Orchestra Hall will make the point: even now, there is a stunning overrepresentation of Europeans and men among the painters, composers, and performers. This is not simply to say that there is a conspiracy of white men at the "top" of the art world, although many will make that point persuasively. Rather, these biases of representation show us something more fundamental about our culture: that the dominance of one race and one gender runs deep in American society. I'd say, in fact, that they show precisely that this dominance is *not* a matter of the conspiracy of a few, but rather a deeply-rooted element of our national character. Frankly, this is much more difficult to swallow than a simplistic conspiracy theory, but it fits better with the facts.

At the same time, we often see in a typical visit to the museum a special exhibit of "Emerging African-American Artists" or "Women of the Arts and Crafts Movement," or "Caribbean Carnival Costume," each giving voice and exposure to a heretofore neglected cultural tradition. And this tells us something, too: that these groups are emerging, gaining force and recognition within the artistic community, finding their way into the public consciousness. Such exhibits were not so common fifty years ago, and it is a measure of social change that we see them in established museums and galleries today.

And it's not only the authorship of the arts that conveys political and social realities. The content of the paintings, photographs, and music also tells us something. How are women represented in 19th-century painting? Are they action figures, suffering saints, sex objects? What does Puccini's opera *Madama Butterfly* say about encounters between the industrialized world and the traditional one? Or about encounters between men and women? Or about Western stereotypes of Asians?

What is considered "acceptable" art in a certain place in a certain time tells us much about the values and ideals of the society that produced it— keeping in mind that art is a production not just of the artist but of the publishers, critics, and viewing or listening public as well. In the 1930's the Nazi regime banned "degenerate" art—that is, modern, Jewish, or politically critical art—allowing only heroic and representational works to be publicly displayed. It's easy for us today to see how wrong that was. But what's our own reaction to gay literature, or anti-American films, or avant-garde music? What does art and our response to it say about us as a people?

All of this aside, we must still address the question of how understanding the political and social realities we learn from art can help us in the "real" world. The answer, of course, is that the real world is full of the very people we've been talking about! Our workplaces are made up of people of different races, genders, sexual identities, political stripes. Even looking at it from a strictly pragmatic standpoint, is it good for our careers to remain ignorant of how things look and sound and feel to our colleagues, clients, patients, students, customers?

1. Art is a window to culture. We are told incessantly that we now live in a global society, and that we shall have to understand the values and beliefs of other cultures in order to be successful in our lives. This may not seem very relevant to us today, because American culture seems so pervasive throughout the world. But this won't last forever. There will come a time when Americans will have to compete in that global marketplace—and not only for resources and markets, but also in terms of language and ideas and values and traditions. What then? We shall have to understand deeply the meanings things have for people of other cultures —what ideals are important, what constitutes beauty, what is considered the best way to live. Our study of aesthetics will help us perceive these diverse points of view, especially if our studies include diverse aesthetic traditions.

But perhaps more important, the arts connect one deeply to one's *own* culture, and that is a fundamental human need. My total immersion in rock music as a teenager was the main way that I *was* a teenager. And we all take on and proclaim our cultural identity all the time through attending concerts, buying records, going to movies, buying clothes, and many other aesthetic activities. My aesthetic choices are a part of who I am— that is, my identification with a community—and it helps both to make me who I am and to communicate it to others. When those medieval serfs looked up at the impossibly soaring and airy space of Chartres cathedral and read the stained-glass windows, they must have felt a profound sense of belonging to something, and of understanding their own identity. These feelings cannot be imparted by words—they require forms of understanding that lie underneath the verbal realm we usually operate in. They require artistic expression and perception.

In the end, the study of aesthetics is the study of the meanings and ideas that make up one's own community, and to understand and appreciate the arts is to understand that community more deeply. I believe one reason many people—and not just students—chafe at understanding the arts is that much of the art we are shown seems to represent a community other than our own. We have already seen that this is true to some extent for people of color, women, and others who are underrepresented or under-appreciated overall in American society. But this hardly argues for a rejection of the study of art, for a retreat to ignorance. In fact, one could argue that this inequity alone justifies a serious effort to learn about the aesthetic dimension of life, simply because it reflects so well the position of various cultural groups in a society.

But curiously, there is a strong tendency even among Euro-Americans to reject learning about their own aesthetic traditions. There is a feeling that the art found in the museums and in the texts is of some other community than one's own, and that it is "shoved down the throats" of students by their professors. I know I experienced it as a younger man; I had to be dragged kicking and screaming to Picasso and Mozart by my professors too. In a sense, they really did represent a community foreign to me; one that I had little interest in and no claim to. But the fact is, so did all the other things I learned in college—the literature, the biology, the math, the philosophy, the political science. They were *all* part of a different world than the one I had inhabited until then: the world of the educated person. To incorporate that knowledge and to study those ideas would be to enter that community—and it would mean changing who I was.

Most of us like ourselves just fine the way we are, and I think the prospect of change in one's identity is a large part of the resistance to learning about the arts. It's more comfortable to hold on to one's own tastes and resist the new because in doing so we can remain our old familiar selves. In fact, this resistance to change tells us all by itself how important the arts are—they help us define and know ourselves. It's difficult to open up to new aesthetic tastes. In fact, we are more willing to explore new ideas about science or politics or ethics or even religion than we are to explore new aesthetic preferences, because they are in some ways more funda-mental to our identity.

But do we come to college to stay the way we are? Isn't this supposed to be a period of exploration and growth? I believe that college is meant to be a life-changing experience; that we are supposed to emerge from our education with a somewhat different identity than the one we entered with. Any less wouldn't be worth the expense. Frankly, I am a different person than the one I was when I entered college, and I don't regret it. Nor have I really had to give anything up; for example, I never did lose my taste for rock music of the 60's and 70's. I've simply gained new inter-ests that I didn't have then. In fact, "It's a bird, it's a plane, it's a Mozart" (Symphony No. 40) is a particular favorite.

Gary Witherspoon (b. 1943) is an anthropologist who studies Navajo art, language, religion, and culture. He is a professor in American Indian studies at the University of Washington in Seattle. In this excerpt from Language and Art in the Navajo Universe *(1977) Witherspoon describes art in the everyday lives of the Navajo as a way of living and generating expression of thought. Is art in this way an expression of external truths or internal truths? According to Witherspoon, how is art different in the lives of the Navajos from that of "Anglos?" In what way is sand painting a particularly telling illustration of how the Navajo view beauty and the function of art? In Navajo society certain of the forms of art are reserved for men or for women alone. How do the art forms of men and women differ in their functions and in their permanency?*

from Navajo Aesthetics

Gary Witherspoon

In the Western world, where mind has been separated from body, where man has been extracted from nature, where affect has been divorced from "fact," where the quest for and focus upon the manipulation and accumulation of things has led man to exploit rather than to respect and admire the earth and her web of life, it is not surprising that art would be divorced from the more practical affairs of business and government and the more serious matters of science, philosophy, and theology. In the Navajo world, however, art is not divorced from everyday life, for the creation of beauty and the incorporation of oneself in beauty represent the highest attainment and ultimate destiny of man. *Hózhó* expresses the Navajo concept of beauty or beautiful conditions. But beauty is not separated from good, from health, from happiness, or from harmony. Beauty—*hózhŏ*—is the combination of all these conditions. It is not an abstractable quality of things or a fragment of experience; it is the normal pattern of nature and the most desirable form of experience.

For the Navajo, beauty is not so much in the eye of the beholder as it is in the mind of its creator and in the creator's relationship to the created (that is, the transformed or the organized). The Navajo does not look for beauty; he generates it within himself and projects it onto the universe. The Navajo says *shit hózhó* "with me there is beauty," *shii' hózhó* "in me there is beauty," and *shaa hózhó* "from me beauty radiates." Beauty is not "out there" in things to be perceived by the perceptive and appreciative viewer; it is a creation of thought. The Navajo experience beauty primarily through expression and creation, not through perception and preservation. Beauty is not so much a perceptual experience as it is a conceptual one.

In the Western world beauty as a quality of things to be perceived is, in essence, static; that is, it is something to be observed and preserved. To the Navajo, however, beauty is an essential condition of man's life and is dynamic. It is not in things so much as it is in the dynamic relationships among things and between man and things. Man experiences beauty by creating it. For the Anglo observer of Navajo sandpaintings, it has always been a source of some bewilderment and frustration that the Navajo "destroy" these sandpaintings in less time than they take to create them. To avoid this overt destruction of beauty and to preserve its artistic value, the Anglo observer always want to take a photograph of the sandpaint-ing, but the Navajo sees no sense and some danger in that. To the Navajo the artistic or aesthetic value of the sandpainting is found in its creation, not in its preservation. Its ritual value is in its symbolic or representa-tional power and in its use as a vehicle of conception. Once it has served that purpose, it no longer has any ritual value.

Navajos take little interest in the display or preservation of their works of art, with the exception of silver and turquoise jewelry. They readily sell them to non-Indians who are looking for beauty in things. Traditionally, they put their works of art to practical use in their daily activities. Now it is more practical to sell them for money and buy stainless steel pots and other more durable but less artistic things. This practice offends the purist's view of aesthetics, but it is, in fact, not a depreciation of aesthetic value at all. It is simply based on the idea that beauty is a dynamic expe-rience in conception and expression, not a static quality of things to be perceived and preserved.

With regard to the two different views of art contrasted above, it is not surprising that Navajo society is one of artists (art creators) while Anglo society consists primarily of nonartists who view art (art consumers). The Navajo find it incomprehensible that we have more art critics than we have artists, and more art collectors than we have art creators. Nearly all Navajos are artists and spend a large part of their time in artistic creation. All Navajos are singers, and most Navajos have composed many songs. Traditionally, over 90 percent of all adult women wove rugs and today, despite limited opportunities to learn this art, a majority of Navajo women over thirty still weave. A large number of Navajo men are skilled at silver work and sandpainting. Some women still make pottery and beautifully designed baskets. Teachers in Navajo schools find that nearly all Navajo students take a special interest in and have an unusual profi-ciency in the graphic arts. Navajos are also very eloquent and often poetic in their use of language.

In white society it is the exceptional and abnormal person that becomes an artist. The artist is usually associated with marginality and noncon-formity with regard to the mainstream of society. From this marginal position the artist dedicates himself almost solely to his artistic creations. The nonartist among the Navajo is a rarity. Moreover, Navajo artists integrate their artistic endeavors into their other activities. Living is not a way of art for them, but art is a way of living.

Navajo artistic interests and talents are enhanced by, if not derived from, the emphasis on the creative nature of thought and the compulsive power of speech. Art is a nondiscursive form of expression, but it involves many of the same processes of symbolic transformation that are found in discursive symbolism. Professor A. D. Richie has noted that "the essential act of thought is symbolization" . . . , and art is as much symbolization as is speech. Art is a symbolic transformation of experience, and, as such, it invests and imbues experience—thus life—with beauty and aesthetic value and meaning.

Navajo culture is not just a food-gathering strategy; it is an artistic way of life. One is admonished to walk in beauty, speak in beauty, act in beauty, sing in beauty, and live in beauty. All things are to be made beautifully, and all activities are to be completed in beauty. The following daily prayer exemplifies the Navajo emphasis on beauty:

> With beauty before me, I walk
> With beauty behind me, I walk
> With beauty above me, I walk
> With beauty below me, I walk
> From the East beauty has been restored
> From the South beauty has been restored
> From the West beauty has been restored
> From the North beauty has been restored
> From the zenith in the sky beauty has been restored
> From the nadir of the earth beauty has been restored
> From all around me beauty has been restored.

The separation of mind and body—or, in the popular idiom, mind and heart—in Western metaphysics has led aesthetic analysis and interpretation into confusion as to what it is that the artist expresses in his work. Experience is divided into fragments which relate to the intellectual realm, the emotional realm, and the aesthetic realm. A major question, then, is whether a particular art work expresses an "idea," whether it expresses the emotions and feelings of the artist who created it, or whether it expresses nothing in the way of ideas or emotions and simply possesses significant and aesthetic form, a pure expression of beauty.

In the Navajo world, where mind and matter, thought and expression are inseparably connected, the aesthetic experience—the creation of beauty—is simultaneously intellectual, emotional, moral, aesthetic, and biological. Navajo life and culture are based on a unity of experience, and the goal of Navajo life—the creation, maintenance, and restoration of *hózhó*—expresses that unity of experience. *Hózhó* expresses the intellectual concept of order, the emotional state of happiness, the moral notion of good, the biological condition of health and well-being, and the aesthetic dimensions of balance, harmony, and beauty. In Navajo art we find all these concepts, states, and conditions expressed.

As the essence of the Navajo conception of life is movement or motion, and the experience of beauty is dynamic and flowing, characteristic themes found in Navajo art express this emphasis on movement and activity. . . .

A Navajo often counts his wealth in the songs he knows and especially in the songs he has created. A poor Navajo is one who has no songs, for songs enrich one's experiences and beautify one's activities. Songs accompany and enrich both ceremonial and nonceremonial activities. There are riding songs, walking songs, grinding songs, planting songs, growing songs, and harvesting songs. There are songs to greet the sun in the morning and songs to bid it farewell in the evening. There are songs for horses, for sheep, and for various other animal species. There are songs for blessing a hogan and songs for taking a sweat bath. In the past there were even songs for bidding visitors farewell. And, of course, there are songs of love and romance. But the most powerful songs are those that are essential parts of ceremonial and ritual activities. The former type is a means by which Navajos maintain *hózhó* in their daily life experiences, while the latter type constitutes a means by which Navajos restore *hózhó* when it has been disrupted.

Professor David McAllester, who has spent over twenty-five years studying Navajo music, says Navajo music is characterized by its vigor, its power, and its acrobatic style. It is intense, at times almost "excessive," compared to Pueblo music which is low, controlled, and rehearsed. Navajo music seems to match the cultural emphasis on energy, activity, and motion. There is hardly ever a "held" note, except at the end of a song. . . .

In analyzing the First Snake Song, Professor McAllester finds that one of its chief characteristics is repetition. Repetition is a motif found all through Navajo life and culture. It is associated with the concepts of renewal, regeneration, rejuvenation, revolution, and restoration. Repetition enhances the compulsive power of the song. The repetitive nature of many Navajo songs is adorned with and enlivened by various modes of variation. . . .

In the First Snake Song there is a significant alternation in the *kind* of melodic activity. This is found between level sections based entirely or largely on the tonic, and active sections characterized by rapid and pulsing movement. McAllester considers this to be the quality in Navajo "chanting" that makes the term a misnomer. . . .

The verses of the First Snake Song also exhibit the principle of alternation. Here are found alternations in colors, in sex, in directions, and in jewel symbols. This is a way of presenting pairs of related objects. . . .

McAllester notes that although the First Snake Song is strophic and framed, it is progressive in that the pitch gradually rises from one song to the next. He relates this progression in pitch to a progression in textually expressed ideas where the movement is from mature male to immature female, from animate snake to inanimate hoop, from "holding," "dangling," "lugging" to "trundling." . . . As noted earlier . . . maturity is often thought of as a static and thus male-linked condition, whereas immaturity is associated with activity, process, and growth and is female-linked in the Navajo metaphor. Since the animate snake is obviously active and the inanimate hoop is static, the progression here seems to go from static to active and from active to static. This is contrasted by the progression of "holding," "dangling," "lugging," and "trundling," which starts from the static "holding" and gets progressively more active. . . .

Where Navajo music, singing, and poetry are artistic endeavors common to both men and women, the other two major domains of Navajo aesthetics, weaving and sandpainting, are sexually bifurcated. Weaving is primarily an activity of women, and sandpainting is primarily an activity of men. Some Navajo men weave, but this associates them with the category of *nádlééhí*, "transvestite." Such a person, however, is usually held in high esteem and is not normally the object of ridicule or unkind behavior. Reichard notes that Left-Handed Singer or Newcomb was a man who wove. She states that he was highly respected, and a person of superior intelligence combined with extreme gentleness and remarkable independence. As an accomplished singer or "medicine man," he wove primarily sandpainting tapestries. . . . Sandpainting is exclusively a male activity. Even female singers do not do sandpainting, although they may supervise the creation of a sandpainting.

It is relevant to note that the composition and design of Navajo sandpaintings are static; that is, the designs are rigidly established and must be created without significant change or alteration if they are to be an effective part of the particular ritual for which they are used. In contrast, a weaver seldom if ever repeats a design. Each rug woven is designed anew, so designs are always changing, flowing and moving. Thus the production of design in sandpainting and weaving seems to be appropriately associated with the generally static nature of male-linked endeavors and the dynamic nature of female-linked endeavors.

Before mass-produced retail goods became available to the Navajo, they had to produce their own blankets, garments, and moccasins. Although buckskin and other skins provided the raw materials to satisfy many of these needs, wool from sheep provided the major source of material for clothing and blankets. However, instead of just producing clothing and blankets to satisfy the pragmatic needs of warmth and protection from the elements, Navajo women turned the production of clothing and blankets into an artistic endeavor. Today, Navajo women weave rugs primarily for the use of non-Indians. Although they sell these rugs for cash, it has been estimated that the average weaver gets less than a quarter an hour for her work. Obviously, then, the motivation to weave is aesthetic as well as economic—probably even primarily aesthetic. Weaving is an effort in creative transformation. Navajo women transform the wool on the back of sheep into beautifully designed and delicately woven rugs. This is done through the processes of shearing, cleaning, dyeing, carding, spinning, and weaving. Additional color is added through vegetal dyes.

Navajo women develop and create designs in their minds, and then project them onto the world of external reality through the art of weaving. The intricate and often complex patterns created by Navajo weavers are generated in the mind and kept there through the whole process from dyeing through weaving. She must know exactly how much dye to use or exactly what amounts of black and white wool to mix in order to get the very exact color combinations and contrasts she has in her mind. . . .

. . . A woven rug is a product of the mind and the body. The inner form of the rug is in the mind; the outer form of the rug is projected onto the loom. . . .

In the patterns found on Navajo rugs, movement and activity are expressed by diagonal and zigzag lines (also associated with lightning), by the active colors of yellow (brown), blue (green), and red (pink), by appendages to various "static" centers, and by diamond shapes. In contrast, a static condition is expressed by straight lines and horizontal and vertical stripes, by squares and rectangles, and by the static colors of white, black, and grey. Motion goes in one of two directions: linear, continuative, incomplete motion, or circular, repetitious, complete, cyclical motion. In Navajo language the former is found in the important and extensively used imperfective and progressive modes and in the continuative aspect of Navajo verbs, while the latter is found in iterative and usitive modes and in the repetitive aspect of Navajo verbs. In addition linear and continuative motion is expressed by the verbal prefix *hi* which renders the idea of succession, while circular and repetitious actions and movements are expressed by the verbal prefixes *náá* and *ná* which express the ideas of repetition, revolution, and restoration.

In the language of Navajo weaving, linear, continuative, and incomplete motion is expressed by the successive alternation of static and active symbols—colors, lines, and designs. Linear movement thus follows the pattern or series of static-active-static-active. Circular and cyclical movement is expressed by the sequence already noted: static-active-active-static. This pattern is found in the sequence of color, direction, and growth, and in the daily and annual path of the sun. It is sunwise motion. There is also an opposite sequence, usually associated with witchcraft and its cure, but also associated with protection and with an emphasis on activity, that goes from active to static and static to active.

The former type of cyclical movement is mainly found in Navajo ritual where control and normality are emphasized, whereas the latter type of cyclical movement is often found in Navajo weaving and other art forms where creativity and activity are emphasized. . . .

Navajo sandpainting is a male-linked art form that accompanies most major Navajo ceremonials. The designs are established parts of the ritual and must not be significantly altered if the ritual is to be effective. These designs are made on the earthen floor of the hogan. The surface upon which the painting is made is cleaned and smoothed. The designs vary from a few inches to more than twenty feet in diameter, with most paintings averaging from three to six feet in diameter. The painting is done by letting dry pigments trickle through the thumb and flexed index finger. The dry pigments are made primarily from red, yellow, and white sandstone and various mixtures of these colors, but pigments made from colored corn meal, plant pollens, crushed flower petals, and charcoal are also used.

The sandpaintings are made by several men under the direction of the chanter or medicine man. Just as Reichard learned to weave, on many occasions I have enjoyed the opportunity to help create a sandpainting.

The sandpaintings depict the *Diyin Dine'é* and other sacred entities. They recall significant episodes of mythical drama. The mythical dramas revolve around a cultural hero's unfortunate plight and diseased condition, and his or her ultimate cure through identification with, and sometimes compulsive control of, a deity or deities. The disease is caused by some sort of disruption in the proper and normal order of things and is cured by a restoration of the proper order. The patient in his or her plight is identified with the cultural hero who contracted a similar disease or plight in the same way the patient did. In the curing ritual the patient follows in the footsteps of the hero of the myth, sings the songs he or she sang, prays the prayers he or she prayed, and ultimately acquires and exerts the power to restore health and order to his or her self and world that the hero acquired and exerted.

The myth, retold in the songs and prayers of the ritual, places the patient's illness in a cultural context where it can be understood and eventually cured. From the myth the patient learns that his or her plight and illness is not new, and that both its cause and treatment are known. To be cured, all the patient has to do is to repeat what has been done before. It has to be done sincerely, however, and this sincerity is expressed in concentration and dedication. The sandpainting depicts the desired order of things, and places the patient in this beautiful and ordered world. The patient thus becomes completely identified with the powerful and curing agents of the universe. The patient undresses to the extent modesty permits (men to a G-string and women to a skirt) and sits on the painting. Where appropriate and possible the patient's body parts—feet, knees, legs, etc.—are placed on the corresponding body parts of the deity with whom the patient is identified. In addition, the medicine man applies sand from the body parts of the depicted deity to corresponding body parts of the patient's body. Spectators and family members may also apply the sand to corresponding parts of their bodies as well. This is done for sanctification, blessing, and protection.

After the sandpainting has fulfilled its aesthetic and ritual purpose, the sand is carefully collected and deposited at some out-of-the-way place to the north. The symbolic representation of various sacred beings and things is considered to be effective in attracting them to the ceremonial hogan and thus enabling the patient to absorb their curative power.

Notwithstanding the important ritual functions of the sandpaintings, they also have great aesthetic appeal to Navajos. The painters take a special interest and pride in the quality of their work, and many men travel from ceremony to ceremony mainly to participate in the art forms—singing, poetry, drama, and painting—of the ritual. The ceremonies are really a symphony of the arts and they have great aesthetic appeal to Navajo participants and spectators. Where else can one go to and participate in a symphony of the arts while simultaneously being physically, morally, and intellectually sanctified and blessed?

The aesthetic appeal of the forms and designs of sandpaintings is also demonstrated in their extensive use in other Navajo art forms. This is particularly true in weaving where many designs and forms are taken from sandpaintings. These designs, however, also appear in Navajo silver work and in the oil paintings and drawings of contemporary Navajo artists. Such replications of these sacred designs and forms are potentially dangerous to their creators, and many purists among the Navajos deplore this secularization and profanation of sacred forms and symbols. Nevertheless, the aesthetic appeal of these designs and forms seems to have, in many cases, overridden the fear of the dangers inherent in the secular use of sacred forms. As elsewhere in Navajo culture, movement, repetition, balance and harmony, and controlled or restrained emotion and force are dominant themes in Navajo sandpaintings. . . .

Navajo art thus expresses Navajo experiences, and Navajo experiences are mediated by the concepts of and orientations to the world found in Navajo language and culture. All experiences are directed toward the ideals of *hózhó*, and *hózhó* is the intellectual, moral, biological, emotional, and aesthetic experience of bèauty. A Navajo experiences beauty most poignantly in creating it and in expressing it, not in observing it or preserving it. The experience of beauty is dynamic; it flows to one and from one; it is found not in things, but in relationships among things. Beauty is not to be preserved but to be continually renewed in oneself and expressed in one's daily life and activities. To contribute to and be a part of this universal *hózhó* is both man's special blessing and his ultimate destiny.

Sandra Marie Schneiders, IHM (Immaculate Heart of Mary), is professor of New Testament studies and Christian spirituality at the Jesuit School of Theology at Berkeley. She is a lecturer on women and religious life and the author of several books. Although this essay is over twenty years old, the ideas expressed may be new to you. Many of us in our spiritual life actually get very little exposure to a theological approach to questions of faith. This selection from Women and the Word *(1986) illustrates what it means to address religious doctrine theologically and also how what we "know," even in a faith tradition, is influenced by culture. It makes us ponder, how is the truth of faith derived? Do you find Schneiders' argument persuasive? Why or why not?*

from Women and the Word
The Gender of God in the New Testament and the Spirituality of Women

Sandra Marie Schneiders

I. The Question about the Gender of God

A. The Modernity of the Question

. . . At the outset of this discussion it is important to be aware that the question of the gender of God is a thoroughly modern issue. No matter how entrenched in the imagination of the average Christian the image of a male God might be, theological tradition has never assigned sex to God.[1] St. Gregory of Nazianzus well represented the tradition when he affirmed that the terms "Father" and "Son" as applied to the persons of the Trinity were not names of natures or essences but of relations[2] and even in this case the terms are used metaphorically. In other words, God is neither a father nor a son but the first person of the Trinity is related to the second person as origin is related to that which is originated. Because the ancients believed that God was indeed personal, and because their defective biology ascribed all agency in procreation or personal originating activity to the male partner, their choice of "father" for the originating person of the Trinity was logical enough. And since they wished to affirm the absolute likeness and equality of the one originated to the divine principle they called the second person the "son." They were, however, quite aware of the metaphorical nature of their language and never intended to impute actual sexuality to the God whom Scripture affirms is pure Spirit (cf. Jn 4:24).

Second, theological tradition has virtually always maintained that the maleness of Jesus is theologically, christologically, soteriologically, and sacramentally irrelevant.[3] It has been suggested, not without reason, that the attempt of the Vatican's Congregation for the Doctrine of the Faith in its "Declaration on the Question of the Admission of Women to the Ministerial Priesthood" (*Inter Insignores*)[4] to assign theological significance to the sex of Jesus by maintaining that women Christians, because they are female, do not resemble Christ is not only non-traditional but also at least theologically confused if not strictly heretical.[5] As patristics scholar R. A. Norris states,

> The argument [against the ordination of women on the grounds that male sex is required for likeness to Christ] is virtually unprecedented. It does not in fact state any of the traditional grounds on which ordination to the presbyterate or episcopate has been denied to women. To accept this argument and its practical consequences, therefore, is not to maintain tradition but to alter it by altering its meaning.[6]

More important, however, than its non-traditionality is the threat it raises to a central theological affirmation about the incarnation, namely, that as Gregory of Nazianzus and numerous other Fathers of the Church have maintained, "*Tò gàr apróslepton atherápeuton*," i.e., "What is not assumed is not redeemed."[7] The Vatican argument attempts to make the maleness of Jesus a necessary precondition to his being who he is, God-with-us, and doing what he does, redeeming us by his paschal mystery. To do so, as Norris says, "is to qualify or deny the universality of his redemption."[8]

In short, the theological tradition of the Church never assigned sex to God and almost never (until the theologically faulty 1977 document) assigned any theological significance to the sex of Jesus. Why, then, is the gender of God such a troubling question for contemporary Christians, especially for women whose consciousness has been raised by the women's movement in our time?

B. The Dilemma for Women

As women have become aware of their inferior status and actual oppression in family, society, and Church, they have also become aware that the gender of God, God's presumed masculinity, has functioned as the ultimate religious legitimation of the unjust social structures which victimize women. First, the maleness of Jesus has been used in Christian cultures as a support from divine revelation for the age-old claim that maleness is normative for humanity and that men are superior to women. Most western languages themselves, in which the generic human is always masculine, testify incessantly to the misconception that humanity is originally and normatively male and that women are a derivative and subordinate, if not actually misbegotten, version of the essentially male species. Male privilege, based on this erroneous assumption of male superiority, is firmly entrenched in virtually every sector of human life.

Second the "fatherhood" of God has been used to justify patriarchy or father-rule, the social system which sacralizes male domination and legitimates virtually all forms of oppression of the weak by the strong. We will return to the topic of patriarchy shortly.

Third, the masculinity of God and of Jesus has been used, in the practical sphere, to deny the likeness of women to God and to Christ and to exclude them from full participation in the life of the Church. Whether this spiritual degradation takes the relatively mild form of excluding little girls from serving at the altar or the more serious forms of exclusion of women from decision-making positions in the Church and enforcement of their sacramental dependence on men, it has a destructive effect on women's spiritual self-image and perverts their relationships with male Christians and with God.

The masculinity of God, in other words, is not primarily an issue in speculative theology. It can easily be established that the God of Judaeo-Christian revelation and Christian theological tradition is not male and that Jesus' maleness is theologically irrelevant. This helps very little, however, because the real problem is not in the area of systematic theology but in the area of religious experience or spirituality.[9] How women experience themselves in relation to God, Christ, and Church is profoundly affected by the imputed masculinity of God which is operative in the imaginations of both male and female believers.

Once their consciousness is raised, women Christians can find themselves impaled on the horns of a dilemma. Either they can continue as Christians, accepting the spiritual consequences of their lack of resemblance to God and Christ and their consequent inferiority to and spiritual dependence on men in the Church (the position advocated by the Vatican Declaration despite its protestations to the contrary), or they can abandon Christianity as a hopelessly patriarchal religion and seek their spiritual home in a religious tradition in which women and women's experience are central and valued.[10] Unless educated and aware women can find a creative and liberating understanding of God and of Jesus, one which does not glorify masculinity at the expense of femininity and does not justify the oppression of women by men, they have no future in institutional Christianity.

II. Preliminary Clarifications

Before undertaking an exploration of the problem of God's "masculinity" and women's spirituality two clarifications are necessary. First, we must distinguish clearly between sex and gender because, as we will see, it is the *gender* of God and the *sex* of Jesus which are the real problems. Second, we have to distinguish between patriarchy (and paternalism) on the one hand and paternity or fatherhood on the other because it is only the former which is problematic. Fatherhood as such, provided that it is not used exclusively, is one appropriate metaphor for God.

A. Sex and Gender

Sex refers to biological identity, the possession of male or female sexual organs and the proportionate activity of male or female hormones which grounds the distinctive roles of men and women in the reproductive process. Gender, however, refers to the experience of self and others in terms of sexual identity. Although sex and gender normally coincide in humans, i.e., females experience themselves and are experienced by others as feminine and males as masculine, this is not always the case, nor is the experience always totally dichotomous. Thus, someone who is biologically a male might experience himself as feminine and might be experienced that way by others. And persons are sometimes experienced as both feminine and masculine, or androgynous. The point is that while sex is biologically determined by observation of empirically available data, gender refers to the way one experiences oneself or others.[11]

God, as we have said, is neither male nor female, i.e., God does not have a body and therefore does not have sex. But because all human persons have gender and we experience God as personal we tend to experience God anthropomorphically as either masculine or feminine or both, i.e., as male and female successively, or as androgynous. Our God-image, as we will explain below, is a function of the imagination, and the Christian religious imagination is deeply influenced by the belief in the personal nature of God, by the overwhelmingly male God-language in the Bible, and by the incarnation of God in the concrete humanity of a male human being, Jesus. Until very recently many if not most Christians, including those who were theologically convinced that God is Spirit, experienced God as almost exclusively masculine. Theologically well-informed people of both sexes have insisted vehemently on the maintenance of exclusively male language for God in public prayer.[12] To a large extent this insistence has more to do with maintaining male dominant power arrangements in family, society, and Church than with theological issues. But for many people the problem is genuinely religious. Their problem is a paralysis of the religious imagination. To imagine God or speak to God as feminine does not simply change the God image for these people; it destroys it.

If God is pure spirit, the same cannot be said about Jesus who was actually a male. However, although biologically male and masculine in gender,

Jesus has also been experienced as distinctly feminine in many ways. Sentimental art provides a perverted testimony to this fact, but the motherhood of Jesus and of Christ is a consistent theme in medieval mystical literature. Bernard of Clairvaux, Julian of Norwich, Anselm of Canterbury, Gertrude of Helfta, Mechtild of Hackeborn, and Mechtild of Magdeburg are among the spiritual writers whose works are explored by medieval scholar Caroline Walker Bynum in her 1982 volume, *Jesus as Mother*.[13] The Gospel portrays Jesus as non-aggressive, non-competitive, meek and humble of heart, a nurturer of the weak, and a friend of the outcast. He manifested and preached a spirituality that was characterized by stereotypically feminine rather than masculine virtues. This femininity of Jesus has often enough proven difficult for men to assimilate, but it has always supported the spirituality of women. For women, the problem is not the gender of Jesus, his masculinity which is so inclusively feminine, but his sex. It is the biological fact that Jesus, by being a man rather than a woman, is irreducibly and irrevocably different from women that seems to exclude women from the fullness of identity with him. Furthermore, the maleness of Jesus cannot help but intensify the experience of God as masculine and of maleness as normative, i.e., as the best and fullest way to be human.

B. Patriarchy and Paternity

A second distinction important for our purposes is that between paternity on the one hand and patriarchy/paternalism on the other. Patriarchy is a social system based on the *patria potestas*, i.e., the absolute and unaccountable power over wives and concubines, children, servants, slaves, animals and real property enjoyed by the *paterfamilias*, i.e., the father who is head of the family, tribe, or clan. To the father of the family belonged, as property, all members of the extended household and all goods. In classical Greek and Roman societies this authority of ownership extended even to the power of life and death. Children, especially girls, were often deemed valueless to the father and left to die. Insubordinate wives or slaves could be sold or killed.[14] While sons, when they became adults, were emancipated and became patriarchs in their own right, daughters were passed, with or without their consent, from the control of the father to that of a husband,[15] i.e., from one patriarch to another.

In the patriarchal system authority and power were strictly coterminous and belonged totally and exclusively to the head of the household unless he delegated it to another. The authority and power of the *paterfamilias* were considered as divinely established, and thus the patriarchal system was unalterable and rebellion against the father was rebellion against God. Furthermore, even though in the absence of a man patriarchal power might sometimes be exercised by a woman, e.g., by a mother or a queen, and unemancipated males, e.g., minor sons and slaves, were as subject to the father's dominion as were females in the family, there is a vital connection in the patriarchal system among power, authority, property, and maleness. Conversely, powerlessness, exclusion from authority, dependence, and femaleness are closely linked. And the entire system is understood as the product and expression of the will of God.

For two reasons patriarchy is not just one social system among others. First, patriarchy is the basic principle of all major relational systems in the western world. As the former president of the World Council of Churches, Dr. W. A. Visser't Hooft, expressed it:

> . . . the patriarchal spirit and the doctrine upon which it is based have had an astonishingly wide influence, penetrating into many different spheres of life. Indeed, it has not been merely one of the many facets of society, but has rather formed its general pattern. . . . [Thus] emancipation [from patriarchy] concerns not only developments in family life, but also those in the state, the church and even in international relations.[16]

Visser't Hooft, like Rosemary Ruether, has pointed out that patriarchy is the basic principle underlying not only the subordination of women to men, but of one race to another, of colonies to master nations, of children to adults, of nations to divine right monarchs, of believers to clergy. In other words, patriarchy is the nerve of racism, ageism, classism, colonialism, and clericalism well as of sexism.[17] Patriarchy is fundamentally a masculine power in which all relationships are understood in terms of superiority and inferiority and social cohesion is assured by the exercise of dominative power.

The second reason why patriarchy is not just one system among others is that patriarchy is essentially hierarchy, i.e., the power and authority exercised over subordinates is believed to derive from the will of God and is exercised in the name of God. The patriarchal structure of the family was understood as divinely established for the good of all. When this structure was extended to other situations they were seen as quasi-families in which there is one adult and all others are minors. The feudal lord, the abbot in his monastery, the divine right monarch, the priest in his parish, the white European in the colonies, the husband in relation to his wife, the slave-holder with his "darkies," the Pope, were all father-figures caring for the "children" over which God had placed them. The difference, of course, between these extensions of patriarchy and its original locus, the family, is that these "children" are adults and, unlike real children, they are expected never to grow up. Thus, in a patriarchal system most people will remain subordinates all their lives and they cannot protest against this arrangement without challenging God "himself" who is the first patriarch and the legitimator of all others.

While not all men are patriarchs, women never are. Where patriarchy reigns women are subject to men. The man may be father, husband, slave-holder, priest, or Pope but the woman is always a minor. It is not surprising, then, that women, once they have analyzed the situation, repudiate patriarchy as the universal social structure and especially its claims to divine legitimacy. A patriarchal God, to feminist women, is at least a legitimator of women's victimization by men if not "himself" the very personification of the oppression of women.

However, it is important to distinguish sharply between patriarchy (including its more benign expression as paternalism) on the one hand, and paternity or fatherhood on the other. The association of fatherhood with patriarchy is so long-standing and widespread that the equation of the two is quite understandable and very often perfectly accurate. However, it is possible for a man to be a father to his minor children without assuming absolute power over them and to remain a father in relation to adult children whose autonomy and equality with himself he fully accepts. Likewise, it is possible for God to be experienced as paternal without being experienced as a patriarch. And a father-God who is not experienced as a patriarch can equally well be experienced as a mother-God without loss of status.

III. Imagination and Spirituality

In what has been said so far I have attempted to locate with some accuracy the problem of the gender of God. The problem is not the sex of God (which does not exist) but our experience of God as masculine; and it is not the masculinity of Jesus (who is anything but a glorification of machismo) but his male sex. However, the reason Jesus' male sex is a problem is because it is seen as a revelatory confirmation of the masculinity of God and therefore of the divinity of maleness. Jesus, the man, is the incarnation of the Son of the Father. Consequently, our primary concern must be with the experienced masculinity of God.

• • •

The tenacity of the patriarchal God-image is such that many feminists have decided that the only course open to women whose self-image has been healed of gender inferiority and whose world-image has been healed of hierarchy in general and patriarchy in particular is to abandon the Christian God altogether. I would like to suggest that just as the self and world images can be healed, so can the God-image. It cannot be healed, however, by rational intervention alone. Repeating the theological truth that God is Spirit may correct our ideas but a healthy spirituality requires a healing of the imagination which will allow us to think not only differently about God but to experience God differently. The imagination is accessible not primarily to abstract ideas but to language, images, interpersonal experience, symbolism, art—all the integrated approaches which appeal simultaneously to intellect, will, and feeling. What must be undertaken is a therapy of the religious imagination, first in regard to God and then in regard to our relationship with Jesus Christ.

• • •

IV. The "Maleness" of God in the Old Testament

• • •

B. Old Testament Metaphors for God[18]

In the Old Testament there are numerous metaphors for God derived from human relationships. The vast majority, although not all, of the vehicles in these metaphors either are necessarily male, e.g., father or husband, or denote roles or activities which were virtually exclusively exercised by males in Israelite society. In the New Testament Jesus frequently used one of these metaphors, namely, father, at least in speaking to God and probably also in speaking about God. Fairly early in Christian history the father metaphor was literalized in religious imagination. The literalized metaphor, it must be remembered, no longer carries its "is not" but simply transfers to the referent all the characteristics of the vehicle. Thus, God the "father" came to be imagined as literally male. All the male metaphors for God in the Old Testament then tended to be drawn into this one metaphor. Since many of the Old Testament God-metaphors such as warlord and king were patriarchal the metaphorical fatherhood of God was not only literalized but patriarchalized. As both theologian Sallie McFague and biblical scholar Johanna Bos have pointed out, the literalized father metaphor for God has not only died but, in its ascription of maleness to God, it has become actually idolatrous.[19] We have created a false god and substituted "him" for the true God of Judaeo-Christian revelation.

It is highly enlightening, then, to examine the father metaphor as it actually occurs in the Old Testament. The most striking characteristic of this metaphor is how seldom it occurs. God is actually referred to as father only twelve times in the Hebrew Scriptures and never in direct address. Father is not a name for God but "a pointer to the free presence of God, which cannot be encapsulated in or manipulated by names."[20] Five of the references to God as father concern the special relation of God to the king. (2 Sam 7:14; 1 Chr 17:13; Ps 89:26; 1 Chr 22: 10; 28:6) and thus do not apply to the ordinary person. The other seven references (Ps 103:13; Dt 32:6, 18; Jer 3:4–5; 31:9; Is 63:16; Mal 1:6) all refer to God in the context of Israel's sin, repentance, and restoration and God's endless forgiveness.[21] The father metaphor in the Old Testament is nowhere used to present God as a patriarch dominating the people or exercising coercive power over them. On the contrary, the father metaphor is evoked precisely to describe the compassionate love of God who is like a parent spurned by ungrateful children but who is endless in patience and loving-kindness toward a rebellious people. The God who is presented as father in the Old Testament is like the father in the New Testament parable of the prodigal son, a paternal rather than patriarchal figure who is in no way a model for or a legitimation of patriarchy.

A second important point about the parental metaphor in the Old Testament is that it is not exclusively masculine. When Israel is referred to as a child the implied parent is sometimes masculine as in Deuteronomy 1:31 where Israel is reminded that "God bore you as a man bears his son." But at other times it is feminine as in Numbers 11:12 where the exasperated Moses demands of God, "Did I conceive all this people? Did I bring them forth, that thou should say to me, 'Carry them in thy bosom . . . ?'" clearly implying that God is the true mother of this people. At other times the metaphor is both masculine and feminine as in Hosea 11: 1–4:

> When Israel was a child, I loved him, and out of Egypt I called my son. The more I called them the more they went from me; they kept sacrificing to Baals, and burning incense to idols. Yet it was I who taught Ephraim to walk, I took them up in my arms; but they did not know that I healed them. I led them with cords of compassion, with the bands of love, and I became to them as one who eases the yoke on their jaws, and I bent down to them and fed them.

Thus, it is to be noted that, while they are not as frequent as even the infrequent paternal metaphors, there are clear maternal metaphors for God in the Old Testament as well as a pervasive maternal climate evoked by imagery based on the womb. In Deuteronomy 32:18 God clearly refers to herself, in feminine language, as "the God who gave you birth." In Isaiah 49:15 Israel is assured that God cherishes her people with a mother's love. In Isaiah 66:13 God says to Israel, "As one whom his mother comforts so will I comfort you." In Psalm 131:2 the psalmist says of reliance on God, "I have calmed and quieted my soul, like a child quieted at its mother's breast." As Phyllis Trible has pointed out[22] the typical Old Testament word for the compassion of God seems to be drawn from *rehem* the Hebrew word for womb, suggesting that God's tenderness is that of a mother for the child to whom she has given birth (cf. Is 63:15; Ex 34:6).[23] In Isaiah 42:14 God compares the divine anguish to that of a woman in the pangs of childbirth.[24]

In sum, an examination of the Old Testament father metaphor reveals that it was by no means a common, much less the preferred or only, metaphor for God, that it was never used to portray God as a patriarch in relation to the people, and that it is complemented by maternal imagery and metaphors which assure us that in no sense was the father metaphor meant to suggest that God is male[25] or that the divine parenthood is exclusively paternal.

Besides the father metaphor which, because of Jesus' use of it, exerted a powerful influence on the Christian imagination, there is one other Old Testament male metaphor for God which has had a major impact on the Christian God-image, namely, the spousal metaphor. Like the paternal metaphor which has been distorted into an exclusive and literalized support for male supremacy and patriarchy, the spousal metaphor has also exercised a perverse influence on the Christian imagination as a degradation of feminine sexuality and a justification of patriarchal marriage.

In some of the prophets, especially Jeremiah and Hosea, the relationship between God and Israel is depicted as marital union. God is the husband and Israel the wife in a marriage founded on love rather than on patriarchal authority and power. The extended metaphor is used, however, to describe the unfaithfulness of Israel to its faithful God. Israel, the wife, is a harlot. As feminist scholars have rightly pointed out, in this metaphor female sexuality is objectified and demonized. The male is assimilated to God and the female to sinful humanity.[26]

However, it must be realized that in the patriarchal culture of ancient Israel a husband could not really sin against his wife since he could do to her with impunity what he willed.[27] Marital fidelity was never absolutely required of men whereas a woman's infidelity was considered an offense against her husband's property rights. In such a culture, therefore, this metaphor could not have been structured in any other way. To make the point that God took the free initiative in choosing Israel, that God entered into a relationship of intimate love with Israel, and that Israel was unfaithful to that covenant, God had to be imaged as the husband who alone could act this way. However, in the husband role God acts not as a patriarch would have acted but as a wife would have acted. A husband who had been betrayed by his wife would at least have divorced her if he had not had her executed. A wife who had been betrayed would be expected, nevertheless, to be faithful and loving. God, in the marital metaphor, is a faithful lover who continually seeks reconciliation through the offer of forgiveness. In other words, the patriarchy of the metaphor is assumed because of the culture, but the message of the metaphor subverts patriarchy.

•   •   •

This brief exploration of the Old Testament language about God and the way this language has been used suggests several conclusions. God is not presented in the Old Testament in exclusively male terms. Even the two necessarily male metaphors, father and husband, are balanced by maternal imagery and the presentation of marital love as a relation of mutuality between equals. It is true that male imagery for God predominates, but this should serve to draw our attention to the unexpected feminine imagery which is perhaps more revelatory precisely because it cannot be adequately explained by the culture. In any case, any literalizing of God metaphors results not only in an impoverishment and distortion of the religious imagination but in a blasphemous assimilation of God to human categories and an idolatrous divinizing of human maleness.

Notes

[1] See Elizabeth A. Johnson, "The Incomprehensibility of God and the Image of God Male and Female," *Theological Studies* 45 (1984) 441–465.

[2] Gregory of Nazianzus, "The Third Theological Oration—on the Son," *Christology of the Later Fathers*, Vol. III, ed. E. R. Hardy (Philadelphia: Westminster, 1954), p. 171. Migne, *Patrologia Graeca* 36:93–96.

[3] The argument that priests had to be male to represent Christ is found in Bonaventure. See J. Rézette, "Le sacerdoce et la femme chez Saint Bonaventure," *Antonianum* 51 (1976) 520–527.

[4] *Acta Apostolicae Sedis* 69 (1977) 98–116; E. T. *Women Priests: A Catholic Commentary on the Vatican Declaration*, ed. L. and A. Swidler (New York: Paulist, 1977), pp. 37–49.

[5] See the excellent article by R. A. Norris, Jr., "The Ordination of Women and the 'Maleness' of Christ," *Supplementary Series of the Anglican Theological Review* 6 (June 1976) 69–80.

[6] Norris, "The Ordination of Women," p. 70.

[7] Gregory of Nazianzus, "Epistle 101," Hardy, *Christology*, p. 218. Migne, *P. G.* 37: 181.

[8] Norris, "The Ordination of Women," p. 74.

[9] See Gail R. Schmidt, "De Divinis Nominibus: The Gender of God," *Worship* 56 (1982) 117–131, for a discussion of how male God language affects liturgical experience.

[10] See, for example, the article by Carol P. Christ, "Why Women Need the Goddess: Phenomenological, Psychological, and Political Reflections," in *Womanspirit Rising: A Feminist Reader in Religion*, ed. C. P. Christ and J. Plaskow (San Francisco: Harper and Row, 1979), 273–287.

[11] Cf. Suzanne J. Kessler and Wendy McKenna, *Gender: An Ethnomethodological Approach* (Chicago: University of Chicago, 1985).

[12] On this subject, see Mary Collins, "Naming God in Public Prayer," *Worship* 59 (1985) 291–304.

[13] Caroline W. Bynum, *Jesus as Mother* (Berkeley: University of California, 1982).

[14] See R. Hamerton-Kelly, *God the Father: Theology and Patriarchy in the Teaching of Jesus* (Philadelphia: Fortress, 1979), pp. 55–60, for a good description of patriarchy in the Judaism of Jesus' time as well as in the Greco-Roman world of first century Christianity.

[15] See W. A. Visser't Hooft, *The Fatherhood of God in an Age of Emancipation* (Geneva: World Council of Churches, 1982), esp. chapters one to three, for a fuller description of this social system.

[16] Visser't Hooft, *Fatherhood*, p. 2.

[17] See Rosemary Ruether, "Feminists Seek Structural Change," *National Catholic Reporter* 20 (April 13, 1984) 4–6.

[18] I am indebted to my colleague, Dr. John Endres, and to Dr. Alice Laffey of Holy Cross College, Worcester, Massachusetts for their help on the Old Testament section of this paper.

[19] Cf. McFague, *Metaphorical Theology*, pp. 145–192; Bos, "When You Pray," p. 12.

[20] Bos, "When You Pray," p. 12.

[21] Cf. Diane Tennis, *Is God the Only Reliable Father?* (Philadelphia: Westminster, 1985), esp. pp. 82–83.

[22] See Phyllis Trible, *God and the Rhetoric of Sexuality* (Philadelphia: Fortress, 1978), pp. 34–56, and "Feminist Hermeneutics and Biblical Studies," *The Christian Century* 99 (Feb. 3–10, 1982)116–118.

[23] Mayer I. Gruber, in "The Motherhood of God in Second Isaiah," *Revue Biblique* 90 (1983) 351–359, challenges Trible's interpretation.

[24] It is interesting that John Paul II in his encyclical *Dives in Misericordia* (Nov. 13, 1980) has a long footnote (#52) in which he explores the feminine significance of *rahamim*.

[25] Cf. Bos, "When You Pray," p. 12.

[26] Cf. T. Drorah Setel, "Prophets and Pornography: Female Sexual Imagery in Hosea," *Feminist Interpretation of the Bible*, ed. Letty M. Russell (Philadelphia: Westminster, 1985) 86–95.

[27] See Phyllis Trible, *Texts of Terror: Literary Feminist Readings of Biblical Narratives* (Philadelphia: Fortress, 1984) for evidences of the male attitude toward women and their rights.

Harold Kushner (b. 1935) is a Jewish rabbi and author of several inspirational books, including the bestsellers When Bad Things Happen to Good People *(1981) and* Living a Life that Matters: Resolving the Conflict Between Conscience and Success *(2001). Again, we consider a theological approach to truth, but in this case about why bad things happen to good people and in doing so the nature of God. One aspect of a liberal arts education is that it challenges you to reconsider beliefs you hold out of habit. How does Kushner's view of the nature of God match your own? Does his analysis change what you think?*

from When Bad Things Happen to Good People

Harold Kushner

Why Do the Righteous Suffer?

There is only one question which really matters: why do bad things happen to good people? All other theological conversation is intellectually diverting; somewhat like doing the crossword puzzle in the Sunday paper and feeling very satisfied when you have made the words fit; but ultimately without the capacity to reach people where they really care. Virtually every meaningful conversation I have ever had with people on the subject of God and religion has either started with this question, or gotten there before long. Not only the troubled man or woman who has just come from a discouraging diagnosis at the doctor's office, but the college student who tells me that he has decided there is no God, or the total stranger who comes up to me at a party just when I am ready to ask the hostess for my coat, and says, "I hear you're a rabbi; how can you believe that . . ."—they all have one thing in common. They are all troubled by the unfair distribution of suffering in the world.

The misfortunes of good people are not only a problem to the people who suffer and to their families. They are a problem to everyone who wants to believe in a just and fair and livable world. They inevitably raise questions about the goodness, the kindness, even the existence of God . . .

One of the ways in which people have tried to make sense of the world's suffering in every generation has been by assumption that we deserve what we get, that somehow our misfortunes come as punishment for our sins:

> Tell the righteous it shall be well with them, for they shall eat the fruit of their deeds. Woe to the wicked, it shall be ill with him, for what his hands have done shall be done to him. (Isaiah 3:10–11)

But Er, Judah's first born, was wicked in the sight of the Lord, and the Lord slew him. (Genesis 38:7)

No ills befall the righteous, but the wicked are filled with trouble. (Proverbs 12:21)

Consider, what innocent ever perished, or where have the righteous been destroyed? (Job 14:7)

This is an attitude we will meet later in the book when we discuss the whole question of guilt. It is tempting at one level to believe that bad things happen to people (especially other people) because God is a righteous judge who gives them exactly what they deserve. By believing that, we keep the world orderly and understandable. We give people the best possible reason for being good and for avoiding sin. And by believing that, we can maintain an image of God as all-loving, all-powerful and totally in control. Given the reality of human nature, given the fact that none of us is perfect and that each of us can, without too much difficulty, think of things he has done which he should not have done, we can always find grounds for justifying what happens to us. But how comforting, how religiously adequate, is such an answer?

The couple whom I tried to comfort, the parents who had lost their only child at age nineteen with no warning, were not profoundly religious people. They were not active in the synagogue; they had not even fasted on Yom Kippur, a tradition which even many otherwise nonobservant Jews maintain. But when they were stunned by tragedy, they reverted back to the basic belief that God punishes people for their sins. They sat there feeling that their daughter's death had been their faults; had they been less selfish and less lazy about Yom Kippur fast some six months earlier, she might still be alive. They sat there angry at God for having exacted His pound of flesh so strictly, but afraid to admit their anger for fear that He would punish them again. Life had hurt them, and religion could not comfort them. Religion was making them feel worse.

The idea that God gives people what they deserve, that our misdeeds cause our misfortune, is a neat and attractive solution to the problem of evil at several levels, but it has a number of serious limitations. As we have seen, it teaches people to blame themselves. It creates guilt even where there is no basis for guilt. It makes people hate God, even as it makes them hate themselves. And most disturbing of all, it does not even fit the facts.

Perhaps if we had lived before the era of mass communications, we could have believed this thesis, as many intelligent people of those centuries did. It was easier to believe then. You needed to ignore fewer cases of bad things happening to good people. Without newspapers and television, without history books, you could shrug off the occasional death of a child or saintly neighbor. We know too much about the world to do that today. How can anyone who recognizes the names Auschwitz and My Lai, or has walked the corridors of hospitals and nursing homes, dare to answer the question of the world's suffering by quoting Isaiah: "Tell the righteous it shall be well with them"? To believe that today, a person would either have to deny the facts that press upon him from every side, or else define what he means by "righteous" in order to fit the inescapable facts. We would have to say that a righteous person was anyone who lived long and well, whether or not he was honest and charitable, and a wicked person was anyone who suffered, even if that person's life was otherwise commendable. . . .

Sometimes we try to make sense of our life's trials by saying that people do in fact get what they deserve, but only over the course of time. At any given moment, life may seem unfair and innocent people may appear to be suffering. But if we wait long enough, we believe, we will see the righteousness of God's plan emerge.

So, for example, the Ninety-second Psalm praises God for the wonderful, flawlessly righteous world He has given us, and hints that foolish people find fault with it because they are impatient and don't give God the time it takes for His justice to emerge.

> How great are Your deeds, O Lord,
> Your thoughts are very deep.
> The ignorant man does not comprehend them,
> Nor does the fool understand them.
> When the wicked spring up like grass,
> And the workers of inequity flourish,
> It is that they may be destroyed forever...
> The righteous shall flourish like the palm tree,
> And grow mighty like a cedar of Lebanon...
> To declare that the Lord is upright,
> My Rock in Whom there is no unrighteousness. (Psalm 92:6–8,13,16) ·

The psalmist wants to explain the world's apparent evil as in no way compromising God's justice and righteousness. He does it by comparing the wicked to grass, and the righteous to a palm tree or cedar. If you plant grass seed and a palm tree seed on the same day, the grass will start to sprout much sooner. At that point, a person who knew nothing about nature might predict that the grass would grow to be higher and stronger than the palm tree, since it was growing faster. But the experienced observer would know that the head start of the grass was only temporary, that it would wither and die in a few months, while the tree would grow slowly, but would grow to be tall and straight and would last for more than a generation.

So too, the psalmist suggests, foolish impatient people see the prosperity of the wicked and the suffering of the upright, and jump to the conclusion that it pays to be wicked. Let them observe the situation over the long run, he notes, and they will see the wicked wither like the grass, and the righteous prosper slowly but surely, like the palm tree or cedar.

If I could meet the author of the Ninety-second Psalm, I would first congratulate him on having composed a masterpiece of devotional literature. I would acknowledge that he has said something perceptive and important about the world we live in, that being dishonest and unscrupulous often gives people a head start, but that justice catches up to them. As Rabbi Milton Steinberg has written, "Consider the pattern of human affairs: how falsehood, having no legs, cannot stand; how evil tends to destroy itself; how every tyranny has eventually invoked its own doom. Now set against this the staying power of truth and righteousness. Could the contrast be so sharp unless something in the scheme of things discouraged evil and favored the good?"

But having said that, I would be obliged to point out that there is a lot of wishful thinking in his theology. Even if I were to grant that wicked people don't get away with their wickedness, that they pay for it in one way or another, I cannot say Amen to his claim that "the righteous flourish like the palm tree." The psalmist would have us believe that, given enough time, the righteous will catch up and surpass the wicked in attaining the good things of life. How does he explain the fact that God, who is presumably behind this arrangement, does not always give the righteous man time to catch up? Some good people die unfulfilled; others find length of days to be more of a punishment than a privilege. The world, alas, is not so neat a place as the psalmist would have us believe. . . .

Often, victims of misfortune try to console themselves with the idea that God has His reasons for making this happen to them, reasons that they are in no position to judge. I think of a woman I know named Helen.

The trouble started when Helen noticed herself getting tired after walking several blocks or standing in line. She chalked it up to getting older and having put on some weight. But one night, coming home after dinner with friends, Helen stumbled over the threshold of the front door, sent a lamp crashing to the floor, and fell to the floor herself. Her husband tried to joke about her getting drunk on two sips of wine, but Helen suspected that it was no joking matter. The following morning, she made an appointment to see a doctor.

The diagnosis was multiple sclerosis. The doctor explained that it was a degenerative nerve disease, and that it would gradually get worse, maybe quickly, maybe gradually over many years. At some point Helen would find it harder to walk without support. Eventually she would be confined to a wheelchair, lose bowel and bladder control, and become more and more of an invalid until she died.

The worst of Helen's fears had come true. She broke down and cried when she heard that. "Why should this happen to me? I've tried to be a good person. I have a husband and young children who need me. I don't deserve this. Why should God make me suffer like this?" Her husband took her hand and tried to console her: "You can't talk like that. God must have His reasons for doing this, and it's not for us to question him. You have to believe that if He wants you to get better, you will get better, and if He doesn't, there has to be some purpose to it."

Helen tried to find peace and strength in those words. She wanted to be comforted by the knowledge that there was some purpose to her suffering, beyond her capacity to understand. She wanted to believe that it made sense at some level. All her life, she had been taught—at religious school and in science classes alike—that the world made sense, that everything happened for a reason. She wanted so desperately to go on believing that, to hold on to her belief that God was in charge of things, because if He wasn't, who was? It was hard to live with multiple sclerosis, but it was even harder to live with the idea that things happened to people for no reason, that God had lost touch with the world and nobody was in the driver's seat.

Helen didn't want to question God or be angry at Him. But her husband's words only made her feel more abandoned and more bewildered. What kind of higher purpose could possibly justify what she would have to face? How could this in any way be good? Much as she tried not to be angry at God, she felt angry, hurt, and betrayed. She had been a good person; not perfect, perhaps, but honest, hard-working, helpful, as good as most people and better than many who were walking around healthy. What reasons could God possibly have for doing this to her? And on top of it all, she felt guilty for being angry at God. She felt alone in her fear and suffering. If God had sent her this affliction, if He, for some reason, wanted her to suffer, how could she ask Him to cure her of it?

•   •   •

Let us consider another question: Can suffering be educational? Can it cure us of our faults and make us better people? Sometimes religious people who would like to believe that God has good reasons for making us suffer, try to imagine what those reasons might be. In the words of one of the great Orthodox Jewish teachers of our time, Rabbi Joseph B. Soloveitchik, "Suffering comes to ennoble man, to purge his thoughts of pride and superficiality, to expand his horizons. In sum, the purpose of suffering is to repair that which is faulty in a man's personality."

Just as a parent sometimes has to punish a child whom he loves, for the child's sake, so God has to punish us. A parent who pulls his child out of a busy roadway, or refuses to give him a candy bar before supper, is not being mean or punitive or unfair. He or she is just being a concerned, responsible parent. Sometimes a parent even has to punish a child, with a spanking or a deprivation, in order to drive home a lesson. The child may feel that he is being arbitrarily deprived of something all the other children have, and he may wonder why an ostensibly loving parent should treat him that way, but that is because he is still a child. When he grows up, he will come to understand the wisdom and necessity of it.

Similarly, we are told, God treats us the way a wise and caring parent treats a naive child, keeping us from hurting ourselves, withholding something we may think we want, punishing us occasionally to make sure we understand that we have done something seriously wrong, and patiently enduring our temper tantrums at His "unfairness" in the confidence that we will one day mature and understand that it was all for our own good. "For whom the Lord loves, He chastises, even as a father does to the son he loves." (Proverbs 3:12). . . .

Consider the case of Ron, a young pharmacist who ran a drugstore with an older partner. When Ron bought into the business, his older colleague told him that the store had recently been the target of a series of holdups by young drug addicts looking for drugs and cash. One day, when Ron was almost ready to close up, a teenage junkie pulled a small-caliber handgun on him and asked for drugs and money. Ron was willing to lose a day's receipts rather than be a hero. He went to open the cash register, his hands trembling as he did so. As he turned , he stumbled and reached for the counter to brace himself. The robber thought he was going for a gun, and fired. The bullet went through Ron's abdomen and lodged in his spinal cord. Doctors removed it, but the damage had been done. Ron could never walk again.

Friends tried to console him. Some held his hand and commiserated with him. Some told him of experimental drugs doctors were using on paraplegics, or of miraculous spontaneous recoveries they had read about. Others tried to help him understand what had happened to him, and to answer his question, "Why me?"

"I have to believe," one friend said, "that everything that happens in life, happens for a purpose. Somehow or other, everything that happens to us is meant for our good. Look at it this way. You were always a pretty cocky guy, popular with girls, flashy cars, confident you were going to make a lot of money. You never really took time to worry about the people who couldn't keep up with you. Maybe this is God's way of teaching you a lesson, making you more thoughtful, more sensitive to others. Maybe this is God's way of purging you of pride and arrogance, and thinking about how you were going to be such a success. It's His way of making you a better, more sensitive person."

The friend wanted to be comforting, to make sense of this senseless accident. But if you were Ron, what would your reaction have been? Ron remembers thinking that if he hadn't been confined to a hospital bed, he would have punched the other man. What right did a normal, healthy person—a person who would soon be driving home, walking upstairs, looking forward to playing tennis—have to tell him that what had happened to him was good and was in his best interest?

The problem with a line of reasoning like this one is that it isn't really meant to help the sufferer or to explain his suffering. It is meant primarily to defend God, to use words and ideas to transform bad into good and pain into privilege. Such answers are thought up by people who believe very strongly that God is a loving parent who controls what happens to us, and on the basis of that belief adjust and interpret the facts to fit their assumption. It may be true that sometimes we have to do painful things to people we love for their benefit, but not every painful thing that happens to us is beneficial.

I would find it easier to believe that I experience tragedy and suffering in order to "repair" that which is faulty in my personality if there were some clear connection between the fault and the punishment. A parent who disciplines a child for doing something wrong, but never tells him what he is being punished for, is hardly a model of responsible parenthood. Yet, those who explain suffering as God's way of teaching us to change are at a loss to specify just what it is about us we are supposed to change.

Equally unhelpful would be the explanation that Ron's accident happened not to make *him* a more sensitive person, but to make his friends and family more sensitive to the handicapped than they would otherwise have been. Perhaps women give birth to dwarfed or retarded children as part of God's plan to deepen and enlarge their souls, to teach them compassion and a different kind of love. . . .

If we cannot satisfactorily explain suffering by saying we deserve what we get, or by viewing it as a "cure" for our faults, can we accept the interpretation of tragedy as a test? Many parents of dying children are urged to read the twenty-second chapter of the Book of Genesis to help them understand and accept their burden. In that chapter, God orders Abraham to take his son Isaac, whom he loves, and offer him to God as a human sacrifice. The chapter begins with the words "It came to pass after all these matters that the Lord tested Abraham." God had Abraham go through that ordeal to test his loyalty and the strength of his faith. When he passed the test, God promised to reward him liberally for the strength he had shown.

For those who have difficulty with the notion of a God who plays such sadistic games with His most faithful follower, proponents of this view explain that God knows how the story will end. He knows that we will pass the test, as Abraham did, with our faith intact (though, in Abraham's case the child did not die). He puts us to the test so that we will discover how strong and faithful we are.

The Talmud, the compilation of the teachings of the rabbis between the years 200 B.C. and A.D. 500, explains Abraham's test this way: If you go to the marketplace, you will see the potter hitting his clay pots with a stick to show you how strong and solid they are. But the wise potter hits only the strongest pots, never the flawed ones. So too, God sends such tests and afflictions only to people He knows are capable of handling them, so that they and others can learn the extent of their spiritual strength.

I was the parent of a handicapped child for fourteen years, until his death. I was not comforted by this notion that God had singled me out because He recognized some special spiritual strength within me and knew that I would be able to handle it better. It didn't make me feel "privileged" nor did it help me understand why God has to send handicapped children into the lives of a hundred thousand unsuspecting families every year.

Writer Harriet Sarnoff Schiff has distilled her pain and tragedy into an excellent book, *The Bereaved Parent*. She remembers that when her young son died during an operation to correct a congenital heart malfunction, her clergyman took her aside and said, "I know that this is a painful time for you. But I know that you will get through it all right, because God never sends us more of a burden than we can bear. God only let this happen to you because He knows that you are strong enough to handle it." Harriet Schiff remembers her reaction to those words: "If only I was a weaker person, Robbie would still be alive."

Does God "temper the wind to the shorn lamb"? Does He never ask more of us that we can endure? My experience, alas, has been otherwise. I have seen people crack under the strain of unbearable tragedy. I have seen marriages break up after the death of a child, because parents blamed each other for not taking proper care or for carrying the defective gene, or simply because the memories they shared were unendurably painful. I have seen some people made noble and sensitive through suffering, but I have seen many more people grow cynical and bitter. I have seen people become jealous of those around them, unable to take part in the routines of normal living. I have seen cancers and automobile accidents take the life of one member of a family, and functionally end the lives of five others, who could never again be the normal, cheerful people they were before disaster struck. If God is testing us, He must know by now that many of us fail the test. If He is only giving us burdens we can bear, I have seen Him miscalculate far too often.

When all else fails, some people try to explain suffering by believing that it comes to liberate us from a world of pain and lead us to a better place. I received a phone call one day informing me that a five-year-old boy in our neighborhood had run out into the street after a ball, had been hit by a car and killed. I didn't know the boy; his family was not part of the congregation. But several children from the congregation had known him and played with him. Their mothers attended the funeral, and some of them told me about it afterwards.

In the eulogy, the family's clergyman had said "This is not a time of sadness or tears. This is a time for rejoicing, because Micheal has been taken out of this world of sin and pain with his innocent soul unstained by sin. He is in a happier land now where there is no pain and no grief; let us thank God for that."

 I heard that, and I felt so bad for Micheal's parents. Not only had they lost a child without warning, they were being told by the representative of their religion that they should rejoice in the fact that he had died so young and innocent, and I couldn't believe that they felt much like rejoicing at that moment. They felt hurt, they felt angry, they felt that God had been unfair to them, and here was God's spokesman telling them to be grateful to God for what had happened.

Sometimes in our reluctance to admit that there is unfairness in the world, we try to persuade ourselves that what has happened is not really bad. We only think that it is. It is only our selfishness that makes us cry because five-year-old Micheal is with God instead of living with us. Sometimes, in our cleverness, we try to persuade ourselves that what we call evil is not real, does not really exist, but is only a condition of not enough goodness, even as "cold" means "not enough heat," or darkness is a name we give to the absence of light. We may thus "prove" that there is really no such thing as darkness or cold, but people do stumble and hurt themselves because of the dark, and people die of exposure to cold. Their deaths and injuries are no less real because of our verbal cleverness.

Sometimes, because our souls yearn for justice, because we so desperately want to believe that God will be fair to us, we fasten our hopes on the idea that life in this world is not the only reality. Sometimes beyond this life is another world where "the last shall be first" and those whose lives were cut short here on earth will be reunited with those they loved, and will spend eternity with them.

Neither I nor any other living person can know anything about the reality of that hope. We know that our physical bodies decay after we die. I for one believe that the part of us which is not physical, the part we call the soul or personality, does not and cannot die. But I am not capable of imagining what a soul without a body looks like. Will we be able to recognize disembodied souls as being the people we had known and loved? Will a man who lost his father at a young age, and then lived a full life, be older, younger, or the same age as his father in the world-to-come? Will the souls of the retarded or the short-tempered be somehow made whole in Heaven?

People who have been close to death and recovered tell of seeing a bright light and being greeted by someone they had loved, now deceased. After our son's death, our daughter dreamed that she had died and was welcomed into Heaven by her brother, now grown normal, and by her grandmother (who had died the year before). Needless to say, we have no way of knowing whether these visions are intimations of reality or products of our own wishful thinking.

Belief in a world to come where the innocent are compensated for their suffering can help people endure the unfairness of life in this world without losing faith. But it can also be an excuse for not being troubled or outraged by injustice around us, and not using our God-given intelligence to try to do something about it. The dictate of practical wisdom for people in our situation might be to remain mindful of the possibility that our lives continue in some form after death, perhaps in a form our earthly imaginations cannot conceive of. But at the same time, since we cannot know for sure, we would be well advised to take this world as seriously as we can, in case it turns out to be the only one we will ever have, and to look for meaning and justice here.

All the responses to tragedy which we have considered have at least one thing in common. They all assume that God is the cause of suffering, and they try to understand why God would want us to suffer. Is it for our own good, or is it a punishment we deserve, or could it be that God does not care what happens to us? Many of the answers were sensitive and imaginative, but none was totally satisfying. Some led us to blame ourselves in order to spare God's reputation. Others asked us to deny reality or to repress our true feelings. We were left either hating ourselves for deserving such a fate, or hating God for sending it to us when we did not deserve it.

There may be another approach. Maybe God does not cause our suffering. Maybe it happens for some reason other than the will of God. The psalmist writes, "I lift mine eyes to the hills; from where does my help come? My help comes from the Lord, maker of Heaven and earth." (Psalm 121:1–2) He does not say, "My pain comes from the Lord," or "my tragedy comes from the Lord." He says "my *help* comes from the Lord."

Could it be that God does not cause the bad things that happen to us? Could it be that He doesn't decide which families shall give birth to a handicapped child, that He did not single out Ron to be crippled by a bullet or Helen by a degenerative disease, but rather that He stands ready to help them and us cope with our tragedies if we could only get beyond the feelings of guilt and anger that separate us from Him? Could it be that "How could God do this to me?" is really the wrong question for us to ask?

• • •

No Exceptions for Nice People

The story is told of the youngster who came home from Sunday School, having been taught the biblical story of the crossing of the Red Sea. His mother asked him what he had learned in class, and he told her: "The Israelites got out of Egypt, but Pharaoh and his army chased after them. They got to the Red Sea and they couldn't cross it. The Egyptian army was getting closer. So Moses got on his walkie-talkie, the Israeli air force bombed the Egyptians, and the Israeli navy built a pontoon bridge so the people could cross." The mother was shocked. "Is that the way they taught you the story?" "Well no," the boy admitted, "but if I told it to you the way they taught it to us, you'd never believe it."

Centuries ago, people found reassuring proof of God in stories of miracles. They would tell of how God divided the sea to let the Israelites cross on dry land. They would recount stories about God sending rain in answer to a righteous person's prayer, or about rivers reversing their courses and the sun moving backward in its flight. They would remember tales of Daniel emerging unhurt from the den of lions, and Shadrach, Meshach, and Abednego surviving the fiery furnace. The point of all these stories was to prove that God cared about us so much that He was willing to suspend the laws of nature to support and protect those whom He favored.

But we today are like the little boy in the Sunday School story. We are told those stories and we are skeptical. If anything, we find proof of God precisely in the fact that laws of nature do not change. God has given us a wonderful, precise, orderly world. One of the things that makes the world livable is the fact that the laws of nature are precise and reliable, and always work the same way. There is gravity: heavy objects always fall toward the earth, so a builder can build a house without having his materials float away. There is chemistry: mixing certain elements in certain proportions always yields the same result, so a doctor can prescribe medication and know what will happen. We can even predict when the sun will rise and set on any given day. We can even predict when the moon will block the sun for certain areas, causing an eclipse. To the ancients, an eclipse was an unnatural event which they interpreted as

God's way of warning them. To us, it is a perfectly natural event, a reminder of how precise a universe God has given us.

Our human bodies are miracles, not because they defy laws of nature, but precisely because they obey them. Our digestive systems extract nutrients from food. Our skins help to regulate body temperature by perspiring. The pupils of our eyes expand and contract in response to light. Even when we get sick, our bodies have built-in defense mechanisms to fight the illness. All these wonderful things happen, usually without our being aware of them, in accordance with the most precise laws of nature. That, not the legendary splitting of the Red Sea, is the real miracle.

But the unchanging character of these laws, which makes medicine and astronomy possible, also causes problems. Gravity makes objects fall. Sometimes they fall on people and hurt them. Sometimes gravity makes people fall off mountains and out of windows. Sometimes gravity makes people slip on ice or sink under water. We could not live without gravity, but that means we have to live with the dangers it causes.

Laws of nature treat everyone alike. They do not make exceptions for good people or for useful people. If a man enters a house where someone has a contagious disease, he runs the risk of catching the disease. It makes no difference why he is in the house. He may be a doctor or a burglar; disease germs cannot tell the difference. If Lee Harvey Oswald fires a bullet at President John Kennedy, laws of nature take over from the moment that bullet is fired. Neither the course of the bullet nor the seriousness of the wound will be affected by questions of whether or not President Kennedy was a good person, or whether the world would be better off with him alive or dead.

Laws of nature do not make exceptions for nice people. A bullet has no conscience; neither does a malignant tumor or an automobile gone out of control. That is why good people get sick and get hurt as much as anyone. No matter what stories we were taught about Daniel or Jonah in Sunday School, God does not reach down to interrupt the workings of laws of nature to protect the righteous from harm. This is a second area of our world which causes bad things to happen to good people, and God does not cause it and cannot stop it.

And really, how could we live in this world if He did? Let us suppose, for purposes of argument, that God was determined not to let anything happen to a good and pious person. If an Oswald shoots at the president, no matter how carefully he aims, God will make the bullet miss. If a wing falls off Air Force One, God will make it land safely. Would this be a better world, if certain people were immune to laws of nature because God favored them, while the rest of us had to fend for ourselves?

Let us suppose, again for purposes of argument, that I was one of those righteous people to whom God would not let anything bad happen, because I was an observant, charitable person with a young family, spending my life helping people. What would that mean? Would I be able to go out in my shirtsleeves in cold weather and not get sick, because God would prevent the workings of nature from doing me harm? Could I cross streets against lights in the face of heavy traffic, and not be injured? Could I jump out of high windows when I was in too much of a hurry to wait for an elevator, and not hurt myself? A world in which good people suffer from the same natural dangers that others do causes problems. But a world in which good people were immune to those laws would cause even more problems.

Insurance companies refer to earthquakes, hurricanes and other natural disasters as "acts of God." I consider that a case of using God's name in vain. I don't believe that an earthquake that kills thousands of innocent victims without reason is an act of God. It is an act of nature. Nature is morally blind, without values. It churns along, following its own laws, not caring who or what gets in the way. But God is not morally blind. I could not worship Him if I thought He was. God stands for justice, for fairness, for compassion. For me, the earthquake is not an "act of God." The act of God is the courage of people to rebuild their lives after the earthquake, and the rush of others to help them in whatever way they can.

If a bridge collapses, if a dam breaks, if a wing falls off an airplane and people die, I cannot see that as God's doing. I cannot believe that He wanted all those people to die and had no choice but to condemn the others along with them. I believe that these calamities are all acts of nature, and that there is no moral reason for those particular victims to be singled out for punishment. Perhaps, as human beings apply their God-given intelligence to the area of natural disasters, we will one day be able to understand the physical processes behind earthquakes, hurricanes, and metal fatigue, and learn how to anticipate them or even prevent them. When that happens, fewer innocent people will fall victim to these so-called "acts of God."

I don't know why one person gets sick, and another does not, but I can only assume that some natural laws which we don't understand are at work. I cannot believe that God "sends" illness to a specific person for a specific reason. I don't believe in a God who has a weekly quota of malignant tumors to distribute, and consults His computer to find out who deserves one most or who could handle it best. "What did I do to deserve this?" is an understandable outcry from a sick and suffering person, but it is not a matter of what God decides that we deserve. The better question is "if this has happened to me, what do I do now, and who is there to help me do it?" As we saw in the previous chapter, it becomes much easier to take God seriously as the source of moral values if we don't hold Him responsible for all the unfair things that happen in the world.

• • •

I believe in God. But I do not believe the same things about Him that I did years ago, when I was growing up or when I was a theological student. I recognize His limitations. He is limited in what He can do by laws of nature and by the evolution of human nature and human moral freedom. I no longer hold God responsible for illness, accident, and natural disasters, because I realize that I gain little and lose so much when I blame God for those things. I can worship a God who hates suffering but cannot eliminate it, more easily than I can worship a God who chooses to make children suffer and die, for whatever exalted reason. Some years ago, when the "death of God" theology was a fad, I remember seeing a bumper sticker that read "My God is not dead; sorry about yours." I guess my bumper sticker reads "My God is not cruel; sorry about yours."

God does not cause our misfortunes. Some are caused by bad luck, some are caused by bad people, and some are simply an inevitable consequence of our being human and being mortal, living in a world of inflexible natural laws. The painful things that happen to us aren't punishments for our misbehavior, nor are they in any way part of some grand design on God's part. Because the tragedy is not God's will, we need not feel hurt or betrayed by God when tragedy strikes. We can turn to Him for help in overcoming it, precisely because we can tell ourselves that God is as outraged by it as we are.

• • •

And finally, to the person who asks "What good is God? Who needs religion, if these things happen to good people and bad people alike?" I would say that God may not prevent the calamity, but He gives us the strength and the perseverance to overcome it. Where else do we get these qualities which we did not have before? The heart attack which slows down a forty-six-year-old businessman does not come from God, but the determination to change his life-style, to stop smoking, to care less about expanding his business and care more about spending time with his family, because his eyes have been opened to what is truly important to him—those things come from God. God does not stand for heart attacks; those are nature's responses to the body's being overstressed. But God does stand for self-discipline and for being part of a family.

The flood that devastates a town is not an "act of God," even if the insurance companies find it useful to call it that. But the efforts people make to save lives, risking their own lives for a person who might be a total stranger to them, and the determination to rebuild their community after the flood waters have receded, do qualify as acts of God.

When a person is dying of cancer, I do not hold God responsible for the cancer or for the pain he feels. They have other causes. But I have seen God give such people the strength to take each day as it comes, to be grateful for a day full of sunshine or one in which they are relatively free of pain.

When people who were never particularly strong become strong in the face of adversity, when people who tended to think only of themselves become unselfish and heroic in an emergency, I have to ask myself where they got these qualities which they would freely admit they did not have before. My answer is that this is one of the ways in which God helps us when we suffer beyond the limits of our own strength.

Life is not fair. The wrong people get sick and the wrong people get robbed and the wrong people get killed in wars and in accidents. Some people see life's unfairness and decide, "There is no God; the world is nothing but chaos." Others sees the same unfairness and ask themselves, "Where do I get my sense of what is fair and what is unfair? Where do I get my sense of outrage and indignation, my instinctive response of sympathy when I read in the paper about a total stranger who has been hurt by life? Don't I get these things from God? Doesn't He plant in me a little bit of His own divine outrage at injustice and oppression, just as He did for the prophets of the Bible? Isn't my feeling of compassion for the afflicted just a reflection of the compassion He feels when He sees the suffering of His creatures?" Our responding to life's unfairness with sympathy and with righteous indignation, God's compassion and God's anger working through us, may be the surest proof of all of God's reality.

Religion alone can affirm the afflicted person's sense of self-worth. Science can describe what has happened to a person; only religion can call it a tragedy. Only the voice of religion, when it frees itself from the need to defend and justify God for all that happens, can say to the afflicted person, "You are a good person, you deserve better. Let me come and sit with you so that you will know that you are not alone."

Kenneth R. Miller (b. 1948) as a scientist has been on the front lines in the public sphere as a defender of evolution. (He testified in a recent court case filed to prevent the Dover, Pennsylvania, school board from requiring science students to read a statement casting doubt on the validity of evolution.) He is a Catholic and a biologist. In this article from the Brown University Alumni Magazine *(1999), which summarizes some of his points in his book* Finding Darwin's God *(1999), he connects a theological way of knowing with that of science. A key tenet of the Catholic intellectual tradition is that faith and reason are not at odds—a viewpoint that Miller shares. Why is it, according to Miller, that creationist thinking (which holds a literalist interpretation of the Bible and denies evolution) is much more dangerous to religion than to science? What does he mean that the creationists have sought God in darkness? Miller also addresses our uneasiness with the indeterminate nature of evolution and its implications for the nature of human existence. Does his answer to this work for you? Would you agree that Miller's analysis provides us with a way to reconcile two ways of knowing: scientific and religious?*

Finding Darwin's God

Kenneth R. Miller

The great hall of the Hynes Convention Center in Boston looks nothing like a church. And yet I sat there, smiling amid an audience of scientists, shaking my head and laughing to myself as I remembered another talk, given long ago, inside a church to an audience of children.

Without warning, I had experienced one of those moments in the present that connects with the scattered recollections of our past. Psychologists tell us that things happen all the time. Five thousand days of childhood are filed, not in chronological order, but as bits and pieces linked by words, or sounds, or even smells that cause us to retrieve them for no apparent reason when something "refreshes" our memory. And just like that, a few words in a symposium on developmental biology had brought me back to the day before my first communion. I was eight years old, sitting with the boys on the right side of our little church (the girls sat on the left), and our pastor was speaking.

Putting the finishing touches on a year of preparation for the sacrament, Father Murphy sought to impress us with the reality of God's power in the world. He pointed to the altar railing, its polished marble gleaming in sunlight, and firmly assured us that God himself had fashioned it. "Yeah, right," whispered the kid next to me. Worried that there might be the son or daughter of a stonecutter in the crowd, the good Father retreated a bit. "Now, he didn't carve the railing or bring it here or cement it in place . . .

but God himself *made* the marble, long ago, and left it for someone to find and make into part of our church."

I don't know if our pastor sensed that his description of God as craftsman was meeting a certain tide of skepticism, but no matter. He had another trick up his sleeve, a can't-miss, sure-thing argument that, no doubt, had never failed him. He walked over to the altar and picked a flower from the vase.

"Look at the beauty of a flower," he began. "The Bible tells us that even Solomon in all his glory was never arrayed as one of these. And do you know what? Not a single person in the world can tell us what makes a flower bloom. All those scientists in their laboratories, the ones who can split the atom and build jet planes and televisions, well, not one of them can tell you how a plant makes flowers." And why should they be able to? "Flowers, just like you, are the work of God."

I was impressed. No one argued, no one wisecracked. We filed out of the church like good little boys and girls, ready for our first communion the next day. And I never thought of it again, until this symposium on developmental biology. Sandwiched between two speakers working on more fashionable topics in animal development was Elliot M. Meyerowitz, a plant scientist at Caltech. A few of my colleagues, uninterested in research dealing with plants, got up to stretch their legs before the final talk, but I sat there with an ear-to-ear grin on my face. I jotted notes furiously; I sketched the diagrams he projected on the screen and wrote additional speculations of my own in the margins. Meyerowitz, you see, had explained how plants make flowers.

The four principal parts of a flower—sepals, petals, stamens, and pistils—are actually modified leaves. This is one of the reasons why plants can produce reproductive cells just about anywhere, while animals are limited to a very specific set of reproductive organs. Your little finger isn't going to start shedding reproductive cells anytime soon. But in springtime, the tip of any branch on an apple tree may very well blossom and begin scattering pollen. Plants can produce new flowers anywhere they can grow new leaves. Somehow, however, the plant must find a way to "tell" an ordinary cluster of leaves that they should develop into floral parts. That's where Meyerowitz's lab took over.

Several years of patient genetic study had isolated a set of mutants that could only form two or three of the four parts. By crossing the various mutants, his team was able to identify four genes that had to be turned on or off in a specific pattern to produce a normal flower. Each of these genes, in turn, sets off a series of signals that "tell" the cells of a brand new bud to develop as sepals or petals rather than ordinary leaves. The details are remarkable, and the interactions between the genes are fascinating. To me, sitting in the crowd thirty-seven years after my first communion, the scientific details were just the icing on the cake. The real message was "Father Murphy, you were wrong." God doesn't make a flower. The floral induction genes do.

Our pastor's error, common and widely repeated, was to seek God in what science has not yet explained. His assumption was that God is best found in territory unknown, in the corners of darkness that have not yet seen the light of understanding. These, as it turns out, are exactly the wrong places to look.

Searching the Shadows

By pointing to the process of making a flower as proof of the reality of God, Father Murphy was embracing the idea that God finds it necessary to cripple nature. In his view, the blooming of a daffodil requires not a self-sufficient material universe, but direct intervention by God. We can find God, therefore, in the things around us that lack material, scientific explanations. In nature, elusive and unexplored, we will find the Creator at work.

The creationist opponents of evolution make similar arguments. They claim that the existence of life, the appearance of new species, and, most especially, the origins of mankind have not and cannot be explained by evolution or any other natural process. By denying the self-sufficiency of nature, they look for God (or at least a "designer") in the deficiencies of science. The trouble is that science, given enough time, generally explains even the most baffling things. As a matter of strategy, creationists would be well-advised to avoid telling scientists what they will never be able to figure out. History is against them. In a general way, we really do understand how nature works.

And evolution forms a critical part of that understanding. Evolution really does explain the very things that its critics say it does not. Claims disputing the antiquity of the earth, the validity of the fossil record, and the sufficiency of evolutionary mechanisms vanish upon close inspection. Even to the most fervent anti-evolutionists, the pattern should be clear—their favorite "gaps" are filling up: the molecular mechanisms of evolution are now well-understood, and the historical record of evolution becomes more compelling with each passing season. This means that science can answer their challenges to evolution in an obvious way. Show the historical record, provide the data, reveal the mechanism, and highlight the convergence of theory and fact.

There is, however, a deeper problem caused by the opponents of evolution, a problem for religion. Like our priest, they have based their search
for God on the premise that nature is *not* self-sufficient. By such logic,
only God can make a species, just as Father Murphy believed only God
could make a flower. Both assertions support the existence of God *only* so
long as these assertions are true, but serious problems for religion emerge
when they are shown to be false.

If we accept a *lack* of scientific explanation as proof for God's existence,
simple logic would dictate that we would have to regard a successful scientific explanation as an argument *against* God. That's why creationist
reasoning, ultimately, is much more dangerous to religion than to science.
Elliot Meyerowitz's fine work on floral induction suddenly becomes a
threat to the divine, even though common sense tells us it should be nothing of the sort. By arguing, as creationists do, that nature cannot be self-
sufficient in the formation of new species, the creationists forge a logical
link between the limits of natural processes to accomplish biological
change and the existence of a designer (God). In other words, they show
the proponents of atheism exactly how to disprove the existence of God—
show that evolution works, and it's time to tear down the temple. This is
an offer that the enemies of religion are all too happy to accept.

Putting it bluntly, the creationists have sought God in darkness. What we
have not found and do not yet understand becomes their best—indeed
their only—evidence for the divine. As a Christian, I find the flow of this
logic particularly depressing. Not only does it teach us to fear the acqui-
sition of knowledge (which might at any time disprove belief), but it suggests that God dwells only in the shadows of our understanding. I
suggest that, if God is real, we should be able to find him somewhere
else—in the bright light of human knowledge, spiritual and scientific.

Faith and Reason

Each of the great Western monotheistic traditions sees God as truth, love,
and knowledge. This should mean that each and every increase in our
understanding of the natural world is a step toward God and not, as many
people assume, a step away. If faith and reason are both gifts from God,
then they should play complementary, not conflicting, roles in our struggle
to understand the world around us. As a scientist and as a Christian, that
is exactly what I believe. True knowledge comes only from a combination
of faith and reason.

A nonbeliever, of course, puts his or her trust in science and finds no
value in faith. And I certainly agree that science allows believer and nonbeliever alike to investigate the natural world through a common lens of
observation, experiment, and theory. The ability of science to transcend

cultural, political, and even religious differences is part of its genius, part of its value as a way of knowing. What science cannot do is assign either meaning or purpose to the world it explores. This leads some to conclude that the world as seen by science is devoid of meaning and absent of purpose. It is not. What it does mean, I would suggest, is that our human tendency to assign meaning and value must transcend science and, ultimately, must come from outside it. The science that results can thus be enriched and informed from its contact with the values and principles of faith. The God of Abraham does not tell us which proteins control the cell cycle. But he does give us a reason to care, a reason to cherish that understanding, and above all, a reason to prefer the light of knowledge to the darkness of ignorance.

As more than one scientist has said, the truly remarkable thing about the world is that it actually does make sense. The parts fit, the molecules interact, the darn thing works. To people of faith, what evolution says is that nature is complete. Their God fashioned a material world in which truly free and independent beings could evolve. He got it right the very first time.

To some, the murderous reality of human nature is proof that God is absent or dead. The same reasoning would find God missing from the unpredictable branchings of an evolutionary tree. But the truth is deeper. In each case, a deity determined to establish a world that was truly independent of his whims, a world in which intelligent creatures would face authentic choices between good and evil, would have to fashion a distinct, material reality and then let his creation run. Neither the self-sufficiency of nature nor the reality of evil in the world mean God is absent. To a religious person, both signify something quite different—the strength of God's love and the reality of our freedom as his creatures.

The Weapons of Disbelief

As a species, we like to see ourselves as the best and brightest. We are the intended, special, primary creatures of creation. We sit at the apex of the evolutionary tree as the ultimate products of nature, self-proclaimed and self-aware. We like to think that evolution's goal was to produce us.

In a purely biological sense, this comforting view of our own position in nature is false, a product of self-inflating distortion induced by the imperfect mirrors we hold up to life. Yes, we are objectively among the most complex of animals, but not in every sense. Among the systems of the body, we are the hands-down winners for physiological complexity in just one place—the nervous system—and even there, a nonprimate (the dolphin) can lay down a claim that rivals our own.

More to the point, any accurate assessment of the evolutionary process shows that the notion of one form of life being more highly evolved than another is incorrect. Every organism, every cell that lives today, is the descendant of a long line of winners, of ancestors who used successful evolutionary strategies time and time again, and therefore lived to tell about it—or, at least, to reproduce. The bacterium perched on the lip of my coffee cup has been through as much evolution as I have. I've got the advantage of size and consciousness, which matter when I write about evolution, but the bacterium has the advantage of numbers, of flexibility, and most especially, of reproductive speed. That single bacterium, given the right conditions, could literally fill the world with its descendants in a matter of days. No human, no vertebrate, no animal could boast of anything remotely as impressive.

What evolution tells us is that life spreads out along endless branching pathways from any starting point. One of those tiny branches eventually led to us. We think it remarkable and wonder how it could have happened, but any fair assessment of the tree of life shows that our tiny branch is crowded into insignificance by those that bolted off in a thousand different directions. Our species, *Homo sapiens*, has not "triumphed" in the evolutionary struggle any more than has a squirrel, a dandelion, or a mosquito. We are all here, now, and that's what matters. We have all followed different pathways to find ourselves in the present. We are all winners in the game of natural selection. *Current* winners, we should be careful to say.

That, in the minds of many, is exactly the problem. In a thousand branching pathways, how can we be sure that one of them, historically and unavoidably, would lead for sure to us? Consider this: we mammals now occupy, in most ecosystems, the roles of large, dominant land animals. But for much of their history, mammals were restricted to habitats in which only very small creatures could survive. Why? Because another group of vertebrates dominated the earth—until, as Stephen Jay Gould has pointed out, the cataclysmic impact of a comet or asteroid drove those giants to extinction. "In an entirely literal sense," Gould has written, "we owe our existence, as large and reasoning animals, to our lucky stars."

So, what if the comet had missed? What if our ancestors, and not dinosaurs, had been the ones driven to extinction? What if, during the Devonian period, the small tribe of fish known as rhipidistians had been obliterated? Vanishing with them would have been the possibility of life for the first tetrapods. Vertebrates might never have struggled onto the land, leaving it, in Gould's words, forever "the unchallenged domain of insects and flowers."

Surely this means that mankind's appearance on this planet was *not* preordained, that we are here not as the products of an inevitable procession of evolutionary success, but as an afterthought, a minor detail, a happenstance in a history that might just as well have left us out. What follows from this, to skeptic and true believer alike, is a conclusion whose logic is rarely challenged—that no God would ever have used such a process to fashion his prize creatures. How could he have been sure that leaving the job to evolution would lead things to working out the "right" way? If it was God's will to produce us, then by showing that we are the products of evolution, we would rule God as Creator. Therein lies the value or the danger of evolution.

Not so fast. The biological account of lucky historical contingencies that led to our own appearance on this planet is surely accurate. What does not follow is that a perceived lack of inevitability translates into something that we should regard as incompatibility with a divine will. To do so seriously underestimates God, even as this God is understood by the most conventional of Western religions.

Yes, the explosive diversification of life on this planet was an unpredictable process. But so were the rise of Western civilization, the collapse of the Roman Empire, and the winning number in last night's lottery. We do not regard the indeterminate nature of any of these events in human history as antithetical to the existence of a Creator; why should we regard similar events in natural history any differently? There is, I would submit, no reason at all. If we can view the contingent events in the families that produced our individual lives as consistent with a Creator, then certainly we can do the same for the chain of circumstances that produced our species.

The alternative is a world where all events have predictable outcomes, where the future is open neither to chance nor to independent human action. A world in which we would always evolve is a world in which we would never be free. To a believer, the particular history leading to us shows how truly remarkable we are, how rare is the gift of consciousness, and how precious is the chance to understand.

Certainty and Faith

One would like to think that all scientific ideas, including evolution, would rise or fall purely on the basis of the evidence. If that were true, evolution would long since have passed, in the public mind, from controversy into common sense, which is exactly what has happened within the scientific community. This is, unfortunately, not the case—evolution remains, in the minds of much of the American public, a dangerous idea, and for biology educators, a source of never-ending strife.

I believe much of the problem is the fault of those in the scientific community who routinely enlist the findings of evolutionary biology in support their own philosophical pronouncements. Sometimes these take the form of stern, dispassionate pronouncements about the meaninglessness of life. Other times we are lectured that the contingency of our presence on this planet invalidates any sense of human purpose. And very often we are told that the raw reality of nature strips the authority from any human system of morality.

As creatures fashioned by evolution, we are filled, as the biologist E. O. Wilson has said, with instinctive behaviors important to the survival of our genes. Some of these behaviors, though favored by natural selection, can get us into trouble. Our desires for food, water, reproduction, and status, our willingness to fight, and our tendencies to band together into social groups, can all be seen as behaviors that help ensure evolutionary success. Sociobiology, which studies the biological basis of social behaviors, tells us that in some circumstances natural selection will favor cooperative and nurturing instincts—"nice" genes that help us get along together. Some circumstances, on the other hand, will favor aggressive self-centered behaviors, ranging all the way from friendly competition to outright homicide. Could such Darwinian ruthlessness be part of the plan of a loving God?

Yes, it could. To survive on this planet, the genes of our ancestors, like those of any other organism, had to produce behaviors that protected, nurtured, defended, and ensured the reproductive successes of the individuals that bore them. It should be no surprise that we carry such passions within us, and Darwinian biology cannot be faulted for giving their presence a biological explanation. Indeed, the Bible itself gives ample documentation of such human tendencies, including pride, selfishness, lust, anger, aggression, and murder.

Darwin can hardly be criticized for pinpointing the biological origins of these drives. All too often, in finding the sources of our "original sins," in fixing the reasons why our species displays the tendencies it does, evolution is misconstrued as providing a kind of justification for the worst aspects of human nature. At best, this is a misreading of the scientific lessons of sociobiology. At worst, it is an attempt to misuse biology to abolish any meaningful system of morality. Evolution may explain the existence of our most basic biological drives and desires, but that does not tell us that it is always proper to act on them. Evolution has provided me with a sense of hunger when my nutritional resources are running low, but evolution does not justify my clubbing you over the head to swipe your lunch. Evolution explains our biology, but it does not tell us what is good, or right, or moral. For those answers, however informed we may be by biology, we must look somewhere else.

What Kind of World?

Like it or not, the values that any of us apply to our daily lives have been affected by the work of Charles Darwin. Religious people, however, have a special question to put to the reclusive naturalist of Down House. Did his work ultimately contribute to the greater glory of God, or did he deliver human nature and destiny into the hands of a professional scientific class, one profoundly hostile to religion? Does Darwin's work strengthen or weaken the idea of God?

The conventional wisdom is that whatever one may think of his science, having Mr. Darwin around certainly hasn't helped religion very much. The general thinking is that religion has been weakened by Darwinism and has been constrained to modify its view of the Creator in order to twist doctrine into conformity with the demands of evolution. As Stephen Jay Gould puts it, with obvious delight," Now the conclusions of science must be accepted *a priori,* and religious interpretations must be finessed and adjusted to match unimpeachable results from the magisterium of natural knowledge!" Science calls the tune, and religion dances to its music.

This sad specter of a weakened and marginalized God drives the continuing opposition to evolution. This is why the God of the creationists requires, above all, that evolution be shown not to have functioned in the past and not to be working now. To free religion from the tyranny of Darwinism, creationists need a science that shows nature to be incomplete; they need a history of life whose events can only be explained as the result of supernatural processes. Put bluntly, the creationists are committed to finding permanent, intractable mystery in nature. To such minds, even the most perfect being we can imagine would not have been perfect enough to fashion a creation in which life would originate and evolve on its own. Nature must be flawed, static, and forever inadequate.

Science in general, and evolutionary science in particular, gives us something quite different. It reveals a universe that is dynamic, flexible, and logically complete. It presents a vision of life that spreads across the planet with endless variety and intricate beauty. It suggests a world in which our material existence is not an impossible illusion propped up by magic, but the genuine article, a world in which things are exactly what they seem. A world in which we were formed, as the Creator once told us, from the dust of the earth itself.

It is often said that a Darwinian universe is one whose randomness cannot be reconciled with meaning. I disagree. A world truly without meaning would be one in which a deity pulled the string of every human puppet, indeed of every material particle. In such a world, physical and biological events would be carefully controlled, evil and suffering could be minimized, and the outcome of historical processes strictly regulated. All things would move toward the Creator's clear, distinct, established goals. Such control and predictability, however, comes at the price of independence. Always in control, such a Creator would deny his creatures any real opportunity to know and worship him—authentic love requires freedom, not manipulation. Such freedom is best supplied by the open contingency of evolution.

One hundred and fifty years ago it might have been impossible not to couple Darwin to a grim and pointless determinism, but things look different today. Darwin's vision has expanded to encompass a new world of biology in which the links from molecule to cell and from cell to organism are becoming clear. Evolution prevails, but it does so with a richness and subtlety its original theorist may have found surprising and could not have anticipated.

We know from astronomy, for example, that the universe had a beginning, from physics that the future is both open and unpredictable, from geology and paleontology that the whole of life has been a process of change and transformation. From biology we know that our tissues are not impenetrable reservoirs of vital magic, but a stunning matrix of complex wonders, ultimately explicable in terms of biochemistry and molecular biology. With such knowledge we can see, perhaps for the first time, why a Creator would have allowed our species to be fashioned by the process of evolution.

If he so chose, the God whose presence is taught by most Western religions could have fashioned anything, ourselves included, *ex nihilo*, from his wish alone. In our childhood as a species, that might have been the only way in which we could imagine the fulfillment of a divine will. But we've grown up, and something remarkable has happened: we have begun to understand the physical basis of life itself. If a string of constant miracles were needed for each turn of the cell cycle or each flicker of a cilium, the hand of God would be written directly into every living thing—his presence at the edge of the human sandbox would be unmistakable. Such findings might confirm our faith, but they would also undermine our independence. How could we fairly choose between God and man when the presence and the power of the divine so obviously and so literally controlled our every breath? Our freedom as his creatures requires a little space and integrity. In the material world, it requires self-sufficiency and consistency with the laws of nature.

Evolution is neither more nor less than the result of respecting the reality and consistency of the physical world over time. To fashion material beings with an independent physical existence, any Creator would have had to produce an independent material universe in which our evolution over time was a contingent possibility. A believer in the divine accepts that God's love and gift of freedom are genuine—so genuine that they include the power to choose evil and, if we wish, to freely send ourselves to Hell. Not all believers will accept the stark conditions of that bargain, but our freedom to act has to have a physical and biological basis. Evolution and its sister sciences of genetics and molecular biology provide that basis. In biological terms, evolution is the only way a Creator could have made us the creatures we are—free beings in a world of authentic and meaningful moral and spiritual choices.

Those who ask from science a final argument, an ultimate proof, an unassailable position from which the issue of God may be decided will always be disappointed. As a scientist I claim no new proofs, no revolutionary data, no stunning insight into nature that can tip the balance in one direction or another. But I do claim that to a believer, even in the most traditional sense, evolutionary biology is not at all the obstacle we often believe it to be. In many respects, evolution is the key to understanding our relationship with God.

When I have the privilege of giving a series of lectures on evolutionary biology to my freshman students, I usually conclude those lectures with a few remarks about the impact of evolutionary theory on other fields, from economics to politics to religion. I find a way to make clear that I do not regard evolution, properly understood, as either antireligious or antispiritual. Most students seem to appreciate those sentiments. They probably figure that Professor Miller, trying to be a nice guy and doubtlessly an agnostic, is trying to find a way to be unequivocal about evolution without offending the University chaplain.

There are always a few who find me after class and want to pin me down. They ask me point-blank: "Do you believe in God?"

And I tell each of them, "Yes."

Puzzled, they ask: "What kind of God?"

Over the years I have struggled to come up with a simple but precise answer to that question. And, eventually I found it. I believe in Darwin's God.

David Freedman is an author and journalist who also speaks to a variety of audiences about science, technology, and management issues. This selection from Discover (June, 1992) is an example of a science journalist writing about the work of a particular scholar, in this case a scientist, Emily Martin. Science is based on empirical truth—that is, derived from direct observation (and inferences from direct observations). We think of science, especially the natural sciences, as being objective. But is that really the case? What does Martin's work reveal about how bias in thought and language has affected research on the biology of reproduction?

The Aggressive Egg

David H. Freedman

Ah, fertilization—that miraculous process to which we all owe our existence. Let's review: first, a wastefully huge swarm of sperm weakly flops along, its members bumping into walls and flailing aimlessly through thick strands of mucus. Eventually, through sheer odds of pinball-like bouncing more than anything else, a few sperm end up close to an egg. As they mill around, the egg selects one and reels it in, pinning it down in spite of its efforts to escape. It's no contest, really. The gigantic, hardy egg yanks this tiny sperm inside, distills out the chromosomes, and sets out to become an embryo.

Or would you have put it differently? Until very recently, so would most biologists. For decades they've been portraying sperm as intrepid warriors battling their way to an aging, passive egg that can do little but await the sturdy victor's final, bold plunge. But the first description is closer to the truth, insists Emily Martin, a 47-year-old researcher at Johns Hopkins who has spent the past seven years examining the metaphors used to describe fertilization. Martin is not a biologist; she's a cultural anthropologist. But her efforts to spotlight the male-skewed imagery that permeates our views of reproduction have placed her at the center of a growing debate about how cultural myths can turn into scientific myths, and vice versa.

Martin didn't set out to skewer biologists. Actually she was studying biology, among other things, at the University of Michigan in 1965 when a course on Japanese music hooked her on investigating other cultures. After picking up a Ph.D. in cultural anthropology from Cornell in 1971, she spent nine years traveling back and forth between the United States, Taiwan, and China, where she was studying Chinese rituals and social organization. Then, having done the study of a foreign culture that's traditionally expected of anthropologists, and being pregnant with her first child, she started casting about for a new project closer to home. "Studying your own culture is harder," she says, "because everything seems so normal to you."

Not until 1982, while attending a class for expectant parents before the birth of her second child, did Martin stumble on her topic. "It suddenly hit me that the way everyone was talking about their bodies was really weird," she recalls. "It was *the* body, *the* uterus, and *the* contraction—as if these things weren't a part of us. I realized that medical science was in need of some sort of interpretation, and my wedge would be reproductive issues." Martin started off by interviewing dozens of women on their feelings about every aspect of reproduction, from menstruation to menopause. Her book *The Woman in the Body*, published in 1987, explored the relation between images of the body and ideas about oneself. But by 1985 Martin realized that she had been looking at these issues from only one point of view. "I decided to do an ethnographic study in a scientific setting, to see how biologists thought about some of these questions," she says. "Also, I thought I should be including male reproductive processes as well." Fertilization research, she realized, would allow her to cover all the bases.

A s she began her background studies, Martin was surprised to find that popular literature, textbooks, and even medical journals were crammed with descriptions of warrior sperm and damsel-in-distress eggs. Martin found that classic biology texts, for example, enthused about the human male's "amazing" productivity—some 200 million sperm every hour—while practically complaining over the "waste" of the 2 million immature eggs present in the human female at birth, only some 400 of which the ovaries ever "shed" for possible fertilization, with the rest destined to "degenerate" over the woman's lifetime. "The real mystery," says Martin, "is why the male's vast production of sperm is not seen as wasteful."

Less mysterious, in Martin's opinion, was the motivation for such biased language. "Men link potency to strong sperm," she says. "You'd like your sperm to be like you; no wonder everyone believed sperm were torpedoes." In all her searching, Martin came up with only a single depiction of less-than-mighty sperm: Woody Allen's portrayal of a neurotic sperm nervous about his imminent ejaculation in the movie *Everything You Always Wanted to Know About Sex But Were Afraid to Ask.*

Woody Allen aside, the durability of the masterful-sperm imagery astonished Martin. It continued to dominate the contemporary technical and popular literature despite a growing body of evidence that the egg plays anything but a passive role. From the early 1970s on, studies of the sperm and eggs of many species have revealed that molecules released by the egg are critical to guiding and "activating" the sperm—that is, triggering the sperm to release proteins that help it adhere to the egg. In fact, the egg might just as well be called eager as passive. Among many species of lizards, insects, some crustaceans, and even turkeys, the egg doesn't always wait for the sperm's arrival. It can begin dividing without fertilization, and females can reproduce without sperm at all.

Yet none of this had made a dent in biologists' language. "When I asked them about it, they told me I had a point," says Martin. "They claimed the imagery came up only when they needed to explain their research, and not in the lab. But I wanted to know what was really going on."

By 1986 Martin had begun hanging out with a team of researchers at Johns Hopkins who were observing sperm mobility in hopes of coming up with a strategy for a new contraceptive. They had started the year before with a simple experiment—measuring human sperm's ability to escape and swim away from a tiny suction pipet placed against the side of the sperm cell's head. To the team's great surprise, the sperm turned out to be feeble swimmers; their heads thrashed from side to side ten times more vigorously than their bodies pushed forward. "It makes sense," says Martin. "The last thing you'd want a sperm to be is a highly effective burrower, because it would end up burrowing into the first obstacle it encountered. You want a sperm that's good at getting away from things."

The team went on to determine that the sperm tries to pull its getaway act even on the egg itself, but is held down against its struggles by molecules on the surface of the egg that hook together with counterparts on the sperm's surface, fastening the sperm until the egg can absorb it. Yet even after having revealed the sperm to be an escape artist and the egg to be a chemically active sperm catcher, even after discussing the egg's role in "tethering" the sperm, the research team continued for another three years to describe the sperm's role as actively "penetrating" the egg.

Meanwhile, Martin was keeping an eye on two other fertilization groups. They too seemed at times to disregard their own observations when writing about fertilization. Researchers at the University of Wisconsin, for example, described the way sea urchin sperm first make contact with an egg by quickly stringing together protein molecules into a filament that extends out until it reaches the egg. But instead of describing this as an innocuous process of assembly and attachment, the group wrote—in a pioneering paper that otherwise points out the egg's ability to actively "clasp" and "entwine"—that the sperm's filament "shoots out and harpoons" the egg. Likewise, when a researcher at the Roche Institute of Molecular Biology in Nutley, New Jersey, wrote in 1987 of his discovery that mouse eggs carry a molecular structure on their coating that fits inside a complementary structure on the sperm, helping bind the two together, he described the two structures, naturally enough, as a lock and key—but he called the egg's protruding structure the lock and the sperm's engulfing structure the key.

Martin doesn't suggest that these researchers willfully distorted their imagery. In fact, she notes that one of the investigators at Johns Hopkins was her politically correct husband, Richard Cone. What's more, Martin concedes that she herself was slow to recognize the disparity between the discoveries at Johns Hopkins and the way the findings were written up. "It didn't strike me for a few years," she says. But innocent or not, she adds, the cultural conditioning these biologists had absorbed early in their careers influenced more than their writing; it skewed their research. "I believe, and my husband believes, and the lab believes, that they would have seen these results sooner if they hadn't had these male-oriented images of sperm. In fact, biologists could have figured out a hundred years ago that sperm are weak forward-propulsion units, but it's hard for men to accept the idea that sperm are best at escaping. The imagery you employ guides you to ask certain questions and to not ask certain others."

People preparing to dismiss Emily Martin as a humorless feminist have their work cut out for them. At once animated and easygoing in her cramped, cactus-strewn office, Martin chuckles as she goes through an inch-thick file of hapless-egg and macho-sperm imagery clipped from magazines. (In one Gary Larson cartoon, a housewife egg fends off a swarm of sperm trying to get past her by posing as phone repairmen, insurance salesmen, and UPS deliverymen.) "I just think this stuff is a riot," she says. In fact, it's the biologists who seem a little stuffy. Though she usually lectures to students, Martin recalls one lecture she gave to biologists at the Woods Hole Oceanographic Institution in 1990. "It was one of the most painful experiences of my life," she says. "I had gotten to the point where the audience is usually rolling in the aisles, and all I got was stony silence. I could see they were furious. On the other hand, I can understand their feelings; I get defensive when someone criticizes cultural anthropology."

One researcher who doesn't bristle at Martin's jabs is Scott Gilbert, a developmental biologist at Swarthmore College. Though he suggests Martin may go a little overboard in stressing the egg's aggressiveness—for example, he prefers to think of the egg as "engaging in a dialog" with the sperm rather than gluing it down—he does believe her views are a vast improvement over the conventional explanations. "Most studies clearly show that the sperm is attracted by the egg and activated by it," says Gilbert. "But if you don't have an interpretation of fertilization that allows you to look at the egg as active, you won't look for the molecules that can prove it. You simply won't find activities that you don't visualize."

Now that the discrepancy between experiment and interpretation is being brought out into the open, the professional literature seems to be coming around—although a recent issue of the biology journal *Cell Differentiation and Development* placed on its cover a Prince Charming sperm delivering a wake-up kiss to a long-eyelashed Sleeping Beauty egg. As for the popular press, Gilbert and Martin cite the same recent example as particularly egregious: an article titled "Sperm Wars" that appeared as a cover story in a national science magazine whose name you'd recognize in a minute, which referred to the sperm cell as "a formidable .00024-inch weapon, tipped with a chemical warhead" (see *Discover*, July 1991). On the other hand, *Developmental Biology*, the most popular college textbook in its subject area, takes great pains to point out the new, equal-opportunity view of fertilization. No wonder: Gilbert wrote it.

One reason the older interpretation is dying hard is that it tends to be self-reinforcing, not only in suggesting ready-made imagery that can skew observations but also in subtly determining who becomes a biologist in the first place. "This business has stopped certain people from entering the field," says Gilbert. "Why would a woman want to continue if people are telling her she's passive?"

Nevertheless, as Martin points out, a growing number of women *are* continuing in biology. But that won't guarantee more evenhanded interpretations. "Scientific training involves a rigorous socialization process that doesn't allow for different perspectives," she says. "It's hard to say that women biologists are any less guilty of these things than men."

Even if biologists do move away from the passive-egg myth, other images are waiting in the wings. These days, says Martin, researchers seem ready to confer a "spider woman" aspect on the egg. "Men have always turned to spider imagery when they are confronted with women who acquire power," she charges. Indeed, her file of magazine clippings contains several images in support of her claim. One striking example: the cartoonish silhouette employed as the emblem of the once-popular *Charlie's Angels* television series, which depicts the three starring female characters, guns and all, unmistakably merged into the eight-limbed shape of a spider.

Though Martin is the first to insist that much of the fertilization imagery is good for a laugh, she doesn't mean to let scientists dismiss it all as a big joke. "People say, 'Oh, what difference does it make?' as if this stuff doesn't affect anyone," she says. "But our culture *is* affected by these powerful visual images. We all put so much faith in science, and so much of the negative load lands on women."

She notes, as another example, that it's been known since the 1960s that women exposed to toxic chemicals bear children who run a higher risk of serious medical problems. Those findings reinforced the cultural notion that women should be sheltered, and some companies have rules to prevent women of reproductive age from working at jobs that might involve exposure to these chemicals. But only in the past few years have comparable studies shown that men exposed to high levels of lead, vinyl chloride, and about a dozen other chemicals also have children who are at higher risk. "It's the notion of invulnerable sperm," she claims, "that made it take so long for scientists and the public to accept the male role in birth defects and infertility."

Martin has recently shifted her focus to metaphors used in other areas of medical research. For example, she says, "when AIDS was seen as affecting only the 'dregs' of society, scientists described it as a monkey virus. Now that well-to-do white women are getting it, all of a sudden researchers are talking about AIDS being an autoimmune disease." There are, of course, other reasons that researchers' language might change, including a growing knowledge of how the AIDS virus in fact wreaks havoc on the host's immune system. Martin is still studying the literature and observing researchers in immunology labs. For now, she concedes, "all you can do is raise a question. It's often impossible to prove causality."

Although she is no longer studying fertilization imagery, Martin still lectures on the topic because, she contends, "the work shows that science can have social effects. When we anthropomorphize the egg and sperm, when we turn them into a miniature bride and groom complete with personalities, what effect does this have on abortion legislation? These effects aren't intended by scientists, but they happen. They blend moral and scientific issues together in a way that makes me want to stand up and say something."

There's further irony in the traditional metaphors. The notion of fiercely battling, competitive sperm suggests that they're battling each other in a "race" to the egg. In fact, says Cone, they have a hard time making their way through the mucus glop, and like a team of bicyclists they "take turns" up front parting strands of mucus. So in a sense sperm are cooperative. The egg, on the other hand, is the real competitive loner. Only one matures each month, and the one out in front suppresses the maturation of all the others. The macho image of sperm not only obscures this reality; it actually reverses what's been observed.

Can biased metaphors be eliminated from science? Martin doesn't think so. Even if they could be, she doesn't think that antiseptically neutral language would be desirable. Metaphor is, after all, a powerful vehicle for creative thinking. "The goal shouldn't be to clean the imagery out," she says, "but to be aware that it's there." It also helps, she adds, to be able to take a joke. "Humor takes away the sting," she says, "along with the potential for inculcating harmful ideas."

Albert Camus (1913–1960), a French author and philosopher, was born and raised in Algeria, a former French colony. He is often associated with Jean-Paul Sartre and Existentialism, but he himself refused this label. Camus wrote novels, plays, short stories, and essays. He is perhaps best known for his two major novels, The Stranger *and* The Plague. *He was awarded the Nobel Prize in literature in 1957, just three years before his death, for his writings against capital punishment. The philosophical notion of the absurd, the idea that the world and the human condition lack clarity and meaning, permeates much of his work as does his commitment to human rights. "The Guest" ("L'Hôte" in French, translates into both the guest and the host, a double meaning which is significant with respect to the two main characters in the story) appeared in Camus' collection of short stories entitled* Exile and the Kingdom *(1957). The plot unfolds in the Algerian desert and is representative of Camus' own moral and intellectual confrontation with the dilemmas posed for him by the Algerian War for Independence (1954–1962). Indeed, the question of choice and who to align himself with, since neutrality is not a viable option, plagues the main character, Daru. How does this story grapple with the notion of truth? In what ways does Daru judge and evaluate the evidence of the "truth" of the situation in which he finds himself? Does he challenge or question authority in his investigation of the truth?*

The Guest

Albert Camus

The schoolmaster was watching the two men climb toward him. One was on horseback, the other on foot. They had not yet tackled the abrupt rise leading to the schoolhouse built on the hillside. They were toiling onward, making slow progress in the snow, among the stones, on the vast expanse of the high, deserted plateau. From time to time the horse stumbled. Without hearing anything yet, he could see the breath issuing from the horse's nostrils. One of the men, at least, knew the region. They were following the trail although it had disappeared days ago under a layer of dirty white snow. The schoolmaster calculated that it would take them half an hour to get onto the hill. It was cold; he went back into the school to get a sweater.

He crossed the empty, frigid classroom. On the blackboard the four rivers of France, drawn with four different colored chalks, had been flowing toward their estuaries for the past three days. Snow had suddenly fallen in mid-October after eight months of drought without the transition of rain, and the twenty pupils, more or less, who lived in the villages scattered over the plateau had stopped coming. With fair weather they would return. Daru now heated only the single room that was his lodging, adjoining the classroom and giving also onto the plateau to the east. Like the class windows, his window looked to the south too. On that side the school was a few kilometers from the point where the plateau began to slope toward the south. In clear weather could be seen the purple mass of the mountain range where the gap opened onto the desert.

Somewhat warmed, Daru returned to the window from which he had first seen the two men. They were no longer visible. Hence they must have tackled the rise. The sky was not so dark, for the snow had stopped falling during the night. The morning had opened with a dirty light which had scarcely become brighter as the ceiling of clouds lifted. At two in the afternoon it seemed as if the day were merely beginning. But still this was better than those three days when the thick snow was falling amidst unbroken darkness with little gusts of wind that rattled the double door of the classroom. Then Daru had spent long hours in his room, leaving it only to go to the shed and feed the chickens or get some coal. Fortunately the delivery truck from Tadjid, the nearest village to the north, had brought his supplies two days before the blizzard. It would return in forty-eight hours.

Besides, he had enough to resist a siege, for the little room was cluttered with bags of wheat that the administration left as a stock to distribute to those of his pupils whose families had suffered from the drought. Actually they had all been victims because they were all poor. Every day Daru would distribute a ration to the children. They had missed it, he knew, during these bad days. Possibly one of the fathers or big brothers would come this afternoon and he could supply them with grain. It was just a matter of carrying them over to the next harvest. Now shiploads of wheat were arriving from France and the worst was over. But it would be hard to forget that poverty, that army of ragged ghosts wandering in the sunlight, the plateaus burned to a cinder month after month, the earth shriveled up little by little, literally scorched, every stone bursting into dust under one's foot. The sheep had died then by thousands and even a few men, here and there, sometimes without anyone's knowing.

In contrast with such poverty, he who lived almost like a monk in his remote schoolhouse, nonetheless satisfied with the little he had and with the rough life, had felt like a lord with his whitewashed walls, his narrow couch, his unpainted shelves, his well, and his weekly provision of water and food. And suddenly this snow, without warning, without the foretaste of rain. This is the way the region was, cruel to live in, even without men—who didn't help matters either. But Daru had been born here. Everywhere else, he felt exiled.

He stepped out onto the terrace in front of the schoolhouse. The two men were now halfway up the slope. He recognized the horseman as Balducci, the old gendarme he had known for a long time. Balducci was holding on the end of a rope an Arab who was walking behind him with hands bound and head lowered. The gendarme waved a greeting to which Daru did not reply, lost as he was in contemplation of the Arab dressed in a faded blue jellaba, his feet in sandals but covered with socks of heavy raw wool, his head surmounted by a narrow, short *chèche*. They were approaching. Balducci was holding back his horse in order not to hurt the Arab, and the group was advancing slowly.

Within earshot, Balducci shouted: "One hour to do the three kilometers from El Ameur!" Daru did not answer. Short and square in his thick sweater, he watched them climb. Not once had the Arab raised his head. "Hello," said Daru when they got up onto the terrace. "Come in and warm up." Balducci painfully got down from his horse without letting go the rope. From under his bristling mustache he smiled at the schoolmaster. His little dark eyes, deep-set under a tanned forehead, and his mouth surrounded with wrinkles made him look attentive and studious. Daru took the bridle, led the horse to the shed, and came back to the two men, who were now waiting for him in the school. He led them into his room. "I am going to heat up the classroom," he said. "We'll be more comfortable there." When he entered the room again, Balducci was on the couch. He had undone the rope tying him to the Arab, who had squatted near the stove. His hands still bound, the *chèche* pushed back on his head, he was looking toward the window. At first Daru noticed only his huge lips, fat, smooth, almost Negroid; yet his nose was straight, his eyes were dark and full of fever. The *chèche* revealed an obstinate forehead and, under the weathered skin now rather discolored by the cold, the whole face had a restless and rebellious look that struck Daru when the Arab, turning his face toward him, looked him straight in the eyes. "Go into the other room," said the schoolmaster, "and I'll make you some mint tea." "Thanks," Balducci said. "What a chore! How I long for retirement." And addressing his prisoner in Arabic: "Come on, you." The Arab got up and, slowly, holding his bound wrists in front of him, went into the classroom.

With the tea, Daru brought a chair. But Balducci was already enthroned on the nearest pupil's desk and the Arab had squatted against the teacher's platform facing the stove, which stood between the desk and the window. When he held out the glass of tea to the prisoner, Daru hesitated at the sight of his bound hands. "He might perhaps be untied." "Sure," said Balducci. "That was for the trip." He started to get to his feet. But Daru, setting the glass on the floor, had knelt beside the Arab. Without saying anything, the Arab watched him with his feverish eyes. Once his hands were free, he rubbed his swollen wrists against each other, took the glass of tea, and sucked up the burning liquid in swift little sips.

"Good," said Daru. "And where are you headed?"

Balducci withdrew his mustache from the tea. "Here, son."

"Odd pupils! And you're spending the night?"

"No. I'm going back to El Ameur. And you will deliver this fellow to Tinguit. He is expected at police headquarters."

Balducci was looking at Daru with a friendly little smile.

"What's this story?" asked the schoolmaster. "Are you pulling my leg?"

"No, son. Those are the orders."

"The orders? I'm not . . ." Daru hesitated, not wanting to hurt the old Corsican. "I mean, that's not my job."

"What! What's the meaning of that? In wartime people do all kinds of jobs."

"Then I'll wait for the declaration of war!"

Balducci nodded.

"O.K. But the orders exist and they concern you too. Things are brewing, it appears. There is talk of a forthcoming revolt. We are mobilized, in a way."

Daru still had his obstinate look.

"Listen, son," Balducci said. "I like you and you must understand. There's only a dozen of us at El Ameur, to patrol throughout the whole territory of a small department and I must get back in a hurry. I was told to hand this guy over to you and return without delay. He couldn't be kept there. His village was beginning to stir; they wanted to take him back. You must take him to Tinguit tomorrow before the day is over. Twenty kilometers shouldn't faze a husky fellow like you. After that, all will be over. You'll come back to your pupils and your comfortable life."

Behind the wall the horse could be heard snorting and pawing the earth. Daru was looking out the window. Decidedly, the weather was clearing and the light was increasing over the snowy plateau. When all the snow was melted, the sun would take over again and once more would burn the fields of stone. For days, still, the unchanging sky would shed its dry light on the solitary expanse where nothing had any connection with man.

"After all," he said, turning around toward Balducci, "what did he do?" And, before the gendarme had opened his mouth, he asked: "Does he speak French?"

"No, not a word. We had been looking for him for a month, but they were hiding him. He killed his cousin."

"Is he against us?"

"I don't think so. But you can never be sure."

"Why did he kill?"

"A family squabble, I think. One owed the other grain, it seems. It's not at all clear. In short, he killed his cousin with a billhook. You know, like a sheep, *kreezk!*"

Balducci made the gesture of drawing a blade across his throat and the Arab, his attention attracted, watched him with a sort of anxiety. Daru felt a sudden wrath against the man, against all men with their rotten spite, their tireless hates, their blood lust.

But the kettle was singing on the stove. He served Balducci more tea, hesitated, then served the Arab again, who, a second time, drank avidly. His raised arms made the jellaba fall open and the schoolmaster saw his thin, muscular chest.

"Thanks, kid," Balducci said. "And now, I'm off."

He got up and went toward the Arab, taking a small rope from his pocket.

"What are you doing?" Daru asked dryly.

Balducci, disconcerted, showed him the rope.

"Don't bother."

The old gendarme hesitated. "It's up to you. Of course, you are armed?"

"I have my shotgun."

"Where?"

"In the trunk."

"You ought to have it near your bed."

"Why? I have nothing to fear."

"You're crazy, son. If there's an uprising, no one is safe, we're all in the same boat."

"I'll defend myself. I'll have time to see them coming."

Balducci began to laugh, then suddenly the mustache covered the white teeth.

"You'll have time? O.K. That's just what I was saying. You have always been a little cracked. That's why I like you, my son was like that."

At the same time he took out his revolver and put it on the desk.

"Keep it; I don't need two weapons from here to El Ameur."

The revolver shone against the black paint of the table. When the gendarme turned toward him, the schoolmaster caught the smell of leather and horseflesh.

"Listen, Balducci," Daru said suddenly, "every bit of this disgusts me, and first of all your fellow here. But I won't hand him over. Fight, yes, if I have to. But not that."

The old gendarme stood in front of him and looked at him severely.

"You're being a fool," he said slowly. "I don't like it either. You don't get used to putting a rope on a man even after years of it, and you're even ashamed—yes, ashamed. But you can't let them have their way."

"I won't hand him over," Daru said again.

"It's an order, son, and I repeat it."

"That's right. Repeat to them what I've said to you: I won't hand him over."

Balducci made a visible effort to reflect. He looked at the Arab and at Daru. At last he decided.

"No, I won't tell them anything. If you want to drop us, go ahead; I'll not denounce you. I have an order to deliver the prisoner and I'm doing so. And now you'll just sign this paper for me."

"There's no need. I'll not deny that you left him with me."

"Don't be mean with me. I know you'll tell the truth. You're from hereabouts and you are a man. But you must sign, that's the rule."

Daru opened his drawer, took out a little square bottle of purple ink, the red wooden penholder with the "sergeant-major" pen he used for making models of penmanship, and signed. The gendarme carefully folded the paper and put it into his wallet. Then he moved toward the door.

"I'll see you off," Daru said.

"No," said Balducci. "There's no use being polite. You insulted me."

He looked at the Arab, motionless in the same spot, sniffed peevishly, and turned away toward the door. "Good-by, son," he said. The door shut behind him. Balducci appeared suddenly outside the window and then disappeared. His footsteps were muffled by the snow. The horse stirred on the other side of the wall and several chickens fluttered in fright. A moment later Balducci reappeared outside the window leading the horse by the bridle. He walked toward the little rise without turning around and disappeared from sight with the horse following him. A big stone could be heard bouncing down. Daru walked back toward the prisoner, who, without stirring, never took his eyes off him. "Wait," the schoolmaster said in

Arabic and went toward the bedroom. As he was going through the door, he had a second thought, went to the desk, took the revolver, and stuck it in his pocket. Then, without looking back, he went into his room.

For some time he lay on his couch watching the sky gradually close over, listening to the silence. It was this silence that had seemed painful to him during the first days here, after the war. He had requested a post in the little town at the base of the foothills separating the upper plateaus from the desert. There, rocky walls, green and black to the north, pink and lavender to the south, marked the frontier of eternal summer. He had been named to a post farther north, on the plateau itself. In the beginning, the solitude and the silence had been hard for him on these wastelands peopled only by stones. Occasionally, furrows suggested cultivation, but they had been dug to uncover a certain kind of stone good for building. The only plowing here was to harvest rocks. Elsewhere a thin layer of soil accumulated in the hollows would be scraped out to enrich paltry village gardens. This is the way it was: bare rock covered three quarters of the region. Towns sprang up, flourished, then disappeared; men came by, loved one another or fought bitterly, then died. No one in this desert, neither he nor his guest, mattered. And yet, outside this desert neither of them, Daru knew, could have really lived.

When he got up, no noise came from the classroom. He was amazed at the unmixed joy he derived from the mere thought that the Arab might have fled and that he would be alone with no decision to make. But the prisoner was there. He had merely stretched out between the stove and the desk. With eyes open, he was staring at the ceiling. In that position, his thick lips were particularly noticeable, giving him a pouting look. "Come," said Daru. The Arab got up and followed him. In the bedroom, the schoolmaster pointed to a chair near the table under the window. The Arab sat down without taking his eyes off Daru.

"Are you hungry?"

"Yes," the prisoner said.

Daru set the table for two. He took flour and oil, shaped a cake in a frying-pan, and lighted the little stove that functioned on bottled gas. While the cake was cooking, he went out to the shed to get cheese, eggs, dates, and condensed milk. When the cake was done he set it on the window sill to cool, heated some condensed milk diluted with water, and beat up the eggs into an omelette. In one of his motions he knocked against the revolver stuck in his right pocket. He set the bowl down, went into the classroom, and put the revolver in his desk drawer. When he came back to the room, night was falling. He put on the light and served the Arab. "Eat," he said. The Arab took a piece of the cake, lifted it eagerly to his mouth, and stopped short.

"And you?" he asked.

"After you. I'll eat too."

The thick lips opened slightly. The Arab hesitated, then bit into the cake determinedly.

The meal over, the Arab looked at the schoolmaster. "Are you the judge?"

"No, I'm simply keeping you until tomorrow."

"Why do you eat with me?"

"I'm hungry."

The Arab fell silent. Daru got up and went out. He brought back a folding bed from the shed, set it up between the table and the stove, perpendicular to his own bed. From a large suitcase which, upright in a corner, served as a shelf for papers, he took two blankets and arranged them on the camp bed. Then he stopped, felt useless, and sat down on his bed. There was nothing more to do or to get ready. He had to look at this man. He looked at him, therefore, trying to imagine his face bursting with rage. He couldn't do so. He could see nothing but the dark yet shining eyes and the animal mouth.

"Why did you kill him?" he asked in a voice whose hostile tone surprised him.

The Arab looked away.

"He ran away. I ran after him."

He raised his eyes to Daru again and they were full of a sort of woeful interrogation. "Now what will they do to me?"

"Are you afraid?"

He stiffened, turning his eyes away.

"Are you sorry?"

The Arab stared at him openmouthed. Obviously he did not understand. Daru's annoyance was growing. At the same time he felt awkward and self-conscious with his big body wedged between the two beds.

"Lie down there," he said impatiently. "That's your bed."

The Arab didn't move. He called to Daru:

"Tell me!"

The schoolmaster looked at him.

"Is the gendarme coming back tomorrow?"

"I don't know."

"Are you coming with us?"

"I don't know. Why?"

The prisoner got up and stretched out on top of the blankets, his feet toward the window. The light from the electric bulb shone straight into his eyes and he closed them at once.

"Why?" Daru repeated, standing beside the bed.

The Arab opened his eyes under the blinding light and looked at him, trying not to blink.

"Come with us," he said.

In the middle of the night, Daru was still not asleep. He had gone to bed after undressing completely; he generally slept naked. But when he suddenly realized that he had nothing on, he hesitated. He felt vulnerable and the temptation came to him to put his clothes back on. Then he shrugged his shoulders; after all, he wasn't a child and, if need be, he could break his adversary in two. From his bed he could observe him, lying on his back, still motionless with his eyes closed under the harsh light. When Daru turned out the light, the darkness seemed to coagulate all of a sudden. Little by little, the night came back to life in the window where the starless sky was stirring gently. The schoolmaster soon made out the body lying at his feet. The Arab still did not move, but his eyes seemed open. A faint wind was prowling around the schoolhouse. Perhaps it would drive away the clouds and the sun would reappear.

During the night the wind increased. The hens fluttered a little and then were silent. The Arab turned over on his side with his back to Daru, who thought he heard him moan. Then he listened for his guest's breathing, become heavier and more regular. He listened to that breath so close to him and mused without being able to go to sleep. In this room where he had been sleeping alone for a year, this presence bothered him. But it bothered him also by imposing on him a sort of brotherhood he knew well but refused to accept in the present circumstances. Men who share the same rooms, soldiers or prisoners, develop a strange alliance as if, having cast off their armor with their clothing, they fraternized every evening, over and above their differences, in the ancient community of dream and fatigue. But Daru shook himself; he didn't like such musings, and it was essential to sleep.

A little later, however, when the Arab stirred slightly, the schoolmaster was still not asleep. When the prisoner made a second move, he stiffened, on the alert. The Arab was lifting himself slowly on his arms with almost the motion of a sleepwalker. Seated upright in bed, he waited motionless without turning his head toward Daru, as if he were listening attentively. Daru did not stir; it had just occurred to him that the revolver was still in the drawer of his desk. It was better to act at once. Yet he continued to observe the prisoner, who, with the same slithery motion, put his feet on the ground, waited again, then began to stand up slowly. Daru was about to call out to him when the Arab began to walk, in a quite natural but extraordinarily silent way. He was heading toward the door at the end of the room that opened into the shed. He lifted the latch with precaution and went out, pushing the door behind him but without shutting it. Daru had not stirred. "He is running away," he merely thought. "Good riddance!" Yet he listened attentively. The hens were not fluttering; the guest must be on the plateau. A faint sound of water reached him, and he didn't know what it was until the Arab again stood framed in the doorway, closed the door carefully, and came back to bed without a sound. Then Daru turned his back on him and fell asleep. Still later he seemed, from the depths of his sleep, to hear furtive steps around the schoolhouse. "I'm dreaming! I'm dreaming!" he repeated to himself. And he went on sleeping.

When he awoke, the sky was clear; the loose window let in a cold, pure air. The Arab was asleep, hunched up under the blankets now, his mouth open, utterly relaxed. But when Daru shook him, he started dreadfully, staring at Daru with wild eyes as if he had never seen him and such a frightened expression that the schoolmaster stepped back. "Don't be afraid. It's me. You must eat." The Arab nodded his head and said yes. Calm had returned to his face, but his expression was vacant and listless.

The coffee was ready. They drank it seated together on the folding bed as they munched their pieces of the cake. Then Daru led the Arab under the shed and showed him the faucet where he washed. He went back into the room, folded the blankets and the bed, made his own bed and put the room in order. Then he went through the classroom and out onto the terrace. The sun was already rising in the blue sky; a soft, bright light was bathing the deserted plateau. On the ridge the snow was melting in spots. The stones were about to reappear. Crouched on the edge of the plateau, the schoolmaster looked at the deserted expanse. He thought of Balducci. He had hurt him, for he had sent him off in a way as if he didn't want to be associated with him. He could still hear the gendarme's farewell and, without knowing why, he felt strangely empty and vulnerable. At that moment, from the other side of the schoolhouse, the prisoner coughed. Daru listened to him almost despite himself and then, furious, threw a pebble that whistled through the air before sinking into the snow. That man's stupid crime revolted him, but to hand him over was contrary to honor. Merely thinking of it made him smart with humiliation. And he cursed at one and the same time his own people who had sent him this

Arab and the Arab too who had dared to kill and not managed to get away. Daru got up, walked in a circle on the terrace, waited motionless, and then went back into the schoolhouse.

The Arab, leaning over the cement floor of the shed, was washing his teeth with two fingers. Daru looked at him and said: "Come." He went back into the room ahead of the prisoner. He slipped a hunting-jacket on over his sweater and put on walking-shoes. Standing, he waited until the Arab had put on his *chèche* and sandals. They went into the classroom and the schoolmaster pointed to the exit, saying: "Go ahead." The fellow didn't budge. "I'm coming," said Daru. The Arab went out. Daru went back into the room and made a package of pieces of rusk, dates, and sugar. In the classroom, before going out, he hesitated a second in front of his desk, then crossed the threshold and locked the door. "That's the way," he said. He started toward the east, followed by the prisoner. But, a short distance from the schoolhouse, he thought he heard a slight sound behind them. He retraced his steps and examined the surroundings of the house; there was no one there. The Arab watched him without seeming to understand. "Come on," said Daru.

They walked for an hour and rested beside a sharp peak of limestone. The snow was melting faster and faster and the sun was drinking up the puddles at once, rapidly cleaning the plateau, which gradually dried and vibrated like the air itself. When they resumed walking, the ground rang under their feet. From time to time a bird rent the space in front of them with a joyful cry. Daru breathed in deeply the fresh morning light. He felt a sort of rapture before the vast familiar expanse, now almost entirely yellow under its dome of blue sky. They walked an hour more, descending toward the south. They reached a level height made up of crumbly rocks. From there on, the plateau sloped down, eastward, toward a low plain where there were a few spindly trees and, to the south, toward outcroppings of rock that gave the landscape a chaotic look.

Daru surveyed the two directions. There was nothing but the sky on the horizon. Not a man could be seen. He turned toward the Arab, who was looking at him blankly. Daru held out the package to him. "Take it," he said. "There are dates, bread, and sugar. You can hold out for two days. Here are a thousand francs too." The Arab took the package and the money but kept his full hands at chest level as if he didn't know what to do with what was being given him. "Now look," the schoolmaster said as he pointed in the direction of the east, "there's the way to Tinguit. You have a two-hour walk. At Tinguit you'll find the administration and the police. They are expecting you." The Arab looked toward the east, still holding the package and the money against his chest. Daru took his elbow and turned him rather roughly toward the south. At the foot of the height on which they stood could be seen a faint path. "That's the trail across the plateau. In a day's walk from here you'll find pasturelands and the first nomads. They'll take you in and shelter you according their law." The Arab had now turned toward Daru and a sort of panic was visible in his expression. "Listen," he said. Daru shook his head: "No, be quiet. Now I'm leaving you." He turned his back on him, took two long steps in the direction of the school, looked hesitantly at the motionless Arab, and started off again. For a few minutes he heard nothing but his own step resounding on the cold ground and did not turn his head. A moment later, however, he turned around. The Arab was still there on the edge of the hill, his arms hanging now, and he was looking at the schoolmaster. Daru felt something rise in his throat. But he swore with impatience, waved vaguely, and started off again. He had already gone some distance when he again stopped and looked. There was no longer anyone on the hill.

Daru hesitated. The sun was now rather high in the sky and was beginning to beat down on his head. The schoolmaster retraced his steps, at first somewhat uncertainly, then with decision. When he reached the little hill, he was bathed in sweat. He climbed it as fast as he could and stopped, out of breath, at the top. The rock-fields to the south stood out sharply against the blue sky, but on the plain to the east a steamy heat was already rising. And in that slight haze, Daru, with heavy heart, made out the Arab walking slowly on the road to prison.

A little later, standing before the window of the classroom, the schoolmaster was watching the clear light bathing the whole surface of the plateau, but he hardly saw it. Behind him on the blackboard, among the winding French rivers, sprawled the clumsily chalked-up words he had just read: "You handed over our brother. You will pay for this." Daru looked at the sky, the plateau, and, beyond, the invisible lands stretching all the way to the sea. In this vast landscape he had loved so much, he was alone.

Novelist, poet, and children's fiction author, Alice Walker (b. 1944) has earned critical and popular acclaim for her portrayals of African-American women and received the Pulitzer Prize for The Color Purple *in 1983. In this piece from* In Search of Our Mothers' Gardens: Womanist Prose *(1974), Walker describes, among other things, coming to understand her mother's garden in new way— determining new truths about the garden. What can happen when the creative spirit has no release? What creative releases were used by the women Walker portrays? Does this experience relate to your or your mother's experiences at all? How? In considering the courageous life of Phillis Wheatly, we connect with the themes of our next unit—community and justice.*

In Search of Our Mothers' Gardens

Alice Walker

I described her own nature and temperament. Told how they needed a larger life for their expression. . . . I pointed out that in lieu of proper channels, her emotions had overflowed into paths that dissipated them. I talked, beautifully I thought, about an art that would be born, an art that would open the way for women the likes of her. I asked her to hope, and build up an inner life against the coming of that day. . . . I sang, with a strange quiver in my voice, a promise song.

—Jean Toomer, "Avey,"
Cane

The poet speaking to a prostitute who falls asleep while he's talking—

When the poet Jean Toomer walked through the South in the early twenties, he discovered a curious thing: black women whose spirituality was so intense, so deep, so *unconscious*, that they were themselves unaware of the richness they held. They stumbled blindly through their lives: creatures so abused and mutilated in body, so dimmed and confused by pain, that they considered themselves unworthy even of hope. In the selfless abstractions their bodies became to the men who used them, they became more than "sexual objects," more even than mere women: they became "Saints." Instead of being perceived as whole persons, their bodies became shrines: what was thought to be their minds became temples suitable for worship. These crazy Saints stared out at the world, wildly, like lunatics—or quietly, like suicides; and the "God" that was in their gaze was as mute as a great stone.

Who were these Saints? These crazy, loony, pitiful women?

Some of them, without a doubt, were our mothers and grandmothers.

In the still heat of the post-Reconstruction South, this is how they seemed to Jean Toomer: exquisite butterflies trapped in an evil honey, toiling away their lives in an era, a century, that did not acknowledge them, except as "the *mule* of the world." They dreamed dreams that no one knew—not even themselves, in any coherent fashion—and saw visions no one could understand. They wandered or sat about the countryside crooning lullabies to ghosts, and drawing the mother of Christ in charcoal on courthouse walls.

They forced their minds to desert their bodies and their striving spirits sought to rise, like frail whirlwinds from the hard red clay. And when those frail whirlwinds fell, in scattered particles, upon the ground, no one mourned. Instead, men lit candles to celebrate the emptiness that remained, as people do who enter a beautiful but vacant space to resurrect a God.

Our mothers and grandmothers, some of them: moving to music not yet written. And they waited.

They waited for a day when the unknown thing that was in them would be made known; but guessed, somehow in their darkness, that on the day of their revelation they would be long dead. Therefore to Toomer they walked, and even ran, in slow motion. For they were going nowhere immediate, and the future was not yet within their grasp. And men took our mothers and grandmothers, "but got no pleasure from it." So complex was their passion and their calm.

To Toomer, they lay vacant and fallow as autumn fields, with harvest time never in sight: and he saw them enter loveless marriages, without joy; and become prostitutes, without resistance; and become mothers of children, without fulfillment.

For these grandmothers and mothers of ours were not Saints, but Artists; driven to a numb and bleeding madness by the springs of creativity in them for which there was no release. They were Creators, who lived lives of spiritual waste, because they were so rich in spirituality—which is the basis of Art—that the strain of enduring their unused and unwanted talent drove them insane. Throwing away this spirituality was their pathetic attempt to lighten the soul to a weight their work-worn, sexually abused bodies could bear.

What did it mean for a black woman to be an artist in our grandmothers' time? In our great-grandmothers' day? It is a question with an answer cruel enough to stop the blood.

Did you have a genius of a great-great-grandmother who died under some ignorant and depraved white overseer's lash? Or was she required to bake biscuits for a lazy backwater tramp, when she cried out in her soul to paint watercolors of sunsets, or the rain falling on the green and peaceful pasturelands? Or was her body broken and forced to bear children (who were more often than not sold away from her)—eight, ten, fifteen, twenty children—when her one joy was the thought of modeling heroic figures of rebellion, in stone or clay?

How was the creativity of the black woman kept alive, year after year and century after century, when for most of the years black people have been in America, it was a punishable crime for a black person to read or write? And the freedom to paint, to sculpt, to expand the mind with action did not exist. Consider, if you can bear to imagine it, what might have been the result if singing, too, had been forbidden by law. Listen to the voices of Bessie Smith, Billie Holiday, Nina Simone, Roberta Flack, and Aretha Franklin, among others, and imagine those voices muzzled for life. Then you may begin to comprehend the lives of our "crazy," "Sainted" mothers and grandmothers. The agony of the lives of women who might have been Poets, Novelists, Essayists, and Short-Story Writers (over a period of centuries), who died with their real gifts stifled within them.

And, if this were the end of the story, we would have cause to cry out in my paraphrase of Okot p'Bitek's great poem:

> O, my clanswomen
> Let us all cry together!
> Come,
> Let us mourn the death of our mother,
> The death of a Queen
> The ash that was produced
> By a great fire!
> O, this homestead is utterly dead
> Close the gates
> With *lacari* thorns,
> For our mother
> The creator of the Stool is lost!
> And all the young women
> Have perished in the wilderness!

But this is not the end of the story, for all the young women—our mothers and grandmothers, ourselves—have not perished in the wilderness. And if we ask ourselves why, and search for and find the answer, we will know beyond all efforts to erase it from our minds, just exactly who, and of what, we black American women are.

One example, perhaps the most pathetic, most misunderstood one, can provide a backdrop for our mothers' work: Phillis Wheatley, a slave in the 1700s.

Virginia Woolf, in her book *A Room of One's Own*, wrote that in order for a woman to write fiction she must have two things, certainly: a room of her own (with key and lock) and enough money to support herself.

What then are we to make of Phillis Wheatley, a slave, who owned not even herself? This sickly, frail black girl who required a servant of her own at times—her health was so precarious—and who, had she been white, would have been easily considered the intellectual superior of all the women and most of the men in the society of her day.

Virginia Woolf wrote further, speaking of course not of our Phillis, that "any woman born with a great gift in the sixteenth century [insert "eighteenth century," insert "black woman," insert "born or made a slave"] would certainly have gone crazed, shot herself, or ended her days in some lonely cottage outside the village, half witch, half wizard [insert "Saint"], feared and mocked at. For it needs little skill and psychology to be sure that a highly gifted girl who had tried to use her gift for poetry would have been so thwarted and hindered by contrary instincts [add "chains, guns, the lash, the ownership of one's body by someone else, submission to an alien religion"], that she must have lost her health and sanity to a certainty."

The key words, as they relate to Phillis, are "contrary instincts." For when we read the poetry of Phillis Wheatley—as when we read the novels of Nella Larsen or the oddly false-sounding autobiography of that freest of all black women writers, Zora Hurston—evidence of "contrary instincts" is everywhere. Her loyalties were completely divided, as was, without question, her mind.

But how could this be otherwise? Captured at seven, a slave of wealthy, doting whites who instilled in her the "savagery" of the Africa they "rescued" her from . . . one wonders if she was even able to remember her homeland as she had known it, or as it really was.

Yet, because she did try to use her gift for poetry in a world that made her a slave, she was "so thwarted and hindered by . . . contrary instincts, that she . . . lost her health. . . ." In the last years of her brief life, burdened not only with the need to express her gift but also with a penniless, friendless "freedom" and several small children for whom she was forced to do strenuous work to feed, she lost her health, certainly. Suffering from malnutrition and neglect and who knows what mental agonies, Phillis Wheatley died.

So torn by "contrary instincts" was black, kidnapped, enslaved Phillis that her description of "the Goddess"—as she poetically called the Liberty she did not have—is ironically, cruelly humorous. And, in fact, has held Phillis up to ridicule for more than a century. It is usually read prior to hanging Phillis's memory as that of a fool. She wrote:

The Goddess comes, she moves divinely fair,
Olive and laurel binds her *golden* hair.
Wherever shines this native of the skies,
Unnumber'd charms and recent graces rise. [My italics]

It is obvious that Phillis, the slave, combed the "Goddess's" hair every
morning; prior, perhaps, to bringing in the milk, or fixing her mistress's
lunch. She took her imagery from the one thing she saw elevated above
all others.

With the benefit of hindsight we ask, "How could she?"

But at last, Phillis, we understand. No more snickering when your stiff,
struggling, ambivalent lines are forced on us. We know now that you
were not an idiot or a traitor; only a sickly little black girl, snatched from
your home and country and made a slave; a woman who still struggled
to sing the song that was your gift, although in a land of barbarians who
praised you for your bewildered tongue. It is not so much what you sang,
as that you kept alive, in so many of our ancestors, *the notion of song*.

Black women are called, in the folklore that so aptly identifies one's status in society, "the *mule* of the world," because we have been handed
the burdens that everyone else—*everyone else*—refused to carry. We have
also been called "Matriarchs," "Superwomen," and "Mean and Evil
Bitches." Not to mention "Castraters" and "Sapphire's Mama." When we
have pleaded for understanding, our character has been distorted; when
we have asked for simple caring, we have been handed empty inspirational appellations, then stuck in the farthest corner. When we have
asked for love, we have been given children. In short, even our plainer
gifts, our labors of fidelity and love, have been knocked down our
throats. To be an artist and a black woman, even today, lowers our status
in many respects, rather than raises it: and yet, artists we will be.

Therefore we must fearlessly pull out of ourselves and look at and identify with our lives the living creativity some of our great-grandmothers
were not allowed to know. I stress *some* of them because it is well known
that the majority of our great-grandmothers knew, even without "knowing" it, the reality of their spirituality, even if they didn't recognize it
beyond what happened in the singing at church—and they never had
any intention of giving it up.

How they did it—those millions of black women who were not Phillis
Wheatley, or Lucy Terry or Frances Harper or Zora Hurston or Nella
Larsen or Bessie Smith; or Elizabeth Catlett, or Katherine Dunham,

either—brings me to the title of this essay, "In Search of Our Mothers' Gardens," which is a personal account that is yet shared, in its theme and its meaning, by all of us. I found, while thinking about the far-reaching world of the creative black woman, that often the truest answer to a question that really matters can be found very close.

In the late 1920s my mother ran away from home to marry my father. Marriage, if not running away, was expected of seventeen-year-old girls. By the time she was twenty, she had two children and was pregnant with a third. Five children later, I was born. And this is how I came to know my mother: she seemed a large, soft, loving-eyed woman who was rarely impatient in our home. Her quick, violent temper was on view only a few times a year, when she battled with the white landlord who had the misfortune to suggest to her that her children did not need to go to school.

She made all the clothes we wore, even my brothers' overalls. She made all the towels and sheets we used. She spent the summers canning vegetables and fruits. She spent the winter evenings making quilts enough to cover all our beds.

During the "working" day, she labored beside—not behind—my father in the fields. Her day began before sunup, and did not end until late at night. There was never a moment for her to sit down, undisturbed, to unravel her own private thoughts; never a time free from interruption—by work or the noisy inquiries of her many children. And yet, it is to my mother—and all our mothers who were not famous—that I went in search of the secret of what has fed that muzzled and often mutilated, but vibrant, creative spirit that the black woman has inherited, and that pops out in wild and unlikely places to this day.

But when, you will ask, did my overworked mother have time to know or care about feeding the creative spirit?

The answer is so simple that many of us have spent years discovering it. We have constantly looked high, when we should have looked high—and low.

For example: in the Smithsonian Institution in Washington, D.C., there hangs a quilt unlike any other in the world. In fanciful, inspired, and yet simple and identifiable figures, it portrays the story of the Crucifixion. It is considered rare, beyond price. Though it follows no known pattern of quilt-making, and though it is made of bits and pieces of worthless rags, it is obviously the work of a person of powerful imagination and deep spiritual feeling. Below this quilt I saw a note that says it was made by "an anonymous Black woman in Alabama, a hundred years ago."

If we could locate this "anonymous" black woman from Alabama, she would turn out to be one of our grandmothers—an artist who left her mark in the only materials she could afford, and in the only medium her position in society allowed her to use.

As Virginia Woolf wrote further, in *A Room of One's Own:*

> Yet genius of a sort must have existed among women as it must have existed among the working class. [Change this to "slaves" and "the wives and daughters of sharecroppers."] Now and again an Emily Brontë or a Robert Burns [change this to "a Zora Hurston or a Richard Wright"] blazes out and proves its presence. But certainly it never got itself on to paper. When, however, one reads of a witch being ducked, of a woman possessed by devils [or "Sainthood"], of a wise woman selling herbs [our root workers], or even a very remarkable man who had a mother, then I think we are on the track of a lost novelist, a suppressed poet, of some mute and inglorious Jane Austen. . . . Indeed, I would venture to guess that Anon, who wrote so many poems without signing them, was often a woman. . . .

And so our mothers and grandmothers have, more often than not anonymously, handed on the creative spark, the seed of the flower they themselves never hoped to see: or like a sealed letter they could not plainly read.

And so it is, certainly, with my own mother. Unlike "Ma" Rainey's songs, which retained their creator's name even while blasting forth from Bessie Smith's mouth, no song or poem will bear my mother's name. Yet so many of the stories that I write, that we all write, are my mother's stories. Only recently did I fully realize this: that through years of listening to my mother's stories of her life, I have absorbed not only the stories themselves, but something of the manner in which she spoke, something of the urgency that involves the knowledge that her stories—like her life—must be recorded. It is probably for this reason that so much of what I have written is about characters whose counterparts in real life are so much older than I am.

But the telling of these stories, which came from my mother's lips as naturally as breathing, was not the only way my mother showed herself as an artist. For stories, too, were subject to being distracted, to dying without conclusion. Dinners must be started, and cotton must be gathered before the big rains. The artist that was and is my mother showed itself to me only after many years. This is what I finally noticed:

Like Mem, a character in *The Third Life of Grange Copeland*, my mother adorned with flowers whatever shabby house we were forced to live in. And not just your typical straggly country stand of zinnias, either. She planted ambitious gardens—and still does—with over fifty different varieties of plants that bloom profusely from early March until late November. Before she left home for the fields, she watered her flowers, chopped up the grass, and laid out new beds. When she returned from the fields she might divide clumps of bulbs, dig a cold pit, uproot and replant roses, or prune branches from her taller bushes or trees—until night came and it was too dark to see.

Whatever she planted grew as if by magic, and her fame as a grower of flowers spread over three counties. Because of her creativity with her flowers, even my memories of poverty are seen through a screen of blooms—sunflowers, petunias, roses, dahlias, forsythia, spirea, delphiniums, verbena . . . and on and on.

And I remember people coming to my mother's yard to be given cuttings from her flowers; I hear again the praise showered on her because whatever rocky soil she landed on, she turned into a garden. A garden so brilliant with colors, so original in its design, so magnificent with life and creativity, that to this day people drive by our house in Georgia—perfect strangers and imperfect strangers—and ask to stand or walk among my mother's art.

I notice that it is only when my mother is working in her flowers that she is radiant, almost to the point of being invisible—except as Creator: hand and eye. She is involved in work her soul must have. Ordering the universe in the image of her personal conception of Beauty.

Her face, as she prepares the Art that is her gift, is a legacy of respect she leaves to me, for all that illuminates and cherishes life. She has handed down respect for the possibilities—and the will to grasp them.

For her, so hindered and intruded upon in so many ways, being an artist has still been a daily part of her life. This ability to hold on, even in very simple ways, is work black women have done for a very long time.

This poem is not enough, but it is something, for the woman who literally covered the holes in our walls with sunflowers:

> They were women then
> My mama's generation
> Husky of voice—Stout of
> Step
> With fists as well as
> Hands
> How they battered down
> Doors
> And ironed
> Starched white
> Shirts
> How they led
> Armies
> Headragged Generals

Across mined
Fields
Booby-trapped
Kitchens
To discover books
Desks
A place for us
How they knew what we
Must know
Without knowing a page
Of it
Themselves.

Guided by my heritage of a love of beauty and a respect for strength—in search of my mother's garden, I found my own.

And perhaps in Africa over two hundred years ago, there was just such a mother; perhaps she painted vivid and daring decorations in oranges and yellows and greens on the walls of her hut; perhaps she sang—in a voice like Roberta Flack's—*sweetly* over the compounds of her village; perhaps she wove the most stunning mats or told the most ingenious stories of all the village storytellers. Perhaps she was herself a poet—though only her daughter's name is signed to the poems that we know.

Perhaps Phillis Wheatley's mother was also an artist.

Perhaps in more than Phillis Wheatley's biological life is her mother's signature made clear.

UNIT 3

Working toward Community
and Justice

Injustice anywhere is a threat to justice everywhere. We are caught in an inescapable network of mutuality tied in a single garment of destiny. Whatever affects one directly affects all indirectly.

Martin Luther King Jr.

Introduction to Working toward Community and Justice

The readings in this final unit are a combination of the theoretical and the personal, but each asks a central question: if, as Martin Luther King Jr. proposes, we are all "caught in an inescapable network," how do we work to heal, mend, strengthen, and enrich that interdependent, interlaced web? Each author in this unit advocates principles to guide us in understanding justice and taking action for the common good.

The work you have done in The Reflective Woman already has been designed to assist you in approaching this final unit with these insights and questions: Who is my neighbor? What vision of our common life is compelling and just? What principles help me determine whether a particular action or decision would help bring that vision into reality? What forces or conditions prevent or delay our communities in achieving that vision?

More importantly, however, the College of St. Catherine is founded on the conviction that educated women have a right and a responsibility to lead and influence for a more just society. As you explore the principles, positions, and strategies of these authors, we invite you to reflect on what you believe the purpose of your life is, how the work you choose to do can best offer your own skills, interests, and understandings, and how you connect with and engage ever-wider circles of community. A liberal arts education is a life-long pursuit to liberate ourselves to know who we are, not just who we are told we are; to seek truths, not passively accept what others would lead us to believe; and to claim our own visions and voices for creating the world we live in and leave for others. This unit connects the concepts of identity and searching for truths with your life's work. As the poet Mary Oliver asks, "What is it you plan to do with your one wild and precious life?"

Ruth Forman is an award-winning African-American poet and the author of We Are the Young Magicians *(1993) (the source of this poem) and* Renaissance *(1997). How does the imagery in this poem symbolize community? What significance do you think poetry plays in describing social injustices?*

Poetry Should Ride the Bus

Ruth Forman

poetry should hopscotch in a polka dot dress
wheel cartwheels
n hold your hand
when you walk past the yellow crackhouse

poetry should wear bright red lipstick
n practice kisses in the mirror
for all the fine young men with fades
shootin craps around the corner

poetry should dress in fine plum linen suits
n not be so educated that it don't stop in
every now n then to sit on the porch
and talk about the comins and goins of the world

poetry should ride the bus
in a fat woman's Safeway bag
between the greens n chicken wings
to be served with Tuesday's dinner

poetry should drop by a sweet potato pie
ask about the grandchildren
n sit through a whole photo album
on a orange plastic covered La-Z-Boy with no place to go

poetry should sing red revolution love songs
that massage your scalp
and bring hope to your blood
when you think you're too old to fight

yeah
poetry should whisper electric blue magic
all the years of your life
never forgettin to look you in the soul
every once in a while
n smile

Mohandas K. Gandhi (1869–1948) was an Indian political activist and spiritual leader who came to be called Mahatma, meaning "Great Soul." Trained as a lawyer in England, he worked in South Africa for civil rights for the Indian population there, and then in his homeland to end the British colonial system. He developed a powerful form of non-violent protest and civil disobedience which came to be called satyagraha. Gandhi explains that his movement initially used the phrase "passive resistance" to describe its methods, but he was uncomfortable with Europeans' understanding of this phrase as connoting weakness, hatred, and the possibility of violence. A newspaper reader suggested satyagraha, *an invented word combining* sat *(truth) and* agraha *(firmness) in the Gujarati language. In these selections Gandhi describes how satyagraha works in practice, a philosophical and spiritual standpoint that later was to influence Dr. Martin Luther King Jr. Gandhi, who was assassinated in 1948, is now called the "Father of India." As you read Gandhi's essay, think about how his movement might be a model for building community. Is a nonviolent approach truly an effective way to achieve social justice?*

from Non-Violent Resistance

Mohandas K. Gandhi

Satyagraha, Civil Disobedience, Passive Resistance, Non-Co-Operation

Satyagraha, then, is literally holding on to Truth and it means, therefore, Truth-force. Truth is soul or spirit. It is, therefore, known as soulforce. It excludes the use of violence because man is not capable of knowing the absolute truth and, therefore, not competent to punish. The word was coined in South Africa [in 1908] to distinguish the non-violent resistance of the Indians of South Africa from the contemporary "passive resistance" of the suffragettes and others. It is not conceived as a weapon of the weak.

Passive resistance is used in the orthodox English sense and covers the suffragette movement as well as the resistance of the nonconformists. Passive resistance has been conceived and is regarded as a weapon of the weak. Whilst it avoids violence, being not open to the weak, it does not exclude its use if, in the opinion of a passive resister, the occasion demands it. However, it has always been distinguished from armed resistance and its application was at one time confined to Christian martyrs.

Civil disobedience is civil breach of unmoral statutory enactments. The expression was, so far as I am aware, coined by Thoreau to signify his own resistance to the laws of a slave state. He has left a masterly treatise on the duty of civil disobedience. But Thoreau was not perhaps an out-and-out champion of non-violence. Probably, also, Thoreau limited his breach of statutory laws to the revenue law, i.e., payment of taxes, whereas the term "civil disobedience" as practiced in 1919 covered a breach of any statutory and unmoral law. It signified the resister's outlawry in a civil, i.e., nonviolent manner. He invoked the sanctions of the law and cheerfully suffered imprisonment. It is a branch of satyagraha.

Non-co-operation predominantly implies withdrawing of co-operation from the state that in the non-co-operator's view has become corrupt and excludes civil disobedience of the fierce type described above. By its very nature, non-co-operation is even open to children of understanding and can be safely practiced by the masses. Civil disobedience presupposes the habit of willing obedience to laws without fear of their sanctions. It can therefore be practiced only as a last resort and by a select few in the first instance at any rate. Non-co-operation, too, like civil disobedience is a branch of satyagraha which includes all non-violent resistance for the vindication of Truth.

Satyagraha—Not Passive Resistance

The force denoted by the term "passive resistance" and translated into Hindi as *nishkriya pratirodha* is not very accurately described either by the original English phrase or by its Hindi rendering. Its correct description is "satyagraha." Satyagraha was born in South Africa in 1908. There was no word in any Indian language denoting the power which our countrymen in South Africa invoked for the redress of their grievances. There was an English equivalent, namely, "passive resistance," and we carried on with it. However, the need for a word to describe this unique power came to be increasingly felt, and it was decided to award a prize to anyone who could think of an appropriate term. A Gujarati-speaking gentleman submitted the word "satyagraha," and it was adjudged the best.

"Passive resistance" conveyed the idea of the Suffragette Movement in England. Burning of houses by these women was called "passive resistance" and so also their fasting in prison. All such acts might very well be "passive resistance" but they were not "satyagraha." It is said of "passive resistance" that it is the weapon of the weak, but the power which is the subject of this article can be used only by the strong. This power is not "passive" resistance; indeed it calls for intense activity. The movement in South Africa was not passive but active. The Indians of South Africa believed that Truth was their object, that Truth ever triumphs, and with this definiteness of purpose they persistently held on to Truth. They put up with all the suffering that this persistence implied. With the conviction that Truth is not to be renounced even unto death, they shed the fear of death. In the cause of Truth, the prison was a palace to them and its doors the gateway to freedom.

Satyagraha is not physical force. A satyagrahi does not inflict pain on the adversary; he does not seek his destruction. A satyagrahi never resorts to firearms. In the use of satyagraha, there is no ill-will whatever.

Satyagraha is pure soul-force. Truth is the very substance of the soul. That is why this force is called satyagraha. The soul is informed with knowledge. In it burns the flame of love. If someone gives us pain through ignorance, we shall win him through love. "Non-violence is the supreme dharma" is the proof of this power of love. Non-violence is a dormant state. In the waking state, it is love. Ruled by love, the world goes on. In English there is a saying, "Might is Right." Then there is the doctrine of the survival of the fittest. Both of these ideas are contradictory to the above principle. Neither is wholly true. If ill-will were the chief motive-force, the world would have been destroyed long ago; and neither would I have had the opportunity to write this article nor would the hopes of the readers be fulfilled. We are alive solely because of love. We are ourselves the proof of this. Deluded by modern western civilization, we have forgotten our ancient civilization and worship the might of arms.

We forget the principle of non-violence, which is the essence of all religions. The doctrine of arms stands for irreligion. It is due to the sway of that doctrine that a sanguinary war is raging in Europe.

In India also we find worship of arms. We see it even in that great work of Tulsidas. But it is seen in all the books that soul-force is the supreme power. . . .

It brings good both to the satyagrahi and his adversary. It is ever victorious. For instance, Harishchandra was a satyagrahi, Prahlad was a satyagrahi, Mirabai was a satyagrahi. Daniel, Socrates and those Arabs who hurled themselves on the fire of the French artillery were all satyagrahis. We see from these examples that a satyagrahi does not fear for his body, he does not give up what he thinks is Truth; the word "defeat" is not to be found in his dictionary, he does not wish for the destruction of his antagonist, he does not vent anger on him; but has only compassion for him.

A satyagrahi does not wait for others, but throws himself into the fray, relying entirely on his own resources. He trusts that when the time comes, others will do likewise. His practice is his precept. Like air, satyagraha is all-pervading. It is infectious, which means that all people—big and small, men and women—can become satyagrahis. No one is kept out from the army of satyagrahis. A satyagrahi cannot perpetrate tyranny on anyone; he is not subdued through application of physical force; he does not strike at anyone. Just as anyone can resort to satyagraha, it can be resorted to in almost any situation.

People demand historical evidence in support of satyagraha. History is for the most part a record of armed activities. Natural activities find very little mention in it. Only uncommon activities strike us with wonder. Satyagraha has been used always and in all situations. The father and the son, the man and the wife are perpetually resorting to satyagraha, one towards the other. When a father gets angry and punishes the son, the son does not hit back with a weapon, he conquers his father's anger by submitting to him. The son refuses to be subdued by the unjust rule of his father but he puts up with the punishment that he may incur through disobeying the unjust father. We can similarly free ourselves of the unjust rule of the Government by defying the unjust rule and accepting the punishments that go with it. We do not bear malice towards the Government. When we set its fears at rest, when we do not desire to make armed assaults on the administrators, nor to unseat them from power, but only to get rid of their injustice, they will at once be subdued to our will.

The question is asked why we should call any rule unjust. In saying so, we ourselves assume the function of a judge. It is true. But in this world, we always have to act as judges for ourselves. That is why the satyagrahi does not strike his adversary with arms. If he has Truth on his side, he will win, and if his thought is faulty, he will suffer the consequences of his fault.

What is the good, they ask, of only one person opposing injustice; for he will be punished and destroyed, he will languish in prison or meet an untimely end through hanging. The objection is not valid. History shows that all reforms have begun with one person. Fruit is hard to come by without *tapasya* [self-sacrifice]. The suffering that has to be undergone in satyagraha is *tapasya* in its purest form. Only when the *tapasya* is capable of bearing fruit, do we have the fruit. This establishes the fact that when there is insufficient *tapasya*, the fruit is delayed. The *tapasya* of Jesus Christ, boundless though it was, was not sufficient for Europe's need. Europe has disapproved Christ. Through ignorance, it has disregarded Christ's pure way of life. Many Christs will have to offer themselves as sacrifice at the terrible altar of Europe, and only then will realization dawn on that continent. But Jesus will always be the first among these. He has been the sower of the seeds and his will therefore be the credit for raising the harvest.

It is said that it is a very difficult, if not an altogether impossible, task to educate ignorant peasants in satyagraha and that it is full of perils, for it is a very arduous business to transform unlettered ignorant people from one condition into another. Both the arguments are just silly. The people of India are perfectly fit to receive the training of satyagraha. India has knowledge of dharma [religious duty], and where there is knowledge of dharma, satyagraha is a very simple matter. The people of India have drunk of the nectar of devotion. This great people overflows with faith. It is no difficult matter to lead such a people on the right path of satyagraha. Some have a fear that once people get involved in satyagraha, they may at a later stage take to arms. This fear is illusory. From the path of satyagraha [clinging to Truth], a transition to the path of a-satyagraha [clinging to untruth] is impossible. It is possible of course that some people who believe in armed activity may mislead the satyagrahis by infiltrating into their ranks and later making them take to arms. This is possible in all enterprises. But as compared to other activities, it is less likely to happen in satyagraha, for their motives soon get exposed and when the people are not ready to take up arms, it becomes almost impossible to lead them on to that terrible path. The might of arms is directly opposed to the might of satyagraha. Just as darkness does not abide in light, soulless armed activity cannot enter the sunlike radiance of soul-force. Many Pathans took part in satyagraha in South Africa abiding by all the rules of satyagraha.

Then it is said that much suffering is involved in being a satyagrahi and that the entire people will not be willing to put up with this suffering. The objection is not valid. People in general always follow in the footsteps of the noble. There is no doubt that it is difficult to produce a satyagrahi leader. Our experience is that a satyagrahi needs many more virtues like self-control, fearlessness, etc., than are requisite for one who believes in armed action. The greatness of the man bearing arms does not lie in the superiority of the arms, nor does it lie in his physical prowess. It lies in his determination and fearlessness in face of death. . . . The strength of a warrior is not measured by reference to his weapons but by his firmness of mind. A satyagrahi needs millions of times more of such firmness than does a bearer of arms. The birth of such a man can bring about the salvation of India in no time. Not only India but the whole world awaits the advent of such a man. We may in the meanwhile prepare the ground as much as we can through satyagraha. . . .

For swaraj, satyagraha is the unfailing weapon. Satyagraha means that what we want is truth, that we deserve it and that we will work for it even unto death. . . .

Truth alone triumphs. There is no dharma [religion] higher than Truth. Truth always wins. We pray to God that in this sacred land we may bring about the reign of dharma by following satyagraha and that thus our country may become an example for all to follow.

There are two methods of attaining one's goal. Satyagraha and *duragraha*. In our scriptures, they have been described, respectively, as divine and devilish modes of action. In satyagraha, there is always unflinching adherence to truth. It is never to be forsaken on any account. Even for the sake of one's country, it does not permit resort to falsehood. It proceeds on the assumption of the ultimate triumph of truth. A satyagrahi does not abandon his path, even though at times it seems impenetrable and beset with difficulties and dangers, and a slight departure from that straight path may appear full of promise. Even in these circumstances, his faith shines resplendent like the midday sun and he does not despond. With truth for his sword, he needs neither a steel sword nor gunpowder. Even an inveterate enemy he conquers by the force of the soul, which is love. Love for a friend is not put to the test. There is nothing surprising in a friend loving a friend; there is no merit in it and it costs no effort. When love is bestowed on the so-called enemy, it is tested, it becomes a virtue and requires an effort, and hence it is an act of manliness and real bravery. We can cultivate such an attitude even towards the Government and, doing so, we shall be able to appreciate their beneficial activities and, as for their errors, rather than feel bitter on their account, point them out in love and so get them rectified. Love does not act through fear. Weakness there certainly cannot be. A coward is incapable of bearing love, it is the prerogative of the brave. Looking at everything with love, we shall not regard the Government with suspicion, nor believe that all their actions are inspired with bad motives. And our examination of their actions, being directed by love, will be unerring and is bound, therefore, to carry conviction with them.

Love can fight; often it is obliged to. In the intoxication of power, man fails to see his error. When that happens, a satyagrahi does not sit still. He suffers. He disobeys the ruler's orders and his laws in a civil manner, and willingly submits to the penalties of such disobedience, for instance, imprisonment and gallows. Thus is the soul disciplined. In this, one never finds that one's time has been wasted and, if it is subsequently realized that such respectful disobedience was an error, the consequences are suffered merely by the satyagrahi and his co-workers. In the event, no bitterness develops between the satyagrahi and those in power; the latter, on the contrary, willingly yield to him. *They discover that they cannot command the satyagrahi's obedience. They cannot make him do anything against his will. And this is the consummation of swaraj, because it means complete independence.* It need not be assumed that such resistance is possible only against civilized rulers. Even a heart of flint will melt in the fire kindled by the power of the soul. Even a Nero becomes a lamb when he faces love. This is no exaggeration. It is as true as an algebraic equation. This satyagraha is India's distinctive weapon. It has had others but satyagraha has been in greater use. It is an unfailing source of strength, and is capable of being used at all times and under all circumstances. It requires no stamp of approval from the Congress or any other body. He who knows its power cannot but use it. Even as the eyelashes automatically protect the eyes, so does satyagraha, when kindled, automatically protect the freedom of the soul.

But *duragraha* is a force with the opposite attributes. . . . The man who follows the path of *duragraha* becomes impatient and wants to kill the so-called enemy. There can be but one result of this. Hatred increases. The defeated party vows vengeance and simply bides its time. The spirit of revenge thus descends from father to son. It is much to be wished that India never give predominance to this spirit of *duragraha*. If the members of this assembly deliberately accept satyagraha and chalk out its program accordingly, they will reach their goal all the more easily for doing so. They may have to face disappointment in the initial stages. They may not see results for a time. But satyagraha will triumph in the end. The *duragrahi*, like the oilman's ox, moves in a circle. His movement is only motion but it is not progress. The satyagrahi is ever moving forward. . . .

The right thing to hope from India is that this great and holy Aryan land will ever give the predominant place to the divine force and employ the weapon of satyagraha, that it will never accept the supremacy of armed strength. India will never respect the principle of might being right. She will ever reserve her allegiance to the principle: "Truth alone triumphs."

On reflection, we find that we can employ satyagraha even for social reform. We can rid ourselves of the many defects of our caste system. We can resolve Hindu-Muslim differences and we can solve political problems. It is all right that, for the sake of convenience, we speak of these things as separate subjects. But it should never be forgotten that they are all closely inter-related. It is not true to say that neither religion nor social reform has anything to do with politics.

Duty, Democracy and Swaraj

You want democracy—the rule of the people, by the people, for the people. Surely, all the 75,000 people of Rajkot* cannot become rulers or administrators. Democracy must in essence, therefore, mean the art and science of mobilizing the entire physical, economic and spiritual resources of all the various sections of the people in the service of the common good of all.

Service of the family has been the motive behind all our activities hitherto. We must now learn to broaden our outlook so as to include in our ambit the service of the people as a whole.

We are familiar with several conceptions of village work. Hitherto it has mostly meant propaganda in the villages to inculcate upon the village masses a sense of their rights. Sometimes it has also meant conducting welfare activity among them to ameliorate their material condition. But the village work that I have now come to place before you consists in educating the villager in his duties.

---

* City in the western state of Gujarat.

Rights accrue automatically to him who duly performs his duties. In fact the right to perform one's duties is the only right that is worth living for and dying for. It covers all legitimate rights. All the rest is garb under one guise or another and contains in it seeds of *himsa*.

The swaraj of my conception will come only when all of us are firmly persuaded that our swaraj has got to be won, worked and maintained through truth and ahimsa alone. True democracy or the swaraj of the masses can never come through untruthful and violent means, for the simple reason that the natural corollary to their use would be to remove all opposition through the suppression or extermination of the antagonists. That does not make for individual freedom. Individual freedom can have the fullest play only under a regime of unadulterated ahimsa.

We cannot afford to have discord in our midst if we are to educate the people. We must all speak with one voice. If we want to weld the various sections into one people—and that is the *sine qua non* of democracy—we may not, in rendering service, make any distinction between those who took part in our struggle and those who did not.

We want to set up democracy in Rajkot. A born democrat is a born disciplinarian. Democracy comes naturally to him who is habituated normally to yield willing obedience to all laws, human or divine. I claim to be a democrat both by instinct and training. Let those who are ambitious to serve democracy qualify themselves by satisfying first this acid test of democracy. Moreover, a democrat must be utterly selfless. He must think and dream not in terms of self or party but only of democracy. Only then does he acquire the right of civil disobedience. I do not want anybody to give up his convictions or to suppress himself. I do not believe that a healthy and honest difference of opinion will injure our cause. But opportunism, camouflage or patched-up compromises certainly will. If you must dissent, you should take care that your opinions voice your innermost convictions and are not intended merely as a convenient party cry.

Today our democracy is choked by our internecine strife. We are torn by dissensions—dissensions between Hindus and Mussalmans, Brahmins and non-Brahmins, Congressmen and non-Congressmen. It is no easy task to evolve democracy out of this mobocracy. Let us not make confusion worse confounded by further introducing into it the virus of sectionalism and party spirit.

I value individual freedom but you must not forget that man is essentially a social being. He has risen to this present status by learning to adjust his individualism to the requirements of social progress. Unrestricted individualism is the law of the beast of the jungle. We have learnt to strike the mean between individual freedom and social restraint. Willing submission to social restraint for the sake of the well-being of the whole society enriches both the individual and the society of which one is a member.

Democracy disciplined and enlightened is the finest thing in the world. A democracy prejudiced, ignorant, superstitious will land itself in chaos and may be self-destroyed.

I hold that self-government is not an end, but only a means to good government. And true democracy is what promotes the welfare of the people. The test of a good government lies in the largest good of the people with the minimum of controls. The test of autocracy, socialism, capitalism, etc., is also people's welfare or good government. In themselves they are of no value. Any system of government can fail if people do not have honesty and a feeling of brotherhood. There may be work, there may be women to do the work and tools with which to do it, yet in my view a system that admits of poverty and unemployment is not fit to survive even for a day.

Democracy is where even the man in the street is heard. When we are out to establish a democratic order, the Viceroy's House, or even Jawaharlal's [Nehru] house, is not the seat of the Government. I have described Jawaharlal as the uncrowned king. And we are a poor nation. We are so poor that we shall walk rather than ride in a car. Even if somebody offers us a lift in his car, we shall decline his offer saying that he can keep his car, we would rather walk. If we are over-hungry, we shall eat a little more. Thus democracy means the rule of the man in the street.

Democracy is an impossible thing until the power is shared by all, but let not democracy degenerate into mobocracy. Even a pariah, a laborer, who makes it possible for you to earn your living, will have his share in self-government. But you will have to touch their lives. Go to them, see their hovels where they live packed like sardines. It is up to you to look after this part of humanity. It is possible for you to make their lives or mar their lives.

In this age of democracy it is essential that desired results are achieved by the collective effort of the people. It will no doubt be good to achieve an objective through the effort of a supremely powerful individual, but it can never make the community conscious of its corporate strength. An individual's success will be like a millionaire doling free food to millions of starving people. We should, therefore, bend our energies to a fulfillment of the thirteenfold constructive programme. It may or may not bring swaraj, but we shall surely have the satisfaction of having done our best.

All Hindus, Muslims, Sikhs, Parsis, Christians and Jews who people this country from Kanyakumari to Kashmir and from Karachi to Dibrugarh in Assam and who have lovingly and in a spirit of service adopted it as their dear motherland, have an equal right to it. No one can say that it has place only for the majority and the minority should be dishonored. Whoever serves it with the purest devotion must have the first right over it. Therefore, anyone who seeks to drive out the Muslims is Delhi's enemy number one and therefore India's enemy number one. We are heading towards that catastrophe. Every Indian must do his bit to ward it off.

What should we do then? If we would see Panchayat Raj, i.e., democracy established, we would regard the humblest and the lowliest Indian as being equally the ruler of India with the tallest in the land. For this everyone should be pure. If they are not they should become so. He who is pure will also be wise. He will observe no distinctions between caste and caste, between touchable and untouchable, but will consider everyone equal with himself. He will bind others to himself with love. To him no one would be an untouchable. He would treat the laborers the same as he would the capitalists. He will, like the millions of toilers, earn his living from service of others and will make no distinction between intellectual and manual work. To hasten this desirable consummation, we should voluntarily turn ourselves into scavengers. He who is wise will never touch opium, liquor or any intoxicants. He will observe the vow of swadeshi and regard every woman who is not his wife as his mother, sister or daughter according to her age, and never see anyone with eyes of lust. He will concede to woman the same rights he claims for himself. If need be he will sacrifice his own life but never kill another.

. . . I have suggested that you [a Hindu majority, in 1947, after independence] should adopt the ways followed by all democratic countries. In democracy, every individual has to abide by the wishes of the people, that is, the Government, and has to direct his own wishes in that light. If every man takes the law into his own hands the State cannot function. It would mean anarchy, which means end of social order. That is, the State would not exist. That is the way to lose our independence. I believe that if you would let the Government carry out its tasks, there is no doubt that every Hindu and Sikh refugee would return home with honor and respect. But you cannot expect these things to happen if you want your Muslim compatriots to be driven out of India. I find any such thing dreadful. You cannot secure justice by doing injustice to the Muslims.

The spirit of democracy, which is fast spreading throughout India and the rest of the world, will, without a shadow of doubt, purge the institution of the idea of predominance and subordination. The spirit of democracy is not a mechanical thing to be adjusted by abolition of forms. It requires change of the heart. If caste is a bar to the spread of that spirit, the existence of five religions in India—Hinduism, Islam, Christianity, Zoroastrianism, and Judaism—is equally a bar. The spirit of democracy requires the inculcation of the spirit of brotherhood, and I can find no difficulty in considering a Christian or a Mohammedan to be my brother in absolutely the same sense as a blood brother, and Hinduism that is responsible for the doctrine of caste is also responsible for the inculcation of the essential brotherhood, not merely of man but even of all that lives.

Dr. Martin Luther King Jr. (1929–1968) was a leader of the United States Civil Rights Movement during the 1950s and 1960s. At the age of thirty-five, he was the youngest man to have ever received the Nobel Peace Prize. He was also a proponent of Gandhi's nonviolent resistance. He was assassinated in 1968. One example of his powerful legacy is the following letter that he wrote while he was in jail for demonstrating without a permit. Do you think it's possible for words to lead to action? What type of arguments did he present and how effective do you think they were in getting his points across? What overall impact do you imagine this letter had on the Civil Rights Movement?

Letter from a Birmingham Jail

Martin Luther King Jr.

Birmingham City Jail
April 16, 1963

Bishop C. C. J. Carpenter
Bishop Joseph A. Durick
Rabbi Milton L. Grafman
Bishop Paul Hardin
Bishop Nolan B. Harmon
The Reverend George M. Murray
The Reverend Edward V. Ramage
The Reverend Earl Stallings

My dear Fellow Clergymen,

While confined here in Birmingham City jail, I came across your recent statement calling our present activities "unwise and untimely." Seldom, if ever, do I pause to answer criticism of my work and ideas. If I sought to answer all of the criticisms that cross my desk, my secretaries would be engaged in little else in the course of the day and I would have no time for constructive work. But since I feel that you are men of genuine good will and your criticisms are sincerely set forth, I would like to answer your statement in what I hope will be patient and reasonable terms.

I think I should give the reason for my being in Birmingham, since you have been influenced by the argument of "outsiders coming in." I have the honor of serving as president of the Southern Christian Leadership Conference, an organization operating in every Southern state with headquarters in Atlanta, Georgia. We have some eighty-five affiliate organizations all across the South—one being the Alabama Christian Movement for Human Rights. Whenever necessary and possible we share staff, educational, and financial resources with our affiliates. Several months ago our local affiliate here in Birmingham invited us to be on call to engage in a nonviolent direct action program if such were deemed necessary. We readily consented and when the hour came we lived up to our promises. So I am here, along with several members of my staff, because we were invited here. I am here because I have basic organizational ties here. Beyond this, I am in Birmingham because injustice is here. Just as the eighth century prophets left their little villages and carried their "thus saith the Lord" far beyond the boundaries of their home town, and just as the Apostle Paul left his little village of Tarsus and carried the gospel of Jesus Christ to practically every hamlet and city of the Graeco-Roman world, I too am compelled to carry the gospel of freedom beyond my particular home town. Like Paul, I must constantly respond to the Macedonian call for aid.

Moreover, I am cognizant of the interrelatedness of all communities and states. I cannot sit idly by in Atlanta and not be concerned about what happens in Birmingham. Injustice anywhere is a threat to justice everywhere. We are caught in an inescapable network of mutuality tied in a single garment of destiny. Whatever affects one directly affects all indirectly. Never again can we afford to live with the narrow, provincial "outside agitator" idea. Anyone who lives inside the United States can never be considered an outsider anywhere in this country.

You deplore the demonstrations that are presently taking place in Birmingham. But I am sorry that your statement did not express a similar concern for the conditions that brought the demonstrations into being. I am sure that each of you would want to go beyond the superficial social analyst who looks merely at effects, and does not grapple with underlying causes. I would not hesitate to say that it is unfortunate that so-called demonstrations are taking place in Birmingham at this time, but I would say in more emphatic terms that it is even more unfortunate that the white power structure of this city left the Negro community with no other alternative.

In any nonviolent campaign there are four basic steps: (1) collection of the facts to determine whether injustices are alive; (2) negotiation; (3) self-purification; and (4) direct action. We have gone through all of these steps in Birmingham. There can be no gainsaying of the fact that racial injustice engulfs this community. Birmingham is probably the most thoroughly segregated city in the United States. Its ugly record of police brutality is known in every section of this country. Its unjust treatment of Negroes in the courts is a notorious reality. There have been more unsolved bombings of Negro homes and churches in Birmingham than any city in this nation. These are the hard, brutal, and unbelievable facts. On the basis of these conditions Negro leaders sought to negotiate with the city fathers. But the political leaders consistently refused to engage in good faith negotiation.

Then came the opportunity last September to talk with some of the leaders of the economic community. In these negotiating sessions certain promises were made by the merchants—such as the promise to remove the humiliating racial signs from the stores. On the basis of these promises Rev. Shuttlesworth and the leaders of the Alabama Christian Movement for Human Rights agreed to call a moratorium on any type of demonstrations. As the weeks and months unfolded we realized that we were the victims of a broken promise. The signs remained. As in so many experiences of the past we were confronted with blasted hopes, and the dark shadow of a deep disappointment settled upon us. So we had no alternative except that of preparing for direct action, whereby we would present our very bodies as a means of laying our case before the conscience of the local and national community. We were not unmindful of the difficulties involved. So we decided to go through a process of self-purification. We started having workshops on nonviolence and repeatedly asked ourselves the questions, "Are you able to accept blows without retaliating?" "Are you able to endure the ordeals of jail?"

We decided to set our direct action program around the Easter season, realizing that with the exception of Christmas, this was the largest shopping period of the year. Knowing that a strong economic withdrawal program would be the by-product of direct action, we felt that this was the best time to bring pressure on the merchants for the needed changes. Then it occurred to us that the March election was ahead, and so we speedily decided to postpone action until after election day. When we discovered that Mr. Connor was in the runoff, we decided again to postpone action so that the demonstrations could not be used to cloud the issues. At this time we agreed to begin our nonviolent witness the day after the runoff.

This reveals that we did not move irresponsibly into direct action. We too wanted to see Mr. Connor defeated; so we went through postponement after postponement to aid in this community need. After this we felt that direct action could be delayed no longer.

You may well ask, "Why direct action? Why sit-ins, marches, etc.? Isn't negotiation a better path?" You are exactly right in your call for negotiation. Indeed, this is the purpose of direct action. Nonviolent direct action seeks to create such a crisis and establish such creative tension that a community that has constantly refused to negotiate is forced to confront the issue. It seeks so to dramatize the issue that it can no longer be ignored. I just referred to the creation of tension as a part of the work of the nonviolent resister. This may sound rather shocking. But I must confess that I am not afraid of the word tension. I have earnestly worked and preached against violent tension, but there is a type of constructive nonviolent tension that is necessary for growth. Just as Socrates felt that it was necessary to create a tension in the mind so that individuals could rise from the bondage of myths and half-truths to the unfettered realm of creative analysis and objective appraisal, we must see the need of having nonviolent gadflies to create the kind of tension in society that will help men rise from the dark depths of prejudice and racism to the majestic heights of understanding and brotherhood. So the purpose of the direct action is to create a situation so crisis-packed that it will inevitably open the door to negotiation. We, therefore, concur with you in your call for negotiation. Too long has our beloved Southland been bogged down in the tragic attempt to live in monologue rather than dialogue.

One of the basic points in your statement is that our acts are untimely. Some have asked, "Why didn't you give the new administration time to act?" The only answer that I can give to this inquiry is that the new administration must be prodded about as much as the outgoing one before it acts. We will be sadly mistaken if we feel that the election of Mr. Boutwell will bring the millennium to Birmingham. While Mr. Boutwell is much more articulate and gentle than Mr. Connor, they are both segregationists dedicated to the task of maintaining the status quo. The hope I see in Mr. Boutwell is that he will be reasonable enough to see the futility of massive resistance to desegregation. But he will not see this without pressure from the devotees of civil rights. My friends, I must say to you that we have not made a single gain in civil rights without determined legal and nonviolent pressure. History is the long and tragic story of the fact that privileged groups seldom give up their privileges voluntarily. Individuals may see the moral light and voluntarily give up their unjust posture; but as Reinhold Niebuhr has reminded us, groups are more immoral than individuals.

We know through painful experience that freedom is never voluntarily given by the oppressor; it must be demanded by the oppressed. Frankly I have never yet engaged in a direct action movement that was "well timed," according to the timetable of those who have not suffered unduly from the disease of segregation. For years now I have heard the word "Wait!" It rings in the ear of every Negro with a piercing familiarity. This "wait" has almost always meant "never." It has been a tranquilizing thalidomide, relieving the emotional stress for a moment, only to give birth to an ill-formed infant of frustration. We must come to see with the distinguished jurist of yesterday that "justice too long delayed is justice denied." We have waited for more than three hundred and forty years for our constitutional and God-given rights. The nations of Asia and Africa are moving with jet-like speed toward the goal of political independence, and we still creep at horse and buggy pace toward the gaining of a cup of coffee at a lunch counter.

I guess it is easy for those who have never felt the stinging darts of segregation to say wait. But when you have seen vicious mobs lynch your mothers and fathers at will and drown your sisters and brothers at whim; when you have seen hate-filled policemen curse, kick, brutalize, and even kill your black brothers and sisters with impunity; when you see the vast majority of your twenty million Negro brothers smothering in an airtight cage of poverty in the midst of an affluent society; when you suddenly find your tongue twisted and your speech stammering as you seek to explain to your six-year-old daughter why she can't go to the public amusement park that has just been advertised on television, and see tears welling up in her little eyes when she is told that Funtown is closed to colored children, and see the depressing clouds of inferiority begin to form in her little mental sky, and see her begin to distort her little personality by unconsciously developing a bitterness toward white people; when you have to concoct an answer for a five-year-old son asking in agonizing pathos: "Daddy, why do white people treat colored people so mean?"; when you take a cross-country drive and find it necessary to sleep night after night in the uncomfortable corners of your automobile because no motel will accept you; when you are humiliated day in and day out by nagging signs reading "white" men and "colored"; when your first name becomes "nigger" and your middle name becomes "boy" (however old you are) and your last name becomes "John," and when your wife and mother are never given the respected title "Mrs."; when you are harried by day and haunted by night by the fact that you are a Negro, living constantly at tip-toe stance never quite knowing what to expect next, and plagued with inner fears and outer resentments; when you are forever fighting a degenerating sense of "nobodiness";—then you will understand why we find it very difficult to wait. There comes a time when the cup of our endurance runs over, and men are no longer willing to be plunged into an abyss of injustice where they experience the bleakness of a corroding despair. I hope, sirs, you can understand our legitimate and unavoidable impatience.

You express a great deal of anxiety over our willingness to break laws. This is certainly a legitimate concern. Since we so diligently urge people to obey the Supreme Court's decision of 1954 outlawing segregation in the public schools, it is rather strange and paradoxical to find us consciously breaking laws. One may well ask, "How can you advocate breaking some laws and obeying others?" The answer is found in the fact that there are two types of laws. There are *just* laws and there are *unjust* laws. I would be the first to advocate obeying just laws. One has not only a legal but moral responsibility to obey just laws. Conversely, one has a moral responsibility to disobey unjust laws. I would agree with Saint Augustine that "An unjust law is no law at all."

Now what is the difference between the two? How does one determine when a law is just or unjust? A just law is a man-made code that squares with the moral law or the law of God. An unjust law is a code that is out of harmony with the moral law. To put it in the terms of Saint Thomas Aquinas, an unjust law is a human law that is not rooted in eternal and natural law. Any law that uplifts human personality is just. Any law that degrades human personality is unjust. All segregation statutes are unjust because segregation distorts the soul and damages the personality. It gives the segregator a false sense of superiority and the segregated a false sense of inferiority. To use the words of Martin Buber, the great Jewish philosopher, segregation substitutes an "I-it" relationship for the "I-thou" relationship, and ends up relegating persons to the status of things. So segregation is not only politically, economically, and sociologically unsound, but it is morally wrong and sinful. Paul Tillich has said that sin is separation. Isn't segregation an existential expression of man's tragic separation, an expression of his awful estrangement, his terrible sinfulness? So I can urge men to obey the 1954 decision of the Supreme Court because it is morally right, and I can urge them to disobey segregation ordinances because they are morally wrong.

Let us turn to a more concrete example of just and unjust laws. An unjust law is a code that a majority inflicts on a minority that is not binding on itself. This is *difference* made legal. On the other hand a just law is a code that a majority compels a minority to follow that it is willing to follow itself. This is *sameness* made legal.

Let me give another explanation. An unjust law is a code inflicted upon a minority which that minority had no part in enacting or creating because they did not have the unhampered right to vote. Who can say the legislature of Alabama which set up the segregation laws was democratically elected? Throughout the State of Alabama all types of conniving methods are used to prevent Negroes from becoming registered voters and there are some counties without a single Negro registered to vote despite the fact that the Negro constitutes a majority of the population. Can any law set up in such a state be considered democratically structured?

These are just a few examples of unjust and just laws. There are some instances when a law is just on its face but unjust in its application. For instance, I was arrested Friday on a charge of parading without a permit. Now there is nothing wrong with an ordinance which requires a permit for a parade, but when the ordinance is used to preserve segregation and to deny citizens the First Amendment privilege of peaceful assembly and peaceful protest, then it becomes unjust.

I hope you can see the distinction I am trying to point out. In no sense do I advocate evading or defying the law as the rabid segregationist would do. This would lead to anarchy. One who breaks an unjust law must do it *openly, lovingly* (not hatefully as the white mothers did in New Orleans when they were seen on television screaming "nigger, nigger, nigger") and with a willingness to accept the penalty. I submit that an individual who breaks a law that conscience tells him is unjust, and willingly accepts the penalty by staying in jail to arouse the conscience of the community over its injustice, is in reality expressing the very highest respect for law.

Of course there is nothing new about this kind of civil disobedience. It was seen sublimely in the refusal of Shadrach, Meshach, and Abednego to obey the unjust laws of Nebuchadnezzar because a higher moral law was involved. It was practiced superbly by the early Christians who were willing to face hungry lions and the excruciating pain of chopping blocks, before submitting to certain very unjust laws of the Roman Empire. To a degree our academic freedom is a reality today because Socrates practiced civil disobedience.

We can never forget that everything Hitler did in Germany was "legal" and everything the Hungarian freedom fighters did in Hungary was "illegal." It was "illegal" to aid and comfort a Jew in Hitler's Germany. But I am sure that, if I had lived in Germany during that time, I would have aided and comforted my Jewish brothers even though it was illegal. If I lived in a communist country today where certain principles dear to the Christian faith are suppressed, I believe I would openly advocate disobeying these antireligious laws.

I must make two honest confessions to you, my Christian and Jewish brothers. First I must confess that over the last few years I have been gravely disappointed with the white moderate. I have almost reached the regrettable conclusion that the Negroes' great stumbling block in the stride toward freedom is not the White Citizens' "Councilor" or the Ku Klux Klanner, but the white moderate who is more devoted to "order" than to justice; who prefers a negative peace which is the absence of tension to a positive peace which is the presence of justice; who constantly says "I agree with you in the goal you seek, but I can't agree with your methods of direct action"; who paternalistically feels that he can set the timetable for another man's freedom; who lives by the myth of time and who constantly advises the Negro to wait until a "more convenient season." Shallow understanding from people of good will is more frustrating than absolute misunderstanding from people of ill will. Lukewarm acceptance is much more bewildering than outright rejection.

I had hoped that the white moderate would understand that law and order exist for the purpose of establishing justice, and that when they fail to do this they become the dangerously structured dams that block the flow of social progress. I had hoped that the white moderate would understand that the present tension in the South is merely a necessary phase of the transition from an obnoxious negative peace, where the Negro passively accepted his unjust plight, to a substance-filled positive peace, where all men will respect the dignity and worth of human personality. Actually, we who engage in nonviolent direct action are not the creators of tension. We merely bring to the surface the hidden tension that is already alive. We bring it out in the open where it can be seen and dealt with. Like a boil that can never be cured as long as it is covered up but must be opened with all its pus-flowing ugliness to the natural medicines of air and light, injustice must likewise be exposed, with all of the tension its exposing creates, to the light of human conscience and the air of national opinion before it can be cured.

In your statement you asserted that our actions, even though peaceful, must be condemned because they precipitate violence. But can this assertion be logically made? Isn't this like condemning the robbed man because his possession of money precipitated the evil act of robbery? Isn't this like condemning Socrates because his unswerving commitment to truth and his philosophical delvings precipitated the misguided popular mind to make him drink the hemlock? Isn't this like condemning Jesus because His unique God consciousness and never-ceasing devotion to His will precipitated the evil act of crucifixion? We must come to see, as federal courts have consistently affirmed, that it is immoral to urge an individual to withdraw his efforts to gain his basic constitutional rights because the quest precipitates violence. Society must protect the robbed and punish the robber.

I had also hoped that the white moderate would reject the myth of time. I received a letter this morning from a white brother in Texas which said: "All Christians know that the colored people will receive equal rights eventually, but is it possible that you are in too great of a religious hurry? It has taken Christianity almost 2000 years to accomplish what it has. The teachings of Christ take time to come to earth." All that is said here grows out of a tragic misconception of time. It is the strangely irrational notion that there is something in the very flow of time that will inevitably cure all ills. Actually time is neutral. It can be used either destructively or constructively. I am coming to feel that the people of ill will have used time much more effectively than the people of good will. We will have to repent in this generation not merely for the vitriolic words and actions of the bad people, but for the appalling silence of the good people. We must come to see that human progress never rolls in on wheels of inevitability. It comes through the tireless efforts and persistent work of men willing to be co-workers with God, and without this hard work time itself becomes an ally of the forces of social stagnation.

We must use time creatively, and forever realize that the time is always ripe to do right. Now is the time to make real the promise of democracy, and transform our pending national elegy into a creative psalm of brotherhood. Now is the time to lift our national policy from the quicksand of racial injustice to the solid rock of human dignity.

You spoke of our activity in Birmingham as extreme. At first I was rather disappointed that fellow clergymen would see my nonviolent efforts as those of the extremist. I started thinking about the fact that I stand in the middle of two opposing forces in the Negro community. One is a force of complacency made up of Negroes who, as a result of long years of oppression, have been so completely drained of self-respect and a sense of "somebodiness" that they have adjusted to segregation, and of a few Negroes in the middle class who, because of a degree of academic and economic security, and because at points they profit by segregation, have unconsciously become insensitive to the problems of the masses. The other force is one of bitterness and hatred and comes perilously close to advocating violence. It is expressed in the various black nationalist groups that are springing up over the nation, the largest and best known being Elijah Muhammad's Muslim movement. This movement is nourished by the contemporary frustration over the continued existence of racial discrimination. It is made up of people who have lost faith in America, who have absolutely repudiated Christianity, and who have concluded that the white man is an incurable "devil." I have tried to stand between these two forces saying that we need not follow the "do-nothingism" of the complacent or the hatred and despair of the black nationalist. There is the more excellent way of love and nonviolent protest. I'm grateful to God that, through the Negro church, the dimension of nonviolence entered our struggle. If this philosophy had not emerged I am convinced that by now many streets of the South would be flowing with floods of blood. And I am further convinced that if our white brothers dismiss us as "rabble rousers" and "outside agitators"—those of us who are working through the channels of nonviolent direct action—and refuse to support our nonviolent efforts, millions of Negroes, out of frustration and despair, will seek solace and security in black nationalist ideologies, a development that will lead inevitably to a frightening racial nightmare.

Oppressed people cannot remain oppressed forever. The urge for freedom will eventually come. This is what has happened to the American

Negro. Something within has reminded him of his birthright of freedom; something without has reminded him that he can gain it. Consciously and unconsciously, he has been swept in by what the Germans call the *Zeitgeist*, and with his black brothers of Africa, and his brown and yellow brothers of Asia, South America, and the Caribbean, he is moving with a sense of cosmic urgency toward the promised land of racial justice. Recognizing this vital urge that has engulfed the Negro community, one should readily understand public demonstrations. The Negro has many pent-up resentments and latent frustrations. He has to get them out. So let him march sometime; let him have his prayer pilgrimages to the city hall; understand why he must have sit-ins and freedom rides. If his repressed emotions do not come out in these nonviolent ways, they will come out in ominous expressions of violence. This is not a threat; it is a fact of history. So I have not said to my people, "Get rid of your discontent." But I have tried to say that this normal and healthy discontent can be channeled through the creative outlet of nonviolent direct action. Now this approach is being dismissed as extremist. I must admit that I was initially disappointed in being so categorized.

But as I continued to think about the matter I gradually gained a bit of satisfaction from being considered an extremist. Was not Jesus an extremist in love? "Love your enemies, bless them that curse you, pray for them that despitefully use you." Was not Amos an extremist for justice—"Let justice roll down like waters and righteousness like a mighty stream." Was not Paul an extremist for the gospel of Jesus Christ—"I bear in my body the marks of the Lord Jesus." Was not Martin Luther an extremist— "Here I stand; I can do none other so help me God." Was not John Bunyan an extremist—"I will stay in jail to the end of my days before I make a butchery of my conscience." Was not Abraham Lincoln an extremist— "This nation cannot survive half slave and half free." Was not Thomas Jefferson an extremist—"We hold these truths to be self-evident that all men are created equal." So the question is not whether we will be extremist but what kind of extremist will we be. Will we be extremists for hate or will we be extremists for love? Will we be extremists for the preservation of injustice—or will we be extremists for the cause of justice? In that dramatic scene on Calvary's hill three men were crucified. We must never forget that all three were crucified for the same crime—the crime of extremism. Two were extremists for immorality, and thus fell below their environment. The other, Jesus Christ, was an extremist for love, truth, and goodness, and thereby rose above His environment. So, after all, maybe the South, the nation, and the world are in dire need of creative extremists.

I had hoped that the white moderate would see this. Maybe I was too optimistic. Maybe I expected too much. I guess I should have realized that few members of a race that has oppressed another race can understand or appreciate the deep groans and passionate yearnings of those that have been oppressed, and still fewer have the vision to see that injustice must be rooted out by strong, persistent, and determined action. I am thankful, however, that some of our white brothers have grasped the meaning of this social revolution and committed themselves to it. They are still all too small in quantity, but they are big in quality. Some like Ralph McGill, Lillian Smith, Harry Golden, and James Dabbs have written about our struggle in eloquent, prophetic, and understanding terms. Others have marched with us down nameless streets of the South. They have languished in filthy, roach-infested jails, suffering the abuse and brutality of angry policemen who look on them as "dirty nigger lovers." They, unlike so many of their moderate brothers and sisters, have recognized the urgency of the moment and sensed the need for powerful "action" antidotes to combat the disease of segregation.

Let me rush on to mention my other disappointment. I have been so greatly disappointed with the white Church and its leadership. Of course there are some notable exceptions. I am not unmindful of the fact that each of you has taken some significant stands on this issue. I commend you, Rev. Stallings, for your Christian stand on this past Sunday, in welcoming Negroes to your service on a non-segregated basis. I commend the Catholic leaders of this state for integrating Springhill College several years ago.

But despite these notable exceptions I must honestly reiterate that I have been disappointed with the Church. I do not say that as one of those negative critics who can always find something wrong with the Church. I say it as a minister of the gospel, who loves the Church; who was nurtured in its bosom; who has been sustained by its spiritual blessings and who will remain true to it as long as the cord of life shall lengthen.

I had the strange feeling when I was suddenly catapulted into the leadership of the bus protest in Montgomery several years ago that we would have the support of the white Church. I felt that the white ministers, priests, and rabbis of the South would be some of our strongest allies. Instead, some have been outright opponents, refusing to understand the freedom movement and misrepresenting its leaders; all too many others have been more cautious than courageous and have remained silent behind the anesthetizing security of stained glass windows.

In spite of my shattered dreams of the past, I came to Birmingham with the hope that the white religious leadership of this community would see the justice of our cause and, with deep moral concern, serve as the channel through which our just grievances could get to the power structure. I had hoped that each of you would understand. But again I have been disappointed.

I have heard numerous religious leaders of the South call upon their worshippers to comply with a desegregation decision because it is the law, but I have longed to hear white ministers say: "Follow this decree because integration is morally right and the Negro is your brother." In the midst of blatant injustices inflicted upon the Negro, I have watched white churches stand on the sideline and merely mouth pious irrelevancies and sanctimonious trivialities. In the midst of a mighty struggle to rid our nation of racial and economic injustice, I have heard so many ministers say, "Those are social issues with which the Gospel has no real concern." and I have watched so many churches commit themselves to a completely otherworldly religion which made a strange distinction between body and soul, the sacred and the secular.

So here we are moving toward the exit of the twentieth century with a religious community largely adjusted to the status quo, standing as a taillight behind other community agencies rather than a headlight leading men to higher levels of justice.

I have travelled the length and breadth of Alabama, Mississippi, and all the other Southern states. On sweltering summer days and crisp autumn mornings I have looked at her beautiful churches with their spires pointing heavenward. I have beheld the impressive outlay of her massive religious education buildings. Over and over again I have found myself asking: "Who worships here? Who is their God? Where were their voices when the lips of Governor Barnett dripped with words of interposition and nullification? Where were they when Governor Wallace gave the clarion call for defiance and hatred? Where were their voices of support when tired, bruised, and weary Negro men and women decided to rise from the dark dungeons of complacency to the bright hills of creative protest?"

Yes, these questions are still in my mind. In deep disappointment, I have wept over the laxity of the Church. But be assured that my tears have been tears of love. There can be no deep disappointment where there is not deep love. Yes, I love the Church; I love her sacred walls. How could I do otherwise? I am in the rather unique position of being the son, the grandson, and the great-grandson of preachers. Yes, I see the Church as the body of Christ. But, oh! How we have blemished and scarred that body through social neglect and fear of being nonconformist.

There was a time when the Church was very powerful. It was during that period when the early Christians rejoiced when they were deemed worthy to suffer for what they believed. In those days the Church was not merely a thermometer that recorded the ideas and principles of popular opinion; it was a thermostat that transformed the mores of society. Wherever the early Christians entered a town the power structure got disturbed and immediately sought to convict them for being "disturbers of the peace" and "outside agitators." But they went on with the conviction that they were a "colony of heaven" and had to obey God rather than man. They were small in number but big in commitment. They were too God-intoxicated to be "astronomically intimidated." They brought an end to such ancient evils as infanticide and gladiatorial contest.

Things are different now. The contemporary Church is so often a weak, ineffectual voice with an uncertain sound. It is so often the arch-supporter of the status quo. Far from being disturbed by the presence of the Church, the power structure of the average community is consoled by the Church's silent and often vocal sanction of things as they are.

But the judgment of God is upon the Church as never before. If the Church of today does not recapture the sacrificial spirit of the early Church, it will lose its authentic ring, forfeit the loyalty of millions, and be dismissed as an irrelevant social club with no meaning for the twentieth century. I am meeting young people every day whose disappointment with the Church has risen to outright disgust.

Maybe again I have been too optimistic. Is organized religion too inextricably bound to the status quo to save our nation and the world? Maybe I must turn my faith to the inner spiritual Church, the church within the Church, as the true *ecclesia* and the hope of the world. But again I am thankful to God that some noble souls from the ranks of organized religion have broken loose from the paralyzing chains of conformity and joined us as active partners in the struggle for freedom. They have left their secure congregations and walked the streets of Albany, Georgia, with us. They have gone through the highways of the South on torturous rides for freedom. Yes, they have gone to jail with us. Some have been kicked out of their churches and lost the support of their bishops and fellow ministers. But they have gone with the faith that right defeated is stronger than evil triumphant. These men have been the leaven in the lump of the race. Their witness has been the spiritual salt that has preserved the true meaning of the Gospel in these troubled times. They have carved a tunnel of hope through the dark mountain of disappointment.

I hope the Church as a whole will meet the challenge of this decisive hour. But even if the Church does not come to the aid of justice, I have no despair about the future. I have no fear about the outcome of our struggle in Birmingham, even if our motives are presently misunderstood. We will reach the goal of freedom in Birmingham and all over the nation, because the goal of America is freedom. Abused and scorned though we may be, our destiny is tied up with the destiny of America. Before the pilgrims landed at Plymouth, we were here. Before the pen of Jefferson etched across the pages of history the majestic words of the Declaration of Independence, we were here. For more than two centuries our foreparents labored in this country without wages; they made cotton "king";

and they built the homes of their masters in the midst of brutal injustice and shameful humiliation—and yet out of a bottomless vitality they continued to thrive and develop. If the inexpressible cruelties of slavery could not stop us, the opposition we now face will surely fail. We will win our freedom because the sacred heritage of our nation and the eternal will of God are surely embodied in our echoing demands.

I must close now. But before closing I am impelled to mention one other point in your statement that troubled me profoundly. You warmly commended the Birmingham police force for keeping "order" and "preventing violence." I don't believe you would have so warmly commended the police force if you had seen its angry violent dogs literally biting six unarmed, nonviolent Negroes. I don't believe you would so quickly commend the policemen if you would observe their ugly and inhuman treatment of Negroes here in the city jail; if you would watch them push and curse old Negro women and young Negro girls; if you would see them slap and kick old Negro men and young Negro boys; if you will observe them, as they have done on two occasions, refuse to give us food because we wanted to sing our grace together. I'm sorry that I can't join you in your praise for the police department.

It is true that they have been rather disciplined in their public handling of the demonstrators. In this sense they have been rather publicly "nonviolent." But for what purpose? To preserve the evil system of segregation. Over the last few years I have consistently preached that nonviolence demands that the means we use must be as pure as the ends we seek. So I have tried to make it clear that it is wrong to use immoral means to attain moral ends. But now I must affirm that it is just as wrong, or even more so, to use moral means to preserve immoral ends. Maybe Mr. Connor and his policemen have been publicly nonviolent, as Chief Prichett was in Albany, Georgia, but they have used the moral means of nonviolence to maintain the immoral end of flagrant racial injustice. T. S. Eliot has said that there is no greater treason than to do the right deed for the wrong reason.

I wish you had commended the Negro sit-inners and demonstrators of Birmingham for their sublime courage, their willingness to suffer, and their amazing discipline in the midst of the most inhuman provocation. One day the South will recognize its real heroes. They will be the James Merediths, courageously and with a majestic sense of purpose, facing jeering and hostile mobs and the agonizing loneliness that characterizes the life of the pioneer. They will be old, oppressed, battered Negro women, symbolized in a seventy-two year old woman of Montgomery, Alabama, who rose up with a sense of dignity and with her people decided not to ride the segregated buses, and responded to one who inquired about her tiredness with ungrammatical profundity: "My feets is tired, but my soul is rested." They will be young high school and college students, young ministers of the gospel and a host of the elders, courageously and nonviolently sitting in at lunch counters and willingly going to jail for conscience sake. One day the South will know that when these disinherited children of God sat down at lunch counters they were in reality standing up for the best in the American dream and the most sacred values in our Judeo-Christian heritage, and thus carrying our whole nation back to great wells of democracy which were dug deep by the founding fathers in the formulation of the Constitution and the Declaration of Independence.

Never before have I written a letter this long (or should I say a book?). I'm afraid that it is much too long to take your precious time. I can assure you that it would have been much shorter if I had been writing from a comfortable desk, but what else is there to do when you are alone for days in the dull monotony of a narrow jail cell other than write long letters, think strange thoughts, and pray long prayers?

If I have said anything in this letter that is an overstatement of the truth and is indicative of an unreasonable impatience, I beg you to forgive me. If I have said anything in this letter that is an understatement of the truth and is indicative of my having a patience that makes me patient with anything less than brotherhood, I beg God to forgive me.

I hope this letter finds you strong in the faith. I also hope that circumstances will soon make it possible for me to meet each of you, not as an integrationist or a civil rights leader, but as a fellow clergyman and a Christian brother. Let us all hope that the dark clouds of racial prejudice will soon pass away and the deep fog of misunderstanding will be lifted from our fear-drenched communities and in some not too distant tomorrow the radiant stars of love and brotherhood will shine over our great nation with all of their scintillating beauty.

Yours for the cause of Peace and Brotherhood

Martin Luther King Jr.

Russell B. Connors Jr. (b. 1948) has been a member of the theology department at the College of St. Catherine since 1995, teaching courses on a variety of topics related to Christian Ethics. He has published three books and a host of scholarly articles, some of them about the similarities and differences between Catholic social teachings (CST) and Catholic teachings about sex. Connors explains seven central convictions that are the basis of CST and then makes connections to three ethical issues of our day. As you read, it may be helpful to analyze Connors' explanation of CST by the categories suggested by Heitzeg. What are the sources for CST? What moral standards does CST suggest? And, what is the scope of Catholic teaching about justice? That is, to whom or what does it apply?

Catholic Social Teaching—
Convictions and Connections[1]

Russell B. Connors Jr.

Introduction: Vignettes

As a state senator, Adam's positions on two issues have been clear and consistent: he has been strongly in favor of state-supported quality health care for all, and he has been opposed—just as strongly—to cutbacks in social services for the poor in recent years. In an interview in the local newspaper, the senator was quite forthright about the connections between his faith and his political life. "Some of my deepest convictions about justice," he explained, "have long been grounded in Catholic social teaching."

One of the students asked Sister MaryAnn how, given her feminist convictions, she remained part of a church that seems so riddled with sexism. Quickly and candidly she replied, "It's largely because of Catholic social teaching that I remain a Catholic, much less a sister. And besides," she went on, "it's my church too."

They were there every Saturday morning, the busiest time at the local grocery store. Their signs marked a protest of the store's continued policy of selling fruits and vegetables grown and picked by non-union farm workers. When asked why they were there each week, some of them referred to Catholic social teaching in their answer.

The pastor, Fr. Jordan, has "taken some heat" from some in the parish for the welcoming things he has been saying in recent Sunday homilies regarding gay and lesbian persons. And he has made church meeting rooms available for a prayer and study program sponsored by a group of gay and lesbian Catholics. As he said in the church bulletin, "There is a direct link between Catholic social teaching and our embrace of gay and lesbian persons."

"In the U.S.," Martina says, "we approach immigration from the point of view of the stresses on our own country. I understand that, but it is wrong. We must see this from the point of view of those who often suffer. The stresses on us are minor compared to the suffering of many who desire to come here." Martina has been called naïve by some of her colleagues at the University, but she does not flinch in her views. A convert to Catholicism, Martina says that one of the most attractive things about the Catholic Church to her was its social teaching, especially its notion of the "option for the poor."

Sheila has enough to do. But several weeks ago she found the time to distribute fliers about her nursing association's opposition to the state initiative to legalize physician-assisted suicide. A member of her church's "Peace and Justice Commission," next week she will be part of a panel discussion at the local public high school on capital punishment. She is similarly opposed to the death penalty. When asked to explain her convictions about these issues, Sheila refers to Catholic social teaching.

"I need to be clear with you, however, before I accept the position as principal of this school. The salaries of our teachers are simply unjust. I will not stop bringing this up until the situation improves dramatically." This is what John had said to the pastor and members of the finance commission as he accepted the position as principal of the Catholic elementary school. And it came to pass. For the past four years, at budget time, John has battled for more just wages for the teachers, grounding a strong and convincing argument in Catholic social teaching.

People make connections between Catholic social teaching and an amazing spectrum of issues, often doing so (as these vignettes make clear) in startlingly diverse ways, in ways that defy categorization as conservative or liberal, Republican or Democrat.

The phrase "Catholic social teaching," refers to the sum total of teachings provided by Catholic leaders—popes, bishops, and sometimes theologians—concerning the social issues of the day, especially over the last 100 years. Christian faith does not shield believers from difficult social issues, but rather, impels them to try to contribute to their solutions. In that spirit, the popes and bishops do not presume to offer simple answers to complex questions, but try to show what the relationship might be between Christian faith and social issues. Catholic teachings are put forth in various types of documents, as the Works Cited pages of this article illustrate. Invariably, those documents include both *convictions* and *connections*. By *convictions* I mean the fundamental presuppositions that ground Catholic involvement in social issues. And by *connections* I mean the way those convictions might be applied to specific questions and concerns. The purpose of this article is to uncover those key *convictions* and to examine how the *connections* get made.

It seems right to state four things very clearly at the start. The first is a bias: I am a Roman Catholic and I am proud of Catholic social teaching (henceforth, CST). As others have observed, it is sadly one of Catholicism's "best kept secrets" (Henriot). To say this is not to claim that it is a tradition that is perfect, completely consistent, or without blind spots. CST is a work-in-progress. Indeed, that is one of its virtues. Secondly, it is important not to reduce Catholicism to its teachings about justice. As important as those are, Catholicism also stands for other things, things like the phenomenon of sacramentality. This is the idea that the created universe is a medium through which we have contact with the divine. Catholic intellectual tradition emphasizes its confidence in humanity's pursuit of truth and wisdom wherever it is to be found. Catholic tradition also celebrates the sacredness and inviolability of conscience, the importance of community, etc. As we proceed I will look for ways to show the connections between CST and some of these other important features of Catholicism. Thirdly, extolling the virtues of CST is not my way of attempting to gloss over the faults and sins of the Catholic Church itself. As we will see, CST is not about what *everyone else* should do. The convictions of justice that are the heart of CST *apply to the church itself.* Indeed, there are some signs that the church is getting a bit better at acknowledging its own injustice and sinfulness and its ongoing need of reformation. The "papal apologies" of Pope John Paul II in 2000 for ". . . the past and present sins of her [the Church's] sons and daughters" may be the most dramatic example (John Paul II, 649; McDonough and Michaud, 103). Fourthly, this is an overview, an introduction. I will have accomplished my goal if, at the end, the reader feels she has tasted of some of the primary flavors of CST. The works cited or recommended at the end will point to a fuller menu.

The remainder of this article is in two unequal parts. After a brief historical introduction, Part One will present what I think are the key *convictions* that are the heart of CST. I will first state the convictions themselves and then elaborate on their sources and their significance. Part One will close with a word about the interpretation and application of the seven major convictions to concrete issues, and with a reflection on the purposes of CST. More briefly, Part Two will explore the *connections* between CST and specific issues. We will do this by focusing simply on two of the key convictions of CST—the dignity and rights of every human being and the option for the poor—seeing how those convictions *connect* to some contemporary questions and concerns.

Part One: Catholic Social Teaching—Convictions

History.[2] Modern CST is commonly thought to have begun with the encyclical letter "Rerum Novarum" ("The Condition of Labor") of Pope Leo XIII in 1891. In that letter the pope faced squarely the conditions of workers in what had become industrialized and urbanized Europe. In a word, conditions were miserable. Many workers (including children) worked long hours in sometimes horrific environments for shockingly small wages—nothing close to a wage that would support a family. Housing and living conditions in the large industrial cities of Europe were equally miserable. Poverty was rampant.

The approach of Leo XIII's letter of concern was new in that rather than simply call for a renewed effort at works of *charity* to assist those in need (although that was indeed part of his message), he called for *social justice.* He called for a change in the social structures and institutions of the day that were the causes of the poverty and misery of the workers. He called for a just and living wage, for working conditions that were safe, and for laws that would prevent the abuse of children in the workforce. Fundamental to all of this was his insistence on the dignity of all people as children of God. He insisted that human dignity must be recognized and respected in the workers of the world.

Since Leo XIII, the Church has taken it to be its responsibility to address the issues of the day that concern the human community—sometimes matters of hunger and poverty, sometimes matters of prejudice and discrimination, sometimes matters of war and peace. Christian faith, the pope and bishops have argued, should not lead us to try to escape these difficult problems, but to try to contribute to their solution in light of the Gospel of Christ. This has given rise over the last 100 years to Catholic social teaching.

Convictions. Many people who discuss CST do so by naming and analyzing some basic moral *principles*. I think it is more helpful to state *convictions*. The word *principles* may suggest to some that what we are dealing with here is theory, philosophically precise but abstract moral principles that await application in the real world. The word *convictions* is better, I think, because it suggests that CST is not only about ideas, but about *passions*, the emotions, attitudes, and dispositions that fuel action on behalf of justice. That is the goal. If there were time for it here (there is not), history would demonstrate that the convictions to follow are not the result of someone's doctoral dissertation; rather, they are the result of the church's reflection on what (in its better moments) it has been *doing*.

At the heart of CST we find seven important convictions:

- *Human Dignity*. The life and dignity of every human being is of incalculable worth and must be recognized, respected, and reverenced. Human rights, "the minimum conditions for life in community," must be protected and promoted in order for human dignity to be respected and for human beings to flourish. (U.S. Catholic Bishops, "Economic Justice for All" par. 17)

- *Community*. Human beings, social by nature, flourish in association with others in community. Everyone has a need, a right, and a responsibility to participate in community life. "Society as a whole, acting through public and private institutions," is responsible for protecting and promoting not only the good of individual persons, but also the common good of the society as a whole. (U.S. Bishops, "Economic Justice for All," par. 18)

- *Equality*. All human beings are fundamentally equal, regardless of race, creed, gender, sexual orientation, and educational or economic status. Every "-ism" that alienates and oppresses people must be opposed and overcome.

- *Work*. Work is critically important for human flourishing. Accordingly, the dignity of work and the rights of workers are the foundation of economic justice.

- *Option for the Poor*. "All members of society have a special obligation to the poor and vulnerable"—not only in our own country, but also around the world. (U.S. Bishops, "Economic Justice for All," par. 16)

- *Peace*. As history sadly demonstrates, war and other forms of violence are the enemies of human well-being. There must be a presumption against war and every other use of force.

- *Care for the Earth*. With increasing conviction, CST calls for the care of the earth itself, for the protection and promotion of the wellbeing of the natural environment not only for the sake of human beings (including future generations), but also for the earth itself and *all* its inhabitants.

Elaboration. Let us explore the significance of these seven convictions, paying attention not only to their sources, but also to some of the issues to which they have been connected over the years.

Human Dignity. Authors who write about the central convictions of CST invariably enumerate and describe them differently. Whether there are seven or nine or nineteen convictions and how they should be stated and described are matters of some opinion. But virtually everyone familiar with this tradition agrees that however many convictions there are, the first and most basic one is about the dignity of human beings. In the introduction to their 1983 pastoral letter on war and peace, the U.S. Catholic Bishops explained the reason for their concern about war and peace by referring to a central conviction about human beings:

> At the center of the Church's teaching on peace and at the center of all Catholic social teaching are the transcendence of God and the dignity of the human person. The human person is the clearest reflection of God's presence in the world; all of the Church's work in pursuit of both justice and peace is designed to protect and promote the dignity of every person. For each person not only reflects God, but is the expression of God's creative work and the meaning of Christ's redemptive ministry. Christians approach the problem of war and peace with fear and reverence (U.S. Catholic Bishops, "The Challenge of Peace: God's Promise and Our Response," par. 15).

With this passage as a starting point, three comments concerning Catholicism's emphasis on human dignity are in order. First, as the statement from the bishops makes clear, the source of CST's emphasis on human dignity is religious in nature. That source is the Christian belief (found also in Judaism and Islam) that each human being is created by God and is a unique reflection of God's holy presence in the world. It is also part of Christian faith that the entire universe, as created by God, is somehow "charged with the grandeur of God," as Gerard Manley Hopkins once put it. CST affirms this, but without embarrassment emphasizes that in a preeminent way *human beings* reflect God's presence in the world. Surely one can be convinced about the dignity of human beings for many reasons. Human intelligence and freedom—our abilities to think and to choose (perhaps especially to love)—as well as some of the amazing accomplishments of humankind (scientific, artistic, altruistic) are certainly good enough reasons to respect human life. CST affirms those reasons. But its deepest convictions about human dignity are rooted in the Christian belief about humanity's relation to God. *In and through* our contact with God's creation—especially (but not exclusively) other human beings—we come into contact with God. Theologian Richard McBrien refers to this as the principle of *sacramentality*. He suggests that it is one of the distinguishing characteristics of Catholicism: the Creator is encountered through the creation (McBrien, pp. 9–11). If this is right, then so too are the bishops: human life is not simply to be respected, but reverenced.

Let us return to the quote above from the U.S. Bishops for a second observation about CST's emphasis on human dignity. As we have seen, the quote is from a pastoral letter on war and peace. But as a matter of fact, one could very easily take out the words *on war and peace* in the opening line and make a wide variety of substitutions. Thus, the sentence could read, "At the center of the Church's teaching [*on economic justice* or *on abortion and euthanasia,* or *on health care reform,* or *on capital punishment,* or *on domestic abuse,* or *on global poverty and hunger,* etc., etc., etc.] and at the center of all Catholic social teaching are the transcendence of God and the dignity of the human person." You get the idea. This emphasis on human dignity grounds CST's interest and involvement in *all* social issues. CST offers no recipe for simple answers to complex questions; it has no formula for ensuring universal agreement on social issues. (It is wise to be suspicious of anyone who does.) What CST does offer is a starting point and a central conviction. In the U.S. political system, for instance, whether one is a liberal democrat or a conservative republican, CST proposes a broad but exceedingly important criterion for moral discernment: the protection and promotion of the dignity of human beings.

Third, CST's conviction about human dignity calls for the recognition of and respect for fundamental *human rights*. Unlike some philosophical approaches to human rights, CST insists that human rights are not conferred upon an individual because they are citizens of a given society. No, the origin of human rights is found in the nature of the human person as such; they are neither given to persons nor (legitimately, at least) taken away from persons by society.

What exactly do we mean by "rights"? Theologian J. Milburn Thompson described human rights as *those basic human goods that are due to human beings so that they can develop themselves fully as persons living in community* (Thompson, pp. 92–102). Some like to think of human rights as the minimum that we have "coming to us" simply because we are human beings. Protection and promotion of human rights is important not simply so that we can survive or "get by" in life, but so that we can strive to flourish as human persons.

It is important to flesh out Catholicism's view of human rights with some examples. Let us consider Pope John XXIII's list of human rights in his 1963 encyclical letter "Pacem in Terris":

- The right to life and a worthy standard of living. These rights include the right to bodily integrity, to food, clothing, shelter, healthcare and necessary social services.

- Rights pertaining to moral and cultural values. These include the right to one's good reputation, the right to search for truth, the right to be informed about public matters of concern, etc.

- The right to worship God according to one's conscience.

- The right to choose one's state in life.

- Economic rights. These include a right to work, to work in a safe environment, and to receive a just wage. Economic rights include a right to private property (and other sources of wealth) as long as this does not interfere with more basic rights of others.

- The right to meet and associate with others.

- The right to emigrate and to immigrate. These rights are especially necessary given the injustices and oppression that exist in some places.

- Political rights. These involve one's ability to take an active part in the civil and political life of one's community.

Obviously a lot of detail is left for interpretation and application—such as what one means by "necessary social services," or what exactly a right to healthcare includes. In the U.S., for example, it would not be hard to imagine both Democrats and Republicans espousing this list of human rights, but disagreeing on how minimally or maximally the government should become involved in seeing to it that they are secured. Even so, by any standard this exposition of human rights sets an agenda for what every society should be concerned about. Flowing from human dignity, CST insists, human rights are important so that we can strive to develop ourselves fully as human beings, in keeping with our common vocation to live as creatures fashioned in the image of God.

Community. If an emphasis on the dignity and rights of every human being is the right hand of CST, emphasis on the importance of community is the left hand. It is only for the sake of simplicity that we discuss them separately here. If Richard McBrien is right, another distinguishing characteristic of Catholicism is its emphasis on the importance of community for human flourishing (McBrien, pp. 12–14). Far different from those aspects of our culture that display a particularly stubborn form of rugged, competitive, and isolating individualism (Bellah), CST insists that the good of the individual is essentially bound up with the good of the community. Following the lead of Catholic social ethicist Thomas Massaro, let us look briefly at three elements of CST's stress on community: *solidarity, common good, and participation* (Massaro, pp. 119–124).

Solidarity is a word that is easier to describe than it is to define. It refers both to an inner conviction and to an outer commitment. The inner conviction involves both the intellectual insight and the affective appreciation of the reality of interdependence: we are all connected; we need one another. CST invites us to believe that at our best moments, simply as human beings, we are able to recognize within ourselves a deep sense of care for one another. When we see the suffering of others (I am thinking especially of the suffering that results from oppression and injustice) it is our sense of solidarity that moves us to "feel for" them and, in some elusive but real way, to share in their suffering. Solidarity enables us to "feel for" others not only because "it could have been me," but because of the nearly mystical conviction that when one person is denied her rights, in some way we all are; when one group is enslaved, none of us is free; when one group suffers from violence and oppression, we are all diminished.

Solidarity begins with this kind of conviction of the heart, but it does not end there. The test of genuine solidarity is that it moves to committed action. Action may vary greatly depending on one's closeness to the situation at hand, as well as one's resources (often more extensive than we think). But real solidarity manifests itself in action on behalf of others, caring, committed action—frequently in the social, political arena—that is aimed at dismantling oppression and building justice.

As is obvious, solidarity presumes an appreciation of the *common good*. Pope John Paul II has written about the connection between these two ideas as follows:

> This then [solidarity] is not a feeling of vague compassion or shallow distress at the misfortunes of so many people, both near and far. On the contrary, it is a *firm and persevering determination* to commit oneself to the *common good*, that is to say to the good of all and of each individual, for we are *all* really responsible for *all* (John Paul II, "On Social Concern," par. 38).

Those with a sense of solidarity, CST suggests, are convinced that one's own individual good is woven into the fabric of the good of others. The common good is "the good of all and of each individual." It presumes that one's individual good must not come at the expense of others: the good of management must not be at the expense of labor, the thriving of the wealthiest must not involve the suffering of the poorest, the well-being of men must not be built upon the oppression of women, the welfare of human beings must not involve the mistreatment of other creatures on the planet. When such inequities exist, CST suggests, we not only have a lack of the common good, but a caricature of individual good. Individual "good" that is the fruit of injustice bears within it the seed of its own destruction.

This understanding of the relationship between the individual good and the common good logically includes an emphasis on the importance of *participation* in social life. CST insists that we all have the right and the responsibility to participate in the life of community. Precisely because of our solidarity with one another, our interdependence, we are called to participate in community life, as much as our abilities enable us to do so. Not only because it is important for us to "speak up on our own behalf," but also because of the contributions we can make to other individuals and to society at large, every human being must be given the opportunity to participate fully in the social institutions and communities. When it is only a powerful few who exercise authority, when it is only the wealthy whose voice is heard, when it is only the men who hold positions of influence (whether in our halls of government or in our places of worship), something is terribly wrong with the picture. Calling the church itself to examine its own conscience, CST suggests that the ability of all to participate and contribute fully in the life of community is very simply a matter of justice.

Equality. The first two convictions of CST that we have just described are on virtually every list of the "basic principles" of Catholic social thought. Equality is not. Nevertheless, it is an important aspect of contemporary Catholic social thought. The following passage from the bishops at the Second Vatican Council (1962–1965) displays well, I think, the church's view on equality:

> Since all . . . possess a rational soul and are created in God's likeness, since they have the same nature and origin, have been redeemed by Christ, and enjoy the same divine calling and destiny, the basic equality of all must receive increasingly greater recognition. True, all . . . are not alike from the point of view of varying physical power and the diversity of intellectual and moral resources. Nevertheless, with respect to the fundamental rights of the person, every type of discrimination, whether social or cultural, whether based on sex, race, color, social condition, language, or religion, is to be overcome and eradicated as contrary to God's intent ("Pastoral Constitution on the Church in the Modern World," par. 29).

The phrase "must receive increasingly greater recognition" should be seen for what it really is: an acknowledgment that not only in society at large but within the church itself, recognition of the fundamental equality of all human beings as persons has been slow in coming. Historically, most of the major institutions of Western Civilization have not been democracies; they have not been grounded in a conviction about the fundamental equality of all people, and they have been slow to recognize those various "isms" that constitute sins against equality. For instance, as Marvin Mich has documented well in his recent book, until fairly recent times, the church (along with other institutions) did not see any great difficulty with slavery, at least not enough to lead the way in dismantling it: ". . . it was common for Catholic laity, bishops, priests, and religious orders to be slaveholders" (Mich, p. 135). In a similar vein, Catholicism's struggle to recognize the equal dignity of women and men and its resistance to allow that recognition to show itself in its own structures displays the fact that whatever equality might mean in Catholic thought, it has not meant (and does not now mean) equal access to all positions of leadership within the church itself. Bishop Ray Lucker from New Ulm, Minnesota, has called for the church to own up to its own sins of racism and sexism, insisting that equality must indeed receive "greater recognition" within the church itself (Lucker). Equality, as one of the key convictions of CST, is a work in progress.

Work. During the last hundred years, the theme of work has received important attention in CST. Catholic social thought looks at work not simply from the perspective of what workers do, but what work does to and for workers. Pope John Paul II has written much about this, especially in his 1981 encyclical letter "Laborem Exercens" ("On Human Work"). Obviously work is important both because many of us spend a high percentage of our lives at our work, and also because it is essential for our livelihood. But CST suggests something more. It is through work that we fulfill a part of our human nature. Work is one of the ways we develop ourselves as persons. It is through our work that we are able to express ourselves, to fulfill ourselves, and to contribute to the human community (Pope John Paul II, "On Human Work," par. 6). These ideas may strike some of us as unrealistic, as ideals that are a long way from reality. Sadly, for too many people that is the case. Work for many is routine, burdensome, and even oppressive. CST argues that that is not as it should be. Workers ought to be given an opportunity to take responsibility for what they do, to make their work their own. The more that happens, the more work can become an opportunity for self-expression, for personal fulfillment, and for the satisfaction that comes from making a genuine contribution, even if a small one, to the well-being of other people. Put differently, if work is for people, and not the other way around, then those responsible for the work that other people do should be looking for ways in which that work can both express and promote human dignity.

Lest all this seems to be too lofty a goal to have in mind regarding human work, the recent *Catechism of the Catholic Church* names several more concrete things that relate to justice for workers. Men and women, first of all, should have *access to employment* in ways that are fair. The professions and the workforce should be ". . . open to all without discrimination" (#2433). Secondly, workers are entitled to a *just wage* for the work that they do. This means a wage that allows one to provide a reasonable and dignified quality of life for oneself and one's family materially, socially, culturally, and spiritually (#2434). The *Catechism* notes that it is not morally sufficient that a contract has been reached between employers and workers. A just wage must meet more stringent criteria; it must take into account the quality of life it allows a person and his or her family to enjoy (#2434). Thirdly, workers should have *recourse to a strike* when it becomes morally legitimate (#2435). Reasons that might warrant strikes include not only unjust wages, but also unsafe or burdensome working conditions. The dignity and rights of persons call for safe working environments. Finally, workers have a right to *social security contributions*, which (in countries like our own) are required by legitimate authority (#2436). The *Catechism* does not include healthcare benefits with this, largely because in many countries healthcare is provided by the state and not linked to employment. In the U.S. access to healthcare (which Pope John XXIII listed as a human right) is linked to employment, an argument could surely be made from CST that employers should be required to see to it that their workers are provided with healthcare benefits. In exchange for all of this, workers indeed have serious obligations to fulfill their own responsibilities to their employers with honesty and integrity. Though it seems accurate to say that the emphasis in CST is clearly on the rights of workers, it is also true that rights and responsibilities go together.

"Option for the Poor." One of the most celebrated and controversial of the key convictions of CST is what has become known as "the option for the poor." Thomas Massaro is right in noting that there is something both new and old about this idea. It is new in that the phrase appears in no official church documents until the 1970s; it is old in that the idea seems evident in Christian tradition from the beginning. Just as in the Old Testament book of Exodus God seemed to intervene in human history to "take the side of" the enslaved Hebrews (Exodus, chapters 3–15), leading them (*in and through* Moses) from oppression to freedom, so too in our day, God is "taking the side of" the poor and oppressed *in and through* all those people (Christians and others) who commit themselves to the social struggle for justice and liberation. Commitment—that is the fundamental meaning of the word "option" in CST. And just as Jesus of Nazareth liberated all people from the bondage of sin and the sting of death, and called his followers to commit themselves, as he had, to "proclaiming glad tidings to the poor" and bringing "liberty to captives" (Luke 4: 18–19), so too, the followers of Jesus are true to their real mission to the extent that they commit themselves to the ongoing work of liberation, the work of helping to fashion God's reign of justice, love and peace (Gutierrez, Boff, Schubeck, *Liberation Ethics*).

The contemporary emphasis on an option for the poor emerges from a very specific historical, political situation: the situation of poverty and injustice in Latin America, poverty and injustice that was and remains essentially linked to social and political structures. Beginning in the 1960s and '70s, Christian theologians in those countries began to make connections between their social/political situation and the essential message of Christianity. What does God want, these theologians asked, in situations of structural poverty and injustice? God wants nothing less than the liberation of all people from any and all things that are the cause of oppression and injustice.

In a fresh and challenging way liberation theology has reminded the Christian community that even though it is true that God loves all people (rich and poor alike, and yes, not only the oppressed, but the oppressors as well), and even though we should try not to pit one group against another or to involve ourselves in violence, Christian faith does call us to make a special option for the poor. Not unlike a parent who loves all her children, but whose love is poured out regularly on behalf of the child most in need, so too "the heart of God" and the passionate care and commitment of Christian people needs to be directed regularly to those most in need, to those who suffer.

If there is something new and fresh about the theme of option for the poor, as it emerged from liberation theology, there is something ancient about the theme as well. Latin American liberation theologians helped the church across the world to recognize that God's option for the poor and our call to make a similar option is implicit in the scriptural stories about God's involvement with humankind, including God's involvement with us through Jesus Christ. By the mid-'70s the option for the poor began to be spoken about directly and forcefully by popes and bishops, enough that today virtually no one writing about CST would leave it off the list of key principles or convictions. (Pope John Paul II, "On the Hundredth Anniversary of 'Rerum Novarum,'" par. 11).

Although liberation theology—and its call for an option for the poor—originated in a specific social situation in Latin America, since the 1980s it has undergone a variety of transformations. The general theme of liberation and the specific call for an option for the poor have been taken up by Christian theologians around the world as they have considered a host of other instances of structural injustice and oppression in society and in the church itself. Drawing on these themes, African-American theologian James Cone has helped to pioneer "black theology," spelled out especially in his influential *A Black Theology of Liberation* (1970). And of course many (not all) feminist theologians have welcomed these same themes and have drawn out their implications for patriarchal cultures, including the Catholic Church. Anne F. Patrick's *Liberating Conscience* (1996) is a fine recent example of a Catholic feminist theology of liberation. The collection of articles called *Liberation Theology,* edited by Curt Cadorette, et. al., displays the wide variety of ways in which liberation theology and its option for the poor have made their mark not only on CST but on Christian theology around the world.

Peace. It should come as a shock to no one: CST is decidedly in favor of peace. Most people, of course, are. Hopefully Christians take it to be part of their responsibility, both as citizens of the earth and as followers of Christ, to do all in their power to eliminate (or at least to minimize) violence in the world and to work for peace.

But there are two things about CST's convictions regarding peace that are distinctive and that deserve attention here: its theology of peace and, for lack of a better phrase, its contributions to "the politics of peace."

Catholicism's theology of peace is captured briefly but clearly in the following two passages from the U.S. Catholic Bishops' pastoral letter on peace in 1983:

> Because peace, like the kingdom of God itself, is both a divine gift and a human work, the Church should continually pray for the gift and share in the

> work. We are called to be a Church at the service of peace, precisely because peace is one manifestation of God's word and work in our midst. ("The Challenge of Peace," par. 23).

> Let us have the courage to believe in the bright future and in a God who wills it for us—not a perfect world, but a better one. The perfect world, we Christians believe, is beyond the horizon, in an endless eternity where God will be all in all. But a better world is here for human hands and hearts and minds to make ("The Challenge of Peace," par. 337).

By the phrase "kingdom of God" or "reign of God" Christians believe that God is "up to something" in the world. Especially through the life, teaching, and dying and rising of Jesus Christ, God has inaugurated a victory of grace over sinfulness, justice over oppression, peace over violence and, most dramatically, life over death. In this way, Christian faith provides believers with a view of history, a very hopeful one. God has been and remains "up to" the transformation of the human race and all of creation. Christian faith daringly insists that God is fashioning a new heaven and a new earth, one which will be characterized by justice, love, and peace. This is what God wants; this is what God is doing.

But how? So far this theology of peace is all about what *God* is doing; it is God's gift, with only glimpses of it on the horizon of human existence. But part of Christian faith concerning the "reign of God" is that we are called to participate in what God is doing through the way in which we live our lives, through the ways in which we work for love and justice and peace. There is not only *discontinuity* between this real world and what lies "beyond the horizon," there is *continuity* as well. A "perfect" world, a *perfectly peaceful* world, Christian faith suggests, is beyond us. But a better world, a more peaceful world, is ours to fashion. *In and through* our peacemaking efforts the "reign of God" is being fashioned. This, I think, is the heart of CST's theology of peace.

But we must speak also (and less poetically) of "the politics of peace." I have two things in mind here: CST's convictions about non-violence and its espousal of just-war theory. These two seemingly conflicting traditions are two different threads woven into the one fabric of Catholicism's approach to peace.

History is important here. In the earliest centuries of Christianity the followers of Jesus were faced with questions concerning how deeply they should become involved in the social, political, and military structures of the culture in which they found themselves, the Roman Empire. Many scholars believe that in the earliest decades after Christ—the decades in which the writings of the New Testament were being formulated—Christians believed that the return of Christ and the end of the world as we know it was on the immediate horizon. In such a context, some of the "hard sayings" attributed to Jesus in the New Testament, particularly the radical call to non-violence (". . . I say to you, offer no resistance to one who is evil. When someone strikes you on your right cheek, turn the other one to him as well" [Matthew 5: 39]) seem to be more palatable. If the world is ending tomorrow, endurance may be an easier pill to swallow. In fact, many of the earliest Christians suffered persecution because of their faith, and so the "hard saying" about non-violence may well have reflected the actual experience of some of Jesus' first followers. All of this contributed to the fact that not only in the first few decades, but also for the first several centuries of the life of the church, non-violence was taken to be the way of Jesus and the way for his followers to live.

Lisa Sowle Cahill (whose book on this topic is a masterful analysis of this part of Catholic tradition) is among those who suggest that once Christianity became "mainstreamed" in the time of Constantine (fourth century), Christians' involvement in the military and justification of the use of force (including killing) on behalf of the state became more widely accepted (Cahill, p. 40). Although peace remained the ideal, justification of the use of force in this less-than-perfect world became widespread. Under the leadership of Augustine (354–430), criteria were developed for determining a just war, and as Massaro notes, "The just-war theory came to form the mainstream of Christian reflection on violence for many centuries" (Massaro, p. 152).

Over the centuries the criteria for determining a just war and for determining just actions within war have evolved. In a contemporary way the 1983 pastoral letter of the U.S. Bishops stated the criteria as follows:

- just cause (protecting innocent persons, securing human rights, etc.)

- competent authority (war must be declared by those with authority for the public order; leaving ambiguous the status of revolutions)

- comparative justice (a criteria that calls for an analysis of which side is sufficiently "right" in a dispute)

- right intention (only the reasons that provide the just cause can be intended, not revenge or violence for its own sake)

- last resort (all possibilities for non-violent resolutions have been tried and exhausted)

- probability of success (there should be some prospect that the use of force will accomplish the goals identified in the just cause)

- proportionality (the damage done to all parties must be proportionate to the good that is hoped for) (U.S. Bishops, "The Challenge of Peace," pars. 86–99).

In addition to these seven criteria for determining when it may be *just to go to war*, the Bishops also provided two criteria for determining what would and would not constitute *just actions within the war* itself:

* proportionality. There must be a proper proportion between the damage one's actions (e.g., bombing) cause to opposing forces, to civilian populations, and to the environment and the good that is likely to be achieved by such actions (103).

* discrimination. "The response to unjust aggression must be discriminate; it must be directed against unjust aggressors, not against innocent people caught up in a war not of their making" (104).

If taken seriously these two criteria are very stringent. Think for a moment of what was done in Hiroshima and Nagasaki at the end of World War II. In a world in which the weapons of war have become capable of ever more massive destruction, not only of opposing forces, but of civilian population centers and the natural environment itself, meeting the criteria of proportionality and discrimination in the conduct of war is very difficult, some think virtually impossible.

It should be obvious that these criteria are far from some simple checklist for determining a just war or for determining just actions within war. Each criterion calls for analysis, and relative to specific situations (e.g., the War in Iraq) each one is open to a variety of interpretations and opinions. As a result, in many circles there is an understandable degree of cynicism about the usefulness of the just war theory itself.

The two traditions of non-violence and just war theory have existed side by side as part of Catholic social thought for centuries. In truth, however, the just-war tradition came to overshadow the tradition of non-violence. Although there have always been challenging, prophetic voices within Catholicism that have attempted to remind the church of the universal call to peace and even the "hard sayings" about non-violence, mostly they have been individual, lonely voices. Today, however, there is a good deal of evidence that that may be changing (Mich, 275–312). CST has given increasing attention to non–violence in recent years. Perhaps as the flaws and the limits of the just war theory become more and more evident (especially in this nuclear age), the presumption against war and the promotion for peace have received greater and greater emphasis. CST still struggles with difficult political situations in which the human rights of innocent people are trampled upon; in such situations, in this sin-riddled world, is violence a regretful but necessary evil? Or does the use of force and violence simply breed more violence? There are no easy answers (Himes).

Care of the Earth. Twenty years ago it would have been unthinkable that someone would list "Care of the Earth" as one of the key convictions of

CST. If any of the convictions being described here are evidence that CST is a work-in-progress, this one is. But with increasing strength in its voice, CST proclaims that that we are all charged to care for the earth. What exactly this means, however, and how precisely this conviction is related to most of those that have been described above, is less clear. To explore this, let us look at Catholicism's approach to "care of the Earth" in three ways (to some extent in historical fashion) by examining three concepts laid out well by Catholic "ecofeminist" theologian Elizabeth A. Johnson: *kingship, stewardship,* and *kinship* (Johnson, pp. 29–40).

KINGSHIP. The idea of kingship is based upon what Johnson describes as hierarchical dualism:

> It is based on hierarchical dualism that sees humanity separated from the earth and placed in a position of absolute dominion over all other creatures who are made for us. In this view, the creatures of the world are ranked . . . with greater value being assigned to those up on the great chain of being. At the lowest level is inorganic matter; next comes vegetative matter, followed by animals, human beings, and non-physical spirits or angels. In the progression from the pebble to the peach to the poodle to the person, with women somewhere between the latter two, the higher order of creatures has the right to use and control the lower . . . This is the patriarchal pyramid again, resulting in a top-down domination of nature by man (Johnson 29).

From the perspective of kingship, the world has been created for us and awaits our dominion and control. Related to this is a 1967 article published by Lynn White, a widely respected historian who taught at Princeton, Stanford and UCLA. It was entitled "The Historical Roots of Our Ecological Crisis," and it argued that the Judeo-Christian tradition—which claimed, with biblical authority (Genesis 1:28), that humans are to subdue the earth and have dominion over all things—is largely to blame for the ecological crisis in which we find ourselves. White's argument corresponds a great deal with Johnson's idea of kingship. At our worst, these thinkers claim (and I would agree), not only has "care of the Earth" not predominated in Catholic thought, but in the past Catholic teaching has contributed to an attitude of dominion that has been part of humanity's irresponsibility and recklessness in regard to the earth.

STEWARDSHIP. But Christian tradition has also espoused stewardship as a way of viewing humanity's relation to the earth. In Johnson's view, stewardship ". . . keeps the structure of hierarchical dualism but calls for human beings to be responsible caretakers or guardians of the earth and all its creatures. . . In this model humanity is still at the top of the pyramid of being but has the duty to protect and preserve what seems weaker and more vulnerable" (Johnson, p. 30). Stewardship is often found in the writings of the pope and bishops. In 1991, for example, the U.S. Catholic bishops wrote that we must be "faithful stewards" of the gift of God's creation. Stewardship, they suggested, means that ". . . we must both care for creation according to standards that are not of our own making and at the same time be resourceful in finding ways to make the earth flourish."(U.S. Catholic Bishops, "Renewing the Earth," 429).

When combined with several of the key convictions we have already discussed—especially convictions about human rights, equality, and the option for the poor—the idea of stewardship can generate and motivate very strong convictions and actions directed to care for the earth. The idea of stewardship, in combination with the human rights tradition, is compatible with the idea that all persons (including future generations of people) have a right to a safe and healthy environment. A commitment to stewardship, combined with CST's conviction that racism is a crime against human dignity and equality, would also lead one to be deeply concerned about "environmental racism"—the phenomenon that people of color are regularly and systematically exposed to a disproportionate degree of environmental harm and hazard (Bullard). To be sure, not all are satisfied with stewardship as the appropriate way to think about our charge to care for the earth. But it is a long way from kingship or dominion. As I see it, stewardship is the predominant way that CST currently calls for environmental responsibility.

KINSHIP. But for Johnson and others, stewardship does not go far enough. The idea of kinship, she argues, takes us where we must go: "If separation is not the ideal but connection is; if dualism is not the ideal but the relational embrace of diversity is; if hierarchy is not the ideal but mutuality is; then the kinship model more closely approximates reality. It sees human beings and the earth with all its creatures intrinsically related as companions in a community of life. . . This kinship attitude does not measure differences on a scale of higher or lower ontological dignity but appreciates them as integral elements in the robust thriving of a whole" (Johnson, p. 30).

Two comments about kinship are important. First, it is an attempt to recognize and celebrate the diversity of all creatures in a way that steadfastly avoids the pattern of "higher" and "lower," or what Johnson has called "hierarchical dualism." The idea of kinship is not that there are no "distinctions between human beings and other forms of life": a rock is not a tree, and a tree is not a person. Instead, the conviction of kinship is that it is both unnecessary and irresponsible to assign "greater" and "lesser" value to diverse creatures. The relation of humanity to the rest of creation should be marked not by superiority, but by the recognition of interconnectedness and mutuality.

The second thing that should be said about Johnson's idea of kinship is that the idea is not entirely new. Although some version of the stewardship model has usually been at the center of Catholic thinking, traces of the kinship model have been part of Catholic social thought all along. In "Creation and an Environmental Ethic," Michael and Kenneth Himes demonstrate how the idea of kinship (they prefer *companionship*) was part of the thinking of St. Augustine, St. Thomas Aquinas, and above all St. Francis of Assisi and is part of a "sacramental vision" that sees ". . . every creature, human and non-human, animate and inanimate" a sign of the love and presence of God (Himes, 112).

To espouse kinship as the right way to envision humanity's relation to the rest of the universe would be a stretch for CST. At first glance it might seem that the first six convictions of CST that we have discussed are so centered on the dignity of human beings that there is little room for the rest of creation in the energy of CST. Admittedly, Catholic social thought—to date at least—has focused on the well-being of human beings. But perhaps scholars like Elizabeth Johnson are helping the Christian community appreciate in fresh ways the intimate connections between the welfare of people and the welfare of the earth and all its inhabitants. It may well be that one of the contributions feminist, non-dualistic, and non-hierarchical thought patterns are starting to make for CST is the ability to emphasize the dignity and sacredness of humankind without compromising the dignity and sacredness of the earth and all its creatures. We are in this together. That conviction, I believe, is "going forward" in many places in our world today, including in CST.

CST: Justice and a Principle of Application. We have come to the end of this reflection on seven key convictions of CST. By way of conclusion, I would like to reflect briefly on two questions. First, what might the word *justice* mean in light of the seven key convictions of CST? Second, how might these seven convictions *connect* with some specific issues? This latter question will lead to two observations: the first regards some principles of application regarding the seven convictions, and the second concerns the purposes of Catholic moral teachings, including CST.

CST and Justice. Justice is hard to define; it involves many things. It is both a virtue of individual persons (so we might say "Nelson Mandela is a just man."); and at the same time it is "larger" than the virtue of individuals (and thus we might also say "South Africa has become a more just society in recent years.") In this latter case, the virtue of individuals is surely involved, but a country is said to be just to the degree that justice is embedded in the *social structures and practices* (the regular way of doing business) of the society itself. Put differently, there is of course a relationship between justice as a virtue and justice as a characteristic of a society: just persons, working together, strive to create just social structures and practices, that is, just communities.

Key to understanding justice is *relationship*. Justice means *right relationship*. Justice exists in a community, large or small, when (and to the extent that) the relationships of the members of the community can be characterized as right relationships. There is not a "one size fits all" formula for determining when right relationships exist. Context is important. But there are a number of criteria from Catholic Social Teaching that can be used to determine when communal or social relationships are "right," that is, when they are just.

Right relationship exists when, and to the extent that, the dignity and sacredness of every living being are recognized and respected. Right relationship exists when, and to the extent that, the well-being and rights of every living being *(especially those who are most vulnerable)* are recognized, protected and promoted. Rights are articulated in different ways in different contexts, but in every context they include a right to life and to the things that are necessary to live with dignity, for one to flourish: a right to food, clothing, shelter, and health care; a right to freedom of relationship, freedom in speech, religion, association and public gatherings; and a right to participate in the economic and political activities of the community, including a right to dignified, meaningful work for a living, just wage. Right relationships exist—justice exists—when, and to the extent that, peace is being promoted.

It must be understood that along with every right there exits a corresponding responsibility. Right relationship exits when, and to the extent that, rights and responsibilities are exercised in a mutual manner.

Right relationship exists when, and to the extent that, the good of individual beings and the common good of all are being protected and promoted. (Notice that "individual beings" includes human beings, persons, but it is not limited to humans. Right relationship has a good deal to do the way human beings treat one another, but it also encompasses human beings' ways of relating to and responding to the earth itself and to others with whom humans share the natural environment.)

None of these observations about justice translate into a formula for simple solutions to complex social and ethical questions. CST yields no such formulas. Nevertheless, the key convictions of CST and the account of justice that accompanies it name some important moral values that should command our attention as well as criteria that may help us think about how we should respond to pressing social and ethic issues.

A Principle of Application. In their 1986 pastoral letter on economic justice, the U.S. Bishops spoke first about general *principles* and then went on to make *applications* to specific issues of economic policy. I have followed this line of thought as I have named general *convictions* of CST and, shortly, will make *connections* to some concrete issues. CST recognizes important differences between principle and application (conviction and connection), acknowledging that the movement from one to the other is neither easy nor obvious. The bishops describe this movement as follows. It is important to quote at some length.

> In focusing on some of the central economic issues and choices in American life in the light of moral principles, we are aware that the movement from principle to policy is complex and difficult and although moral values are essential in determining public policies, they do not dictate specific solutions. They must interact with empirical data, with historical, social, and political realities, and with competing demands on limited resources. The soundness of our prudential judgments depends not only on the moral force of our principles, but also on the accuracy of our information and the validity of our assumptions. Our judgments and recommendations on specific economic issues, therefore, do not carry the same moral authority as our statements of universal moral principles and formal church teaching; the former are related to circumstances which can change or which can be interpreted differently by people of good will. We expect and welcome debate on our specific policy recommendations. Nevertheless, we want our statements on these matters to be given serious consideration by Catholics as they determine whether their own moral judgments are consistent with the Gospel and with Catholic social teaching. We believe that differences on complex economic questions should be expressed in a spirit of mutual respect and open dialogue (U.S. Bishops, "Economic Justice for All," pars. 134–135).

In a church with a reputation for its emphasis on authority, these words from the bishops have a refreshing humility about them, indeed realism (which, in the end, is what humility really is). Keenly aware of the complexity of the economic issues they were addressing, the bishops proceeded by naming some general, but admittedly somewhat abstract moral principles that should govern economic policy choices. Two examples suffice: "Every economic decision and institution must be judged in light of whether it protects or undermines the dignity of the human person" (par. 13); "All members of society have a special obligation to the poor and vulnerable" (par. 16). The bishops acknowledged that there is a difference between general principles and specific recommendation regarding economic policy. People of good will—Catholic or otherwise—may agree that we have special obligations to the poor, but disagree profoundly regarding which revisions in, say, a taxation plan would best meet the needs of the poor. And yes, (as much as it might pain me at times to admit this) both Democrats and Republicans can espouse the convictions of CST, but disagree about many matters of public policy. This doesn't mean that CST means nothing, only that it may mean more than one thing. CST provides critical criteria for assessing public policy. Does a proposed taxation plan help or hinder the quality of life of the poor and vulnerable? CST is convinced that that is the right question, even as it admits that the answer is far from obvious.

Purposes of CST. I think it can be said that the purposes of CST—and of all of the church's moral teachings—are twofold. First, they are intended to lift up the moral dimension of important issues of the day and in that way to contribute to public discussion of issues that effect the common good. Second, they exist to help form the consciences of Catholic people so that they might make judgments and choices that are not only wise, but which bear the mark of Christian faith convictions.

In the introduction to their pastoral letter on economic justice the bishops noted that they intended to speak both because they were Americans and also because they were pastors. As Americans, they strove to address public issues in ways that would make sense to all Americans. Groups as diverse as the National Organization for Women and the National Rifle Association do the same: they address public issues, attempting to persuade others concerning their values and convictions. So too, CST is often addressed to "the public," attempting to lift up the moral dimensions of important social issues.

As pastors, the bishops addressed members of the Catholic Church. As part of their teaching office, it is the responsibility of the pope and bishops to make connections between Catholic faith and important moral issues in order to guide the consciences of Catholics. In the pastoral letter quoted above, the bishops stated that they hoped both their general principles and their specific policy applications would be "given serious consideration by Catholics as they determine whether their own moral judgments are consistent with the Gospel and with Catholic social teaching" (par. 135). That captures well what Catholic teaching is concerning the responsibilities of Catholics regarding the moral teachings of the church. In the words of the bishops at Vatican II, in forming their consciences, Catholics are to "pay careful attention to" the moral teachings of the church ("Declaration on Religious Liberty," par. 14). Catholicism is not "in the business" of assuming moral responsibility for others; or at least it ought not be. But it is "in the business" of naming the moral aspects of important social issues and contributing to consciences that are wise and just.

Part Two: Catholic Social Teaching—Connections

In the concluding part of this article (much more brief than Part One) it is neither possible nor necessary to try to even touch on the wide array of social issues that have commanded the attention of CST in recent years. My purpose here is simply this: I would like to show how some of CST's key convictions—especially about human dignity and the option for the poor—*connect* to three specific issues: capital punishment, immigration, and the place of gay and lesbian persons in the church. What should emerge is the fact that CST is not simply a matter of general or vague convictions, but includes the drive to make connections with the important issues of the day.

Capital Punishment: Does Every Life Count? Catholic Social Teaching is opposed to the use of the death penalty as a legitimate means of punishment. That simple sentence captures the way CST's conviction about the dignity of every human being connects with this perennially difficult issue. Having said that, however, it is also true that there is nothing simple about Catholic teaching on capital punishment. As James Megivern's recent 600-page history on this issue illustrates, Catholic convictions have changed dramatically on this issue. In what follows let us simply take note of some of the historical features of this issue, examine the "why" of current Catholic opposition to capital punishment, and see how CST's contemporary stance on the death penalty connects with other issues in which human life is at stake.

Toward the end of his historical treatment of Catholicism's view of the death penalty, Megivern quotes from a 1960 article by Jesuit theologian Antonio Messineo as a way of summarizing the predominant stance of the church:

> The Church, from the Fathers to St. Thomas Aquinas down to our own day, with unswerving unanimity, taught the legitimacy of capital punishment, and that therefore it could confidently be affirmed that the death penalty was in perfect accord with Christian thought (Megivern, p. 460).

As Megivern chronicles, the *reasons* for the church's predominant approval (there were always "voices of dissent") of the legitimacy of the death penalty evolved over the centuries. In the fourth and fifth centuries, as Christianity became the "established" religion of the Roman Empire, it was virtually unthinkable that the state could not exercise lethal force, including the exercise of capital punishment (3). From the eleventh through the seventeenth centuries the church invoked various arguments to explain why the death penalty could be seen as a justifiable way of dealing with heresy, more precisely with heretics (3–4). This period saw the establishment of the Inquisition, which involved both the torture and death of heretics. And it was during this period that St. Thomas Aquinas invoked the image of a "diseased organ" to explain the justifiability of capital punishment: just as a surgeon removes a diseased organ for the welfare of the total body, so too the state may "remove" a "diseased member" for the overall good of the community (Megivern, pp. 115–116). In more recent centuries the argument tended to move toward just defense: the state may exercise capital punishment as a necessary way of defending itself against those prone to heinous crimes against the state and its citizens. As recently as 1952, Pope Pius XII, attempting to uphold both the inviolability of the right to life and the justifiability of the death penalty, argued that the state, in exercising capital punishment, does not/can not take away the right to life from an individual. Instead, through the death penalty the state deprives the criminal of the *good* of life "after he by his crime has already been dispossessed of his right to life" (Megivern, p. 459).

Given this history, why is it that the church *today* is opposed to the use of capital punishment? Pope John Paul II's words from "The Gospel of Life" (1995) are important here. After affirming the rightful place of punishment the pope argued as follows:

> . . . the nature and extent of the punishment must be carefully evaluated and decided upon, and ought not go to the extreme of executing the offender except in cases of absolute necessity: in other words, when it would not be possible otherwise to defend society. Today however, as a result of steady improvements in the organization of the penal system, such cases are very rare, if not practically non-existent ("The Gospel of Life," par. 56).

Noteworthy is the fact that the pope did not quibble with the state's theoretical right to capital punishment. Instead, his argument focused on the rightness of the *use* of capital punishment in ordinary circumstances today. Under normal circumstances, he argued, capital punishment is not right precisely because it is not necessary; the rightful purposes of punishment can be served otherwise. This argument, essentially that of the U.S. Bishops in a 1980 statement on the issue, expresses current CST on the matter.

For some, more important and more convincing than the pope's argument for the non-use of the death penalty, is the fact that the church's current teaching emphasizes the conviction that every human life is sacred, yes, even the life of those whose actions have violated life. For many, our call to recognize the dignity of every human being and the value of every human life is upheld in a powerful way through CST's stand against the death penalty. Perhaps no one has dramatized this conviction more effectively than Helen Prejean, CSJ, in her book (and later the film) *Dead Man Walking: An Eyewitness Account of the Death Penalty in the United States.* She and others like her argue that there are a host of things wrong with the death penalty: judicial errors *do* take place that result in the execution of innocent people; there is evidence of racial bias at work in the disproportionate way people of color are sent to their death; and the notion that capital punishment deters others from violent crime seems largely unsubstantiated. But beyond these arguments there is something more. Does not capital punishment simply continue a senseless circle of violence? Does it not make us killers ourselves? And do we not deaden a voice within us that calls us to mercy, even for those who have offended us so terribly? Prejean and others answer yes to these questions. They think that yes, part of the core of Christian faith, is also accessible to all people of good will. I believe they are right.

A final word about CST's current stance on capital punishment is this: it is part of what the late Cardinal Joseph Bernardin (Chicago) called "a consistent ethic of life." This is the idea that there is fundamental value that grounds Catholic teaching on all issues related to life: the dignity and inviolability of the life of every human being. Put differently, the fundamental value CST is attempting to protect and promote in its teachings on abortion, euthanasia, assisted-suicide and capital punishment is the value of every human life. Even more precisely, as the teaching on abortion makes explicit, we ought not discriminate or "cut corners" on the dignity of human life because of its stage of development (Congregation for the Doctrine of the Faith, "Declaration on Procured Abortion," par. 11). To be sure, CST recognizes the value of the life and well-being of a mother in an unplanned and unwanted pregnancy; it embraces the virtue of compassion that motivates those who propose assisted-suicide or euthanasia as a way to respond to the suffering of a loved one; and it stands in awe in the face of the rage and devastation of those who have lost a loved one through violent crime. But with all that, CST suggests that the taking of life through abortion, assisted-suicide or euthanasia, or through capital punishment pits values and even human lives against one another in ways that cause us not to flourish, but to diminish. On these issues CST constitutes "hard sayings." That is obvious. But the "consistent ethic of life" is not simply about what CST opposes; it is about a conviction it wishes to celebrate: every life counts.

Immigration: Who Is a Neighbor? Catholic Social Teaching, seeing immigration from the point of view of those whose social condition of poverty or oppression leads them to emigrate, argues that such persons have a right to emigrate and that countries that are able have a responsibility to provide residence, indeed welcome. This sentence captures the way CST makes a *connection* between its convictions about human dignity and the option for the poor and the issue of immigration.

There are religious roots for the concern about immigration in both Judaism and Christianity. Perhaps the most important of all the stories in the Hebrew Scriptures is the story of the Exodus (Exodus, chapters 3–15). In the story, God heard the cries of the Jews suffering from slavery and oppression in Egypt and God did something about it. In and through the leadership of Moses, the story goes, God enabled the Jews to flee from oppression and led them safely (eventually!) to their own land. The "moral lesson" is that God cares for those who suffer, God cares for migrants and refugees. God's people should do the same.

By almost anyone's standard, the story of the Good Samaritan in the New Testament is one of the classic texts in all of literature. I won't do justice to it here. But among other things, the story is about an encounter between two people who are "set up" to be enemies, to despise one another. The one who has been beaten, presumably a Jew, is ignored by his own religious leaders. And then a Samaritan (stereotypically a bitter enemy of the Jews) enters the scene. In a remarkably grace-filled moment, he is "moved with pity" and proceeds to go out of his way, to inconvenience himself, to take practical steps to tend to the man's needs. In Luke's Gospel, after Jesus' instructions to love our neighbor as ourselves, this story is told in response to the question "And who is my neighbor?" (Luke 10: 25–29). So among the "moral lessons" of the story there is this one: we should consider carefully what it means to be a neighbor. "Neighbor" is not simply about living close to someone else; and it is not simply about "feeling comfortable" with others. In the Good Samaritan story "neighbor" is more of a verb than a noun. The word "neighbor," the story suggests, describes the way we respond to the "the other," "the stranger," particularly the stranger who suffers.

What this faith tradition provides for CST is not a detailed set of proposals regarding immigration policies. Rather, it provides a perspective, a starting point. CST enters discussions about immigration from the perspective of those whose poverty or oppression causes them to leave their home, suggesting that when it is necessary the ability "to emigrate to other countries and to take up residence there" is a matter of human rights (Pope John XXIII, "Peace on Earth," par. 25). Motivated by a conviction about the dignity of *all* persons and, even more, by its option for the poor, CST argues that the right to emigrate calls for a corresponding responsibility for those who are able to provide a safe haven for those who need it, and indeed to provide the social services that may be necessary to secure a quality of life that befits human dignity. Put more simply, we are to be "neighbor" to those who suffer. And as in the New Testament story, "being neighbor" may involve overcoming racism and other forms of discrimination that are often at work in our personal attitudes toward refugees and migrants as well as in our institutional and national policies (Pope John Paul II, "On Human Work," par. 23).

None of this is to say, as Catholic theologians William O'Neill and William Spohn have noted, that there should not be a fair distribution of both the burdens (which countries should offer asylum) and benefits (which countries should benefit from immigration of skilled workers) of immigration policies internationally (O'Neill and Spohn, 100–101). Indeed, there may be reasons to limit immigration. However, CST suggests that such limitation has a condition: "Efforts to stem migration that do not effectively address its root causes are not only ineffectual, but permit the continuation of the political, social, and economic inequities that cause it" (U.S. Bishops Committee on Migration, "One Family Under God," 13).

It should be clear that CST does not offer a detailed proposal regarding immigration policies nationally or internationally. What it does offer is a perspective we might adopt regarding migrants and refugees. Who are these people? They are our brothers and sisters. Their ability to flee from poverty and oppression is a matter of human rights. Our call to provide welcome, to "be neighbor," is a matter of human responsibility. Many questions remain, but that is a start, a challenging one.

Gay and Lesbian Persons in the Church: Who Belongs at the Table?
Catholic Social Teaching recognizes that gay and lesbian persons, created in the image and likeness of God and brothers and sisters to us all, unfortunately often suffer from discrimination and violence, even murder. Every form of prejudice or oppression directed against gay and lesbian persons—whether in society at large or within the Christian community itself—is an offense against human dignity and human rights and should be eradicated. Gay and lesbian persons should receive a particular welcome in the church—not only because of what the Christian community may offer them, but also because of the way their particular experiences can enrich the church.

I am well aware of the complexity and the controversy of the issue at hand. Had I asked, I know there are many who would have suggested that I conclude with something else. But the issue is important, very important. And as the opening paragraph above suggests (a paragraph that belongs well within the bounds of official Catholic teaching on the connections between homosexuality and justice), some of Catholicism's most important convictions relative to homosexuality are more about justice than they are about sex. Knowing that many questions will remain when I have finished, let me offer just two comments on the place of gay and lesbian persons within the church.

As we have seen, two of the most important convictions of CST are about human dignity/human rights and an option for the poor and vulnerable. The Christian community has special obligations to gay and lesbian persons. There is no need to document the ways in which gay and lesbian persons often suffer from discrimination (or something worse) precisely because of their sexual orientation. Gay and lesbian persons have experienced everything from raised eyebrows to laughter to ridicule to marginalization to the denial of human rights to violence to murder. Without question, their human dignity has often been defaced. And they remain "vulnerable" in a variety of ways. CST's convictions about the dignity of *all* persons and the desire to "take the side" of the poor and vulnerable are the reason the church should muster its best energies to help eradicate such discrimination both in society and in the Christian community. That should begin by providing a special degree of welcome in the church itself, as the U.S. Bishops put it, "a special degree of pastoral under-standing and care" ("To Live in Christ Jesus," par. 4; Peddicord). To say this differently, gay and lesbian persons belong at *all* our tables. As the pastor in one of this article's opening vignettes seems to understand, the church must do much better extending hospitality toward gay and les-bian persons, especially at the nourishing table of the Eucharist.

But there is another, equally important reason for such hospitality. To put it simply, the Catholic Church has unfinished business regarding its own teaching on homosexuality. The unfinished business will not be attended to well without the voice of gay and lesbian persons themselves. Now there are many who think that the church's current teaching about homo-sexuality (briefly, that a homosexual orientation does not involve any moral fault, but that homosexual relations *do* precisely because *all* sexual relations, for *all* people, belong exclusively within the context of hetero-sexual marriage) is just right. But of course there are many who do not. Some think that the church's teaching on this needs to be expressed bet-ter, more cogently, more compassionately. Others think that the teaching is so riddled with "heterosexism" that we must "erase the board and start over." The tensions, indeed divisions, within the church on this issue are more pronounced than ever. In my view, the experience—especially the moral experience—of gay and lesbian persons must be "factored in" to Catholic theological reflection about homosexuality more than it ever has before. If, as I believe, Christian ethics is reflection on moral experience in the light of Christian faith, then Christian ethical reflection about homo-sexuality cannot help but be well served by paying particularly close attention to the experience and narratives of gay and lesbian persons themselves.

As I hope this article has made clear, CST—indeed Catholic teaching on all matters of morality—is an evolving reality. In my view, that is not a weakness of Catholic teaching, but one of its strengths. Good teaching requires good listening. So, as CST urges, let us make sure that gay and lesbian persons know they are welcome at our table. And let us not only speak, let us listen.

Works Cited and Recommended Sources

Bellah, Robert N., Madsen, Richard, Sullivan, William M., Swindler, Ann, Tipton, Steven M. *Habits of the Heart: Individualism and Commitment in American Life.* New York: Harper & Row, 1985.

Bernardin, Joseph Cardinal. *Consistent Ethic of Life.* Thomas G. Fuecht-mann, Ed. Kansas City, MO: Sheed & Ward, 1988.

Boff, Leonardo. *Jesus Christ Liberator.* Maryknoll, NY: Orbis Books, 1978.

Bullard, Robert D., Ed. *Confronting Environmental Racism: Voices from the Grassroots.* Boston, MA: South End Press, 1993.

Cadorette, Curt, Giblin, Marie, Legge, Marilyn J., Snyder, Mary H. *Liberation Theology: An Introductory Reader.* Maryknoll, NY: Orbis Press, 1992.

Cahill, Lisa Sowle. *Love Your Enemies: Discipleship, Pacifism, and Just War Theory.* Minneapolis, MN: Fortress Press, 1994.

Catechism of the Catholic Church. English Ed., United States Catholic Conference, Inc.- Libreria Editrice Vaticana, 1994.

Congregation for the Doctrine of the Faith. "Declaration on Procured Abortion" (1974). Excerpts. *Medical Ethics: Sources of Catholic Teachings.* Kevin D. O'Rourke, OP, and Philip Boyle, OP., Eds. St. Louis, MO: Catholic Health Association. 1989, 37–39.

Elsbernd, Mary, and Bieringer, Reimund. *When Love Is Not Enough.* Collegeville, MN: The Liturgical Press, 2002.

Gutierrez, Gustavo. *A Theology of Liberation.* London: SCM Press, LTD, 1974.

Henriot, Peter J., DeBerri, Edward P., Schultheis, Michael J. *Catholic Social Teaching: Our Best Kept Secret.* Maryknoll, NY: Orbis Books, 1992.

Himes, Kenneth R., OFM. "The Morality of Humanitarian Intervention." *Theological Studies.* March 1994 Vol. 55, No. 1. 82–105.

Himes, Michael J. and Himes, Kenneth R. , OFM. "Creation and an Environmental Ethic." *Fullness of Faith: The Public Significance of Theology.* Mahwah, NJ: Paulist Press, 1993 104–124.

Hopkins, Gerard Manley. "God's Grandeur." *The Norton Anthology of English Literature,* Revised, Vol. 2. New York: W. W. Norton & Co., 1968, 1433.

Johnson, Elizabeth A. *Women, Earth, and Creator Spirit.* Mahwah, NJ: Paulist Press, 1993.

Keenan, James F., SJ. "The Open Debate: Moral Theology and the Lives of Gay and Lesbian Persons." *Theological Studies.* V. 64, No. 1. March, 2003. 127–150.

Lucker, Raymond A. "Justice in the Church: The Church as Example." *One Hundred Years of Catholic Social Thought: Celebration and Challenge.* John A. Coleman, SJ, Ed. New York: Orbis Books, 1991, 88–100.

Massaro, Thomas, SJ. *Living Justice: Catholic Social Teaching in Action.* Franklin, Wisconsin: Sheed & Ward, 2000.

McBrien, Richard P. "What Is Catholicism?" *Catholicism*. Revised ed. New York: Harper, 1994, 3–17.

McCormick, Patrick T. *A Banqueter's Guide to the All-Night Soup Kitchen of the Kingdom of God*. Collegeville, MN: The Liturgical Press, 2004.

McDonough, William C., and Michaud, Catherine R., CSJ, "Papal Apologies Embody and Advance Vatican II on 'the Tradition Poured Out in the Church,'" Ch. 6 of *Revelation and the Church: Vatican II in the Twenty-first Century*. Maryknoll, NY: Orbis Books, 2003. 103–122.

Megivern, James J. *The Death Penalty: An Historical and Theological Survey*. Mahwah, NJ: Paulist Press 1997.

Mich, Marvin L. Krier. *Catholic Social Teaching and Movements*. Mystic, CT: Twenty-Third Publications 1998.

O'Neill, William R., SJ, and Spohn, William C. "Rights of Passage: The Ethics of Immigration and Refugee Policy." *Theological Studies*. March, 1998. Vol. 59, No. 1 84–106.

Patrick, Anne E. *Liberating Conscience: Feminist Explorations in Catholic Moral Theology*. New York: Continuum 1996.

Peddicord, Richard, OP. *Gay and Lesbian Rights — A Question: Sexual Ethics or Social Justice?* Kansas City, MO: Sheed & Ward, 1996.

Prejean, Helen, CSJ. *Dead Man Walking: An Eyewitness Account of the Death Penalty in the United States*. New York: Random House 1993.

Pope John XXIII. "Pacem in Terris" ("Peace on Earth") (1963). *Catholic Social Thought: The Documentary Heritage*. Ed. David J. O'Brien and Thomas A. Shannon. Maryknoll, NY: Orbis Books, 1997.

Pope John Paul II. "Centesimus Annus" ("On the Hundredth Anniversary of 'Rerum Novarum'") (1991). *Catholic Social Thought: The Documentary Heritage*.439–488.

Pope John Paul II. "Evangelium Vitae" ("The Gospel of Life") (1995). Vatican City: Libreria Editrice Vaticana 1995.

Pope John Paul II. "Jubilee Characteristic: The Purification of Memory." *Origins* 29/40. (March 23, 2000). 648–650.

Pope John Paul II. "Laborem Exercens" ("On Human Work") (1981). *Catholic Social Thought: The Documentary Heritage* 352–392.

Pope John Paul II. "Peace With All Creation" (January 1, 1990). *Origins*, Vol. 19 465–468.

Pope John Paul II. "Sollicitudo Rei Socialis" ("On Social Concern") (1987). *Catholic Social Thought: The Documentary Heritage* 395–436.

Pope Leo XIII. "Rerum Novarum" ("The Condition of Labor") *(1891)*. *Catholic Social Thought: The Documentary Heritage* 14–39.

Schubeck, Thomas L., SJ. *Liberation Ethics: Sources, Models, and Norms*. Minneapolis, MN: Fortress Press 1993.

Thompson, J. Milburn. *Justice & Peace: A Christian Primer*. Maryknoll, NY: Orbis Books, 1997 179–205.

U.S. Catholic Bishops. "The Challenge of Peace: God's Promise and Our Response" (1983). *Catholic Social Thought: The Documentary Heritage* 489–571.

U.S. Catholic Bishops. "Economic Justice for All" (1986). *Catholic Social Thought: The Documentary Heritage* 572–680.

U.S. Catholic Bishops. "Renewing the Earth" (November 14, 1991). *Origins*, Vol. 21, 425–432.

U.S. Catholic Bishops. "Statement on Capital Punishment." Washington, DC: U.S.CC 1980.

U.S. Catholic Bishops. "To Live as Christ Jesus." Washington, DC: U.S.CC 1976.

U.S. Catholic Bishops. Committee on Migration. "One Family Under God." Washington, DC: U.S.CC, 1998.

Vatican II, Catholic Bishops. "Dignitatis Humanae" ("Declaration on Religious Liberty") (1965). Documents of Vatican II. Ed. Austin P. Flannery. Grand Rapids, MI: Eerdmans, 1975).

Vatican II, Catholic Bishops. "Gaudium et Spes" ("Pastoral Constitution on the Church in the Modern World") (1965). *Catholic Social Thought: The Documentary Heritage* 166–237.

White, Lynn. "The Historical Roots of our Ecological Crisis." Ch. 2 of *Environmental Ethics: Readings in Theory and Application*, Third Edition, Louis P. Pojman, editor. Belmont, CA: Wadsworth/Thomson Learning, 2001. 13–19.

Notes

[1] This is a modest revision of my article (with the same title) that appeared first in *The Global Search for Justice:* The College of St. Catherine. Acton, MA: Copley Custom Publishing Group, 2000.

[2] As is the case with several sections of this article, this history is drawn from my *In the Breath of God: Christian Morality*, Ch. 7 "Christian Morality and Social Responsibility" (Chicago: Loyola Press, 2000).

Beverly Daniel Tatum (b. 1954) is currently the president of Spelman College. An academic and author, Tatum gained national attention in 1997 when her book Why Are All the Black Kids Sitting Together in the Cafeteria? *was published. Her writing focuses on the psychology of racism. In reading the following excerpt ask yourself if prejudice is the same as racism? How does racism lead to social injustice? How can one work toward combating both prejudice and racism? Can you think of examples of both racism and prejudice from the readings in Unit 1?*

Defining Racism
"Can We Talk?"

Beverly Daniel Tatum

Early in my teaching career, a White student I knew asked me what I would be teaching the following semester. I mentioned that I would be teaching a course on racism. She replied, with some surprise in her voice, "Oh, is there still racism?" I assured her that indeed there was and suggested that she sign up for my course. Fifteen years later, after exhaustive media coverage of events such as the Rodney King beating, the Charles Stuart and Susan Smith cases, the O. J. Simpson trial, the appeal to racial prejudices in electoral politics, and the bitter debates about affirmative action and welfare reform, it seems hard to imagine that anyone would still be unaware of the reality of racism in our society. But in fact, in almost every audience I address, there is someone who will suggest that racism is a thing of the past. There is always someone who hasn't noticed the stereotypical images of people of color in the media, who hasn't observed the housing discrimination in their community, who hasn't read the newspaper articles about documented racial bias in lending practices among well-known banks, who isn't aware of the racial tracking pattern at the local school, who hasn't seen the reports of rising incidents of racially motivated hate crimes in America—in short, someone who hasn't been paying attention to issues of race. But if you are paying attention, the legacy of racism is not hard to see, and we are all affected by it.

The impact of racism begins early. Even in our preschool years, we are exposed to misinformation about people different from ourselves. Many of us grew up in neighborhoods where we had limited opportunities to interact with people different from our own families. When I ask my college students, "How many of you grew up in neighborhoods where most of the people were from the same racial group as your own?" almost every hand goes up. There is still a great deal of social segregation in our communities. Consequently, most of the early information we receive

320

about "others"—people racially, religiously, or socioeconomically different from ourselves—does not come as the result of firsthand experience. The secondhand information we do receive has often been distorted, shaped by cultural stereotypes, and left incomplete.

Some examples will highlight this process. Several years ago one of my students conducted a research project investigating preschoolers' conceptions of Native Americans.[1] Using children at a local day care center as her participants, she asked these three- and four-year-olds to draw a picture of a Native American. Most children were stumped by her request. They didn't know what a Native American was. But when she rephrased the question and asked them to draw a picture of an Indian, they readily complied. Almost every picture included one central feature: feathers. In fact, many of them also included a weapon—a knife or tomahawk—and depicted the person in violent or aggressive terms. Though this group of children, almost all of whom were White, did not live near a large Native American population and probably had had little if any personal interaction with American Indians, they all had internalized an image of what Indians were like. How did they know? Cartoon images, in particular the Disney movie *Peter Pan*, were cited by the children as their number-one source of information. At the age of three, these children already had a set of stereotypes in place. Though I would not describe three-year-olds as prejudiced, the stereotypes to which they have been exposed become the foundation for the adult prejudices so many of us have.

Sometimes the assumptions we make about others come not from what we have been told or what we have seen on television or in books, but rather from what we have *not* been told. The distortion of historical information about people of color leads young people (and older people, too) to make assumptions that may go unchallenged for a long time. Consider this conversation between two White students following a discussion about the cultural transmission of racism:

"Yeah, I just found out that Cleopatra was actually a Black woman."

"What?"

The first student went on to explain her newly learned information. The second student exclaimed in disbelief, "That can't be true. Cleopatra was beautiful!"

What had this young woman learned about who in our society is considered beautiful and who is not? Had she conjured up images of Elizabeth Taylor when she thought of Cleopatra? The new information her classmate had shared and her own deeply ingrained assumptions about who is beautiful and who is not were too incongruous to allow her to assimilate the information at that moment.

Omitted information can have similar effects. For example, another young woman, preparing to be a high school English teacher, expressed her dismay that she had never learned about any Black authors in any of her English courses. How was she to teach about them to her future students when she hadn't learned about them herself? A White male student in the class responded to this discussion with frustration in his response journal, writing "It's not my fault that Blacks don't write books." Had one of his elementary, high school, or college teachers ever told him that there were no Black writers? Probably not. Yet because he had never been exposed to Black authors, he had drawn his own conclusion that there were none.

Stereotypes, omissions, and distortions all contribute to the development of prejudice. *Prejudice* is a preconceived judgment or opinion, usually based on limited information. I assume that we all have prejudices, not because we want them, but simply because we are so continually exposed to misinformation about others. Though I have often heard students or workshop participants describe someone as not having "a prejudiced bone in his body," I usually suggest that they look again. Prejudice is one of the inescapable consequences of living in a racist society. Cultural racism—the cultural images and messages that affirm the assumed superiority of Whites and the assumed inferiority of people of color—is like smog in the air. Sometimes it is so thick it is visible, other times it is less apparent, but always, day in and day out, we are breathing it in. None of us would introduce ourselves as "smog-breathers" (and most of us don't want to be described as prejudiced), but if we live in a smoggy place, how can we avoid breathing the air? If we live in an environment in which we are bombarded with stereotypical images in the media, are frequently exposed to the ethnic jokes of friends and family members, and are rarely informed of the accomplishments of oppressed groups, we will develop the negative categorizations of those groups that form the basis of prejudice.

People of color as well as Whites develop these categorizations. Even a member of the stereotyped group may internalize the stereotypical categories about his or her own group to some degree. In fact, this process happens so frequently that it has a name, *internalized oppression*. Some of the consequences of believing the distorted messages about one's own group will be discussed in subsequent chapters.

Certainly some people are more prejudiced than others, actively embracing and perpetuating negative and hateful images of those who are different from themselves. When we claim to be free of prejudice, perhaps what we are really saying is that we are not hatemongers. But none of us is completely innocent. Prejudice is an integral part of our socialization, and it is not our fault. Just as the preschoolers my student interviewed are not to blame for the negative messages they internalized, we are not at fault for the stereotypes, distortions, and omissions that shaped our thinking as we grew up.

To say that it is not our fault does not relieve us of responsibility, however. We may not have polluted the air, but we need to take responsibility, along with others, for cleaning it up. Each of us needs to look at our own behavior. Am I perpetuating and reinforcing the negative messages so pervasive in our culture, or am I seeking to challenge them? If I have not been exposed to positive images of marginalized groups, am I seeking them out, expanding my own knowledge base for myself and my children? Am I acknowledging and examining my own prejudices, my own rigid categorizations of others, thereby minimizing the adverse impact they might have on my interactions with those I have categorized? Unless we engage in these and other conscious acts of reflection and reeducation, we easily repeat the process with our children. We teach what we were taught. The unexamined prejudices of the parents are passed on to the children. It is not our fault, but it is our responsibility to interrupt this cycle.

Racism: A System of Advantage Based on Race

Many people use the terms *prejudice* and *racism* interchangeably. I do not, and I think it is important to make a distinction. In his book *Portraits of White Racism*, David Wellman argues convincingly that limiting our understanding of racism to prejudice does not offer a sufficient explanation for the persistence of racism. He defines racism as a "system of advantage based on race."[2] In illustrating this definition, he provides example after example of how Whites defend their racial advantage—access to better schools, housing, jobs—even when they do not embrace overtly prejudicial thinking. Racism cannot be fully explained as an expression of prejudice alone.

This definition of racism is useful because it allows us to see that racism, like other forms of oppression, is not only a personal ideology based on racial prejudice, but a *system* involving cultural messages and institutional policies and practices as well as the beliefs and actions of individuals. In the context of the United States, this system clearly operates to the advantage of Whites and to the disadvantage of people of color. Another related definition of racism, commonly used by antiracist educators and consultants, is "prejudice plus power." Racial prejudice when combined with social power—access to social, cultural, and economic resources and decision-making—leads to the institutionalization of racist policies and practices. While I think this definition also captures the idea that racism is more than individual beliefs and attitudes, I prefer Wellman's definition because the idea of systematic advantage and disadvantage is critical to an understanding of how racism operates in American society.

In addition, I find that many of my White students and workshop participants do not feel powerful. Defining racism as prejudice plus power has little personal relevance. For some, their response to this definition is the following: "I'm not really prejudiced, and I have no power, so racism has nothing to do with me." However, most White people, if they are really being honest with themselves, can see that there are advantages to being White in the United States. Despite the current rhetoric about affirmative action and "reverse racism," every social indicator, from salary to life expectancy, reveals the advantages of being White.[3]

The systematic advantages of being White are often referred to as White privilege. In a now well-known article, "White Privilege: Unpacking the Invisible Knapsack," Peggy McIntosh, a White feminist scholar, identified a long list of societal privileges that she received simply because she was White.[4] She did not ask for them, and it is important to note that she hadn't always noticed that she was receiving them. They included major and minor advantages. Of course she enjoyed greater access to jobs and housing. But she also was able to shop in department stores without being followed by suspicious salespeople and could always find appropriate hair care products and makeup in any drugstore. She could send her child to school confident that the teacher would not discriminate against him on the basis of race. She could also be late for meetings, and talk with her mouth full, fairly confident that these behaviors would not be attributed to the fact that she was White. She could express an opinion in a meeting or in print and not have it labeled the "White" viewpoint. In other words, she was more often than not viewed as an individual, rather than as a member of a racial group.

This article rings true for most White readers, many of whom may have never considered the benefits of being White. It's one thing to have enough awareness of racism to describe the ways that people of color are disadvantaged by it. But this new understanding of racism is more elusive. In very concrete terms, it means that if a person of color is the victim of housing discrimination, the apartment that would otherwise have been rented to that person of color is still available for a White person. The White tenant is, knowingly or unknowingly, the beneficiary of racism, a system of advantage based on race. The unsuspecting tenant is not to blame for the prior discrimination, but she benefits from it anyway.

For many Whites, this new awareness of the benefits of a racist system elicits considerable pain, often accompanied by feelings of anger and guilt. These uncomfortable emotions can hinder further discussion. We all like to think that we deserve the good things we have received, and that others, too, get what they deserve. Social psychologists call this tendency a "belief in a just world."[5] Racism directly contradicts such notions of justice.

Understanding racism as a system of advantage based on race is antithetical to traditional notions of an American meritocracy. For those who have internalized this myth, this definition generates considerable discomfort. It is more comfortable simply to think of racism as a particular form of prejudice. Notions of power or privilege do not have to be addressed when our understanding of racism is constructed in that way.

The discomfort generated when a systemic definition of racism is introduced is usually quite visible in the workshops I lead. Someone in the group is usually quick to point out that this is not the definition you will find in most dictionaries. I reply, "Who wrote the dictionary?" I am not being facetious with this response. Whose interests are served by a "prejudice only" definition of racism? It is important to understand that the system of advantage is perpetuated when we do not acknowledge its existence.

Racism: For Whites Only?

Frequently someone will say, "You keep talking about White people. People of color can be racist, too." I once asked a White teacher what it would mean to her if a student or parent of color accused her of being racist. She said she would feel as though she had been punched in the stomach or called a "low-life scum." She is not alone in this feeling. The word *racist* holds a lot of emotional power. For many White people, to be called racist is the ultimate insult. The idea that this term might only be applied to Whites becomes highly problematic for after all, can't people of color be "low-life scum" too?

Of course, people of any racial group can hold hateful attitudes and behave in racially discriminatory and bigoted ways. We can all cite examples of horrible hate crimes which have been perpetrated by people of color as well as Whites. Hateful behavior is hateful behavior no matter who does it. But when I am asked, "Can people of color be racist?" I reply, "The answer depends on your definition of racism." If one defines racism as racial prejudice, the answer is yes. People of color can and do have racial prejudices. However, if one defines racism as a system of advantage based on race, the answer is no. People of color are not racist because they do not systematically benefit from racism. And equally important, there is no systematic cultural and institutional support or sanction for the racial bigotry of people of color. In my view, reserving the term *racist* only for behaviors committed by Whites in the context of a White-dominated society is a way of acknowledging the ever-present power differential afforded Whites by the culture and institutions that make up the system of advantage and continue to reinforce notions of White superiority. (Using the same logic, I reserve the word *sexist* for men. Though women can and do have gender-based prejudices, only men systematically benefit from sexism.)

Despite my best efforts to explain my thinking on this point, there are some who will be troubled, perhaps even incensed, by my response. To call the racially motivated acts of a person of color acts of racial bigotry and to describe similar acts committed by Whites as racist will make no sense to some people, including some people of color. To those, I will respectfully say, "We can agree to disagree." At moments like these, it is not agreement that is essential, but clarity. Even if you don't like the definition of racism I am using, hopefully you are now clear about what it is. If I also understand how you are using the term, our conversation can continue—despite our disagreement.

Another provocative question I'm often asked is "Are you saying all Whites are racist?" When asked this question, I again remember that White teacher's response, and I am conscious that perhaps the question I am really being asked is, "Are you saying all Whites are bad people?" The answer to that question is of course not. However, all White people, intentionally or unintentionally, do benefit from racism. A more relevant question is what are White people as individuals doing to interrupt racism? For many White people, the image of a racist is a hood-wearing Klan member or a name-calling Archie Bunker figure. These images represent what might be called *active racism*, blatant, intentional acts of racial bigotry and discrimination. *Passive racism* is more subtle and can be seen in the collusion of laughing when a racist joke is told, of letting exclusionary hiring practices go unchallenged, of accepting as appropriate the omissions of people of color from the curriculum, and of avoiding difficult race-related issues. Because racism is so ingrained in the fabric of American institutions, it is easily self-perpetuating.[6] All that is required to maintain it is business as usual.

I sometimes visualize the ongoing cycle of racism as a moving walkway at the airport. Active racist behavior is equivalent to walking fast on the conveyor belt. The person engaged in active racist behavior has identified with the ideology of White supremacy and is moving with it. Passive racist behavior is equivalent to standing still on the walkway. No overt effort is being made, but the conveyor belt moves the bystanders along to the same destination as those who are actively walking. Some of the bystanders may feel the motion of the conveyor belt, see the active racists ahead of them, and choose to turn around, unwilling to go to the same destination as the White supremacists. But unless they are walking actively in the opposite direction at a speed faster than the conveyor belt—unless they are actively antiracist—they will find themselves carried along with the others.

So, not all Whites are actively racist. Many are passively racist. Some, though not enough, are actively antiracist. The relevant question is not whether all Whites are racist, but how we can move more White people from a position of active or passive racism to one of active antiracism? The task of interrupting racism is obviously not the task of Whites alone. But the fact of White privilege means that Whites have greater access to the societal institutions in need of transformation. To whom much is given, much is required.

It is important to acknowledge that while all Whites benefit from racism, they do not all benefit equally. Other factors, such as socioeconomic status, gender, age, religious affiliation, sexual orientation, mental and physical ability, also play a role in our access to social influence and power. A White woman on welfare is not privileged to the same extent as a wealthy White heterosexual man. In her case, the systematic disadvantages of sexism and classism intersect with her White privilege, but the privilege is still there. This point was brought home to me in a 1994 study conducted by a Mount Holyoke graduate student, Phyllis Wentworth.[7] Wentworth interviewed a group of female college students, who were both older than their peers and were the first members of their families to attend college, about the pathways that lead them to college. All of the women interviewed were White, from working-class backgrounds, from families where women were expected to graduate from high school and get married or get a job. Several had experienced abusive relationships and other personal difficulties prior to coming to college. Yet their experiences were punctuated by "good luck" stories of apartments obtained without a deposit, good jobs offered without experience or extensive reference checks, and encouragement provided by willing mentors. While the women acknowledged their good fortune, none of them discussed their Whiteness. They had not considered the possibility that being White had worked in their favor and helped give them the benefit of the doubt at critical junctures. This study clearly showed that even under difficult circumstances, White privilege was still operating.

It is also true that not all people of color are equally targeted by racism. We all have multiple identities that shape our experience. I can describe myself as a light-skinned, well-educated, heterosexual, able-bodied, Christian African American woman raised in a middle-class suburb. As an African American woman, I am systematically disadvantaged by race and by gender, but I systematically receive benefits in the other categories, which then mediate my experience of racism and sexism. When one is targeted by multiple isms—racism, sexism, classism, heterosexism, ableism, anti-Semitism, ageism—in whatever combination, the effect is intensified. The particular combination of racism and classism in many communities of color is life-threatening. Nonetheless, when I, the middle-class Black mother of two sons, read another story about a Black man's unlucky encounter with a White police officer's deadly force, I am reminded that racism by itself can kill.

The Cost of Racism

Several years ago, a White male student in my psychology of racism course wrote in his journal at the end of the semester that he had learned a lot about racism and now understood in a way he never had before just how advantaged he was. He also commented that he didn't think he would do anything to try to change the situation. After all, the system was working in his favor. Fortunately, his response was not typical. Most of my students leave my course with the desire (and an action plan) to interrupt the cycle of racism. However, this young man's response does raise an important question. Why should Whites who are advantaged by racism *want* to end that system of advantage? What are the *costs* of that system to them?

A *Money* magazine article called "Race and Money" chronicled the many ways the American economy was hindered by institutional racism.[8] Whether one looks at productivity lowered by racial tensions in the workplace, or real estate equity lost through housing discrimination, or the tax revenue lost in underemployed communities of color, or the high cost of warehousing human talent in prison, the economic costs of racism are real and measurable.

As a psychologist, I often hear about the less easily measured costs. When I ask White men and women how racism hurts them, they frequently talk about their fears of people of color, the social incompetence they feel in racially mixed situations, the alienation they have experienced between parents and children when a child marries into a family of color, and the interracial friendships they had as children that were lost in adolescence or young adulthood without their ever understanding why. White people are paying a significant price for the system of advantage. The cost is not as high for Whites as it is for people of color, but a price is being paid.[9] Wendell Berry, a White writer raised in Kentucky, captures this psychic pain in the opening pages of his book, *The Hidden Wound*:

> If white people have suffered less obviously from racism than black people, they have nevertheless suffered greatly; the cost has been greater perhaps than we can yet know. If the white man has inflicted the wound of racism upon black men, the cost has been that he would receive the mirror image of that wound into himself. As the master, or as a member of the dominant race, he has felt little compulsion to acknowledge it or speak of it; the more painful it has grown the more deeply he has hidden it within himself. But the wound is there, and it is a profound disorder, as great a damage in his mind as it is in his society.[10]

The dismantling of racism is in the best interests of everyone.

A Word about Language

Throughout this chapter I have used the term *White* to refer to Americans of European descent. In another era, I might have used the term *Caucasian*. I have used the term *people of color* to refer to those groups in America that are and have been historically targeted by racism. This includes people of African descent, people of Asian descent, people of Latin American descent, and indigenous peoples (sometimes referred to as Native Americans or American Indians).[11] Many people refer to these groups collectively as non-Whites. This term is particularly offensive because it defines groups of people in terms of what they are not. (Do we call women "nonmen?") I also avoid using the term *minorities* because it represents another kind of distortion of information which we need to correct. So-called minorities represent the majority of the world's population. While the term *people of color* is inclusive, it is not perfect. As a workshop participant once said, White people have color, too. Perhaps it would be more accurate to say "people of more color," though I am not ready to make that change. Perhaps fellow psychologist Linda James Myers is on the right track. She refers to two groups of people, those of acknowledged African descent and those of unacknowledged African descent, reminding us that we can all trace the roots of our common humanity to Africa.

I refer to people of acknowledged African descent as Black. I know that *African American* is also a commonly used term, and I often refer to myself and other Black people born and raised in America in that way. Perhaps because I am a child of the 1960s "Black and beautiful" era, I still prefer *Black*. The term is more inclusive than *African American*, because there are Black people in the United States who are not African American—Afro-Caribbeans, for example—yet are targeted by racism, and are identified as Black.

When referring to other groups of color, I try to use the terms that the people themselves want to be called. In some cases, there is no clear consensus. For example, some people of Latin American ancestry prefer *Latino*, while others prefer *Hispanic* or, if of Mexican descent, *Chicano*.[12] The terms *Latino* and *Hispanic* are used interchangeably here. Similarly, there are regional variations in the use of the terms *Native American*, *American Indian*, and *Indian*. *American Indian* and *Native people* are now more widely used than *Native American*, and the language used here reflects that. People of Asian descent include Pacific Islanders, and that is reflected in the terms *Asian/Pacific Islanders* and *Asian Pacific Americans*. However, when quoting others I use whichever terms they use.

My dilemma about the language to use reflects the fact that race is a social construction.[13] Despite myths to the contrary, biologists tell us that the only meaningful racial categorization is that of human. Van den Berghe defines race as "a group that is socially defined but on the basis of *physical* criteria," including skin color and facial features.[14]

Racial identity development, a central focus of this book, usually refers to the process of defining for oneself the personal significance and social meaning of belonging to a particular racial group. The terms *racial identity* and *ethnic identity* are often used synonymously, though a distinction can be made between the two. An ethnic group is a socially defined group based on *cultural* criteria, such as language, customs, and shared history. An individual might identify as a member of an ethnic group (Irish or Italian, for example) but might not think of himself in racial terms (as White). On the other hand, one may recognize the personal significance of racial group membership (identifying as Black, for instance) but may not consider ethnic identity (such as West Indian) as particularly meaningful.

Both racial and ethnic categories are socially constructed, and social definitions of these categories have changed over time. For example, in his book *Ethnic Identity: The Transformation of White America*, Richard Alba points out that the high rates of intermarriage and the dissolution of other social boundaries among European ethnic groups in the United States have reduced the significance of ethnic identity for these groups. In their place, he argues, a new ethnic identity is emerging, that of European American.[15]

Throughout this book, I refer primarily to racial identity. It is important, however, to acknowledge that ethnic identity and racial identity sometimes intersect. For example, dark-skinned Puerto Ricans may identify culturally as Puerto Rican and yet be categorized racially by others as Black on the basis of physical appearance. In the case of either racial or ethnic identity, these identities remain most salient to individuals of racial or ethnic groups that have been historically disadvantaged or marginalized.

The language we use to categorize one another racially is imperfect. These categories are still evolving as the current debate over Census classifications indicates.[16] The original creation of racial categories was in the service of oppression. Some may argue that to continue to use them is to continue that oppression. I respect that argument. Yet it is difficult to talk about what is essentially a flawed and problematic social construct without using language that is itself problematic. We have to be able to talk about it in order to change it. So this is the language I choose.

Notes

[1] C. O'Toole, "The effect of the media and multicultural education on children's perceptions of Native Americans" (senior thesis, Department of Psychology and Education, Mount Holyoke College, South Hadley, MA, May 1990).

[2] For an extended discussion of this point, see David Wellman, *Portraits of White Racism* (Cambridge: Cambridge University Press, 1977), ch. 1.

[3] For specific statistical information, see R. Farley, "The common destiny of Blacks and Whites: Observations about the social and economic status of the races," pp. 197–233 in H. Hill and J. E. Jones, Jr. (Eds.), *Race in America: The Struggle for Equality* (Madison: University of Wisconsin Press, 1993).

[4] P. McIntosh, "White Priveledge: Unpacking the Invisible Knapsack," *Peace and Freedom* (July/August 1989): 10–12.

[5] For further discussion of the concept of "belief in a just world," see M. J. Lerner, "Social Psychology of Justice and Interpersonal Attraction," in T. Huston (Ed.), *Foundations of Interpersonal Attraction* (New York: Academic Press, 1974).

[6] For a brief historical overview of the institutionalization of racism and sexism in our legal system, see "Part V: How It Happened: Race and Gender Issues in U.S. law," in P. S. Rothenberg (Ed.), *Race, Class, and Gender in the United States: An Integrated Study*, 3rd. ed. (New York: St. Martin's Press, 1995).

[7] P. A. Wentworth, "The identity development of non-traditionally aged first-generation women college students: An exploratory study" (master's thesis, Department of Psychology and Education, Mount Holyoke College, South Hadley, MA, 1994).

[8] W. I. Updegrave, "Race and Money," *Money* (December 1989): 152–72.

[9] For further discussion of the impact of racism on Whites, see B. Bowser and R. G. Hunt (Eds.), *Impacts of Racism on White Americans* (Thousand Oaks, CA: Sage, 1981); P. Kivel, *Uprooting Racism: How White People Can Work for Racial Justice* (Philadelphia: New Society Publishers, 1996); and J. Barndt, *Dismantling Racism: The Continuing Challenge to White America* (Minneapolis: Augsburg Press, 1991).

[10] W. Berry, *The Hidden Wound* (San Francisco: North Point Press, 1989), pp. 3–4.

[11] It is important to note here that these groups are not necessarily mutually exclusive. For example, people of Latin America descent may have European, African, and Native American ancestors. The politics of racial categorization has served to create artificial boundaries between groups with shared ancestry.

[12] It is difficult to know which is the preferred term to use because different sub-groups have different preferences. According to Amado Padilla, younger U.S.-born university-educated individuals of Mexican ancestry prefer *Chicano(a)* to *Mexican American* or *Hispanic*. On the other hand, *Latino* is preferred by others of Mexican ancestry or other Latin American origin. Those of Cuban ancestry may prefer *Cuban American* to *Latino*, wheras recent immigrants from Central America would rather be identified by their nationality (e.g., *Guatematecos* or *Salvadorenos*). A. Padilla (Ed.), *Hispanic Psychology* (Thousand Oaks, CA: Sage 1995).

[13] For an expanded discussion of the social construction of race, see M. Omi and H. Winant, *Racial Formation in the United States*, 2nd ed. (New York: Routledge, 1994).

[14] P. L. Van den Berghe, *Race and Racism* (New York: Wiley, 1967).

[15] See R. Alba, *Ethnic Identity: The Transformation of White America* (New Haven: Yale University Press, 1990).

[16] For a discussion of the census classification debate and the history of racial classification in the United States, see L. Wright, "One Drop of Blood," *The New Yorker* (July 25, 1994): 46–55.

Wendell Berry (b. 1934) is an academic, cultural and economic critic, as well as a farmer. Furthermore, he has been a strong activist in the environmental movement. He is a prolific author of novels, short stories, poems, and essays. He is also an elected member of the Fellowship of Southern Writers. This poem is from The Country of Marriage *(1973).What message is he attempting to get across here? Why might he have chosen a poem instead of an essay to deliver this message? How does it resonate with you in regard to the communities in your life? Does this poem consider that some of our communities might be involuntary and/or negative in nature?*

Manifesto:
The Mad Farmer Liberation Front

Wendell Berry

Love the quick profit, the annual raise,
vacation with pay. Want more
of everything ready made. Be afraid
to know your neighbors and to die.
And you will have a window in your head.
Not even your future will be a mystery
any more. Your mind will be punched in a
 card
and shut away in a little drawer.
When they want you to buy something
they will call you. When they want you
to die for profit they will let you know.
So, friends, every day do something
that won't compute. Love the Lord.
Love the world. Work for nothing.
Take all that you have and be poor.
Love someone who does not deserve it.
Denounce the government and embrace
the flag. Hope to live in that free
republic for which it stands.
Give your approval to all you cannot
understand. Praise ignorance, for what man
has not encountered he has not destroyed.
Ask the questions that have no answers.
Invest in the millennium. Plant sequoias.
Say that your main crop is the forest
that you did not plant,

that you will not live to harvest.
Say that the leaves are harvested
when they have rotted into the mold.
Call that profit. Prophesy such returns.
Put your faith in the two inches of humus
that will build under the trees
every thousand years.
Listen to carrion—put your ear
close, and hear the faint chattering
of the songs that are to come.
Expect the end of the world. Laugh.
Laughter is immeasurable. Be joyful
though you have considered all the facts.
So long as women do not go cheap
for power, please women more than men.
Ask yourself: Will this satisfy
a woman satisfied to bear a child?
Will this disturb the sleep
of a woman near to giving birth?
Go with your love to the fields.
Lie easy in the shade. Rest your head
in her lap. Swear allegiance
to what is nighest your thoughts.
As soon as the generals and the politicos
can predict the motions of your mind,
lose it. Leave it as a sign
to mark the false trail, the way
you didn't go. Be like the fox
who makes more tracks than necessary,
some in the wrong direction.
Practice resurrection.

Barbara Kingsolver (b. 1955) is an American fiction writer. She has written several novels, poems, short stories, and essays, and established the Bellwether Prize for "literature of social change." Among her most famous works to date are Animal Dreams *(1990) and* The Poisonwood Bible *(1998), as well as the recent* Animal, Vegetable, Miracle *(2007). As you read this particular story, from* High Tide in Tucson *(1995), determine what a "jabberwocky" is. Do you think it is used as a metaphor? What does Kingsolver say about the connection between art, politics, and one's role in society?*

Jabberwocky

Barbara Kingsolver

Once upon a time, a passing stranger sent me into exile. I was downtown in front of the Federal Building with a small crowd assembled to protest war in the Persian Gulf; he was in a black Ford pickup. As the truck roared by he leaned most of his upper body out the window to give me a better view of his finger, and he screamed, "Hey, bitch, love it or leave it!"

So I left.

He wasn't the first to give me that instruction; I've heard it since I was a nineteen-year-old in a scary barbershop haircut. Now I was thirty-four, mother of a child, with a decent reputation and pretty good hair. Why start listening *now*? I can only say he was finally one too many. I was on the verge of having a special kind of nervous breakdown, in which a person stalks through a Kmart parking lot ripping yellow ribbons off car antennas.

I realize that would have been abridging other people's right to free expression. What was driving me crazy was that very term "right to free expression," and how it was being applied in a nation at war. We were supposed to behave as though we had refrigerators for brains. Open, shove in a slab of baloney, close, stay cool. No questions. Our leaders told us this was a *surgical* war. *Very clean.* The language of the event was a perfect construct of nonmeaning. "Delivering the ordnance," they called it on the nightly news, which sounds nearly friendly. . . . "Why, here is your ordnance, friends, just sign on the line." "Deliver the ordnance" means "Drop the bomb."

But we bought the goods, or we kept our mouths shut. If we felt disturbed by the idea of pulverizing civilizations as the best way to settle our differences—or had trouble explaining that to our kids as adult behavior—we weren't talking about it. Typically, if I raised the debate, I was advised that if I liked Saddam so much I could go live in Iraq. As a matter of fact I *didn't* like Saddam, *or* the government of Kuwait. The two countries appeared practically indistinguishable; I doubt if many Americans could have guessed, a few years earlier (as we flooded Iraq with military aid), which one would turn out to be the Evil Empire, and which would require us to rush to its defense in the name of democracy. If *democracy* were really an issue we considered when going into that war, Iraq might have come out a nose ahead, Kuwait being a monarchy in which women held rights approximately equal to those of livestock. (*Since* the war, women's status in Kuwait has actually declined.) But the level of discourse allowed on this subject was "We're gonna kick butt." A shadow of doubt was viewed as treason.

I'm lucky enough to have a job that will follow me anywhere, so I left. I could contemplate from a distance these words on patriotism, written by the wise Garry Wills: "Love of one's country should be like love of one's spouse—a give-and-take criticism and affection. Although it is hoped one prefers one's spouse to other people . . . one does not prove that one loves one's wife by battering other women."

Give-and-take criticism and affection, out the window. And the battery was severe. Upon moving to Spain I read in the papers what was common knowledge, apparently, everywhere but in the U.S.: from the first night onward we bombed Iraqis relentlessly in their homes, killing thousands of civilians every day. Within months, more than 250,000 would be dead—most of them children—because of bombed-out water and sewer systems, hospitals with no antibiotics, hospitals with no roofs. To my horror I read that infections of hands and feet were rampant among Iraqi children, because of bombing debris, and the only available treatment was amputation. It had been an air war on civilians. The Commission of Inquiry for the International War Crimes Tribunal is still compiling the gruesome list of what the United States bombed in Iraq: all the country's major dams and most of its drinking water facilities; enough sewage treatment facilities to contaminate the Tigris River with waterborne killers; virtually all communications systems, leaving civilians unwarned of danger and unable to get help; civilian cars, buses, and taxis; 139 auto and railway bridges; food-processing, storage, and distribution systems; 100 percent of irrigation systems; wheat and grain fields (with incendiary bombs); 28 civilian hospitals and 52 community health centers; clothing factories; a cosmetics factory; an infant formula factory; 56 mosques; more than 600 schools. This was our surgical war.

Soon after the bombing ended, Ramsey Clark wrote a book called *The Fire This Time*, a meticulously researched account of the many ways the U.S. violated the Geneva Convention and perpetrated crimes against civilians in the Persian Gulf War. Clark, as a former U.S. Attorney General, had once been appointed trustee of the nation's conscience. Now he asked us to reckon with some awful responsibilities. But he encountered a truly American form of censorship: free enterprise in the hands of a monkey called See No Evil. His manuscript was rejected by eleven publishers— every major New York house. The editors did not turn it down for lack of merit, they said, but on grounds that it wouldn't be popular. (At length it was released by a small publisher called Thunder's Mouth; hurray for the alternative presses.)

No such hard luck for the memoirs of generals or celebrities, or O. J. Simpson's thoughts from jail while awaiting his verdict. The publisher of the latter (Little, Brown) claimed no moral qualms about providing a forum for Simpson at a time when he already commanded more media attention than has ever been held, probably, by any human being on the planet. The first printing was half a million copies.

This is a spooky proposition: an information industry that narrows down what we'll get to read and know about, mainly on the basis of how eagerly we'll lap it up. Producers and publishers who make these choices seem inclined, if confronted, to throw up their hands and exclaim, "I can't help it if that's what the people want!" A mother could say the same while feeding her baby nothing but jelly beans day after day; so could a physician who administers morphine for head colds. Both would be convicted of criminal neglect. Why is there no Hippocratic Oath for the professionals who service our intellects? Why is it that I knew, without wanting to, every possible thing about a figure skater who got whacked on the leg with a pipe—a melodrama that in the long run, let's face it, is utterly without consequence to anyone but the whackers and the whackee—but I had to go far out of my way to dig up the recent historical events that led to anarchy in Somalia and Haiti? (I learned, it's worth noting, that the U.S. did embarrassing things in both places.) News stations will move heaven and earth to get their own reporters into the likes of California vs. O. J. Simpson, or backstage with Tonya Harding, but not into hearings on the Clean Air Act. Producers will blame consumers, but blame is hardly the point if we are merrily dying of ignorance, and killing others with our apathy. Few U.S. citizens are aware, for example, that our government has routinely engineered assassinations of democratically elected heads of state in places like Chile and Guatemala, and replaced them with such monstrous confederates as Augusto Pinochet and Castillo Armas. Why do those dictators' names fail even to ring a bell in most red-blooded American heads? Possibly because our heads are too crowded with names like O. J. and Tonya. The guilt for that may not rest entirely with the producers or the consumers, but the crime has nevertheless occurred. To buy or to sell information as nothing more than a consumer product, like soda pop, is surely wrong. Marketed in that way, information's principal attribute must be universal palatability.

This is not to say we only get to tune in to *happy* news—there are wrecks and murders galore. But it's information that corroborates a certain narrow view of the world and our place in it. Exhaustive reports of rare, bizarre behaviors among the wealthy support the myth that violent crime is a random, unpreventable disaster, and obscure the blunt truth that most crime is caused by poverty. There's not much in the news to remind us, either, that poverty is a problem we could decently address, as all other industrialized countries have done. The safest marketing technique is to dispense with historical analysis, accountability, and even—apparently—critical thought.

When the Smithsonian deferred to what it called "public pressure" and canceled an exhibit on the historical use of the atomic bomb in Hiroshima and Nagasaki, Smithsonian Secretary I. Michael Heyman explained, "Veterans and their families were expecting, and rightly so, that the nation would honor and commemorate their valor and sacrifice. They were not looking for analysis, and, frankly, we did not give enough thought to the intense feeling that such analysis would evoke." *Analysis* in that case meant the most elementary connection between cause and effect: what happens when the Ordnance gets Delivered.

As a member of that all-important public, I'd like to state for the record that I'm offended. Give me the chance and I'll spend my consumer dollar on the story that relates to what kind of shape the world will be in fifty years from now. I'll choose analysis, every time, over placebo news and empty salve for my patriotic ego. I'm offended by the presumption that my honor as a citizen will crumple unless I'm protected from knowledge of my country's mistakes. I'm made of sturdier stuff than that, and I imagine, if he really thought about it, so is that guy who leaned out of a truck to give me the finger. What kind of love is patriotism, if it evaporates in the face of uncomfortable truths? What kind of honor sits quietly by while a nation's conscience flies south for a long, long winter?

A rtists are as guilty as anyone in the conspiracy of self-censorship, if they succumb to the lure of producing only what's sure to sell. The good ones don't, and might still sell anyway, for humans have long accepted subconsciously that good art won't always, so to speak, match the sofa. "Poets are the unacknowledged legislators of the race," Percy Shelley said. They are also its margin of safety, like the canaries that used to be carried into mines because of their sensitivity to toxic gases; their silence can be taken as a sign of imminent danger.

The artist's maverick responsibility is sometimes to sugarcoat the bitter pill and slip it down our gullet, telling us what we didn't think we wanted to know. But in the U.S. we're establishing a modern tradition of tarpapering our messengers. The one who delivers the bitter pill, whether the vehicle is a war-crime documentary or a love story, is apt to be dismissed as a "political artist."

It's a Jabberwockish sort of label, both dreaded and perplexing. Technically the term "political" refers to campaigns, governments, and public institutions. But *Police Academy* was not called political. Barry Lopez is called political, and he writes about dying ecosystems and great blue herons and wolves, for heaven's sake. It took me years to work out what it is that earns this scalding label for an artist or an act.

Now I know, and this is how I know: during the Gulf War some young friends of mine wanted to set up a table in the shopping mall and hand out information about the less cheerful aspects of the war. The administrators of the mall refused permission. My friends contended, "But you let people hand out yellow ribbons and flags and 'We kick butt' bumper stickers!" The mall administrators explained their charter forbids anything political. "Handing out yellow ribbons is public service," they said, "but what *you* want to do is *political.*"

Now you know. This subterfuge use of the word "political," which doesn't show up in my Random House Unabridged, means only that a thing runs counter to prevailing assumptions. If 60 percent of us support the war, then the expressions of the other 40 percent are political—and can be disallowed in some contexts for that reason alone. The really bad news is that the charter of the shopping mall seems to be standing in as a national artistic standard. Cultural workers in the U.S. are prone to be bound and gagged by a dread of being called political, for that word implies the art is not quite pure. Real art, the story goes, does not endorse a point of view. This is utter nonsense, of course (try to imagine a story or a painting with no point of view), and also the most thorough and invisible form of censorship I've ever encountered. When I'm interviewed about writing, I spend a good deal of time defending the possibility that such things as environmental ruin, child abuse, or the hypocrisy of U.S. immigration policy are appropriate subjects for a novel. I keep waiting for the interviewer to bring up *art* things, like voice and metaphor; usually I'm still waiting for that when the cows come home.

In rural Greece some people believe that if you drink very cold water on a very hot day, you will die; here, we have that kind of superstition about mixing art with conscience. It's a quaintly provincial belief that fades out fast at our borders. Most of the rest of the world considers social criticism to be, absolutely, the most legitimate domain of art. If you think I'm overstating this, look who's been winning Nobel Prizes in literature for the last ninety years:

Nadine Gordimer, who has spent her life writing against racism and apartheid in South Africa. Joseph Brodsky, who spent some years in Siberia because of his criticism of Soviet society. Wole Soyinka, who has also logged time in jail because of his criticisms of colonialism in Africa. Gabriel García Márquez, who is possibly the most gifted social critic in a whole continent of social-critic-writers. Czeslaw Milosz, who was active in the anti-Nazi underground and whose poetry is thoroughly ideological. Pablo Neruda, Aleksandr Solzhenitsyn, Miguel Asturias, Thomas Mann, George Bernard Shaw.

U.S. prizewinners do not dominate this list (as they do the Nobel categories of Physics, Chemistry, and Medicine), especially since the 1950s. It's not for lack of great writers, but perhaps because we've learned to limit our own access to serious content. The fear of being perceived as ideologues runs so deep in writers of my generation it undoubtedly steers us away from certain subjects without our knowing it. The fear is that if you fall short of perfect execution, you'll be called "preachy." But falling short of perfection when you've plunged in to say what needs to be said—is that so much worse, really, than falling short when you've plunged in to say what *didn't* need to be said?

And if you should by chance succeed—oh, then. Art has the power not only to soothe a savage breast, but to change a savage mind. A novel can make us weep over the same events that might hardly give us pause if we read them in a newspaper. Even though the tragedy in the newspaper happened to real people, while the one in the novel happened in an author's imagination.

A novel works its magic by putting a reader inside another person's life. The pace is as slow as life. It's as detailed as life. It requires you, the reader, to fill in an outline of words with vivid pictures drawn subconsciously from your own life, so that the story feels more personal than the sets designed by someone else and handed over via TV or movies. Literature duplicates the experience of living in a way that nothing else can, drawing you so fully into another life that you temporarily forget you have one of your own. That is why you read it, and might even sit up in bed till early dawn, throwing your whole tomorrow out of whack, simply to find out what happens to some people who, you know perfectly well, are made up. It's why you might find yourself crying, even if you aren't the crying kind.

The power of fiction is to create empathy. It lifts you away from your chair and stuffs you gently down inside someone else's point of view. It differs drastically from a newspaper, which imparts information while allowing you to remain rooted in your own perspective. A newspaper could tell you that one hundred people, say, in an airplane, or in Israel, or in Iraq, have died today. And you can think to yourself, "How very sad," then turn the page and see how the Wildcats fared. But a novel could take just one of those hundred lives and show you exactly how it felt to be that person rising from bed in the morning, watching the desert light on the tile of her doorway and on the curve of her daughter's cheek. You would taste that person's breakfast, and love her family, and sort through her worries as your own, and know that a death in that household will be the end of the only life that someone will ever have. As important as yours. As important as mine.

At the height of the Gulf War, I found in the *New York Times* this quote from Loren Thompson, director of the national security program at Georgetown University, explaining why the Pentagon wasn't releasing information about deaths in Iraq. When bomb damage is listed only in technical terms, he said, "you avoid talking about lives lost, and that serves both an esthetic and a practical purpose."

The esthetic and practical purpose, of course, is the loss of empathy. We seem to be living in the age of anesthesia and it's no wonder. Confronted with knowledge of dozens of apparently random disasters each day, what can a human heart do but slam its doors? No mortal can grieve that much. We didn't evolve to cope with tragedy on a global scale. Our defense is to pretend there's no thread of event that connects us, and that those lives are somehow not precious and real like our own. It's a practical strategy, to some ends, but the loss of empathy is also the loss of humanity, and that's no small tradeoff.

Art is the antidote that can call us back from the edge of numbness, restoring the ability to feel for another. By virtue of that power, it is political, regardless of content. If *Jane Eyre* is a great romance, it has also given thousands of men a female experience, and a chance to feel the constraints that weighed upon women of Jane's time. Through art, a woman can give a male reader the unparalleled athletic accomplishment of childbirth, or the annihilation of being raped; if every man knew both those things, I would expect the world to change tomorrow. We have all heard plenty about each other's troubles, but evidently it's not enough to be told, it has to be lived. And art is so very nearly the same as life.

I *know*, for example, that slavery was heinous, but the fate of sixty million slaves is too big a thing for a heart to understand. So it was not until I read Toni Morrison's *Beloved* that I honestly felt that truth. When Sethe killed her children rather than have them grow up in slavery, I was so far from my sheltered self I knew the horror that could make infanticide an act of love. Morrison carved the tragedy of those sixty million, to whom the book is dedicated, into something small and dense and real enough to fit through the door, get in my heart, and explode. This is how a novel can be more true than a newspaper.

One of my favorite writings about writing is this excerpt from Ursula K. Le Guin's introduction to her science-fiction novel *The Left Hand of Darkness*, in which she discusses fiction's role in what we call the truth:

Open your eyes; listen, listen. That is what the novelists say. But they don't tell you what you will see and hear. All they can tell you is what they have seen and heard, in their time in this world, a third of it spent in sleep and dreaming, another third of it spent in telling lies.

. . . Fiction writers, at least in their braver moments, do desire the truth: to know it, speak it, serve it. But they go about it in a peculiar and devious way, which consists in inventing persons, places, and events which never did and never will exist or occur, and telling about these fictions in detail and at length and with a great deal of emotion, and then when they are done writing down this pack of lies, they say, There! That's the truth!

. . . In reading a novel, any novel, we have to know perfectly well that the whole thing is nonsense, and then, while reading, believe every word of it. Finally, when we're done with it, we may find that we're a bit different from what we were before we read it, that we have been changed a little . . . crossed a street we never crossed before. But it's very hard to *say* just what we learned, how we were changed.

The artist deals with what cannot be said in words.

The artist whose medium is fiction does this *in words*. The novelist says in words what cannot be said in words.

This baffling manifesto is a command that rules my writing life. I believe it means there are truths we all know, but can't make ourselves feel: Slavery was horrible. Love thy neighbor as thyself, or we'll all go to hell in a handbasket. These are things that cannot be said in words because they're too familiar to move us, too big and bald and flat to penetrate our souls. The artist must craft missiles to deliver these truths so unerringly to the right place inside of us we are left panting, with no possibility of doubting they are true. The novelist must do this in story, image, and character. And make the reader believe.

To speak of this process as something that must fall either into the camp of "political" or "pure" is frankly absurd. Good art is political, whether it means to be or not, insofar as it provides the chance to understand points of view alien to our own. Its nature is the opposite of spiritual meanness, bigotry, and warfare. If it is disturbing at times, or unpalatable, it may be a good idea to buy it anyway.

In time, I came back from political exile. Not with my tail between my legs, having discovered the U.S.A. was after all the greatest place in the world. On the contrary, I loved the new experience of safety, the freedom to walk anywhere I pleased at any time of day, and the connected moral comfort of a society that cares for all its children, provides universal health care, and allows no one to be destitute. All these foreign things, and more, I loved: the sound of the ocean in my window, and the towering poinsettia trees that blossomed along the roadsides from Christmas till Easter. I missed a few things: Mexican food, certain familiar music on the radio, the blush of a Tucson sunset running hot and sweet up the face of the Santa Catalina Mountains. And I missed the sound of my mother tongue. By accident, it turns out, I've been apprenticed as a writer to my own language and culture. In the midst of a deeply American novel, high and dry in the Canary Isles, I had to beg friends back home for mundanities I couldn't recall—figures of speech, car makes, even commercial jingles.

More than anything, though, I missed people, the beloved relatives and friends I left behind. I had new friends, but it was finally on account of the old ones that I prepared to give up the expatriate's life.

As the time drew near, my feet balked. I dreaded leaving my kind new place to return to the land of the free (*free* to live behind locks at all times; *free* to walk in the evenings from library to parked car with sheer terror in my heart) and the home of the brave (well, yes, *brave*). The land where 7 percent of the world's souls guzzle the lion's share of the world's goods, pitch out a yearly average of sixteen hundred pounds of garbage apiece, and still can drive past homeless neighbors with little awareness of wrongdoing or alternatives. The place I was told to love or leave.

I found I could do neither. Not wholeheartedly. But like the boy who fought the Jabberwock in *Through the Looking Glass*, I took my vorpal sword in hand. For the sake of people who love me and the sight of mountains that move my soul, I would come galumphing back, to face the tyranny of words without meaning and monsters beyond my ken.

I came back because leaving was selfish. A country can be flawed as a marriage or a family or a person is flawed, but "Love it or leave it" is a coward's slogan. There's more honor in "Love it and get it right." Love it, love it. Love it and never shut up.

Audre Lorde (1934–1992) was born to parents of West Indian descent in New York. She was a self described "black feminist lesbian poet." Her essays and poetry have made an integral contribution to the contemporary feminist movement. In this work, from The Cancer Journals (1980), *she challenges each of us to speak out despite our fears to do so. What harm can silence do to our own lives? What consequence can it have on the people and communities in our lives?*

The Transformation of Silence into Language and Action

Audre Lorde

I have come to believe over and over again that what is most important to me must be spoken, made verbal and shared, even at the risk of having it bruised or misunderstood. That the speaking profits me, beyond any other effect. I am standing here as a Black lesbian poet, and the meaning of all that waits upon the fact that I am still alive, and might not have been. Less than two months ago I was told by two doctors, one female and one male, that I would have to have breast surgery, and that there was a 60 to 80 percent chance that the tumor was malignant. Between that telling and the actual surgery, there was a three-week period of the agony of an involuntary reorganization of my entire life. The surgery was completed, and the growth was benign.

But within those three weeks, I was forced to look upon myself and my living with a harsh and urgent clarity that has left me still shaken but much stronger. This is a situation faced by many women, by some of you here today. Some of what I experienced during that time has helped elucidate for me much of what I feel concerning the transformation of silence into language and action.

In becoming forcibly and essentially aware of my mortality and of what I wished and wanted for my life, however short it might be, priorities and omissions became strongly etched in a merciless light, and what I most regretted were my silences. Of what had I *ever* been afraid? To question or to speak as I believed could have meant pain, or death. But we all hurt in so many different ways, all the time, and pain will either change or end. Death, on the other hand, is the final silence. And that might be coming quickly, now, without regard for whether I had ever spoken what needed to be said, or had only betrayed myself into small silences, while I planned someday to speak, or waited for someone else's words. And I began to recognize a source of power within myself that comes from the knowledge that while it is most desirable not to be afraid, learning to put fear into a perspective gave me great strength.

I was going to die, if not sooner then later, whether or not I had ever spoken myself. My silences had not protected me. Your silence will not protect you. But for every real word spoken, for every attempt I had ever made to speak those truths for which I am still seeking, I had made contact with other women while we examined the words to fit a world in which we all believed, bridging our differences. And it was the concern and caring of all those women which gave me strength and enabled me to scrutinize the essentials of my living.

The women who sustained me through that period were Black and white, old and young, lesbian, bisexual, and heterosexual, and we all shared a war against the tyrannies of silence. They all gave me a strength and concern without which I could not have survived intact. Within those weeks of acute fear came the knowledge—within the war we are all waging with the forces of death, subtle and otherwise, conscious or not—I am not only a casualty, I am also a warrior.

What are the words you do not yet have? What do you need to say? What are the tyrannies you swallow day by day and attempt to make your own, until you will sicken and die of them, still in silence? Perhaps for some of you here today, I am the face of one of your fears. Because I am woman, because I am Black, because I am lesbian, because I am myself— a Black woman warrior poet doing my work—come to ask you, are you doing yours?

And of course I am afraid, because the transformation of silence into language and action is an act of self-revelation, and that always seems fraught with danger. But my daughter, when I told her of our topic and my difficulty with it, said, "Tell them about how you're never really a whole person if you remain silent, because there's always that one little piece inside you that wants to be spoken out, and if you keep ignoring it, it gets madder and madder and hotter and hotter, and if you don't speak it out one day it will just up and punch you in the mouth from the inside."

In the cause of silence, each of us draws the face of her own fear—fear of contempt, of censure, or some judgment, or recognition, of challenge, of annihilation. But most of all, I think, we fear the visibility without which we cannot truly live. Within this country where racial difference creates a constant, if unspoken, distortion of vision, Black women have on one hand always been highly visible, and so, on the other hand, have been rendered invisible through the depersonalization of racism. Even within the women's movement, we have had to fight, and still do, for that very visibility which also renders us most vulnerable, our Blackness. For to survive in the mouth of this dragon we call America, we have had to learn this first and most vital lesson—that we were never meant to survive. Not as human beings. And neither were most of you here today, Black or not. And that visibility which makes us most vulnerable is that which also is the source of our greatest strength. Because the machine will try to grind you into dust anyway, whether or not we speak. We can sit in our corners mute forever while our sisters and our selves are wasted, while our children are distorted and destroyed, while our earth is poisoned; we can sit in our safe corners mute as bottles, and we will still be no less afraid.

In my house this year we are celebrating the feast of Kwanza, the African-American festival of harvest which begins the day after Christmas and lasts for seven days. There are seven principles of Kwanza, one for each day. The first principle is Umoja, which means unity, the decision to strive for and maintain unity in self and community. The principle for yesterday, the second day, was Kujichagulia—self-determination—the decision to define ourselves, name ourselves, and speak for ourselves, instead of being defined and spoken for by others. Today is the third day of Kwanza, and the principle for today is Ujima—collective work and responsibility—the decision to build and maintain ourselves and our communities together and to recognize and solve our problems together.

Each of us is here now because in one way or another we share a commitment to language and to the power of language, and to the reclaiming of that language which has been made to work against us. In the transformation of silence into language and action, it is vitally necessary for each one of us to establish or examine her function in that transformation and to recognize her role as vital within that transformation.

For those of us who write, it is necessary to scrutinize not only the truth of what we speak, but the truth of that language by which we speak it. For others, it is to share and spread also those words that are meaningful to us. But primarily for us all, it is necessary to teach by living and speaking those truths which we believe and know beyond understanding. Because in this way alone we can survive, by taking part in a process of life that is creative and continuing, that is growth.

And it is never without fear—of visibility, of the harsh light of scrutiny and perhaps judgment, of pain, of death. But we have lived through all of those already, in silence, except death. And I remind myself all the time now that if I were to have been born mute, or had maintained an oath of silence my whole life long for safety, I would still have suffered, and I would still die. It is very good for establishing perspective.

And where the words of women are crying to be heard, we must each of us recognize our responsibility to seek those words out, to read them and share them and examine them in their pertinence to our lives. That we not hide behind the mockeries of separations that have been imposed upon us and which so often we accept as our own. For instance, "I can't possibly teach Black women's writing—their experience is so different from mine." Yet how many years have you spent teaching Plato and Shakespeare and Proust? Or another, "She's a white woman and what could she possibly have to say to me?" Or, "She's a lesbian, what would my husband say, or my chairman?" Or again, "This woman writes of her sons and I have no children." And all the other endless ways in which we rob ourselves of ourselves and each other.

We can learn to work and speak when we are afraid in the same way we have learned to work and speak when we are tired. For we have been socialized to respect fear more than our own needs for language and definition, and while we wait in silence for that final luxury of fearlessness, the weight of that silence will choke us.

The fact that we are here and that I speak these words is an attempt to break that silence and bridge some of those differences between us, for it is not difference which immobilizes us, but silence. And there are so many silences to be broken.

Thomas H. West (b. 1942) has been a professor of theology at the College of Saint Catherine since 1979. West is also the author of Ultimate Hope without God: The Atheistic Eschatology of Ernst Bloch *(1991) and other works. In this excerpt he revisits the story of the "good Samaritan." What qualities does it take to be considered as such? What is agapic love and how does it lead to social justice?*

Love into Justice: The Good Samaritan Revisited

Thomas H. West

Most Christians would say that the foundation of social justice is love, especially love of neighbor, *agape*. But how do we get from agape to an active commitment to social justice? We do not answer this question well if we say simply that agapic love and social justice are the same thing. They are not. Yet I want to argue that work for social justice is a necessary expression of agapic love.

In the New Testament, the epitome of agapic love is the Good Samaritan. We do not ordinarily think of the Good Samaritan as practicing social justice. We see him as practicing compassion, performing an act of charity, carrying out a mission of mercy, not, surely, working for social justice. What the Good Samaritan did and what a social reformer like Martin Luther King, Jr. did are clearly very different things.

But is social justice so sharply different from agapic love? In this chapter I shall argue that there is indeed a distinction between agapic love and social justice, but it is a distinction within a unity.

Luke's Parable of the Good Samaritan

Here is the parable of the Good Samaritan as told in Luke's gospel:

> Just then a lawyer stood up to test Jesus. "Teacher," he said, "what must I do to inherit eternal life?" He said to him, "What is written in the law? What do you read there?" He answered, "You shall love the Lord your God with all your heart, and with all your soul, and with all your strength, and with all your mind; and your neighbor as yourself." And he said to him, "You have given the right answer; do this, and you will live."
>
> But wanting to justify himself, he asked Jesus, "And who is my neighbor?" Jesus replied, "A man was going down from Jerusalem to Jericho, and fell into the hands of robbers, who stripped him, beat him, and went away, leaving him half dead." Now by chance a priest was going down the road; and when he saw him, he passed by on the other side. So likewise a Levite, when he came to the place and saw him, passed by on the other side. But a Samaritan

348

while traveling came near him; and when he saw him, he was moved with compassion. He went to him and bandaged his wounds, having poured oil and wine on them. Then he put him on his own animal, brought him to an inn, and took care of him. The next day he took out two denarii, gave them to the innkeeper, and said, "Take care of him; and when I come back, I will repay you whatever more you spend" (Luke 10:25–35).

Luke situates the parable of the Good Samaritan within the "travel narrative" (Luke 9: 51–19: 27) that follows Jesus' journey from Galilee to Jerusalem.[1]

During the journey Jesus frequently pauses to instruct his followers in the way of discipleship. One day he instructed them by telling the parable of the Good Samaritan.

The Good Samaritan parable is classified by Joachim Jeremias as a "parable of realized discipleship,"[2] though it is not a parable in the narrow or typical sense. Rather, it is an *example story*, not an extended metaphor or simile where the figures and events symbolize something else, as when the mustard seed symbolizes the reign of God (see Mt. 13: 31–32) or the generous vineyard owner (see Mt. 20: 1–16), God's unconditional love.[3] The Good Samaritan parable does not refer beyond itself in this way. Jesus is not saying that "God acts like the Good Samaritan," but rather, "You should act like the Good Samaritan."

The Good Samaritan story does, however, display other elements typical of a parable, most obviously the element of surprise. The surprise is not that the priest and the Levite (a Temple official subordinate to the priests) pass by an injured man. Out in the countryside, "anti-clericalism" was widespread among Jews. That Jesus would portray Temple officials as morally callous would evoke a knowing murmur from his Jewish audience. His audience would then expect Jesus to finish off his story by having an Israelite layperson like themselves stop and do the right thing.[4] Instead, the *Samaritan* stops, and, "moved with compassion," does the right thing. This is a major surprise to Jesus' Jewish audience. John Donahue reminds us: "Centuries of pious reflection have dulled our sensibilities to the hatred that existed between Jews and Samaritans." Jews regarded Samaritans not only as a mongrel people who had intermarried with pagan invaders, but as deserters of the Jewish religion.[5] That a Jew could love the Samaritan as a neighbor, and a Samaritan could love the Jew as a neighbor, well, it's a scandal, it's out of the question. When the lawyer asked Jesus, "Who is my neighbor?" he was being serious. There was genuine debate among Jews at this time about who was included under "neighbor." According to Jeremias, "It was generally agreed that the term connoted fellow countrymen, including full proselytes."[6] It did not include Samaritans. Jesus defines *neighbor* to include the hated

Samaritan, depicting the Samaritan as one who is a neighbor precisely by treating the injured Jew as a neighbor. This is a surprise. This is a shock.

In the parable of the Good Samaritan, Jesus offers an example of agapic love in action. Such love imitates the love shown by Jesus, and Jesus' love is in turn an imitation of God's love. Such is the nature of Jesus' radical moral demand on those called to the mission of bringing people into the reign of God. In the parable, agapic love shows the following qualities:

- It is unconditional. The Samaritan does not demand that the person injured fulfill any conditions before the Samaritan is willing to give help.
- This love is universal. The Samaritan does not care to which gender, race, class, religion, or ethnic group the injured person belongs. A human being is hurt. This Samaritan would have reached out to any human being who was suffering.
- This love is unconcerned with merit or just deserts. The Samaritan does not say to himself, "This person in the ditch half dead does not deserve my help because he had it coming. He didn't take sufficient care to avoid the threat of robbery." The Samaritan does not say to himself, "There is probably some past sin in the victim's life. God through this violent assault and robbery is punishing him."
- It is love moved by compassion. The Samaritan is moved by feeling. Indeed, one can imagine him seized by feeling and impelled to the ditch beside the road.
- It is a love that is spontaneous and uncalculating. The Samaritan is moved to act, quickly. He is not shown pondering the pros and cons. He is not shown engaging in subtle calculations about precisely what he should do. He spends no time in rational analysis.
- It is a love that goes beyond the minimum one would expect of even the most decent person. That is, it is supererogatory; it goes beyond what is asked. He doesn't just bandage the injured man's wounds and get him to the next town, but stays with him, takes care of him, pays his lodging, and then—and here is the special touch—says to the innkeeper: "If it comes to more than this, I'll pay the difference on my way back." Here the Samaritan shows himself to be a virtuoso of the supererogatory.[7]

These qualities constitute agapic, that is, Christian, love in action, in the public sphere, among strangers, who through love become neighbors and friends.

Now if the Christian moral life were simply a matter of letting oneself be moved to uncalculating love towards any human being in special need, we would have no need for lengthy books on Christian morality and justice. But the Christian moral life often requires us to go beyond spontaneous acts of agapic love. Morality then becomes more complex, and when it does, it begins to move from agapic love pure and simple to agapic love that expresses itself in the work of justice.

2. Love into Interpersonal Justice

The great American theologian Reinhold Niebuhr said that Christian love becomes justice when there are three or more people in the room.[8] Expanding on the story of the Good Samaritan, let us imagine that the Samaritan, instead of discovering one robbery victim in the ditch, discovers three. The Samaritan is moved by compassion to go over to the three victims, but as soon as he arrives, he finds himself having to step back from the situation and from his feeling in order to engage in some rational analysis and calculation. He finds himself engaged in what we today call *triage*. Triage is a system of principles and rules by which one judges how one can best treat victims like these, given one's resources. Whenever my family calls our Health Maintenance Organization after hours, we talk first to the triage nurse; using a complex system of principles and rules she decides what the HMO can and should do for us given our ailments and given their resources.

Coming upon the three victims, the Good Samaritan must also practice triage. The principles and rules of triage he uses will be undoubtedly less explicit and formalized than those of the HMO triage nurse; nevertheless, if he is to do *justice* to these three victims he will have to turn his thoughtful attention to *some* principles and rules, however rudimentary they might be.

In practicing triage, the Samaritan does not completely turn from feeling to thought, but he does distance himself enough to allow a rational analysis of the situation. If he lets himself be ruled only by feeling, he might spontaneously attend first to the victim who is screaming and moaning the loudest, but to do so would be unjust. One of the first principles of triage is that one should attend first to the victim who is most seriously injured and then make a judgment about whether one has the resources to help him or her. The Samaritan coolheadedly turns his attention very self-consciously towards this principle and sets about putting it into practice. He first gathers empirical data about the condition of the victims. He discovers that the victim screaming the loudest is a teenage boy holding his ankle. A second victim is very quiet, is not bleeding, but he has a weak pulse. A third victim is bleeding profusely from the neck. He decides to help her first, and bandages her wounds, and stops the bleeding. On her he decides to concentrate his maximum effort. He has acted justly.

Yet it would be unfair, it would be unjust, if he were to cease thinking about the other two. They, after all, are human beings, with their inherent dignity and worth. He can*not* give them his *maximum* effort in this situation, but he feels bound to give them at least a minimum of attention. But what precisely is the minimum he owes them in this situation? The answer requires another calculation on his part. To the boy holding his ankle, he decides that the injury is not that serious, and he limits himself to wrapping the ankle and uttering words of comfort. And he double-checks the person with the weak pulse to make sure that he still is alive.

At this point the Samaritan is now expressing his love in the form of justice, and specifically, *interpersonal* justice. Interpersonal justice refers to the justice that is practiced by one individual to another in a situation where the person practicing the justice has to distance himself somewhat from his feelings, consult a set of principles and rules, gather data about this situation, and make a rational decision about what should be done. Interpersonal justice requires attention to the questions of what is equal treatment, what is fair treatment, what is the minimum one owes each individual who is present, and what is the maximum one can offer, given one's resources. This kind of analysis tells the Samaritan that it would be wrong, it would violate the principles of interpersonal justice, if he were to spend himself totally in selfless and supererogatory love on only one of the victims that now confront him. He must therefore carefully and rationally distribute his efforts in an equal yet fair manner, giving the most he can give to one without at the same time totally neglecting the others.

Interpersonal justice is not only practiced in the kind of extraordinary situation in which the Samaritan finds himself. It is in fact the stuff of ordinary daily life, in a way that heedless agapic love can never be. Every day we have many encounters with our fellow human beings. Not every encounter is, or should be, an occasion for agapic love in the pure form. Rather, we should treat those individuals we encounter every day with a simple, interpersonal justice, with a basic respect for their worth, dignity, and autonomy.[9] There is a minimum that we owe everyone. Some might require more than the minimum from us. We must weigh matters and decide what we can give. Knowing how this is done takes much training and learning. Some people take to this very well and show an acute ethical intelligence.

Let us return to our story. The Samaritan has bound the wounds of the woman bleeding, attended to the man with the weak pulse, and calmed the boy with the injured ankle. Somehow, after making a whole series of further decisions, all accompanied by considerable rational analysis, he gets them to the nearest town and arranges for their care, though this time a check of his financial resources precludes an offer to pay the innkeeper and the local physician. He has done justice to these people.

But the whole experience has left him angry. For the fourth time this month he has encountered victims of brutal robberies left to die in the ditch. What would have happened to these poor people had he not happened along? The Samaritan thinks on the many others who were passed by and left to suffer and die. This tragic situation is more than he as an individual can manage. He is moved to conclude that one-to-one agapic love and interpersonal justice are not enough. He decides to move into social justice.

3. Love into Social Justice

The Good Samaritan decides to involve the larger community and attempt a more systematic solution to this terrible problem of assault and robbery.[10] He decides thereby to make the move from *interpersonal* justice to the work of *social* justice. Social justice is justice practiced by a group or community towards individuals or other groups or communities. Social justice is a social endeavor, which involves the creation of *social structures.*

Social structures have two elements: the mental and the institutional. The *first* element is concerned with the consciousness, the mind, the attitude, the ethos, of the community. It is obvious to the Samaritan that many people are passing by these victims in the ditch and not doing anything to help. "There is a deeply faulty ethos in these parts," he says to himself. "People around here are indifferent to this kind of human misery."

The Good Samaritan resolves to change the ethos, to raise consciousness, to change the mentality. On his next trip down this road, he stops at each village and gives a little talk to the villagers, alerting them to the suffering of the victims of these robberies and urging them not to pass by the victims. He talks about the basic dignity and equality of all human beings. All human beings, he insists, have a claim on our love and justice, especially those who are suffering. He even includes in his talk a rudimentary introduction to triage. In his efforts to create a new social mentality, the Samaritan enjoys some success. People become more sensitized. More people than before are reaching out with agapic love and interpersonal justice.

In one village this new consciousness becomes so pervasive that helping robbery victims becomes what sociologists call an *institution*, that is, an *established pattern of behavior*, which is the *second* element of a social structure.[11] Helping victims is something that villagers practice without hesitation. The institution in this case is a *custom*, a pattern of behavior that establishes itself quite spontaneously and lacks formal organization.

Nevertheless, this proves to be not enough. There are still many victims and many people are passing them by. The ethos of reaching out to help is indeed deeper and more widespread, but it is far from pervasive. Human beings, after all, are free to defy ethos and custom and are especially prone to do so when they are asked to go outside themselves for someone else's sake. And so the Samaritan decides to move beyond custom and create a more formal institution.

He decides to create an institution in which groups of volunteers will patrol the road in shifts in search of victims.[12] To insure that these volunteers will be skilled in applying triage, he arranges for training sessions. He rents several buildings in the villages in which to hold these sessions. Since those who conduct the sessions will be engaged in virtually full-time work, he decides to pay them. Realizing that he does not have enough money for rent and salaries, he sets out to raise money, trusting that the ethos he created earlier is wide and deep enough to produce people willing to contribute. He organizes a fund drive, to occur on a regular basis. His institution comes thereby to depend on both the willingness of people to volunteer their time to work on the patrols and their willingness to contribute money on a regular basis. And since the contributions of time and money depend on the continued vitality of the ethos, the Samaritan must continue to give talks to raise ethical consciousness; that is, he must continue to be concerned with the element of mentality.

The Samaritan has thus created not only a new mentality, but also new institutions. And many robbery victims are helped.

Yet, many victims continue to die in the ditch, unhelped. The crime rate is up. Also, there are difficulties with the Samaritan's institutional structure. The patrols are staffed largely by unpaid volunteers, who are free to cease volunteering, and quite regularly one or more will suddenly and unpredictably pull out. On nights before holidays, the most dangerous nights, whole patrols have to be canceled for lack of volunteers.

Funding is a continuing problem. The regional economy fluctuates wildly and along with that, financial contributions fluctuate wildly. Sometimes the Samaritan has the funds to do the training, sometimes not. A fickleness and unpredictability pervade the institution making for a fickle and unpredictable service to the victims along the road. One of the principles of justice is universality of coverage: all persons will receive the minimum due them. This institution is failing to provide that coverage, which causes acute pangs of conscience in the Samaritan. The compassion that moved him to that first act of agapic love has now moved him towards the work of justice that aims to reach all those suffering, but he is *not* reaching them all in any consistent way.

For a while the Samaritan considers going to what we now call the free-market approach. In order to guarantee more predictable and reliable staff he could staff the patrols with paid professionals. To pay for them, he could market their services by charging the victims—with some provision for their ability to pay—or by selling their services to villages along the road or to groups of travelers. To raise the initial capital outlay for this service, he could sell shares to the enterprise and then pay the shareholders out of the profits.

But he decides against going into the market. He is not opposed to the market as such, for he is a businessperson and believes firmly that some goods and services are best delivered to people through the market. But he has come to believe that a robbery victim in the ditch has not just a *need* for help, but also a *right* to help. A right means that the victim has an absolute claim on the community for a consistent, predictable, and skilled response to his or her suffering. The free market approach introduces the profit motive and with that the inevitable tendency to provide the best service to those who have the most money to pay for it. But this is the kind of service that every human being has a right to, irrespective of wealth or social position.

So the Samaritan chooses another step, namely, he decides to go to the state, that is, to the institutions of government. This road is in a province under the jurisdiction of Rome. He decides to go to the Roman governor and ask that a new social structure be created. While talking with the governor and his aides, he learns that the problems occurring along this road are occurring on roads throughout the province. The governor is responsive. He petitions Rome for the permission to create a new structure and collect a tax to pay for it. The Roman senate passes a law, the emperor approves it, and the governor's bureaucrats work out detailed policies, that is, principles and rules, to guide the new institution in its service. Paid governmental patrols are put in place along the roads. They deliver medical help more quickly and predictably and thus provide coverage that approaches universal. Because the government owns the means of legalized violence, it equips the patrols with the physical means to pursue, subdue, and arrest the violent robbers who are causing so much human suffering.[13] And since the taxes are set and levied by law, funding is more predictable year-to-year.

The Good Samaritan is quite satisfied with his work. He has moved from agapic love to interpersonal justice, and finally, to social justice. To be sure, he has not ceased practicing agapic love—indeed, just the other night an opportunity again presented itself and he reached out to help a victim—but he has spent most of his time these past several years on the long march through social structures.

Despite his general satisfaction, the Samaritan has frequently found the work of social justice tedious and boring. Giving ethical pep talks, finding buildings to rent, training volunteers, writing up detailed policy suggestions for the governor—more than once during all this he has felt a slackening in his original agapic motivation. Indeed there have been moments when he becomes wistful for the spontaneous purity of that original act of agapic love. He recalls the deep joy and peace he felt after he had paid the innkeeper, knowing that he had done the right thing.

In addition, he is no naïve reformer. He has seen the negative side of this movement from agapic love to social justice. He worries, for example, about the impersonality of the new government structure. He has talked with some members of the patrols and found that quite a few are not motivated by the desire to help their neighbors but by the desire to advance their careers. Some government administrators appear less interested in providing a good service than in protecting their turf and increasing their budgets. He worries that with the movement to a government structure, the community ethos will decline. There is already much grumbling about the new taxes. Taxes, after all, are coercive. They are extracted by law and backed by the organized violence of the state. The other day he heard someone say, "They're confiscating my hard-earned money to pay for these patrols—I never even take those roads. It's not fair!" He fears that giving this work of social justice over to the state will diminish the motivating energy of agapic love to the point where individuals will pass by victims in the ditch with the excuse, "I don't need to stop, a patrol will be by soon." He has even heard rumors that some patrols are abusing their power and using their instruments of violence not to protect the victims but to blackmail them. Social justice, when it is carried out by the structures of government, has its dark side.

But all in all, despite these concerns, the Samaritan remains cautiously proud of his work. He is convinced that this new social structure has reduced the total amount of human suffering. Social justice has accomplished more than his individual acts of agapic love ever could.

As we watch the Samaritan move from agapic love to social justice from our perspective, we notice something missing from his vision and practice. At no time does the Samaritan engage in an in-depth social, political, and economic analysis of his society. He does not ask himself why there are so many robberies. He does not link the rise in the crime rate with the high concentration of wealth in the hands of a few large absentee landowners. He fails to bring into view the many tenant farmers who live in virtual slavery.[14] Many are so poor that they are drawn to lives of crime. As he journeys to see the governor, he does not wonder if perhaps his work of social justice wouldn't be more effective if this region were not under imperial rule and if Jews and Samaritans were independent peoples with grassroots, egalitarian political structures more immediately responsive to crime and its victims. This kind of analysis might very well have led the Samaritan to a vision of radical and sweeping change in the social, economic, and political structures of his day. But this kind of analysis, and the radical vision that often goes with it, is a relatively recent development in the history of ethical intelligence. Jesus did not undertake this kind of analysis.[15] Nor did the early Church. And the Catholic Church was indifferent, sometimes even hostile, to this kind of analysis until late in the nineteenth century. In our day, however, virtually all Christians engaged in the work of social justice are aware of the need for complex social analysis.

I hope that my revisit of the Good Samaritan story has shown that the distinctions among agapic love, interpersonal justice, and social justice are real, but not hard and fast. Agapic love, Christian love, is not *replaced* by interpersonal and social justice, but continues to accompany both as their motivational fount, energizing both,[16] preventing each from becoming impersonal and bloodless. Justice has been described as the *public* expression of love, a definition that strikes me as particularly apt. The movement from agapic love to social justice is continuous and necessary. Any theology that draws too sharp a separation between love and justice, or which sees them as belonging to utterly different spheres, or which sees them in opposition, is a deeply flawed theology.

Just as there is a natural movement from agapic love to social justice, so too is there a natural move from social justice to agapic love. Even the most intense, one-to-one expression of agapic love does not occur in a social vacuum. Social structures—mentality, ethos, custom, laws, institutions—all pre-shape even the most private actions. The Good Samaritan, after all, is a member of a schismatic Jewish sect whose members followed the Torah, the Jewish law found in the first five books of the Hebrew Bible. The heart of this law is the two-fold commandment to love God and love your neighbor as yourself. This two-fold law was part of the Samaritan ethos and passed on to the Good Samaritan through the institutions of religious learning and instruction. The religious and ethical logic of the two-fold law led him to oppose a mentality that would forbid him to help an injured Jew. And therefore his spontaneous act of agapic love as told in Jesus' story did not arise solely out of his own spontaneity, it was not utterly his own, *sui generis*, but in part was the consequence of a social structure. Indeed the very spontaneity of his action is partly a sign of how thoroughly he was socialized by the redemptive elements of this structure.[17] And we must not forget, the parable of the Good Samaritan was told by Jesus, who was raised a Jew and was taught the same two-fold law of love.

We must, therefore, be wary of drawing overprecise distinctions among Christian love, interpersonal justice, and social justice. The distinctions are real, but within an unfolding unity. In his story of the Good Samaritan, Jesus beautifully captured the first and decisive moment of agapic love. Yet we can well imagine that the logic of love carried the Good Samaritan, as it should carry us, into the work of justice.

But with all this talk of social justice we dare not forget that the direction of agapic love is not only out into the public sphere of social structures.[18] There is the other direction, towards the intimacy of full mutuality, towards friendship, romantic love, and family. What is the final purpose of just social structures if not a world where mutuality can flourish? Mutuality with God and mutuality with others. The full terror of a corrupt social structure is the way its destructive power makes even the intimacy of mutuality impossible. Agapic love achieves public expression in justice, but its fulfillment in mutual self-giving.[19]

Notes

[1] See John Donahue, *The Gospel in Parable: Metaphor, Narrative, and Theology in the Synoptic Gospels* (Philadelphia: Fortress Press, 1988), 126ff.

[2] Joachim Jeremias, *The Parables of Jesus* (New York: Charles Scribner's Sons, 2nd rev. ed., 1972), 198ff.

[3] Donahue, *The Gospel in Parable*, 12f.

[4] Jeremias, *The Parables of Jesus*, 204.

[5] Donahue, *The Gospel in Parable*, 130f., supplies a short history of the relations between Jews and Samaritans to show why they were such enemies.

[6] Jeremias, *The Parables of Jesus*, 202.

[7] Donahue, *The Gospel in Parable*, tells us that the Samaritan's extra help at the inn is more than just a sign of the supererogatory: "As a paradigm for compassionate entry into the world of an injured brother or sister, this final action is indispensable. According to the law at the time, a person with an unpaid debt could be enslaved until the debt was paid (see Matt. 18:23–35). Since the injured man was robbed and stripped—deprived of all resources—he could have been at the mercy of the innkeeper, a profession that had a bad reputation for dishonesty and violence. The parable assures the injured man's freedom and independence" (133).

[8] Actually, Niebuhr said it more abstractly than that: "An immediately felt obligation towards obvious need may be prompted by the emotion of pity. But a continued sense of obligation rests upon and expresses itself in rational calculations of the needs of others as compared with our own interests. A relation between the self and one other may be partly ecstatic; and in any case the calculation of relative interests may be reduced to a minimum. But as soon as a third person is introduced into the relation even the most perfect love requires a rational estimate of conflicting needs and interests." Reinhold Niebuhr, *The*

Nature and Destiny of Man: A Christian Interpretation. Volume II: Human Destiny, (New York: Charles Scribner's Sons, 1943), 248.

9 Following the rules of common courtesy can fulfill more than a small part of interpersonal justice on a day-to-day level. It is amazing how much of the advice that Ms. Manners gives in her syndicated newspaper column can be seen as the application of interpersonal justice. She shows an acute sense for the intersection of morality and manners. Though insofar as her rulings on courtesy precipitate a widespread pattern of behavior in society, she is creating a social structure; that is, she is doing the work of social justice.

10 Another re-telling of the Good Samaritan story, which makes much the same move to social justice as I make here, is that of Stephen Mott. See his *Biblical Ethics and Social Change* (New York: Oxford University Press, 1982), 58f. I am not indebted to Mott's re-telling, but the parallel is striking. For the Mott reference I am indebted to Garth L. Hallet, *Christian Neighbor Love: An Assessment of Six Rival Positions* (Washington, D.C.: Georgetown University Press, 1989), 118.

11 On institutionalization, see Peter L. Berger and Thomas Luckmann, *The Social Construction of Reality: A Treatise on the Sociology of Knowledge* (New York: Doubleday Anchor Books, 1967), 54–61.

12 A volunteer patrol is a good example of what Catholic social teaching calls a "mediating structure" or an "intermediate structure." Such structures carry out the "principle of subsidiarity," which could be summed up this way: before creating larger, governmental structures, first create smaller, local, nongovernmental structures. See Fred Kammer, *Doing Faithjustice: An Introduction to Catholic Social Thought* (New York: Paulist Press, 1991), 184.

13 Here we have an example of the twin functions of government. On the one hand, it has the more positive function of extending medical help to all who need it. On the other hand, it has the more negative function of countering violence with violence, of enforcing order against the forces of anarchy and destruction. There are two traditions in Western political theory that tend to focus on one function at the expense of the other. Martin Luther (and before him Augustine and after him Hobbes) tends to reduce government to the "negative" function, that is, "to bear the secular sword and punish the wicked" (see "Secular Authority: To What Extent it Should be Obeyed," in John Dillenberger, ed., *Martin Luther Selections from his Writings* [New York: Doubleday Anchor Books, first published in 1523, this edition, 1961] 363–402, here 374). Government indeed is willed by God, but by God's "left hand." Its work is God's work, yet an "alien work" (377). If there had been no sin there would be no government. The scriptural source for this tradition can be found in Rom. 13:4 and 1 Pet. 1: 13. Another tradition, going back to Plato and Aristotle, stresses that government is a good, and natural to human life. Christian socialists and welfare state liberals add to this the agapic motivation and welcome government structures in their "positive" function of meeting a broad range of human needs. Reinhold Niebuhr keeps these two traditions in good balance: "All structures of justice do indeed presuppose the sinfulness of man, and are all partly systems of restraint which prevent the conflict of wills and interests from resulting in a consistent anarchy. But they are also all mechanisms by which

men fulfill their obligations to their fellow men, beyond the possibilities offered in direct and personal relationships. The Kingdom of God and the demands of perfect love are therefore relevant to every political system and impinge upon every social situation in which the self seeks to come to terms with the claims of other life." See *The Nature and Destiny of Man: A Christian Interpretation. Volume II: Human Destiny*, 192.

[14] One of the effects of the widespread indebtedness among the peasants in Palestine was virtual slavery for those who could not pay their debts. Many took to banditry. See Richard A. Horsley, *Sociology and the Jesus Movement* (New York: Crossroad, 1989), 88–90.

[15] I am not denying that people in Jesus' time could not have visions of a new world where life would be radically different. Jesus had that vision, as did the many other "millenarian prophets" of his time. What I don't see is the combination of radical vision and social analysis, as epitomized, for example, in the work of Karl Marx.

[16] In the words of Fred Kammer: "Instead of a tension between love and justice, love as the soul of justice gives the Christian passion for building a more just order." See *Doing Faithjustice: An Introduction to Catholic Social Thought* (New York: Paulist Press, 1991), 181.

[17] An extraordinary example of agapic love practiced spontaneously more because of communal ethos than individual heroic virtue is the story of the French mountain village of Le Chambon, whose 5000 inhabitants sheltered 5000 Jews during World War II. The documentary, produced by Pierre Sauvage, that tells the story has many interviews with individuals who participated in this good work. What is remarkable is how self-effacing they are. Indeed, they appear somewhat baffled by the attention. What emerges out of the interviews is that these people performed individual acts of love because that is what one does if one is a member of that community. There appears to have been very little agonizing over the risks. It was the triumph of an ethos and thus of the work of social justice. See also Philip P. Hallie, *Lest Innocent Blood Be Shed: The Story of the Village of Le Chambon and How Goodness Happened There* (New York: Harper and Row, 1979). And yet reading Hallie's book reveals how mysteriously complex all this is. For the ethos of Le Chambon would not have attained its spontaneous strength without the inspired work of two individuals, the pastor and his wife, André and Magda Trocmé. For a very interesting philosophical examination of both the village ethos and the moral achievement of the Trocmés, see Lawrence A. Blum, *Moral Perception and Particularity* (New York: Cambridge University Press, 1994), 73–4, 85–9, 91–2, 151–2, 175–80.

[18] Within the public sphere of social justice there are several sub-spheres that correspond to different kinds of social justice. These sub-spheres are: 1) basic human rights and freedoms: freedom of speech, of worship, of movement, and so on; 2) economic justice: the duty of society to ensure that goods and services are fairly and equally distributed and the duty of individuals to contribute to the production of goods and services; 3) political justice: the duty of society to ensure that political power is fairly and equally distributed and the duty of individuals to contribute to political decision-making; 4) criminal justice: the

duty of the society to fairly and equally enforce the law and the duty of individuals to obey the law; 5) environmental justice: the duty to protect the inorganic and organic world so that all being will flourish, not just human being; 6) intergenerational justice: duty of the present generation to pass on just social structures to the next generation and not overburden the next generation with debt and environmental degradation; 7) international justice: the duty of nations to live in comity with other nations and to create international social structures to solve social problems that are global in their effects. To all these duties are corresponding rights; indeed, one of the tasks of social justice is to find the proper balance of duties (responsibilities) and rights (entitlements), or to put it another way, the proper mix of what the larger society should distribute to sub-societies and individuals, and what individuals and sub-societies should contribute to the larger society.

[19] The works of two contemporary theorists of agapic love show these two tendencies. Gene Outka in his *Agape: an Ethical Analysis* (New Haven: Yale University Press, 1972), defines agapic love as "universal equal regard." Although he does accept mutuality as a proper fulfillment of agape, his understanding of agape leads his analysis more naturally towards justice. Stephen Post, in his *A Theory of Agape: On the Meaning of Christian Love* (Lewisburg, PA: Bucknell University Press, 1990) shows agapic love as seeking out mutual response in "special relations." My own view is that both tendencies must be kept together in dialectical unity. I like the words of Gilbert Meilander: "We ought not give up the desire for mutual love and try to be stoics. Neither ought we permit our love to be limited to the small circle of those who return it." See *Friendship: A Study in Theological Ethics* (South Bend: University of Notre Dame Press, 1981), 50.

In this essay William Andrew Myers proposes that our individual actions in the world express what we most want the world to be. What does this thesis say about ideals people claim to hold but fail to act on? Do you think political activism and political apathy express different visions of the world? Is Myers right about the difference between a consumer and a citizen?

Individual Action and a Global Ethic

William Andrew Myers

Consider the idea that whatever we do, whatever action we deliberately take, is an expression of what we want the world to be. To help a stranger with car trouble is to say that we want to live in a world in which people with car trouble get helped, and also it is to create that kind of world. To stand by passively while people use violence in disputes is to say that we want a world in which violence is unchallenged, and it is to create that kind of world. The way we live and interact with people around us makes the world what we want it to be.

The day the Berlin Wall opened, November 10, 1989, I was in Warsaw participating in the founding of the International Society for Universalism, a worldwide group of scholars working on ways to create and foster dialogue across boundaries of culture, ideology, religion, philosophy, and language. As we academics from five continents began discussions about the bases for communication and understanding across borders, the geopolitical world began the upheaval which is redefining the borders themselves. At the first ISU meeting and the ones which followed in Berlin, London, and St. Catherine's, Ontario, the idealism of the participants was complemented by the belief that geopolitical changes were going to make it possible in a practical way to change the way the peoples of the earth relate to each other.

Years later, the rich conversation among universalists which began at that 1989 meeting continues, through conferences and the ISU journal, Dialogue and Universalism. But we are more sober about the possibilities. Perpetual wars, and worries about nuclear proliferation all point to continued willingness to use violent force for political ends and the failure of leaders to construct viable contexts for dialogue. Of course from the standpoint of the so-called realists in politics, dialogue can never replace violence as an instrument of national policy.

From a universalist point of view, however, building the bridges which make dialogue the normal basis for relationships, rather than violence and the threat of force, is not mere ivory tower idealism: it is a practical mandate upon which depend our prospects for species survival. The conditions of human life have changed fundamentally over the last century, with the result that a universalist ethics—a framework for assessing the rights, responsibilities, and consequences of human actions—must become the conceptual basis for large-scale human interactions.

It is commonplace to observe that we live in a different world than our parents and grandparents did. But it is not so often made clear what the momentous changes in human life in the twentieth century mean for humans as ethical agents. I think the human condition itself—the fundamentals of human living—have changed in ways that also change who we are in relation to the rest of creation. Think of just five areas of fundamental change:

First, we have seen since World War I the development of weapons of mass destruction and intellectual justifications for their use on civilian populations. Centuries of development of a theory intended to limit the means used in warfare, called Just War Theory, which had historically influenced politicians in forming international agreements to observe non-combatant immunity, seemed to have no effect on the planners who perfected aerial bombardment during World War II and its logical outgrowth, the intercontinental nuclear missiles. Every human being on earth has become a viable target in the eyes of strategists. The superpower arms race as ended; but nothing fundamental has changed as long as the weapons and the strategic theories which would justify their use are accepted as givens of international relations.

Second, we have developed means of communication across borders that allow creation of a global culture in which information, and more important, systems of understanding, can be delivered to anyone with access to a computer. Whereas it took three days for news of President Lincoln's assassination to cross the continent in 1865, in 1981 three-fifths of the population of the earth watched a broadcast of the British royal wedding as it happened. Third, since the 1920s and the invention of effective antibiotics, we have made progress in medical technology which gives those with access to it greater life expectancy and higher quality of life than ever before possible. For members of intact developed societies, medicine gives average people an expectation of healthy longevity previous generations would not dream of.

Fourth, our various technologies, from industry, farming, and natural resource extraction to consumer waste habits, military testing, and energy production, have produced enormous and long lasting toxic pollution which will threaten human health and well-being for generations to come.

Fifth, the post World War II era has seen the spread of universal concepts of human rights. The United Nations Universal Declaration of Human Rights, produced in 1949 and as of 1976 part of international law, sets out a long list of specific rights that governments are bound to protect. These rights are said to pertain to people as such, not merely to persons as members of specific societies which happen to recognize certain rights. They are thus asserted to be universal possessions of all human beings regardless of whether their governments recognize them as rights or not.

These five areas of change, I contend, add up to changes in the basic circumstances of human life. The implication for our ethical responsibilities is that we must assess the consequences of actions and policies in a much larger context than before, because our ability to affect the lives of others is more vast than before. And because of the communicability of actions, it is not only direct consequences we should be aware of but also the effects of modeling certain kinds of action that we should assess.

Those with positional power and those responsible for holding them accountable for their actions and policies need new norms of conduct based on a long-term, large scale idea of human flourishing. The idea of flourishing is a description of what it means for human beings to live well, to bring about their best potentials in a full life. To think globally about the prospects for all humanity to achieve the maximum possible level of human flourishing is the work of universalist ethicists.

But ethical understanding develops in local settings, not universally. As Carol Bly has argued, for ethical character to develop, we need lots of discussion of ethical ideas around the dinner table. It is in face to face interaction that we become who we are and undertake the responsibilities that mark our moral characters. Without interconnection in a locality, universalism threatens to become hopelessly abstract and vague. Our actions can affect remote others as never before; but we still learn how to act in our own families, neighborhood, and workplaces.

In American life, many forces push us toward apathy, indifference and passivity. The very idea of the consumer is an idea of human life at a biological minimum. I can consume goods without being a citizen, without interacting much with others,without being a functioning member of a community. But if I am to act as a fully formed ethical person, I must be much more than a mere consumer.

Citizen politics is the idea that individuals control democratic process by engaging in myriad small processes of partnership and egalitarian decision making. It is primarily individuals taking responsibility for what happens in their neighborhoods, homes, and workplaces by insisting that leadership be shared, that hierarchical decision structures be leveled, that policies be developed through consultative processes rather than through executive fiat.

By expressing values of cooperation, egalitarian partnership, and shared power in organizations, we express locally and personally the world we want to live in; in fact, we create that world. We do the same thing negatively to the extent that we live in relationships constituted by dominance and allow those with positional power to act arbitrarily and without accountability. If dialogue is to become the norm in international relations rather than threats of violence, then we have to do the hard and time consuming work in our everyday lives of listening to others and building dialogue, especially with people whose ideas we disagree with.

If democratic process is universally viable, we create the potential for that universal by modeling it in everyday practical relationships, in homes, churches, classrooms, jobs, and local government. In the end, the long term well-being of the "global village" will depend on the quality of ethical interactions among individuals in the local settings we all live in.

Ursula K. Le Guin (b. 1929) is a feminist science fiction writer. She is the author of numerous poems, plays, short stories, and novels. "The Ones Who Walk Away from Omelas" won a Hugo Award for best short story in 1974. In reading this excerpt, does this sound like any community that you have ever been a part of or witnessed elsewhere? What specific injustice is taking place? What does the child represent? What needs to be accomplished to bring about social change?

The Ones Who Walk Away from Omelas

Ursula K. Le Guin

With a clamor of bells that set the swallows soaring, the Festival of Summer came to the City of Omelas, bright-towered by the sea. The rigging of the boats in harbor sparkled with flags. In the streets between houses and red roofs and painted walls, between old moss-grown gardens and under avenues of trees, past great parks and public buildings, processions moved. Some were decrous: old people in long stiff robes of mauve and grey, grave master workmen, quiet, merry women carrying their babies and chatting as they walked. In other streets the music beat faster, a shimmering of gong and tambourine, and the people went dancing, the procession was a dance. Children dodged in and out, their high calls rising like the swallows' crossing flights over the music and the singing. All the processions wound towards the north side of the city, where on the great water-meadow called the Green Fields boys and girls, naked in the bright air, with mud-stained feet and ankles and long, lithe arms, exercised their restive horses before the race. The horses wore no gear at all but a halter without bit. Their manes were braided with streamers of silver, gold, and green. They flared their nostrils and pranced and boasted to one another; they were vastly excited, the horse being the only animal who has adopted our ceremonies as his own. Far off to the north and west the mountains stood up half encircling Omelas on her bay. The air of morning was so clear that the snow still crowning the Eighteen Peaks burned with white-gold fire across the miles of sunlit air, under the dark blue of the sky. There was just enough wind to make the banners that marked the racecourse snap and flutter now and then. In the silence of the broad green meadows one could hear the music winding through the city streets, farther and nearer and ever approaching, a cheerful faint sweetness of the air that from time to time trembled and gathered together and broke out into the great joyous clanging of the bells.

Joyous! How is one to tell about joy? How describe the citizens of Omelas?

They were not simple folk, you see, though they were happy. But we do not say the words of cheer much any more. All smiles have become archaic. Given a description such as this one tends to make certain assumptions. Given a description such as this one tends to look next for the King, mounted on a splendid stallion and surrounded by his noble knights, or perhaps in a golden litter borne by great-muscled slaves. But there was no king. They did not use swords, or keep slaves. They were not barbarians. I do not know the rules and laws of their society, but I suspect that they were singularly few. As they did without monarchy and slavery, so they also got on without the stock exchange, the advertisement, the secret police, and the bomb. Yet I repeat that these were not simple folk, not dulcet shepherds, noble savages, bland utopians. They were not less complex than us. The trouble is that we have a bad habit, encouraged by pedants and sophisticates, of considering happiness as something rather stupid. Only pain is intellectual, only evil interesting. This is the treason of the artist: a refusal to admit the banality of evil and the terrible boredom of pain. If you can't lick 'em, join 'em. If it hurts, repeat it. But to praise despair is to condemn delight, to embrace violence is to lose hold of everything else. We have almost lost hold; we can no longer describe a happy man, nor make any celebration of joy. How can I tell you about the people of Omelas? They were not naïve and happy children—though their children were, in fact, happy. They were mature, intelligent, passionate adults whose lives were not wretched. O miracle! but I wish I could describe it better. I wish I could convince you. Omelas sounds in my words like a city in a fairy tale, long ago and far away, once upon a time. Perhaps it would be best if you imagined it as your own fancy bids, assuming it will rise to the occasion, for certainly I cannot suit you all. For instance, how about technology? I think that there would be no cars or helicopters in and above the streets; this follows from the fact that the people of Omelas are happy people. Happiness is based on a just discrimination of what is necessary, what is neither necessary nor destructive, and what is destructive. In the middle category, however— that of the unnecessary but undestructive, that of comfort, luxury, exuberance, etc.—they could perfectly well have central heating, subway trains, washing machines, and all kinds of marvelous devices not yet invented here, floating light-sources, fuelless power, a cure for the common cold. Or they could have none of that; it doesn't matter. As you like it. I incline to think that people from towns up and down the coast have been coming to Omelas during the last days before the Festival on very fast little trains and double-decked trams, and that the train station of Omelas is actually the handsomest building in town, though plainer than the magnificent Farmers' Market. But even granted trains, I fear that Omelas so far strikes some of you as goody-goody. Smiles, bells, parades, horses, bleh. If so, please add an orgy. If an orgy would help, don't hesitate. Let us not, however, have temples from which issue beautiful nude priests and priestesses already half in ecstasy and ready to copulate with any man or woman, lover or stranger, who desires union with the deep godhead of the blood, although that was my first idea. But really it would be better not to have any temples in Omelas—at least, not manned temples. Religion yes, clergy no. Surely the beautiful nudes can just wander about, offering themselves like divine soufflés to the hunger of the needy and the rapture of the flesh. Let them join the processions. Let tambourines be struck above the copulations, and the glory of desire be proclaimed upon the gongs, and (a not unimportant point) let the offspring of these delightful rituals be beloved and looked after by all. One thing I know there is none of in Omelas is guilt. But what else should there be? I thought at first there were no drugs, but that is puritanical. For those who like it, the faint insistent sweetness of *drooz* may perfume the ways of the city, *drooz* which first brings a great lightness and brilliance to the mind and limbs, and then after some hours a dreamy languor, and wonderful visions at last of the very arcana and inmost secrets of the Universe, as well as exciting the pleasure of sex beyond belief; and it is not habit-forming. For more modest tastes I think there ought to be beer. What else, what else belongs in the joyous city? The sense of victory, surely, the celebration of courage. But as we did without clergy, let us do without soldiers. The joy built upon successful slaughter is not the right kind of joy; it will not do; it is fearful and it is trivial. A boundless and generous contentment, a magnanimous triumph felt not against some outer enemy but in communion with the finest and fairest in the souls of all men everywhere and the splendor of the world's summer: this is what swells the hearts of the people of Omelas, and the victory they celebrate is that of life. I really don't think many of them need to take *drooz*.

Most of the processions have reached the Green Fields by now. A marvelous smell of cooking goes forth from the red and blue tents of the provisioners. The faces of small children are amiably sticky; in the benign gray beard of a man a couple of crumbs of rich pastry are entangled. The youths and girls have mounted their horses and are beginning to group around the starting line of the course. An old woman, small, fat, and laughing, is passing out flowers from a basket, and tall young men wear her flowers in their shining hair. A child of nine or ten sits at the edge of the crowd, alone, playing on a wooden flute. People pause to listen, and they smile, but they do not speak to him, for he never ceases playing and never sees them, his dark eyes wholly rapt in the sweet, thin magic of the tune.

He finishes, and slowly lowers his hands holding the wooden flute.

As if that little private silence were the signal, all at once a trumpet sounds from the pavilion near the starting line: imperious, melancholy, piercing. The horses rear on their slender legs, and some of them neigh in answer. Sober-faced, the young riders stroke the horses' necks and soothe them, whispering, "Quiet, quiet, there my beauty, my hope . . . ." They begin to form in rank along the starting line. The crowds along the race-course are like a field of grass and flowers in the wind. The Festival of Summer has begun.

Do you believe? Do you accept the festival, the city, the joy? No? Then let me describe one more thing.

In a basement under one of the beautiful public buildings of Omelas, or perhaps in the cellar of one of its spacious private homes, there is a room. It has one locked door, and no window. A little light seeps in dustily between cracks in the boards, secondhand from a cobwebbed window somewhere across the cellar. In one corner of the little room a couple of mops, with stiff, clotted, foul-smelling heads, stand near a rusty bucket. The floor is dirt, a little damp to the touch, as cellar dirt usually is. The room is about three paces long and two wide: a mere broom closet or dis-used tool room. In the room a child is sitting. It could be a boy or a girl. It looks about six, but actually is nearly ten. It is feeble-minded. Perhaps it was born defective, or perhaps it has become imbecile through fear, malnutrition, and neglect. It picks its nose and occasionally fumbles vaguely with its toes or genitals, as it sits hunched in the corner farthest from the bucket and the two mops. It is afraid of the mops. It find them horrible. It shuts its eyes, but it knows the mops are still standing there; and the door is locked; and nobody will come. The door is always locked; and nobody ever comes, except that sometimes—the child has no under-standing of time or interval—sometimes the door rattles terribly and opens, and a person, or several people, are there. One of them may come in and kick the child to make it stand up. The others never come close, but peer in at it with frightened, disgusted eyes. The food bowl and the water jug are hastily filled, the door is locked, the eyes disappear. The people at the door never say anything, but the child, who has not always lived in the tool room, and can remember sunlight and its mother's voice, sometimes speaks. "I will be good," it says. "Please let me out. I will be good!" They never answer. The child used to scream for help at night, and cry a good deal, but now it only makes a kind of whining "eh-haa, eh-haa" and it speaks less and less often. It is so thin there are no calves to its legs; its belly protrudes; it lives on a half-bowl of corn meal and grease a day. It is naked. Its buttocks and thighs are a mass of festered sores, as it sits in its own excrement continually.

They all know it is there, all the people of Omelas. Some of them have come to see it, others are content merely to know it is there. They all know that it has to be there. Some of them understand why, and some do not, but they all understand that their happiness, the beauty of their city, the tenderness of their friendships, the health of their children, the wisdom of their scholars, the skill of their makers, even the abundance of their harvest and the kindly weathers of their skies, depend wholly on this child's abominable misery.

This is usually explained to children when they are between eight and twelve, whenever they seem capable of understanding; and most of those who come to see the child are young people, though often enough an adult comes, or comes back, to see the child. No matter how well the matter has been explained to them, these young spectators are always shocked and sickened at the sight. They feel disgust, which they had thought themselves superior to. They feel anger, outrage, impotence, despite all the explanations. They would like to do something for the child. But there is nothing they can do. If the child were brought up into the sunlight out of that vile place, if it were cleaned and fed and comforted, that would be a good thing, indeed; but if it were done, in that day and hour all the prosperity and beauty and delight of Omelas would wither and be destroyed. Those are the terms. To exchange all the goodness and grace of every life in Omelas for that single, small improvement: to throw away the happiness of thousands for the chance of the happiness of one: that would be to let guilt within the walls indeed.

The terms are strict and absolute; there may not even be a kind word spoken to the child.

Often the young people go home in tears, or in a tearless rage, when they have seen the child and faced this terrible paradox. They may brood over it for weeks or years. But as time goes on they begin to realize that even if the child could be released, it would not get much good of its freedom: a little vague pleasure of warmth and food, no doubt, but little more. It is too degraded and imbecile to know any real joy. It has been afraid too long ever to be free of fear. Its habits are too uncouth for it to respond to humane treatment. Indeed, after so long it would probably be wretched without walls about it to protect it, and darkness for its eyes, and its own excrement to sit in. Their tears at the bitter injustice dry when they begin to perceive the terrible justice of reality, and to accept it. Yet it is their tears and anger, the trying of their generosity and the acceptance of their helplessness, which are perhaps the true source of the splendor of their lives. Theirs is no vapid, irresponsible happiness. They know that they, like the child, are not free. They know compassion. It is the existence of the child, and their knowledge of its existence, that makes possible the nobility of their architecture, the poignancy of their music, the profundity of their science. It is because of the child that they are so gentle with children. They know that if the wretched one were not there snivelling in the dark, the other one, the flute-player, could make no joyful music as the young riders line up in their beauty for the race in the sunlight of the first morning of summer.

Now do you believe in them? Are they not more credible? But there is one more thing to tell, and this is quite incredible.

At times one of the adolescent girls or boys who go to see the child does not go home to weep or rage, does not, in fact, go home at all. Sometimes also a man or woman much older falls silent for a day or two, and then leaves home. These people go out into the street, and walk down the street alone. They keep walking, and walk straight out of the city of Omelas, through the beautiful gates. They keep walking across the farmlands of Omelas. Each one goes alone, youth or girl, man or woman. Night falls; the traveler must pass down village streets, between the houses with yellow-lit windows, and on out into the darkness of the fields. Each alone, they go west or north, towards the mountains. They go on. They leave Omelas, they walk ahead into the darkness, and they do not come back. The place they go towards is a place even less imaginable to most of us than the city of happiness. I cannot describe it at all. It is possible that it does not exist. But they seem to know where they are going, the ones who walk away from Omelas.

Eyes Open on a World was written as part of the 150th anniversary of the arrival of the Sisters of St. Joseph in St. Paul. In it, the sisters reflect on the many changes that have taken place in the world over the past several decades and, hence, in their very own community. As you absorb this final reading, ponder how the CSJs have embodied the College's mission of seeking social justice and evoking hope for all. Has this effort influenced your education? Have you been inspired to continue to carry out this mission?

Eyes Open on a World:
Responding to Societal Needs

A Collaboration by the Sisters of St. Joseph of Carondelet
St. Paul Province

The story of Sister Rita Steinhagen reflects the evolution of many sisters from institutionally based ministries to direct social services and then to social justice issues and political action. As Sister Rita explains, "One thing led to another." After illness demanded she leave her work as a medical technologist, Sister Rita opened a Free Store on the West Bank in Minneapolis, a place where people could "shop" for what they needed. She became acquainted with many people, including runaway youth who spent their days and nights on the streets. One day a youth asked her, "Why don't you get us a place to stay?" So Sister Rita founded the Bridge, a shelter for runaway youth, not far from the Free Store.

"I was learning about the oppressive and unjust systems—what it is like to be poor with a constant struggle just to survive," recalls Sister Rita. Because many of the people she met spoke Spanish, "I decided it was time to learn that language. So I went to a small language school in El Paso, Texas, and worked at a nearby shelter for refugees. It was there that I first learned about the School of the Americas." After hearing the refugees' stories, Sister Rita went to Central America as a Witness for Peace and lived in the war zones in northern Nicaragua.

When she returned home, Sister Rita worked for seven years at the Center for Victims of Torture. Haunted by her experience of seeing the results of torture and by her knowledge of U.S. complicity in training Latin American soldiers in methods of torture, she went to Fort Benning, Georgia, to participate in demonstrations opposing the School of the Americas. Because she "crossed the line a second time," a judge sentenced her to six months in federal prison, where "I got a crash course in our prison system and the unfairness of it all." Now, besides continuing to work to close the School of the Americas, she is involved with changing prison policies that are especially harsh on women with children.

Like Sister Rita, many sisters have become active in social justice movements. With the growing understanding in the 1960s that our religious vow of obedience meant much more than listening to the directives of our superiors and included being open to the Spirit by listening to the people and events of our times, we felt called to confront injustices wherever we saw them.

Like our first sisters in France we continue to give direct service to those in need and work for systemic change. Sister Florence Steichen uses the phrase "walking on the two feet of justice," a metaphor developed in the 1970s to describe this dual task. Our stories from the past fifty years show how leadership has emerged whenever sisters have seen needs and responded to them.

Sisters, of course, have been responding to needs all along. Sister Lillian Meyer went to political caucuses in the early 1950s, subscribed to the *Congressional Record*, and vigorously contributed her knowledge and opinions in Saturday classes on current affairs she took at the College of St. Catherine. In the 1940s and 1950s Sister Julienne Foley taught Mexican children and adults. Downtown St. Paul merchants and cab drivers recognized her resolute gait as she fearlessly approached them for food and clothing for "her people" or asked for free rides. Throughout the years sisters visited students and families in their homes and provided clothing and other necessities. They also visited those who were poor and elderly at the Ramsey County "poor farm," in hospitals, and in prisons, as our earliest members had done.

Some of our sisters worked at the Catholic Infant Home, a residence program for pregnant girls. The sisters provided child care and personal and spiritual enrichment classes for the girls, while other organizations provided health care services. As attitudes toward single pregnant women changed, so did the program. This ministry, now called Seton Center, is no longer a residence and offers a variety of services for single parents and married couples.

As social issues and reform movements surfaced in the 1960s, our community experienced transition from total separation to deep involvement in world affairs and ambivalence over our sisters being involved in public issues. By the end of the decade, however, we had a clear affirmation from our congregational leaders and from one another that social activism is part of our call. We welcomed the pastoral letter *Justice in the World*, issued by the U.S. bishops in 1971. One statement reinforced our conviction that working for justice is not an optional pursuit but is integral to the gospel:

"Action on behalf of justice and participation in the transformation of the world appear to us as a constitutive dimension of the preaching of the gospel, or, in other words, of the church's mission for the redemption of the human race and its liberation from every oppressive situation." We celebrated this liberating statement as a landmark.

Sisters participated in political caucuses and demonstrations, including vigils for slain civil rights workers and protests against the Vietnam War and the Gulf War. Some also protested Honeywell's production of cluster bombs. Sisters Char Madigan and Rita Foster were among the early organizers of nonviolent protests there. In the early 1990s when Honeywell moved its weapons making to Alliant Technical Systems in Hopkins, the protesters moved there, too. Several sisters took part in antiwar demonstrations protesting the U.S. bombing of Iraq, the sanctions on Iraq, and intervention in Yugoslavia.

Societal conditions and movements provided impetus for political action. Some sisters became active in the Civil Rights movement, which in the beginning was primarily concerned with voting rights of African Americans. The notion of civil rights soon expanded to include the right to be born, to be housed adequately, and to be employed. Civil rights further evolved to encompass Native Americans and other ethnic minorities, sexual minorities, and women.

The *Roe v. Wade* Supreme Court decision in 1973 legalizing abortion in every state brought our deep convictions about the sacredness of life to the forefront. As a community we support all efforts to reverence and enhance the life of each person from beginning to end. Some of us are active in the prolife movement. Others focus their energy on abolishing the death penalty. After Sister Helen Prejean, a Sister of St. Joseph from the Medaille congregation and a well-known author and advocate for abolishing the death penalty, spoke at a gathering of the Federation of Sisters of St. Joseph in St. Louis in 2000, the 1,550 sisters present released a public statement on their stand against capital punishment. Also in the summer of 2000 Sister Mary Mark Mahoney, retired for many years, and Sister Carol Neuburger testified at a court appeal in Oklahoma and tried, unsuccessfully, to commute the death sentence of a prisoner with whom Sister Mary Mark had been corresponding for three years. She continues her special ministry by corresponding with other prison "pen pals."

As we moved from convents and from institutions into neighborhoods, many of us became more involved in public issues. When some of us moved from the College of St. Catherine into neighborhood housing in 1968, the college's student publication, *The Catherine Wheel* (May 10, 1968, p. 8) described the experience as not a departure from traditional religious living but rather as an opportunity to open up new possibilities of religious life in the spirit of renewal.

Moving into different living situations brought us into new ministries and political involvement. In the mid-1970s, Sisters Jean Campbell and Jackie Slater moved into the Cedar-Riverside housing project in Minneapolis, a multiracial, multi-economic, integrated community. Sister Jackie's work there led her to run for the city council. She reported: "A few of the older and more traditional Catholics were upset about my candidacy for office. They were concerned that a nun would have a hard time in the nasty world of politics, or they were clinging to the notion that sisters should be either teachers or nurses. But there were also many who were very much in favor of it and they gave me their support and votes" (*Minneapolis Star Tribune*, December 24, 1977). Jackie won the election and became an influential as well as controversial council member. After her sudden death in 1984, the city of Minneapolis honored her by naming a renovated block of housing near downtown Minneapolis Slater Square.

Sister Jackie was not the first sister from the St. Paul Province to seek public office. Running on a prolife platform, Sister Elizabeth Regnier narrowly missed being elected to the North Dakota state legislature in 1972. Two years earlier in Jamestown, North Dakota, Sister Rose Alma Woychik lost the election to a ward precinct post by two votes.

While some sisters sought to influence public policy through elected office, Sister Mary Madonna Ashton received a state appointment from Minnesota Governor Rudy Perpich. During her tenure as Commissioner of Health from 1983 to 1991, Minnesota led the nation in addressing major health concerns by implementing tobacco control programs and HIV/AIDS prevention measures.

A number of us received our political initiation when Senator Eugene McCarthy from Minnesota sought the Democratic nomination for president in 1968. At the precinct caucus so many sisters showed up that we overwhelmed the proceedings. Some of us remember how upset the politician who chaired the meeting was when he saw all of us. Suspicious of the sisters' unaccustomed activism, he told us in no uncertain terms that he expected us to continue to come to the subsequent caucuses, and we did.

Some of us believed that protesting was part of our mission. In addition to her political involvement, Sister Rose Alma Woychik protested at missile bases in Jamestown, North Dakota, beginning in the mid-1960s. In a 1975 letter to Sister Frances Babb, she expressed the pivotal shift from suspicion of the world and withdrawal from it to wholehearted engagement with the world, which came to characterize the thinking of many sisters in the remaining decades of the twentieth century. She wrote: "I am not willing to admit that being interested in politics necessarily means that I am less interested in the love of God and my neighbor, or the spread of the gospel."

While some sisters protested against the Vietnam War and others demon-strated against legalized abortion, still others lobbied for fair housing, jobs, health care, education, and welfare legislation. Seeing government cuts in human services and increases in military spending, we insisted that enormous expenditures for weapons to protect the national security were creating havoc in our cities. As Sister Rita Steinhagen keeps saying, "One thing led to another." We did social analysis, asking who benefits and who suffers. We learned from our sisters in Peru that multinational success and security for developed countries meant tragic insecurity to the majority in developing countries.

When Sister Char Madigan began working in a downtown parish in the 1970s, she realized she was saying good night to people at 5:00 P.M. know-ing they had no home to go to. Sisters Rita Steinhagen, Laura Geyer, and Char Madigan began offering shelter in their upper flat convent. That even-tually led to the opening of St. Joseph's House, Ascension Place, and Incar-nation House, all in Minneapolis, which were transitional housing shelters designed to empower women to live healthy, independent lives. In Novem-ber 2000, Incarnation House began a new phase of service to women and children as it held an open house to celebrate its partnership with Wayside, a Minneapolis-based program designed to help women achieve their full potential and become productive members of the community.

Experience in these newly established shelters and runaway centers led Sister Marguerite Corcoran and three of the McDonald sisters, Rita, Brigid, and Jane, to question what was going on in the broader world community. A fourth McDonald sister, Kate, who along with others taught English to refugees and immigrants, had the same question. Her sister, Sister Brigid, while working at Incarnation House, connected us with Women Against Military Madness (WAMM) to pressure legislative bodies to direct gov-ernment funds to welfare rights instead of to military spending. A grow-ing interest in liberation theology, which focuses on the struggles of those who are poor and encourages religious people to champion nonviolent resistance, motivated many sisters to support WAMM's work.

Sisters have joined in solidarity with our Native American sisters and brothers seeking to preserve their cultural beliefs. At the invitation of Ojibwe elder woman Bea Swanson, Sister Jane McDonald helps staff an intergenerational and interracial prayer lodge at All Nations Church in Minneapolis. That experience led her to stand in solidarity with Native American struggles against land pollution—for example, the pollution of Prairie Island Indian land with the storing of nuclear waste. In the late 1990s Sisters Jane McDonald, Jan Dalsin, and Mary O'Brien and others joined the Native American protest against a highway reroute that sacri-ficed sacred sites, including trees and spring-fed waters, for the sake of a highway expansion. Other sisters helped Native Americans adjust to urban life by providing basic necessities and connecting them with social service agencies.

For twenty years our sisters have worked with the Resource Center of the Americas and other Sanctuary movements, both for indigenous peoples in other lands and with refugees fleeing those lands. While serving as director of a sanctuary house in Waco, Texas, Sister Marie Richard King worked to provide temporary safe haven for undocumented persons from Mexico. Sisters have been arrested, and some imprisoned, for such "illegal" activities as supporting the César Chavez United Farm Workers grape boycott in 1968, standing with Salvadoran refugees who sought sanctuary in the Cathedral of St. Paul, and demonstrating against the manufacture of nuclear weapons. After more than twenty years of involvement in human rights issues, Sister Betty McKenzie connected sisters to the St. Paul Ecumenical Alliance of Churches (SPEAC), an ecumenical effort to work locally for housing, fair wages, and environmental issues.

The plight of persons who are homeless continues to be of deep concern to us. In one instance, both serendipity and providence played a part in the opening of an overnight shelter. Sister Dolore Rochon, an administrator at St. Joseph's Hospital in downtown St. Paul, was having coffee with Sister Rita Steinhagen one blizzardy December day in 1981. Sister Rita, then working at the nearby Dorothy Day Center, expressed concern that so many homeless people were sleeping in downtown doorways and in caves near the river. Sister Dolore, aware there was an empty floor in Mary Hall, the nurses' residence at the hospital, persuaded hospital and province leaders to convert this space into overnight housing for homeless persons. A week later, on New Year's Eve, with a wind chill of seventy degrees below zero, the doors of Mary Hall opened. Sisters volunteered to spend nights with the guests until Catholic Charities assumed responsibility for the residence.

Another dream became reality when Sister Rose Tillemans established Peace House, a space where people gather during the day for sharing and prayer. To her, Peace House is "one answer to the seldom looked-at question of what do the poor and disadvantaged do after they have some food, clothing, and shelter." She set up a storefront in 1985 on Franklin Avenue in Minneapolis, and since then people have come each day for coffee, food, and meditation. Together, they form community in a safe atmosphere built on acceptance, a sense of belonging, friendship, dignity, and mutuality of service.

Our commitment to supporting people who experience poverty, abuse, torture, mental illness, or discrimination remains strong. In Minneapolis, sisters are involved in INSTEP, a child care program that helps low-income parents pursue work and/or educational opportunities to become more self-sufficient. When the Derham Convent building in St. Paul became available in the 1990s, the province opened Sarah's Oasis, a temporary home for women, including refugees, some of whom come from the Center for the Victims of Torture in Minneapolis. At Sarah's women live in a safe environment that fosters relationships, reflection, and self-empowerment.

As a psychologist, Sister Karen Hilgers worked with many adult women who had survived abuse. She dreamed of a peaceful residence—not a hospital—where women in crisis could spend a few days with a supportive staff to regain their equilibrium. In collaboration with a small group of other psychologists Sister Karen developed this new approach to treatment. In 1996, Cornelia Place opened its doors in Minneapolis, providing the care and support the women needed. Although the model Sister Karen and her colleagues created proved to be a successful crisis management model, the residential portion of the program closed because of lack of funding. Cornelia Place now operates as a mental health clinic specializing in the treatment of women with posttraumatic stress disorder.

Through our experiences in pastoral and social ministries, we realized that unjust economic systems are significant factors leading to the oppression of people. This insight led Sister Mary Ellen Foster to complete a master's degree at the New School for Social Research in New York City, a school that critiques economic systems with an eye towards social transformation. Following her studies, Sister Mary Ellen began to teach classes in economics stressing the impact of economic systems on the world and urging her students to engage in activities that lead to systemic change.

Clearly, our concerns for social justice extend beyond the U.S. boundaries. Recognizing needs around the globe, sisters have responded in various ways. While Sister Florence Steichen served as registrar at Bethlehem University in the occupied West Bank, the Israeli military governor closed the university for three years because of the *Intifada*, the struggle of Palestinian young people to gain independence. Sister Florence played a major role in arranging for off-campus classes to help Palestinian students continue their education. She and other sisters who taught at Bethlehem University returned home with a commitment to further Palestinian rights by speaking, writing, contacting legislators, and seeking funds for Bethlehem University from our Partners in Justice fund. Continuing her advocacy for peace in the Middle East, Sister Florence works with Minnesota Middle East Peace Now and the Middle East Committee of Women Against Military Madness.

Representing our province at the United Nations Fourth World Conference on Women in Beijing in 1995, Sister Susan Oeffling learned firsthand about the status and plight of women throughout the world. While she was in Beijing, at the invitation of Minnesota Public Radio, Sister Susan called in regularly to report on the conference and answer listeners' questions. Upon returning home, she gave numerous talks on her Beijing experience to parish, school, corporate, and religious groups and published an article entitled "Keep on Keeping On" in *Sisters Today*. She joined the nonviolence working group of the Justice Commission, which then changed its name to Beyond Beijing: Women and Violence to focus on implementation of the Beijing platform.

As we struggled to "walk on the two feet of justice" in these last fifty years, we realized that we needed education and support in our efforts. As coordinator of the Social Justice Secretariat from 1979 to 1982, Sister Kathy Roehl kept us informed about justice issues and actions we could take to address the issues. We then established the Social Justice Task Force in 1982, which evolved into the Justice Commission in 1984. Sister Carol Neuburger, the first chair of the commission, brought energy and initiative to the work of justice. With her guidance, the province developed a process for sisters in the province to take a "corporate stand," that is, to make a public statement in the name of the Sisters of St. Joseph of the St. Paul Province. The process ensured that a corporate stand would represent the will of a majority of sisters, not a small group within the province. We took our first corporate stand in 1986 as a strong symbolic action for peace: "To declare as nuclear-free zones properties owned by the Sisters of St. Joseph in the St. Paul Province."

The province hired Joänne Tromiczak-Neid, a former Sister of St. Joseph, in 1992 as the full-time justice coordinator to help us address issues of social justice discussed at the congregational chapter and written in our Acts of Chapter. In addition to networking with local and national justice groups, Joanne was instrumental in starting Women Religious for Justice, a collaborative effort of area religious communities. Among the founders of www.Sistersonline.org, a collaborative venture begun in 1996 with other communities of women religious in Minnesota, Joänne sees the website as facilitating outreach "to women and children who suffer from the multiple manifestations of injustice" (*Together*, November 1999, p. 13). As part of a global movement of women who care deeply about what is happening with the world, the earth, and its people, Sistersonline's 1999–2000 focus included debt relief and women in prison.

The role of women in the church is the concern of many of us. Sister Frances Babb, throughout her long life, was an ardent feminist. At the age of six in 1912, she handed out women's suffrage pamphlets with her mother. From the age of sixteen, she was certain that she had a vocation to the ordained priesthood, and throughout her life she was a persuasive spokeswoman for the ordination of women. In 1975 she spoke eloquently and painfully, with her commanding voice and strong Maine accent, of her desire to be a priest when she presented a petition to the official board for the Permanent Diaconate asking that the St. Paul and Minneapolis Archdiocese permit women to enter the Permanent Diaconate Training program. No action was taken on her petition.

Our first public efforts on behalf of gay, lesbian, bisexual, and transgendered (GLBT) persons were undertaken by Sister Sarah O'Neill, who dedicated much of her time and energy to seeking reconciliation and support between the Catholic Church and Catholic gays and lesbians. She worked tirelessly to assist with the founding of the Catholic Pastoral Committee on Sexual Minorities (CPCSM). In the years since Sister Sarah's death, some sisters have participated in demonstrations against repression of GLBT persons and sought to help families/friends both understand the church's position on GLBT persons and respect the individual's conscience. In June of 1999, twenty-two sisters and consociates marched in the Twin Cities Gay Pride Parade. They carried a large banner stating, "Sisters of St. Joseph of Carondelet, St. Paul, MN, Justice Commission, Standing for Human Rights and Justice." It was the first time we had walked in the parade so publicly.

As we look to the future, we recognize that the need to "walk on the two feet of justice" at times exceeds our ability to be involved personally and directly. In recent years we have found additional ways to support our quest for justice. After we sold St. John's Hospital in Fargo, North Dakota, we established the Giving Board in 1987, which allowed sisters to request grants for persons with immediate needs such as child care and living expenses. The sale of St. Mary's Hospital in Minneapolis presented us with a unique opportunity and challenged us to use the money generated to fulfill our mission. We developed a focus statement to guide our vision: "We, the community of the Sisters of St. Joseph [of the St. Paul Province], in keeping with our commitment to the gospel, choose, in dialogue with one another to use our spiritual, material, and personal resources in collaborative efforts to support those in need."

An Allocations Task Force recommended that the funding of ministries be spread across a range of categories representing a continuum of risk, from sponsored institutions and affiliated ministries to new, ongoing, or collaborative projects and individual radical responses to the gospel. As a result of the work of the task force, we established the Partners in Justice fund, which supports ministries that respond uniquely to unmet needs of the economically oppressed and to ministries that further our historical commitment to women and children.

Another vehicle for funding our ministries, the Partners in Ministry fund of our Ministries Foundation, "seeks to make a difference in the lives of those in need by generating and allocating funds to support present and future ministries of the Sisters of St. Joseph of Carondelet" (Ministries Foundation mission statement, 1995). Foundation board members, both sisters and laypeople, dedicate their time and efforts to ensuring that our mission and ministries continue into the future.

As we look back on the last fifty years we see how we have divided the city and sought to be attentive to the needs of our neighbors. Although, at times, tensions existed among us and we do not always agree on how to address the needs, we have grown in respect for one another as we realized that there are many ways to do the works of justice. Our Congregation of the Sisters of St. Joseph of Carondelet "encourages each sister [and consociate] to witness in areas of concern according to the dictates of an informed conscience and supports the rights of members to take a public stand on matters of justice" (Complementary Document 1984, p. 12). As needs continue to manifest themselves, we are confident that, like our foremothers, our sisters, consociates, and partners in ministry will divide the city and stand with the dear neighbor.

Resources

College of St. Catherine
Mission, Leadership, and Roman
Catholic Identity Statements

Mission Statement

The College of St. Catherine educates women to lead and influence. Founded by the Sisters of St. Joseph of Carondelet in 1905, the College integrates liberal arts and professional education within the Catholic traditions of intellectual inquiry and social teaching. Committed to excellence and opportunity, the College engages students from diverse backgrounds in a learning environment uniquely suited to women. Education at the College of St. Catherine prepares graduates to demonstrate ethical leadership grounded in social responsibility.

Leadership Statement

The College of St. Catherine is committed to the development of effective, ethical leaders. Through study, practice, and life experience, individuals have opportunities to enrich the knowledge, refine the skills, and clarify the attitudes essential for responsible action. In varied roles and settings, the College of St. Catherine leader:

- lives a commitment to the values of justice and caring;
- acts from a strong self-concept;
- thinks critically and creatively;
- communicates and interacts effectively within groups;
- takes risks willingly;
- exercises power appropriately;
- articulates a positive sense of direction; and
- evokes hope.

The Roman Catholic Identity Statement

Throughout the history of the College of St. Catherine, founded by the Sisters of St. Joseph of Carondelet, we have been dedicated as a campus community to our Roman Catholic heritage and identity. In light of the rich and diverse history of the Church and the vision of Vatican II, we affirm aspects of that identity that are particularly appropriate to higher education. From the Church's intellectual tradition, which has equated the search for truth with true liberation, we value an open atmosphere of critical inquiry, cross-cultural studies, and interdisciplinary teaching. From its social tradition, with its consistent commitment to the poor and outcast, we value and reach out to those marginalized by our society and churches, and in particular, we seek to promote women's leadership.

From its sacramental tradition, which has emphasized ritual, symbol, and the use of material things as signs of grace, we value the integration of the material and spiritual, and the use of creative rituals for prayer and celebration. From the tradition that has stressed both communal participation and the worth of the individual, we value dialogue, respect for diversity, and the nurturing of personal conscience. From the call of Jesus himself, that all should be one (John 17:21), we value ecumenism and collaboration among all faiths.

Drawing on those traditions, we seek to promote, through our student services, campus ministry, administration, faculty, and staff, a common search for wisdom and the integration of our daily lives and work with our spirituality. Without being exclusive of other ecclesial and spiritual traditions, we will continue to ask ourselves how this Catholic heritage enhances the people we serve and the well-being of our planet.

Goals of a Liberal Arts Education
at the College of St. Catherine

The College of St. Catherine has identified seven themes of a St. Catherine's education encompassing the knowledge, skills, and attitudes that it seeks to develop in its graduates. Based on our commitment to women, the liberal arts, and the Catholic traditions of intellectual inquiry and social teaching, an education at the College of St. Catherine emphasizes:

Leadership and Collaboration

The ability to lead and influence for ethical and responsible action and for systemic change; the ability to work well with others, especially in joint intellectual effort.

Students will demonstrate leadership and collaboration by their ability to:

a) act from a strong self-concept;

b) transform information into knowledge and knowledge into judgment and action;

c) make timely and relevant decisions based on sound reasoning;

d) discern consequences, including ethical consequences, of decisions and actions;

e) articulate a positive sense of direction and evoke hope;

f) work well in teams and work groups of diverse composition, building consensus and integrating conflict resolution strategies.

Ethics and Social Justice

The ability to apply ethical standards to judge individual and collective actions; the development of attitudes and behaviors that reflect integrity, honesty, compassion, and justice in one's personal and professional life.

Students will demonstrate a commitment to ethics and social justice by their ability to:

a) understand principles of ethics and social justice from multiple perspectives;

b) understand Catholic Social Teaching and the Catholic commitment to social justice;

c) apply ethical and justice frameworks to contemporary issues;

d) exhibit personal and academic integrity;

e) practice social responsibility through community engagement, citizenship, and advocacy.

Diversity and Global Perspectives

The ability to understand and analyze the impact of diversity and systems of power and privilege on the individual and society; the ability to decipher and honor multiple and global perspectives in creating mutual understanding; the ability to imagine and take action toward justice.

Students will demonstrate a commitment to diversity and global perspectives by their ability to

a) understand the experiences and contributions of women across history and cultures;

b) recognize the historic and current relationships within and among cultural communities, locally, nationally, and globally;

c) identify and critically analyze the impact of race/ethnicity, gender, social class, religion, sexual orientation, age, ability, and other differences on identity, experience, and systems of power and privilege;

d) understand how economic, social, religious, and political systems interact and how those systems vary across societies;

e) understand the interrelationships between nature and humans and develop eco-centric perspectives;

f) increase critical cultural competencies and responsiveness through engaging with multiple communities;

g) take action to dismantle systems of oppression and build a more just world.

Critical and Creative Inquiry

The ability to gather, analyze, and critically evaluate information to develop reasonable arguments, sound judgments, and effective solutions. This ability is founded on a broad knowledge of the achievements of human creativity and of the variety of disciplinary approaches for exploring truths.

Students will demonstrate critical and creative inquiry by their ability to:

a) locate appropriate information from a variety of sources and evaluate its relevance and reliability;

b) organize, describe, interpret, and integrate both qualitative and quantitative information;

c) shape ideas and discern meaning from experience, observation, imagination, and passion;

d) analyze complex issues and arguments in various intellectual contexts (scientific, aesthetic, philosophical, etc.) and evaluate the validity and soundness of such arguments;

e) develop and evaluate action plans for solving significant social and intellectual problems;

f) demonstrate breadth of knowledge of the major accomplishments of human endeavors and of the distinct methods of exploring truths (in the natural sciences, social sciences, and the arts and humanities);*

g) identify and interpret similarities and differences among various disciplinary approaches and examine the relationships among them.

Breadth of knowledge applies to all degrees except the graduate degrees, where the focus is on in-depth development of disciplinary skills.

Discipline-Based Competence**

The ability to demonstrate in-depth knowledge, values, and skills in at least one major field of study and to relate disciplinary approaches to those of other fields.

Students will demonstrate discipline-based competence by their ability to:

a) use in-depth knowledge and engage key ideas in at least one field of study;

b) exercise disciplinary methods and skills, and carry out research or learn independently in that field;

c) develop disciplinary perspective and identity, including an understanding of the route to acquiring knowledge in that discipline;

d) identify and analyze similarities and differences between the student's major field and other disciplinary approaches.

***Discipline-Based Competence applies to all degree programs except the Associate of Arts Degree Program*

Effective Communication in a Variety of Modes

The ability to read, write, speak, view, and listen effectively; the ability to present information in a clear and engaging manner.

Students will demonstrate effective communication by the ability to:

a) read, view, and listen with understanding and critical discernment;

b) organize, evaluate, and communicate ideas effectively through writing and public speaking to various audiences;

c) prepare and present information visually and through the use of technology;

d) find expression in fine, literary, and performing arts;

e) develop and put into practice interpersonal, group, and cross-cultural communication skills and listening skills;

f) show competency in a second language (applies only to bachelor's degree).

Purposeful Life-long Learning

The ability to continue personal and professional development based on ongoing self-assessment, feedback from others, and new learning.

Students will demonstrate a commitment to purposeful life-long learning by:

a) assuming responsibility for their own learning;

b) engaging in and reflecting on opportunities that prepare for life after college;

c) practicing a variety of methods of learning, including reading and research, observing and listening, self assessment and feedback, work and life experience;

d) developing knowledge and strategies for maintaining a balance of body, mind, and spirit;

e) reflecting on and developing a meaningful, purposeful, and spiritual life.

The coauthors of this article have both worked extensively at the College of St. Catherine to design The Reflective Woman course and first year advising program. Suzanne Hendricks is a professor of Family, Consumer, and Nutrition Sciences and former Director of the Core Curriculum. Ellen Richter-Norgel is Director of Retention.

The Catherine Connection:
A Tool for Engagement and Commitment

Suzanne Hendricks and Ellen Richter-Norgel

> When I first came to St. Kate's, all I cared about was getting my degree. I just wanted to get in and get out. Just do my schoolwork, and that was it. But, now I feel differently. As the year has gone by, I've invested into issues and relationships; I've encouraged and tutored younger students. I have grown to care about bearing good fruit at St. Kate's. I have grown to feel like I want to give everything I can to this College community and get all that I am suppose to out of being here at this school.
>
> Kathleen Woodbury, TRW, 2000

As you begin your college education, we are well aware of the many opportunities that await you. No doubt, having to make choices about your educational options seems a bit daunting. We join you in your anticipation and we are eager to provide you with some guidance about embarking on this journey. This journey, which you will design with your academic advisor, will involve traveling beyond the classroom to what is commonly referred to as the co-curriculum. The co-curriculum includes the diverse offering of programs and services that support your learning as well as contributes to your development as a whole person. These programs and services, such as social justice trips, service learning activities, and internships, can strongly affect your development. These experiences will open your eyes to a different worldview. Through your work both inside and outside the classroom, you will build skills related to your professional and personal development.

> The most valuable piece (of information) to me was the Catherine Connection folder everyone received from their advisors. It made me realize all the connections. . . .
>
> Shannon Murphy, current student

The Catherine Connection serves as a navigational tool to guide you through all the learning experiences available at the College; both you and your advisor have a copy and can access it online at the College Web site. It is designed to highlight significant opportunities and options that are appropriate at particular points in your journey, whether you are a traditional day student, an associate of arts student, a Weekend College student, or a transfer student. While the Catherine Connection may look like a folder, it is much more than that. You will want to carefully examine the pages within, as they contain a wealth of information and identify resources that guide you through your journey here.

Three overall objectives guide the Catherine Connection. (1) It creates a conceptual "map" that helps you think concretely about a sequenced and integrated college experience. (2) It identifies and articulates the best of the curricular and co-curricular opportunities available at the College. (3) It offers implementation strategies for achieving the College of St. Catherine's learning goals. Think of the Catherine Connection as a tool that helps you take charge of your education; it focuses on specific activities that we believe represent prime opportunities for you both within and outside the classroom.

> I like this plan. You can find your place here . . . it gets you involved with your faculty and advisor. It provided me with ideas of what to get involved in and how early I could sign up for activities.
>
> Maya Dalberg, Class of 2003

Gateways

Each of the four years is organized around a theme. "Gateways," the first year theme introduced in the Reflective Woman, encourages you to create connections to classmates and to the CSC community at large. For instance, you read Adrienne Rich's, "Claiming an Education" (1979) along with an excerpt from *More than a Dream: 85 years at the College of St. Catherine* (1992). These readings provide a historical and philosophical context for your education at this college and a sense of the community to which you now belong. The focus of the first year is also to help you develop a "sense of place," and form the foundation to explore interests and examine talents in light of career possibilities. Early in your first year you will have opportunities to attend departmental open houses, explore majors that interest you, and identify clubs or organizations of interest at the annual Activities Fair.

As you meet with your advisor you can discuss resources that will help you get on the right track for success. From the start, you have the opportunity to build your academic skills at the O'Neill Center for Academic Development or the Learning Center on the Minneapolis campus if you are in the Associate of Arts program. If you are unsure about what you want to choose as a major, or just want to explore career options, you might want to enroll in INDI 200, Career Development for Women. Associate of Arts students will want to attend the annual Health Care Career Fair. Additionally, whatever your faith tradition, you will want to discover and cultivate your spirituality through programs offered in Campus Ministry. You can also consider pursuing the Honor's program or explore the requirements for election to Phi Beta Kappa, the national liberal arts honor society.

Pathways

"Pathways" is the theme for the second year, which focuses on identifying strategies that allow you to begin to develop career goals. For traditional day students, you will begin the year by attending the "Sophomore Send-off" program where you will meet your new major advisor. For transfer, Associate of Arts, and Weekend College students, you will want to connect with your advisor early in the fall and talk about your academic plans for the year. You can begin taking courses at higher levels; perhaps explore another discipline that sparks your interest. As you do so, you will want to meet again with your advisor and consider how your interests impact your academic planning. You can register for the Shadow Program and spend a day with an alumna in the field you are considering. If you are still choosing a major, you can meet with a career counselor to explore your interests and how they relate to possible majors, or arrange informational sessions with professors in different disciplines.

Now is a good time to look for ways to build on your leadership skills. Take a leadership role in the classroom in a small group discussion or study group, or in a club or organization, student government or in your campus employment. Consider being an Orientation Leader or joining the Lead Team. You are also encouraged to act on St. Kate's commitment to social justice through service-learning opportunities including America Reads and the Spring Break Outreach trips coordinated by Campus Ministry.

Remember that as a sophomore student, you will also have the opportunity to delve into focused interdisciplinary work by participating in one of several core minors with the added benefit of belonging to a learning community. Make sure you explore with your advisor the necessary prerequisites for enrolling in these core minors.

Avenues

The third year theme, "Avenues," stresses making solid connections with an academic major. This includes tasks such as investigating and completing an internship, conducting a research project with a faculty member, joining a special interest club such as Amnesty International or Poetry Circle, an honor society or an organization affiliated with your major, and attending a career fair or gathering graduate school information. Consider applying for a research, program, or teaching assistantship through the Centers of Excellence (AMP) where you can develop a mentoring relationship with a faculty or staff member. Perhaps you will want to meet with your faculty advisor to plan an internship experience. The intent is to insure that you are developing both a theoretical and hands-on understanding of your chosen discipline.

During this year consider developing an electronic portfolio, a thoughtful, organized collection of artifacts that illustrates your skills, abilities, and the defining experiences of your St. Catherine education to date. You are encouraged to enroll in the workshop series on "Building Your Professional E-Portfolio."

Bridges

"Bridges," the fourth year theme, focuses on the steps you need to prepare for graduation. Suggested activities include completing a second internship, engaging in a work-study position that requires high-level skills, finishing your portfolio, and/or applying for graduate school. You will want to take advantage of a capstone or seminar course in your major to integrate all that you have learned in your major's coursework. You will have structured opportunities to learn about and complete the steps necessary for a successful job search and attend an appropriate job fair. You will want to attend the yearlong programs and workshops in the "From Backpack to Briefcase" program, or schedule interviews with alumnae in the field you have chosen. You are also encouraged to mentor underclass students and help them develop in leadership roles. Additionally, during this year you may also consider taking a leadership role in designing or leading a Justice and Outreach trip or spirituality retreat through Campus Ministry.

> I have laid the ground work and started to pave a path at St. Kate's . . . with a few bumps of course . . . all of the pages of the Catherine Connection are in place; it is up to me to fill them with each gateway, pathway, avenue, and bridge I encounter.
>
> Shannon Murphy, current student

In many ways, the Catherine Connection provides the warp for weaving an individualized tapestry of learning that takes place both in and outside the classroom throughout the four-year college experience. Perhaps the most concrete evidence of this tapestry is the portfolio, which is threaded and developed throughout each of the four years. From the beginning, you are encouraged to start to compile your portfolio with examples of work completed in the Reflective Woman along with other courses and out of class experiences. By your senior year, you are able to use the portfolio to demonstrate knowledge and competence in your discipline as well as provide evidence of the integration of broad liberal arts skills. In addition, the portfolio encompasses and validates your St.

Catherine experience and provides a language to share the learning with publics beyond the College, including graduate school admission committees as well as employers.

The Catherine Connection infers that as you move through each year, you need to keep in mind that your education at St. Catherine is holistic; it means that you need to attend to not only to your intellectual growth, but also to your spiritual, physical, emotional and social growth. While difficult at times for anyone, you are encouraged to take the time to nurture these facets with the resources and vast opportunities available in this community. Attending to this will not only add to your success at St. Catherine, but will contribute to your success as a lifelong learner.

References

Rich, A. (1979). Claiming an Education. In *On Lies, Secrets, and Silence: Selected Prose 1966–1978*. (pp. 231–235). New York: Norton.

Ryan, R., and Wolkerstofter, J. C. (1992). *More Than a Dream: Eighty-Five Years at the College of St. Catherine*. Minneapolis, MN: Cooperative Printing.

Joanne Cavallaro is an associate professor of English at the College of St. Catherine and Director of the Women's Studies program. She has also served as Director of the Writing Center and of the Writing Intensive Program.

How Writing Works

Joanne Cavallaro

Writing is a complex process. Indeed, it often seems mysterious or magical to people who don't write much. Often, people assume that a good writer is somehow born that way. Well, some people may be born with a talent for putting words together in interesting and evocative ways, but most good writers, whether published novelists or good student writers, have learned how to write through practice and feedback. Writing is a skill anyone can learn. We may not all end up published writers, but we can all learn enough to handle well any writing task we may encounter in college or on the job.

"How do I know what I think until I see what I say?"—E. M. Forster

Writing is a process of discovery. Despite what you may have been told before, most writers, when they start a project, do not usually have a complete picture of what they will write. Generally, they discover what it is they want to say as they go through the process of writing. They gather ideas and facts, start writing, see where the writing leads them, get feedback, write some more, get more facts and ideas, write again, revise, rewrite, change, add, delete, edit.

This process may seem messy and meandering, but if you learn to trust it, it works. Writing helps us give form to thought. When we try to write something down, we soon discover whether we really understand it or not. When we write our ideas down, we can examine them from different angles; we can question them, see where they lead us. By writing, we not only discover what we have to say, we also learn to say it better.

Sometimes writing takes place far away from pen and paper, or computer and printer. As we drive to school, wait for the bus, stand in line for a sandwich at the Grill, we can continue to work on our writing by thinking about it. Many of the best introductions I have written have come to me as I've showered in the morning. They've just popped into my head, probably because I went to bed the night before thinking about what I was writing. I also constantly write down ideas for papers on napkins, receipts, anything I find handy when an idea appears. Good writers often continue to work at their writing even away from the desk.

Good writers also know that writing is hard work. Someone once said that writing a college essay is cognitively one of the hardest things most of us are ever asked to do. The hard work comes from thinking things out. And it's only when we've written down our ideas and tried to develop them that we can see if they make sense and are worth keeping.

> "I suffer always from fear of putting down that first line. It is amazing the terrors, the magics, the prayers, the straightening shyness that assails one."
> —John Steinbeck

Sometimes the hardest part about writing is just getting started, so many writers use "tricks" to get started and keep themselves going to produce a first draft. The following section includes a list of some of these tricks that might be useful to you. Most writers know that they will be able to work things out if they just get started and keep going. They know they will revise their first drafts, so they don't need to worry about getting it all perfect the first time. In fact, they know that the quest for perfection early in the process will stymie their creativity and thinking. They write freely for the first draft, not worrying about spelling and punctuation for now. And they know that if they hit a stumbling block, they can mark it on the draft and come back to it later when they revise.

Planning what you want to write before you begin your draft helps make the writing easier, so most writers have some sort of plan before they sit down to write their draft. It may be an outline, or it may be a list of ideas on a sheet of scratch paper. They use the information they have gathered before they started to write the draft to help them create their plan. And for most writers, whatever plan they produce is tentative. Since we usually discover more about our topic as we write, any plan needs to be flexible, able to be refined and revised during the process of writing.

> "I have never thought of myself as a good writer. Anyone who wants reassurance of that should read one of my first drafts. But I'm one of the world's great revisers."—James Michener

Writing is rewriting, as Donald Murray says. Good writing rarely appears full blown on a first draft. To produce strong writing, writers have to revise, often going through several drafts. Hemingway claimed he rewrote the ending to *A Farewell to Arms* 39 times. When asked why, he answered, "To get the words right." Revising is an opportunity to get the words right. It's also an opportunity to gain an entirely new perspective on your subject, an opportunity to delve more deeply into your ideas. It may mean adding lots of new material or cutting out lots of stuff you've already written (always a difficult thing to do!). It may mean moving things around or rewriting whole sections. It may mean starting all over. The following section contains some strategies that might be useful for you as you revise.

"Well, it's a beautiful feeling, even if it's hard work."—Anne Sexton

Writing the Draft

As you write your first draft, it is best to focus on what you want to say first and worry about how it looks later. Remember, this is a draft, so you will have an opportunity to go back and change it later. If you find that you worry so much about spelling and mechanics that you sometimes forget what you were trying to say, it might be best to stop worrying about those things for now. Worry about spelling and punctuation and precise word choice and other sentence-level matters only after you're satisfied that you've said what you want to say. It's not very efficient to stop and carefully fix all the possible errors in a paragraph that you may well delete later when you revise. Leave the editing until later.

1. Focus on your ideas first. As you write your draft, keep rereading what you've written and ask yourself: What am I trying to tell my reader? What's my point, my story here? What else needs to be added? What's no longer necessary? If you're stuck for a word or a transition, leave a blank or a mark that will remind you to come back to that spot later.

2. Allow yourself time. If a paper is due next week, start it this week, even if you don't yet have all the data or ideas you want. Beginning to write, if only for 10 minutes, will start the incubation process in your own mind. You'll find that once you start it, you'll actually be working on the paper in your subconscious as you go through your day. Plan to do more than one draft; very few writers can create a good paper in their first draft.

3. Imagine a real audience as you write and revise. Think of your classmates or teacher as your audience unless you have a more specific audience you are writing to. Ask yourself what information they will need in order to follow what you're trying to say. You already know that information and probably take it for granted; does your audience know it? If not, put it in.

4. Play with titles, introductions, and conclusions. These are important, highly visible points in any paper. Provocative titles catch readers' attention; good introductions keep readers going; strong conclusions leave strong memories in readers' minds. But these same elements work on the writer as well as the reader, for a good title, introduction or conclusion can suggest changes for what follows or precedes. Sometimes these elements come early in the process, as controlling ideas. Sometimes they come later. In any case, they can capture the essence of your paper, telling you what to keep and what to cut.

5. Use a word processor. Some people write out their first draft by hand and then type it on a computer. Others compose directly onto the computer. Use whatever way suits you best, but do use a computer. Computers make all the difference when it comes to making changes easy. You can move things around, add and delete easily. When writers go to revise their drafts, most find it more efficient to print the drafts out and read them on paper rather than on the screen. It is much easier to see the whole picture when you read it on paper. It's also easier on paper to find your mistakes when you come to the editing and proofreading stage.

Some General Strategies for Revision

Once you've written your draft, take some time away from it; let it rest for a few hours at least. If you can, leave it overnight or a few days before you look at it again. That way, you can approach it more objectively, the way your reader will, without already knowing exactly what it says.

You may already have some ideas about what you want to change in your draft. That's a good place to start. Even if you do know what you want to change, it's a good idea to sit down and reread the entire thing, making notes as you go along.

Re-Reading Your Draft

1. Read the whole thing first. Read it straight through to see what it says, to find its central point. You may be surprised to find that it doesn't say exactly what you thought you were saying. That's OK right now. At this point, it's helpful to first get an overall sense of what your draft actually says. One way to do this is to outline your draft. The outline needn't be too detailed, just one that summarizes the main point of each paragraph. In addition to an outline, try writing down what the purpose of your essay is, who the audience is, and what strategy you have used in each paragraph to achieve your purpose (in other words, what each paragraph does). Jot down problem areas or things to return to later. As you read, keep asking yourself, "What am I trying to say here?"

2. Try to read the draft as your reader would. Remember, your reader doesn't know everything that was in your head as you wrote the essay. As you read, you might know the background information necessary to fully understand your points, but will the reader know that information? Ask yourself what information the reader needs to know that you take for granted.

3. It's difficult to be objective about one's own writing, so getting someone else to read your draft is very helpful. Give it to a friend, or even better take it to the Writing Center. Either way, ask your reader or tutor to

tell you if there are any parts that are difficult to understand, that need more elaboration, more support. Are there any connections that are not clear? Start by asking about the clarity and development of your ideas; leave the grammar issues for later. Make notes on the paper as you listen to your readers' reactions. Most good writers ask others to read and react to their work before the final copy is due.

Revising Your Draft

When you sit down to revise, don't try to do it all at once. Break the process up into stages. Look at the whole first and then move on to parts.

1. Start with the big picture, the main points, your overall purpose. Think about what you want to say. Does the draft say what you want it to? Is your thesis clear? Can the reader tell easily what your main points are? Do you develop your ideas enough? Do you support your points rather than just state them? Do you need to add more information? Have you thought through your ideas thoroughly? What are you really trying to say? Have you said it? Have you said it all?

Writers often don't get to the point they really want to make until the end of the first draft. If that happens to you, if you find you've gotten to your main point at the end of the draft, then use that main point. Begin a new draft with that point as your thesis. Use ideas and information from your first draft if they're relevant, but don't be afraid to throw things out if they don't belong. Cutting our own words is often hard to do, but almost always necessary. If you find it difficult, create a file (on your computer or in a file folder) and put the sentences or phrases you cut into this file to be used in a later paper.

2. Check your writing for clarity and coherence. Can your reader easily follow what you are saying? Is the organization logical? Is it clear to the reader as well as to you? Are there transitions that show the connections among your ideas?

3. Move on to style only after you have made your major revisions. Look at your sentences. Do you like the way they sound? Is your tone appropriate to your content? Reading your essay out loud is helpful in really hearing what you have said. Try reading it aloud to a friend or to a tutor in the Writing Center; you'll be amazed at how much you notice about your own writing style.

4. Finally, proofread for grammatical errors. It's best to leave this stage until the end; after all, what's the use of correcting sentences that you may well change later? Also, too much attention to errors too early in the writing process can limit your ideas and creativity. As with revision, it's more effective if you leave some time after you've written the final draft to read it over for spelling, punctuation, mechanics, grammar.

Using Your Instructor's Comments

If you are lucky enough to have an instructor who will read and comment on your draft, use the comments wisely. They are an indication of what your instructor thinks is important. When you receive your draft back, read it and the comments over carefully. Start with the substantive comments, ones about your ideas, about how well you explain them, about how clearly you state them. If you do not understand any comment, ask your instructor for clarification. If you are still unsure or if you cannot ask your instructor, bring the draft to the Writing Center.

As with revision in general, work on the big things first, the content, organization and clarity. If there are questions in the comments, be sure you have answered them in your revision. This may mean adding more information, elaborating on the ideas you already have, or even doing more research.

Once you have revised your essay to your satisfaction and have addressed the comments of your instructor, go on to look at the errors corrected or comments about grammar and usage. You may well have changed the sentence the original correction was in, but look at the correction anyway and see if you understand why your instructor made it. What was the error? How can you correct it? How can you work to avoid that error next time you write?

Remember, you are not your draft. When other people comment on your work, especially when they criticize it, they are not attacking or criticizing you. They are merely commenting on a draft, on an unfinished product, not on you.

Helen Humeston is an assistant professor in the Master of Library and Information Sciences program. She has taught classes at the College of St. Catherine since 1995 in information management, library science, and The Reflective Woman.

How to Harness an Octopus: Researching the Structured Controversy Project

Helen Humeston

Introduction

When you begin researching the structured controversy assignment, you may feel as if you are trying to harness an octopus. As soon as you grasp one part, the thing seems to move in seven other directions at once. The purpose of this article is to help you to take control of the research process. Remember, no one is born knowing how to do research. Most of us have learned through long, sometimes painful, experience. I hope that by offering you a few tips, your research will be both efficient and effective.

Three major issues will be addressed: choosing a topic, designing an effective research strategy, and evaluating sources. This is intended only as a general introduction to library research. For more detail, I recommend Thomas Mann's *The Oxford Guide to Library Research.* (New York: Oxford University Press, 1998.)

Choosing a Topic

It is, unfortunately, easy to write a bad paper on a good topic. It is much more difficult to write a good paper on a bad topic. Your choice of which controversial issue to present is crucial. There are three basic questions you should ask yourself about your topic. First, is this issue interesting? You will be working on this project for several weeks, so the topic should engage you at some level. If, moreover, the subject bores you, the chances are that your audience will respond to it in the same way.

Second, are there at least two clearly opposing views on the issue? If not, there is no controversy. In several of my TRW classes, teams discovered that there was overwhelming support for one side of a topic and virtually none on the other. The pros and cons of tribal fishing rights in Minnesota is a case in point. The team advocating tribal fishing rights had no difficulty in finding evidence to support their side, even though most of the articles were published in a newspaper designed for Native Americans.

The opposing team was hard pressed to find any information about why tribal fishing rights should be abolished or curtailed. A little preliminary research should tell you whether there is enough information about both sides of the topic to constitute a controversy.

The third question is whether you can cover the major points of the issue in the time allotted. Students usually find that they must narrow their topics to fit the amount of class time used for presentations. Obviously it is more efficient to refine the topic before you have spent a great deal of time looking for information and taking notes.

The best way to determine whether the issue is interesting, controversial, and manageable is to look up a few articles about it in general encyclopedias such as *Encyclopedia Americana, Britannica,* or the *American Academic Encyclopedia.* Most encyclopedias give a brief overview of the topic, list the major issues involved, and include a few recommended readings. Even more importantly, encyclopedia articles will give you terms that you can use when researching the topic. If your subject is not included in the general encyclopedias, try looking in some of the specialized, or subject, encyclopedias. There are special encyclopedias on virtually every academic discipline, such as the *Encyclopedia of Religion, Encyclopedia of Philosophy, Encyclopedia of Psychology, Encyclopedia of Social Sciences* and many more. There are, however, no encyclopedias of abortion, gun control, assisted-suicide, or similar issues. You may find articles on these topics in the special encyclopedias listed above or in other special encyclopedias. Ask a reference librarian for help in locating a useful encyclopedia that may include information on your topic.

If encyclopedias are the best place to begin reading about your topic, the World Wide Web is the worst. The reason is that you will probably find too much information, which may or may not be accurate and seldom provides the kind of overview of the topic that you need before you begin your research. There are, however, some Internet-based resources such as *FirstSearch* that you may wish to consult in the early stages of your work.

Diagramming the Research Strategy

You probably would not start driving across the country without a map. For the same reason, you should design a map or diagram to guide your research. The purpose of doing a diagram is to assure that you are connecting the research topic or thesis statement to the types of library materials that are likely to contain the information that you are seeking and to the access tools that you can use to locate this information. There are four basic steps to diagramming a research strategy as listed below.

Step 1

Write your topic or thesis statement in the center of a sheet of paper and draw a circle or oval around it. Underline the key terms. Leave space at the top of the page to write subject headings from *Library of Congress Subject Headings* and/or another thesaurus such as *ERIC, The Thesaurus of Psychological Index Terms*, etc. Getting the right subject headings is vital to the success of your search. Reference librarians will be happy to help you. Please see Figure 1. I am using homeschooling only as an example. Your topic and sources may be quite different, but the general approach should be applicable. Although I am illustrating how to diagram a research project in four steps, each builds upon the previous one. By the end of this exercise, you will have only one page that should look like Figure 4.

Figure 1

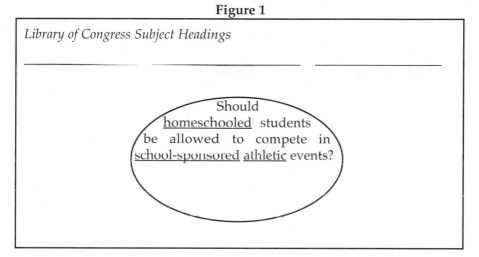

Library of Congress Subject Headings

Should homeschooled students be allowed to compete in school-sponsored athletic events?

Step 2

The next step is to think about all of the possible *types* of library materials that might offer information on your subject. Arrange these around the periphery of the oval in the center of the page. Background sources include encyclopedias, almanacs, and other general reference works that you might consult early in the research process.

I have not included Internet resources here because there are so many of them and they are so diverse. I found, for example, more than one hundred thousand Web sites on the topic or homeschooling alone. This is not good news for a harried TRW student who is trying to get the research finished in a reasonable amount of time.

Figure 2

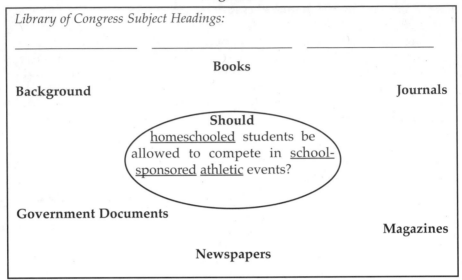

Library of Congress Subject Headings:

Books

Background   **Journals**

Should
homeschooled students be
allowed to compete in school-
sponsored athletic events?

Government Documents

                                                              Magazines

Newspapers

Step 3

The third step is to jot down some titles of materials that you might examine. You might not know the exact title, particularly of books. That is fine, because you are merely trying to brainstorm about possible areas of inquiry. This task may seem rather difficult at first, but you can always add or delete titles later. "CSC Periodical and Subject Heading List" can be very helpful in locating periodicals. The first half of this source lists all of the journals and magazines in the CSC libraries in alphabetical order. The second half arranges them according to academic discipline.

Figure 3

Library of Congress Subject Headings:

_____   _____   _____

Other lists of subject headings:

ERIC

_____   _____   _____

Books

Should
homeschooled students be
allowed to compete in school-
sponsored athletic events?

Background
Encyclopedia Americana
Academic American Encyclopedia
International Encyclopedia of Education
West's Encyclopedia of Law

Government Documents
U.S. Department of Education
Congressional Information Service
Minnesota Legislative documents
Court cases

Journals
Journal of Education
Journal of Psychology

Magazines
Time
Newsweek
U.S. News & World Report

Newspapers
Education newsletters
New York Times
Los Angeles Times
Washington Post
Wall Street Journal
Christian Science Monitor

Step 4

The final step is the one that will save you the most time. This involves thinking of indexes that will help you to find information quickly. Nearly everything in a library is indexed somewhere if you know where to look.

Figure 4

Library of Congress Subject Headings:

_____   _____   _____

Other lists of subject headings:

ERIC

_____   _____   _____

Books
(Online catalog)
(Bibliography of Bibliographies)

Should homeschooled students be allowed to compete in school-sponsored athletic events?

Background	**Journals**
Encyclopedia Americana	*Journal of Education*
Academic American Encyclopedia	*Journal of Psychology*
International Encyclopedia of Education	Homeschooling Journal?
West's Encyclopedia of Law	School Athletics Journal?
(Ask at the reference desk)	*(Ulrich's International Periodicals Directory)*
(*ERIC* on CD-ROM)	
(First Stop: The Master Index to	*(Social Science Index)*
Subject Encyclopedias)	*(Education Index/Abstracts)*
(ARBA Guide to Subject Encyclopedias)	
(Guide to Reference Books)	

Government Documents	**Magazines**
U.S. Department of Education	*Time*
Congressional Information Service	*Newsweek*
Minnesota Legislative documents	*U.S. News & World Report*
Court cases	
(Monthly Catalog of U.S.	On CD-ROM:
Government Publications)	*The Magazine Index;*
(CIS/Index)	*Business Index:*

(LEXIS on CD-ROM)	*InfoTrac; General* *Periodicals Index;* *Expanded Academic Index* *NEXIS*)

Newspapers
Education Newsletters
New York Times
Los Angeles Times
Washington Post
Wall Street Journal
Christian Science Monitor
Many of the newspapers are indexed in the sources for
magazines or see *National Newspaper Index.*

Once you have read a few background articles in reference books and have sketched a diagram to guide your research, you are ready to begin finding materials. A reference librarian is an invaluable ally as you begin looking for information on your topic. No one knows better than a librarian that libraries are not particularly easy to use. People become reference librarians because they want to help others to find the information they need. Librarians will not think that you are stupid if you ask a question. The worst way to use a library is to spend an inordinate amount of time looking for something when a librarian can put you on the right track in a few minutes.

Evaluating Sources

One of the most daunting questions in research is whether the information found is trustworthy. The fact is virtually everything that is written is biased, if only because of what the author chose to omit. Most writers, moreover, have a particular point of view and are trying to persuade readers to accept the author's position. There is nothing wrong with taking a stance. Using inaccurate or misleading information to support an argument is, of course, intellectually dishonest.

Most encyclopedias, scholarly journals, and books published by reputable publishing houses go through a thorough editorial review. Editors know that their publications must be accurate or they will not be in business very long. Please note, however, that the information contained in these sources is out of date by as much as a year by the time of publication. That means any kind of statistical data about a current topic will probably not be accurate.

Well-known magazines and newspapers are reasonably reliable, although many have an editorial slant. Larger problems occur with small newsletters directed to a targeted audience. Bubba Smith's *The Commies in Washington Are Trying to Take Our Guns Away*, for example, will not present an even-handed treatment of gun control.

There are no checks on what individuals post on the Web. You may, of course, use these sources but you should weigh them against what you have read in more conventional publications.

Government documents can be a cornucopia of excellent information. Finding the documents is not always easy. Please refer to the list in Figure 4 for sources that can help you to begin to search government publications.

Conclusion

I hope that this brief survey of how to research the structured controversy assignment has provided some useful tips on choosing a topic, designing a research strategy, and evaluating sources. You control the process. Now you know how to harness an octopus.

The O'Neill Center for Academic Development addresses the diverse academic needs and interests of students. The professional and student staff offer programs, services, and facilities designed to promote academic achievement through the Writing/Reading Center, the Math/Science Center, and the Resources for Disabilities Center.

Avoiding Plagiarism

O'Neill Center for Academic Development

Plagiarism is the act of passing off someone else's work as your own. It includes such dishonest practices as buying, borrowing or stealing a paper to turn in as your own or simply copying someone else's words without putting them in quotation marks and identifying the author and source. Most students are not so dishonest as to buy or steal a paper. Many students, however, inadvertently plagiarize because they do not realize that what they are doing is, in fact, plagiarism and thus dishonest. Avoiding plagiarism is much more complicated than simply not copying other people's work.

In an attempt to avoid plagiarizing, students often paraphrase the passages they want to use. Basically, paraphrasing is stating something in different words. As such, it is a useful device. The problem is that it can lead you to unintentional plagiarism if it is not done properly. Changing a few words in a passage and then using it in your paper without documentation is plagiarism. Changing a few words and then using it in your paper even *with* proper documentation is also plagiarism. When you paraphrase other people's ideas, you have two choices: 1) you may quote the passage exactly, put it in quotation marks, and cite it; or 2) you may change the wording of the passage so that the ideas are explained substantially in your own words *and cite it.* Anything in between is plagiarism.

One reason some students inadvertently plagiarize is the pressure they feel to come up with new ideas, to be original, even with topics that they know little about. In academic settings such as college courses, it is difficult if not impossible to come up with totally original ideas, especially on topics with which you are unfamiliar. When an instructor asks for original thinking, she often means thinking through ideas to find your own perspective on them and then expressing those ideas in your own way. In doing so, you may and often should use other people and their ideas to add to or support your own. When you do so, however, you must give them credit.

Some examples might help at this point. Below are several paraphrases of some material. Two constitute plagiarism; the third shows one correct way of using other people's ideas.

The original material:

> It is not generally recognized that at the same time when women are making their way into every corner of our work-world, only one percent of the professional engineers in the nation are female. A generation ago this statistic would have raised no eyebrows, but today it is hard to believe. The engineering schools, reacting to social and governmental pressures, have opened wide their gates and are recruiting women with zeal. The major corporations, reacting to even more intense pressures, are offering attractive opportunities to practically all women engineering graduates.

> from Samual C. Florman, "Engineering and the Female Mind,"
> *Harper's Magazine* (1974)

Case 1: Overt Plagiarism

> Because women seem to be taking jobs of all kinds, few people realize that only 1 percent of the professional engineers in the nation are female. A generation ago this would have raised no eyebrows, but today it is hard to believe. The engineering schools, reacting to social and governmental pressures, have opened wide their gates and are recruiting women with zeal. The major corporations, reacting to even more intense pressures, are offering attractive opportunities to practically all women engineering graduates.

After adding a bit to the first sentence, the writer here merely copies the original source word for word, an obvious case of plagiarism. And she doesn't even cite her source! She could avoid plagiarism here by putting quotation marks around the borrowed passage and citing her source. The problem is that there is no pressing reason to quote this passage, and if she does this often, she will produce a paper full of quotations, a paper that has more of other people than of her. Not a good thing.

Case II: Plagiarism Caused by Improper Paraphrasing

> Few people realize, now that women are making inroads into every corner of the work-world, only a small percentage (1%) of professional engineers in the United States are female. A generation ago, this fact would not have surprised anyone, but today it is hard to believe. Engineering schools, reacting to pressure from the government and society, are recruiting women with zeal. And many major corporations, reacting to even more pressures, offer attractive employment opportunities to just about any women who is an engineering graduate.

Although this writer does not copy word for word, she only substitutes her own words in a few cases and does not substantially change the original. The ideas appear in the same order and are expressed in basically the same words. She also does not cite her source. Again, this is plagiarism. She could improve this by acknowledging and citing her source, something she must do to be academically honest. Even with that improvement, however, the charge of plagiarism would still stand because the expression is not substantially her own.

Case III: Proper Paraphrasing

> In the last twenty years, women certainly have made great gains in the world of employment. There are now more women working as doctors, lawyers, legislators, and janitors than probably ever before. In one area, however, they still lag far behind men, at least in terms of numbers in the field. That area is engineering. Samuel Florman (1974) points out that of all the professional engineers in the U.S., only one percent are women. He adds that engineering schools and major corporations alike have responded to social and governmental pressure to increase the number of female engineers from this surprisingly low rate. They are now actively recruiting women into both the schools and the corporations.

This writer weaves the information supplied by Florman into her own paragraph, paraphrases it and gives proper credit to him through her citation. She summarizes Florman's ideas so that they fit in with hers and then acknowledges that she has done so. .

If you have any questions about how to use your sources without plagiarizing, talk to your instructor or go to the Writing Center (basement of the Chapel). The Writing Center has tutors to help you and additional handouts about citing your sources.

Sources

Sources

pp. 3–10: Presentation for the College of St. Catherine Faculty/Staff Workshop, August 30, 1994, by Joan Mitchell, CSJ.

pp. 11–29: From *More than a Dream: Eighty-five Years at the College of St. Catherine* by Rosalie Ryan, CSJ and Joan Christine Wolkerstorfer. Copyright © 1992 by the College of St. Catherine, St. Paul, Minnesota.

pp. 30–33: From *On Lies, Secrets, and Silence: Selected Prose 1966–1978* by Adrienne Rich. Copyright © 1979 by W. W. Norton and Company. Reprinted by permission of the publisher.

pp. 34–42: From *Let Your Life Speak: Listening for the Voice of Vocation* by Parker Palmer. Copyright © 2000 by Jossey-Bass, Inc. Reprinted by permission of the publisher via the Copyright Clearance Center.

pp. 43–47: Reprinted with permission of Simon & Schuster Adult Publishing Group from *Boundaries* by Maya Lin. Copyright © 2000 by Maya Lin Studio, Inc.

p. 48: From *Carnival Evening: New and Selected Poems 1968–1998* by Linda Pastan. Copyright © 1978 by Linda Pastan. Used by permission of W. W. Norton & Company, Inc.

pp. 49–50: Copyright © 1980 by Lucille Clifton. First appeared in *Two-Headed Woman*, published by The University of Massachusetts Press. Now appears in *Good Woman: Poems and a Memoir 1969–1980*, published by BOA Editions, Ltd.(1987). Reprinted by permission of Curtis Brown, Ltd.

pp. 60–63: "Being Poor: A Look Inside This Secret Society" by Alia Ganaposki appeared in *About Campus*, November/December 2001. Copyright © 2001 by John Wiley and Sons, Inc. Reprinted by permission of the publisher via The Copyright Clearance Center.

pp. 71–76: Copyright © 1990 by Amy Tan. First appeared in *The Threepenny Review*. Reprinted by permission of the author and the Sandra Dijkstra Literary Agency.

pp. 77–90: "Cathedral" reprinted by permission of International Creative Management, Inc. Copyright © 1981 by Raymond Carver.

pp. 91–103: From "Working Paper #189 of the Wellesley College Center for Research on Women" by Peggy McIntosh. Copyright © 1988 by Peggy McIntosh. Reprinted by permission of the author.

pp. 104–108: From *Do You Know Me Now? An Anthology of Minnesota Multicultural Writings* edited by Elisabeth Rosenberg. Copyright © 1997 by Pamela Fletcher. Reprinted by permission.

pp. 183–191: From *Language and Art in the Navajo Universe* by Gary Witherspoon. Copyright © 1977 by University of Michigan Press. Reprinted by permission of the publisher.

pp. 192–203: From *Women and the Word* by Sandra Marie Schneiders. Copyright © 1986 by Saint Mary's College, Notre Dame, Indiana. Reprinted by permission of Paulist Press.

pp. 204–218: From *When Bad Things Happen to Good People* by Harold S. Kushner. Copyright © 1981 by Harold S. Kushner. Preface Copyright © 2001 by Harold S. Kushner. Used by permission of Schocken Books, a division of Random House, Inc.

pp. 219–229: As appeared in the *Brown Alumni Magazine*, November/December, 1999. Copyright © 1999 by Kenneth R. Miller. Reprinted by permission of the Brown Alumni Magazine.

pp. 230–236: From *Discover*, June 1992. Copyright © 1992 by David Freedman. Reprinted by permission of the author.

pp. 237–248: From *Exile and the Kingdom* by Albert Camus, translated by Justin O'Brien. Copyright © 1957, 1958 by Alfred A. Knopf, a division of Random House, Inc. Reprinted by permission.

pp. 249–257: From *In Search of our Mothers' Gardens: Womanist Prose* by Alice Walker. Copyright © 1974 by Alice Walker.

pp. 261–262: From *We Are All Magicians* by Ruth Forman. Copyright © 1993 by Ruth Forman. Reprinted by permission of the author.

pp. 263–273: From *Non-Violent Resistance* by Mohandas K. Gandhi. Copyright © 1951 by Navajivan Trust. Reprinted by permission.

pp. 274–288: Reprinted by arrangement with The Heirs to the Estate of Martin Luther King, Jr., c/o Writers House, Inc. as agent for the proprietor. Copyright © 1963 by Martin Luther King, Jr., copyright renewed 1991 by Coretta Scott King.

pp. 320–332: From *Why Are All the Black Kids Sitting Together in the Cafeteria?* by Beverly Daniel Tatum. Copyright © 1997 by Perseus Books Group. Reprinted by permission of the publisher via the Copyright Clearance Center.

pp. 333–334: From *The Country of Marriage* by Wendell Berry. Copyright © 1971 by Wendell Berry.

pp. 335–343: From *High Tide in Tucson* by Barbara Kingsolver. Copyright © 1995 by Barbara Kingsolver. Reprinted by permission of HarperCollins Publishers, Inc.

pp. 344–347: From *The Cancer Journals* by Audre Lorde. Copyright © 1980 by Aunt Lute Books. Reprinted by permission of the publisher.

pp. 362–365: First published in the *Institute for Leadership Review* as "Creating the World We Want to Live in," December 1994, pp. 16–17. Copyright © 1994 by William Myers.

pp. 366–371: First appeared in *The Wind's Twelve Quarters* by Ursula K. LeGuin. Copyright © 1973 by Ursula K. LeGuin. Reprinted by permission of the author and the author's agents, the Virginia Kidd Agency, Inc.

pp. 372–381: From *Eyes Open on a World: The Challenges of Change* by the Sisters of St. Joseph of Carondelet. Copyright © 2001 by North Star Press of Saint Cloud, Inc.

Author Index

Author Index